MW01075530

Trails of the
Sawtooth and Boulder-White Cloud Mountains

Warbonnet Peak

Trails of the

Sawtooth and Boulder-White Cloud Mountains

Updated and expanded

143 hikes in the Sawtooth, White Clouds, Hemingway-Boulders and Jim McClure-Jerry Peak Wildernesses and surrounding areas

by Margaret Fuller

TRAIL GUIDE BOOKS

Published by
Trail Guide Books
P.O. Box 148
Weiser, Idaho 83672

Updated and expanded sixth edition
© 2017 Margaret Fuller

Manufactured in the United States

Edited by Wayne Fuller
Maps by Jerry Painter
Cover, maps and book design by Jerry Painter of Trail Guide Books

All photographs by the author unless otherwise noted

Cover photograph: El Capitan and Alice Lake by Chris Fuller, Chris Fuller photos ©

Library of Congress Catalog Card Number: GV199.42.122S2944 1988
917.96'04'3   88-31851

Fuller, Margaret, 1935–

ISBN 978-0-9911561-2-2

For Ryan, Chris, Sierra, Ivy, Grace, Natalya and Fiona

FOREWORD

By Cecil D. Andrus
former Idaho Governor and Secretary of the Interior and
Chairman, The Andrus Center for Public Policy, Boise State University

The Sawtooth National Recreation Area, in the center of Idaho, is one of those rare spots that remain serenely remote, even though it is near popular vacation destinations. I know it well for I have spent many hours in its soul-satisfying confines.

Only a few miles from the popular Sun Valley area, the Sawtooth National Recreation Area provides access to wild backcountry for many visitors every year.

My efforts to preserve this region, when I was first governor of Idaho, are some of my most satisfying accomplishments. Therefore, it was with the greatest pleasure that I saw Margaret Fuller produce the Sawtooth National Recreation Area's first comprehensive guide in 1979. In writing it, Margaret compiled descriptions of all the trails she had hiked with her family in the Sawtooth, White Cloud, and Boulder Mountains - the Sawtooth NRA's three rugged ranges. In later editions she added hikes in the part of the Smoky Mountains that are in the Sawtooth National Recreation Area.

Now she has again revised and expanded Trails of the Sawtooth and White Cloud Mountains and added the word Boulder to the title. Those who travel only by motorized vehicle won't benefit as much from the new edition as those who travel by foot or on horseback. But this is the perfect reference and trail companion for those who explore this section of the Idaho backcountry.

On the following pages, Margaret details many Idaho trails in the Sawtooth - White Cloud - Boulder Mountain area, The book now contains 70 more hikes than in the original edition, and 16 more than were in the 5th edition.

For each trail or route she lists mileage, elevation gain, highest point, and an estimate of the time it will take. Her book again includes a discussion of the area and its history and natural history. It also contains tips on safety, equipment, and leave-no-trace travel.

The Sawtooth National Recreation Area and is immediate surroundings now contains four wildernesses instead of just the Sawtooth that existed in 1979, when the first edition of Margaret; book was published. On August 7, 2015, President Barack Obama signed a bill that created three new wildernesses in the Boulder-White Clouds. The bill passed both houses of Congress unanimously. Designating these wildernesses took a 45-year-long effort and compromises by many people. The new wildernesses mean that the area has at last received the degree of protection its beauty and wildness deserve. The new areas are the White Clouds, the Hemingway-Boulders, and the Jim McClure-Jerry Peak.

If you've never tried an Idaho mountain trail, this book provides valuable information. If you've tried many trails but would like to experience some new ones, this book gives you some ideas of where to go.

It is my hope that this guide will continue to encourage visitors to the Sawtooth NRA to try the less-used trails and campsites and will help disperse the public enjoyment throughout the area.

This region is special to me. I hope this edition of Margaret's guide will help you find and share the very special Idaho experiences in store for visitors to the Sawtooth National Recreation Area. It's a worthwhile addition to literature on how to enjoy Idaho's unique quality of life. Margaret's book is one that has proved its value to me many times over the years.

Cecil D. Andrus

ACKNOWLEDGMENTS

I would like to thank all those who helped me with this revision of the book, including Jay Dorr, Liese Dean, and Ed Cannady of the Sawtooth National Recreation Area staff. A special thanks goes to Jerry Painter for the maps and layout. I couldn't have done the hikes for the book without the help of more than 60 of my friends and family over the years. My immediate family deserves the most credit: my husband Wayne, our daughters, Leslie (Fuller) Smith, and Hilary Fuller Renner, our sons, Doug, Neal and Stuart Fuller, and our children's families. Without the help and support of all these people I could never have written this book. I would also especially like to thank former Idaho governor Cecil Andrus for writing the foreword.

Many people have helped with this book over the years. One of them was Donna Parsons, former director of the Snake River Regional Studies Center at the College of Idaho; Others have been Louise Marshall, founder of Signpost Books; and Dave Lee, the first chief wilderness ranger for the SNRA. Another wilderness ranger who helped earlier was Mose Shrum. I want to thank Cliff and Mary Ann Cameron of Signpost Books for publishing the first three editions.

I would also like to thank those who have helped me over the years with publicity for the book such as Pete Zimowsky, of The Idaho Statesman; Lou Florence of Sawtooth Mountaineering, the Idaho Lung Association, and the more than 250 organizations and businesses who have invited me to give slide shows. The most important people to thank are the many businesses in Stanley, Ketchum, Boise, McCall, and elsewhere who buy my books to sell to their customers.

Margaret Fuller

Preserve · Protect · Enhance
SAWTOOTH SOCIETY

The Sawtooth Society wishes to congratulate Margaret Fuller on the updated sixth edition of her hiking guide, "Trails of the Sawtooth and Boulder-White Cloud Mountains," which includes 16 new hikes!

We know you will enjoy this guide that over the years has helped visitors follow well-trod trails and find "secret" spots throughout Central Idaho.

A way to give back to this spectacular and iconic part of Idaho is to become a supporter of the Sawtooth Society's efforts to preserve, protect, and enhance the Sawtooth National Recreation Area. To become a donor, please go to our website at sawtoothsociety.org or fill out the form below and mail it to our Stanley office.

Thank you, Margaret, for all you are doing to help us better enjoy and appreciate this remarkable area and congratulations on your wonderful new book!

Become a Sawtooth Society Donor
* By contributing an annual donation
* By attending the annual fundraiser, the Sagebrush Soiree
* By donating an auction item for the fundraiser
* By getting involved in one of our many volunteer/stewardship projects

Name: _____

Address: _____

City/St/Zip: _____

Phone: _____

Email: _____

I would like to hep by: _____

_____ Check enclosed (payable to Sawtooth Society)

Charge my donation to _____ Visa _____ MasterCard _____ American Express

Card #_____ Exp. _____

Signature _____

P.O. Box 209, Stanley, ID 83278 • 208.721.2909
www.sawtoothsociety.org • gary@sawtoothsociety.org

Castle Peak from Chamberlain Divide

Playing on Stanley Lake

TABLE OF CONTENTS

FOREWORD 6
ACKNOWLEDGMENTS 7

INTRODUCTION
About the Area 18
Purposes of This Guide 20
How to Reach the Sawtooth National Recreation Area 20
New in recent years 20
Volunteer Help 21
About This Guidebook 22
Visitor Services 22

HISTORY

Fur Trapping 23
Mining 23
Ranching 27
The Forest Service 27
Exploration 27
Formation of the Sawtooth National Recreation Area 28
Formation of the Three new Wildernesses

GEOLOGY

The Sawtooth Mountains 28
The White Cloud and Boulder Mountains 29

PLANTS AND ANIMALS

Plants, Trees, and Shrubs 30
The Mountain Pine Beetle and Douglas Fir Beetle Epidemic 33
Wildlife 34
Birds 34
Threatened and Endangered Species 35

ACTIVITIES 35

BACKCOUNTRY TRAVEL 36
Horse Travel 37
Llamas 38
Pack Goats 38
Outfitters 38
Mountain Biking 39
Preventing the Spread of Noxious Weeds 40
SAFE HIKING 40
SAFETY FOR ALL WILDERNESS TRAVELERS 42
The Twelve Essentials 44
Maps 44

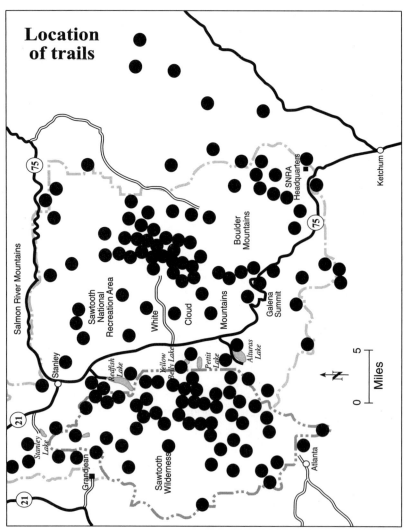

Location of trails

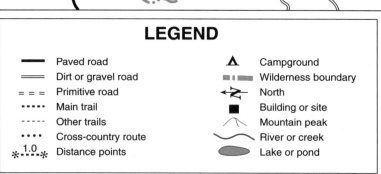

LEGEND

——— Paved road		▲	Campground
=== Dirt or gravel road		▓▬▓	Wilderness boundary
= = = Primitive road		⭠N	North
••••• Main trail		■	Building or site
- - - - Other trails		⌒	Mountain peak
•••• Cross-country route		∿	River or creek
••1.0•• Distance points		⬭	Lake or pond

GPS Readings 45
Emergencies 45
Leave No Trace Travel 48
Planning Your Trip 50
Regulations in the Wildernesses 51
Your Responsibility 51

TRAILS IN THE SAWTOOTH MOUNTAINS 53
Trails new in this edition are starred
ALTURAS LAKE AREA 54
* 1. Mill Gulch 54
2. Frenchman Creek 56
3. Smiley Creek Trail 57
4. Alpine Creek Lakes 59
5. Eureka Gulch 62
6. Mattingly Creek Divide 64
7. Mattingly Creek 66
8. Cabin Lakes 70

PETTIT LAKE AREA 71
9. Alice Lake 71
*10. Pettit Lake Over Ridge to McDonald Lake 74
11. From Alice Lake over Snowyside Pass to Toxaway Lake 75
12. Yellow Belly Lake 77
13. Farley Lake 78
14. Toxaway Lake 79
15. Edith Lake 82
16. Toxaway Lake to Edna Lake 83
17. Edna Lake to Ardeth and Spangle Lakes 84
18. Sand Mountain Pass to Imogene Lake 85

HELL ROARING AREA 86
19. Mays Creek Trail to McDonald Lake 86
20. Hell Roaring Lake 88
*21. Huckleberry Creek 90
22. Hell Roaring Lake to Decker Creek and Lakes 92
23. Decker Creek to Redfish Inlet Transfer Camp 94
24. Imogene Lake 96
25. Profile Lake 97
*26. Bull Moose Trail 98

REDFISH LAKE AREA 100
27. Grand Mogul Trail 100
28. The Lily Pond (Lily Lake) 103
*29. Unnamed Lake 7,100 (Lake Jon) 104
30. Fishhook Creek Meadow 105
31. The Alpine Way from Redfish Lake to Marshall Lake and Iron Creek 106
*32. Thompson Cirque (Profile) Lake 107
33. Bench Lakes 109
34. Redfish Inlet to Flatrock Junction 111

13

35. Saddleback Lakes 112
36. Flatrock Junction to Cramer Lakes 113
37. Cramer Lakes to Edna Lake 115
38. Flatrock Junction to Alpine Lake 116
39. Alpine Lake to Baron Lakes 116
40. Upper Redfish Lakes 117

IRON CREEK AREA **119**
41. Alpine, Sawtooth, and McGown Lakes 119
42. Goat Falls and Lake 121
43. The Alpine Way from Iron Creek to Stanley Lake ... 123

STANLEY LAKE AREA **126**
44. Bridalveil Falls and Hanson Lakes 126
45. Elk Meadow 127
46. Observation Peak 129
47. Marten and Kelly Lakes 130
48. Elizabeth Lake 131

GRANDJEAN AREA **133**
49. Trail Creek Lakes 133
50. Baron Creek Trail to Baron Lakes 137
51. North Baron Trail to Sawtooth Lake 138
52. South Fork Payette River: Grandjean to Elk Lake ... 141
53. South Fork Payette River: Elk Lake to Hidden Lake Junction 142
54. Tenlake Creek Trail to Ardeth Lake 144

GRAHAM AREA **144**
55. Bayhouse and Johnson Creek Trails 144

QUEENS RIVER AREA **147**
56. Queens River Canyon to Pats Lake Junction ... 147
57. Pats Lake Junction to Everly and Plummer Lakes ... 151
58. Pats Lake Junction to Pats Lake 152
59. Little Queens River to Scenic Lakes Junction ... 153
60. Scenic Lakes 154
61. Scenic Lakes Junction to Browns Lake, High Pass, and Johnson
Lake Junction 156
62. Johnson Lake Junction to Johnson Lake and Pats Lake ... 157

ATLANTA AREA **158**
63. Middle Fork Boise River: Powerplant Campground
to Rock Creek 158
64. Leggit Lake 162
65. Timpa Lake 163
66. Middle Fork Boise River: Rock Creek to Spangle Lakes ... 165
67. Ingeborg, Rock Slide, and Benedict Lakes 166
68. Camp and Heart Lakes 167

THE SALMON RIVER MOUNTAINS **168**
69. Sawtooth View and Nip Peak 169

14

TRAILS IN THE WHITE CLOUD MOUNTAINS 172
    GERMANIA CREEK AREA 175
    70. South Fork Champion Creek and Rainbow Lake 175
    71. Champion Lakes 176
    72. Washington Basin 178
    73. Washington Basin Lake 180
    74. Washington Peak 181
    75. Germania Creek Trail: Three Cabins Creek to Chamberlain Creek 183
    76. Chamberlain Lakes from Three Cabins Creek 186
    77. Horton Peak 187

    FOURTH OF JULY CREEK AREA 189
    78. Champion Creek 189
    79. Heart Lake and Six Lakes 191
    80. Phyllis Lake 192
    81. Lightning Lake 194
    82. Fourth of July and Washington Lakes 195
    83. Born (Boorn) Lakes 196
    84. Born Lakes to Quiet Lake through Four Lakes Basin 199
    85. Washington Lake to Castle Divide and Baker Lake Junction 200

    OBSIDIAN AREA 202
    86. The Meadows on Warm Springs Creek 202
    87. Williams Creek Trail 204

    CASINO CREEK AREA 206
    88. Boundary Creek, Casino Lakes, and Big Casino Creek 206
    89. Little Casino Creek 209

    ROUGH CREEK AREA 210
    90. Rough and Garland Lakes 210
    91. Lookout Mountain 213

    SUNBEAM AREA 215
    92. Lower Warm Springs Creek 215

    SLATE CREEK AREA 216
    93. Hoodoo Lake 216
    94. Crater Lake 219
    *95. Mill-Holman Creek Loop 220
    *96. French Creek 221

    CLAYTON AREA 223
    97. Sullivan Lake 223

    EAST FORK OF THE SALMON RIVER AREA 224
    98. Jimmy Smith Lake 224
    99. Railroad Ridge 226
    100. Walker Lake 229
    101. Big Boulder Lakes 230

102. Sheep and Slide Lakes 232
103. Island and Goat Lakes 233
104. Livingston Mill to Frog Lake 234
105. Frog Lake and the Boulder Chain Lakes 235
106. little Boulder Creek Trail to the Boulder Chain Lakes 238
107. Baker Lake 240
108. Castle Lake 241
109. Baker Lake to Noisy and Quiet Lakes 244
110. The Boulder Chain Lakes to Shallow, Scree, Quiet Lakes 246
111. Germania Creek from East Fork Salmon River to Chamberlain Creek 247

TRAILS IN THE SMOKY MOUNTAINS **249**
GALENA AREA **250**
112. Headwaters of the Salmon River 250
113. Titus Lake and Titus Creek 253
114. The Old Toll Road 256

PRAIRIE CREEK AREA **257**
115. Mill Lake 257
116. Miner Lake 259
117. Prairie Lakes 260
118. West Fork Prairie Creek 262

NORTH FORK AREA **263**
119. The Harriman Trail 263

TRAILS IN THE BOULDER MOUNTAINS **268**
POLE CREEK AREA **269**
*120. The Governors Punchbowl From Pole Creek 269
121. Grand Prize Gulch 272
122. Galena Gulch 273

GALENA AREA **276**
123. Gladiator Pass 276
124. Galena Lodge Trails: The Galena Grinder 277

EASLEY AREA **278**
125. Silver Lake 278
126. Boulder Basin 281

NORTH FORK BIG WOOD RIVER AREA **283**
127. Murdock Creek 283
128. East Fork North Fork Big Wood River 285
129. West Fork North Fork Big Wood River and Window Lake 286
130. Amber Lakes 289
131. North Fork Big Wood River 290
132. West Pass Creek Divide from the North Fork Big Wood River 291

BOWERY AREA **294**
133. East Fork Salmon River Trail 294

16

Stanley from Lower Stanley

134. Bowery Cutoff   298
135. West Pass Creek Divide from the East Fork Salmon River   299

OUTSIDE THE SAWTOOTH NATIONAL RECREATION AREA
TRAIL CREEK AREA   **303**
136. Big Fall Creek Lake   303
*137. Toolbox Creek   304
138. North Fork Lake   306

JIM MCCLURE-JERRY PEAK WILDERNESS
EAST FORK SALMON RIVER AREA   **308**
*139. Lake Basin   308
*140. Upper Lake Creek Campground   313
*141. Bowery Creek   314
*142. Sage Creek   317
*143. East Pass Creek from Hunter Creek Summit   318

APPENDIX   **322**
OTHER TRAILS AND ROUTES   **322**
GUIDE TO TRIPS   **326**
SOURCES OF INFORMATION   **330**
SUGGESTED READING   **330**
BASIC BACKPACKING EQUIPMENT   **332**
ABOUT THE AUTHOR   **334**
INDEX   **336**

INTRODUCTION

ABOUT THE AREA

A few miles north of Sun Valley, Idaho, the Sawtooth Mountains rise thousands of feet above the headwaters of the Salmon River, like the sharp edges of crosscut saws. Across Sawtooth Valley from them, behind fir and sagebrush hills a section of the White Clouds resembles mountains of vanilla ice cream. The highest of the White Clouds, Castle Peak (11,815 feet), has one face that is half white. Closer to Sun Valley, pink and gray stripes of the Boulder and Smoky Mountains swirl above the Big Wood River. The lack of crowds adds to the appeal of these ranges. This book covers hikes in all four ranges that are administered by the Sawtooth National Recreation Area and the Salmon-Challis National Forest and Challis office of the Bureau of Land Management. The trips vary in difficulty, from short day hikes suitable for children and older people to multi-day trips for the fittest backpackers. On August 7, 2015, President Obama signed the Sawtooth National Recreation and Jerry Peak Wilderness Additions Act. It had just passed both houses of Congress with unanimous consent. The passage of this act occurred after more than 40 years of negotiations and previous bills. Congressman Mike Simpson had first introduced a version of this bill in 2004. The new wildernesses are the White Cloud, Hemingway-Boulder, and Jim McClure-Jerry Peak. The Jim McClure-Jerry Peak Wilderness is in the Salmon-Challis Forest and on Bureau of land Management land. For information on it , call the Middle Fork District of that forest, or the BLM field office in Challis.

The headwaters of the Salmon River separate the Sawtooths on the west from the White Clouds on the east. At Stanley, the young river turns east. At this turn, a tributary, Valley Creek, flows south into the river from a chain of meadows known as Stanley Basin. This basin separates the northern Sawtooths on the west from the Salmon River Mountains of the Frank Church - River of No Return Wilderness on the east. In June, the flowering camas transforms these meadows into carpets of blue.

Big sagebrush colors the dry parts of these valleys with a soft gray green. Bright green meadows and willows follow the coils of Valley Creek and the Salmon River. An occasional sheepherder's wagon with curved white top shows that traditional ranching lives on here. The area's remoteness brought few settlers until the twentieth century. Even today Stanley's population is listed as only 63 on the state map.

At the west edge of the valleys, forested moraines embrace large glacial lakes like Alturas, Pettit, Yellow Belly, Redfish, and Stanley. Five-mile long Redfish is the best known and most popular. From it, needles of buff, gray, and peach-colored rock march up the canyon of its main inlet. The entrance to the canyon is guarded on the south by

Fishing at Alturas Lake

the triangular pinnacles of the Grand Mogul and on the north by the pleated crown of Mt. Heyburn.

PURPOSES OF THIS GUIDEBOOK

This guidebook was written to help disperse visitors by giving them information on little-used trails as well as standard ones, and by encouraging experienced hikers to explore trailless areas. Another purpose is to advertise the beauty of the Sawtooth, White Cloud and Boulder Mountains.

HOW TO REACH THE SAWTOOTH NATIONAL RECREATION AREA (SNRA)

Idaho Highway 75 bisects the area. This highway begins at Shoshone and goes north past Ketchum and Sun Valley over Galena Summit. From there it descends the Sawtooth Valley to Stanley, then goes down the Salmon River to Challis. By road, Stanley is 60 miles northwest of Sun Valley, 130 miles northeast of Boise, and 135 miles north of Twin Falls. Along Idaho 21, which goes 130 miles to Stanley from Boise, unpaved side roads lead to Grandjean (7 miles) and Atlanta (47 miles.)

NEW IN RECENT YEARS

In this sixth edition the titled is changed to Trails of the Sawtooth and Boulder-White Cloud Mountains, 16 hikes have been added and one (Alturas Shore) removed because of a large amount of downed timber. The first edition in 1979, has been followed by new revised editions in 1988, 1998, 2005 and 2011. For each one I consulted with the rangers, checked trailheads and re-hiked trails where needed. This edition contains 143 hikers in contrast with the 73 of the first edition. Then there was only one wilderness. Now there are four.

Hikes in this book in the White Cloud Wilderness are Chamberlain Lakes from Three Cabins Creek, Born Lakes, Born Lakes to Quiet Lake Through Four Lakes Basin, Washington Lake to Castle Divide and Baker Lake Junction (part), Lower Warm Springs Creek, Hoodoo Lake, Crater Lake, Walker Lake, Big Boulder Lakes, Sheep Lake, Island and Goat Lakes, Frog Lake to the Boulder Chain Lakes, part of the Little Boulder Creek Trail to the Boulder Chain Lakes, Baker Lake, Castle Lake, Baker Lake to Quiet and Noisy Lakes, The Boulder Chain Lakes to Shallow, Scree, and Quiet Lakes

Hikes in this book in the Hemingway-Boulder Wilderness are Murdock Creek, East Fork North Fork Big Wood River, West Fork North Fork Big Wood River and Window Lake, Amber Lakes, North Fork Big Wood River, West Pass Creek Divide from the North Fork Big Wood River, West Pass Creek Divide from East Fork Salmon River.

Hikes in the book in the Jim McClure-Jerry Peak Wilderness are Bowery Creek, Hunter Creek Summit and East Pass Creek, Lake Basin, Sage Creek, Toolbox Creek, and Upper Lake Creek Campground.

If a section of the trail described is only part of a route to a desti-

20

nation, the notation: "this one-way section, ___miles" appears at the beginning of the hike. Under Access, the miles are given both from Stanley and Ketchum where relevant. The description of what you'll see on the hike is now labeled: what you'll see. The author doesn't attempt to rate the hikes on quality because preferences vary. Some people want views of high cliffs. Others love waterfalls. Some seek fish; others solitude. For some, steep rocky climbs in the hot sun spoil any scenery they may see; others don't mind the hard climb.

Mention of non-system trails and paths was removed in the third edition. For off-trail hikes, only the terrain and landmarks are described. The maps show the routes, but in many cases there is no path, or there are several. Paths in trailless areas may be animal paths and mislead you. Or they may lead to dangerous slopes. Instead of trying to follow paths, go cross-country, using landmarks and a topographic map to find the way. To be sure of finding an off trail lake or peak summit, get its GPS co-ordinates off Google Earth before you start out, Using a GPS unit, walk to those co-ordinates, detouring around obstacles as needed. The mileages in the descriptions have carefully been rechecked with those on the maps,

To prevent erosion, on any non-system trails or paths walk your own zigzag path beside them. In trailless areas, walk on rock whenever possible. Spread out any large party to avoid creating a new path.

In 2005, the Valley Road Fire burned the Fourth of July Creek, Champion Creek, Fisher Creek, and Warm Springs Creek drainages in the White Clouds. In 2006, the Trailhead Fire burned the Trail Creek Lakes and McGown Lakes areas, In 2014 the whole drainage of the Little Queens River and the lower five miles of the Queens River burned. Since then other fires have occurred . Burned trees often fall on windy days, so it is a good idea to stay out of burned areas when a strong wind is blowing. The many dead trees killed by mountain pine beetle and Douglas fir beetle also fall on windy days and even when there is no wind. The trail crews and volunteers can't keep up with clearing dead trees, so allow extra time for going over or around them if your trail is not a main trail. Even if it is, be sure to check with the Forest Service first or you may find 36 downed trees in a mile as I did early last summer.

VOLUNTEER HELP

A non-profit organization called the Sawtooth Society raises money to be used within the SNRA for trail improvement and for preserving its world-class scenery. Several of the trailheads have been improved with money raised by this society. It has paid to install several vault toilets. It also organizes various volunteer projects including rebuilding log worm fences.

Another non-profit group, the Sawtooth Interpretive and Historical Association (SIHA) runs the Stanley Museum and the Redfish Visitors Center and puts on a lecture series at the museum in the summer. It also works on historical preservation and oral histories of long time area residents.

Campfires are prohibited in some drainages in the wildernesses. These areas and lakes are listed in the appendix. In the Sawtooth

Wilderness where fires are permitted they must be built on a fire pan or fire blanket and the cool ashes scattered. Stock is prohibited in the Sawtooth drainages of Alpine Creek and of Goat Creek (near Grandjean) and dogs are prohibited in the Goat Creek drainage.

All parties entering the Sawtooth Wilderness must carry a free permit, which they can get at trailheads. In addition, in the Sawtooth Wilderness parties of 8 or more and those with stock staying overnight must obtain a special permit at an SNRA office. There are size limits for a party (10) and for the number of stock (20). For Sawtooth and other wildernesses permit information contact the SNRA Headquarters 8 miles north of Ketchum on Idaho 75, or the Stanley Ranger Station 5 miles south of Stanley on Idaho 75. Regulations for the new wilderness areas are still being prepared.

ABOUT THIS GUIDEBOOK

The author is a hiker, so the book gives information and times for foot travel, but horses can use most of these trails and mountain bikers can manage many of the non-wilderness ones. Mountain bikes are not allowed in the wildernesses.

The first edition was published in 1979 and a complete revision, containing 26 new hikes, was published in 1988. For that edition the author hiked again all but seven of the original hikes.

The third edition contained five new hikes, but one hike in the second edition was removed at the request of the Forest Service to protect wildlife. For the fourth edition, the author hiked some of the trails for a fourth time and did 20 new hikes. That edition added four hikes in the Smokies that also appear in Trails of Western Idaho.

For the fifth edition, the author checked every trailhead in person for changes, and took its GPS reading.

There are 16 new hikes in this sixth edition.

VISITOR SERVICES

The main business district of Stanley, the SNRA's largest town , has log buildings and dirt streets. The town is adjacent to the sharp towers and snow-filled chimneys of the Sawtooths. Only three blocks long by two blocks wide at its heart, the town has grown along its two highways, Idaho 21 and Idaho 75. There are new residences on the hill across Valley Creek and behind the City Park, which is on the hill beside the airport. Food, gasoline, lodging, gift shops, and guide services are located in Stanley and Lower Stanley. Some services are available at Redfish Lake, and Smiley Creek (also called Sawtooth City), and to the east at Sunbeam and Clayton, and on the west side of the Sawtooths at Grandjean and Atlanta.

The Forest Service has developed large campgrounds at Alturas, Redfish and Stanley Lakes and along the Wood River north of Ketchum. Smaller ones are located at Iron Creek, Pettit Lake, Atlanta, Grandjean, and along Highway 21 and the Salmon River Canyon. You can also camp at undeveloped sites along the backcountry roads.

`New visitor maps with the new wildernesses and updated maps of the Sawtooth and Salmon-Challis forests should be available in 2018.

Free motor vehicle maps that show permitted uses on the roads and trails are available now.

HISTORY

FUR TRAPPING

Mountain Shoshoni Indians, also called Sheepeaters, lived along the Salmon River and its tributaries for centuries before Alexander Ross visited the area with his fur trappers in 1824. On his trip across the divide between the Big Wood River and the headwaters of the Salmon River, he discovered and named a small pond, Governors Punchbowl. He named it for the "governor" of the Hudson Bay Company for which he trapped. Other trappers soon arrived: Warren Ferris of the American Fur Company in 1831, John Work of the Hudson Bay Company in 1832, and Captain Benjamin Bonneville in 1833.

MINING

When gold was discovered 30 years later, miners began to arrive. In 1863, as Boise Basin miners began to spread out from Idaho City, they soon found gold and silver quartz lodes. The discovery of gold on the South Fork of the Boise River, southwest of today's SNRA, started the town of Rocky Bar. Prospectors from Rocky Bar and elsewhere soon found gold in the Sawtooths. In 1864, placer gold was discovered in the Stanley Basin and placer and lode gold at Atlanta. The basin was named for John Stanley, one of those prospectors.

In 1865, a wagon road was built from Rocky Bar to Yuba City near Atlanta on the west side of the Sawtooths. It acquired the name, Boiler Grade, when a boiler being packed along it fell off the road. Because the area was remote, the first stamp mill didn't reach Atlanta until 1867, and the first three mills made little profit. By the mid-1870's, the Monarch and Buffalo mines were smelting ore at Atlanta. This first boom had declined by 1884, but Atlanta has had several more: from 1902-11, in 1916, 1932-36, and from 1980 to the present. The peak from 1932-36 was the most profitable. In those years Atlanta produced more gold than any other Idaho area, reaching $6 million by 1938.

Near Atlanta on the North Fork of the Boise River, silver was found on Silver Mountain in the 1860s. Little mining occurred until Matthew Graham, a miner at Atlanta and Rocky Bar, had ore from Silver Mountain assayed in 1885. The ore was so high-grade that he built a mine and a road to Silver Mountain from Trappers Flat in 1887. A 20-stamp mill and mile-long tram were installed in 1888. By then the area population had reached 350, most of it in Graham. When the venture failed in 1889, the mine, tram, and buildings were sold at sheriffs' sales for

23

Exploring in Washington Basin

$500 and the mill for $9,500. On nearby Black Warrior Creek, mining occurred from 1900 to 1910 at the Double Standard, Rice Mammoth, and Overlook Mines.

In 1864, a road was built from Idaho City to Banner, near Lowman, and a pack trail led from there to Cape Horn in the Stanley Basin. By 1869, miners were placer mining in Stanley Basin and hydraulic mining at Robinson Bar down the Salmon River from Stanley. By this time, Stanley had a store, which was run by Arthur McGown. When mining on the Yankee Fork of the Salmon River began in 1876, miners from that area also spread into the Stanley Basin and Sawtooth Valley.

They soon made rich discoveries. Levi Smiley found a quartz lode at the head of Smiley Creek in 1878, and in 1879 E.M. Wilson discovered the lode of the Vienna Mine nearby. By 1880, the Pilgrim, Columbia, and Beaver mines operated at Sawtooth City, and a toll road led from there to Ketchum. Eastern developers provided a 20-stamp mill for the Vienna Mine at Vienna, which at its height had 800 residents.

There were also mines along Alturas Creek and in Eureka Gulch. By the winter of 1883-84, the road to Ketchum was kept open all winter. A trail from Sawtooth City to Atlanta was "improved" in 1885 for a total of $450 paid to 10 men for 11 days work. When the work was completed, a traveler could take the stage at 6:00 A.M. in Ketchum to Sawtooth City, arriving there at 1:00 P.M. Then he could ride in the daily pack train to Atlanta, reaching there by 6 P.M. The boom at Sawtooth City and Vienna ended in 1892 when the last mine operating, the Silver King, burned, However, after construction of a 75-ton flotation plant, the Vienna Mine operated for a few years in the 1930s.

Mining also occurred in the White Clouds, but was much later and less extensive. The lead-silver deposits of the Livingston Mine, the most successful, at $2.3 million, were located by A.S. and W.S. Livingston in 1882. Its first ore was shipped by pack train. In 1922 a road, 200- ton mill and three-mile tramway were built and the mine ran until 1930. Some activity still persists on the patented claims. The first claims in Washington Basin at the head of Washington Creek were located in 1882. There were two mills, but only $50,000 in lead and silver was produced. Blackman Peak is named for a black miner, George Z. Blackmon, although they didn't spell his name right. He mined in Washington Basin, beginning in the 1880s. He was one of the workmen who helped outdoor photographer and Idaho promoter Bob Limbert build Redfish Lake Lodge in 1929.

Jess Baker located claims at Baker Lake near the head of Little Boulder Creek in the White Clouds in 1922, and in 1939, molybdenum was discovered there. In 1967, the American Mining, Smelting and Refining Company (ASARCO) obtained these claims and located 50 more. In 1970, environmentalists opposed their application for a road. The controversy over the proposed mine led to the formation of the SNRA in 1972.

In the Boulders, the settlement of Galena, near today's Galena Lodge, was founded in 1879 around lead and silver claims. Soon the mines had a 20-ton smelter, 800 people, four general stores, and a stage line to Hailey. A few miles south of Galena, the town of Boulder City was the second town established in the Wood River Valley. It produced

25

Traditional log worm fence

$1 million in gold, silver, copper, and lead from 1900 through 1980. Although located at 9,000 feet, it once had a store, hotel, post office, saloon, several cabins, and a mill. In September 2004, two families who owned the heart of the city donated their three claims to the Sawtooth National Forest.

RANCHING

In Sawtooth Valley, David Clark started the first year-round ranch in 1899 at a hot spring. He served as postmaster of the first post office, called Pierson, which opened in 1902. Its name was later changed to Obsidian and moved to that village, where it operated until the early 1970s at two different locations.

Nearby on Fisher Creek in 1901, Frank Shaw was the second settler in the valley, and his cabin now stands in the Stanley City Park. A few sheep grazed Stanley Basin by 1879. Frank Gooding (later governor) brought in large bands of sheep around 1887. By 1907 the area was being overgrazed: there were 364,000 sheep in the Sawtooth Forest Reserve.

THE FOREST SERVICE

In 1908 when the Forest Reserves were changed to National Forests, the Sawtooth Forest was split, with the western part becoming the Boise National Forest. Emil Grandjean, a professional forester from Denmark, became its first Supervisor and kept the position until 1923. The Sawtooth Reserve then included several ranger districts including Wood River, Salmon River, and Boise River.

One of these districts was the Pole Creek District in Sawtooth Valley. William Horton served as its ranger for 20 years. His log ranger station, built in 1909, is the site of an interpretive trail. By 1913, it had the first telephone in the area. The fenced space around the station shows the difference in vegetation between areas that have been grazed and those that haven't. You can see the contrast in vegetation 150 yards south of the Pole Creek Road on the east side of the fenced area. Within the fence only Horton's few horses have ever grazed.

From 1933 to 1941, the Civilian Conservation Corps constructed many Forest Service buildings, roads, trails, and campgrounds. CCC camps were located at Redfish, Ketchum, and on Big Smoky Creek just south of the Sawtooths. During those years, a drought caused many fires in Idaho. The 1,424-acre Germania Creek fire was one of the first to be fought. Extinguishing it cost $1,054.

EXPLORATION

The first to explore the Sawtooths extensively was a taxidermist, photographer and guide named Robert Limbert. In the 1920s he successfully lobbied for a national monument for Craters of the Moon. He also built Redfish Lake Lodge in 1929, and with John Ewald, made first ascents of several Sawtooth peaks

In 1934 and 1935, the famous American mountaineers, Robert and Miriam Underhill climbed at least 20 of the major Sawtooth Peaks, including Mt. Heyburn. They were guided and packed in by a local

27

rancher, Dave Williams. Articles written by the Underhills attracted more climbers, including members of the Iowa Mountaineers. Paul Petzoldt, founder of the National Outdoor Leadership School, and five others from the Iowa Mountaineers, made the first ascent of Warbonnet in 1947. Beginning in the late 1940s, the northwest mountaineer, Fred Beckey, also made first ascents, such as Big Baron Spire and North Raker. Louis Stur made the first ascent of the Finger of Fate, with Jerry Fuller, in 1958. Stur is best known for the route he pioneered on Mt. Heyburn, called the Stur Chimney.

FORMATION OF THE NATIONAL RECREATION AREA

The beauty of the rugged peaks led people to campaign to set the area aside for public enjoyment. As early as 1911, women's organizations in Idaho proposed a national park in the Sawtooths, but a series of bills to establish a park failed in Congress. In 1937, the Forest Service established the 200,042-acre Sawtooth Primitive Area to keep the Sawtooths pristine. In 1972, after studies and public hearings, Congress created the Sawtooth National Recreation Area to be administered by the U.S. Forest Service. The law also designated the Sawtooth Primitive Area as a 216,383-acre wilderness in the National Wilderness System. It stated that the purpose of the Sawtooth National Recreation Area was to protect the plants, trees, wildlife, and fish, especially the salmon, and to conserve and develop the area for public recreation and enjoyment.

The land once designated as the Sawtooth Primitive Area was made a wilderness under the provisions of the 1964 Wilderness Act. The act directed the Secretary of Agriculture to determine what other areas in the SNRA should be made wilderness. It directed the Secretary of the Interior to study the area and the adjacent Pioneer Mountains for a national park. Completed in 1976, the study recommended 686,080 acres for a pair of national parks and the land around them for a national recreation area. The parks have never been established because most Idahoans feel park status would bring too many problems.

GEOLOGY

THE SAWTOOTH MOUNTAINS

The Sawtooth Range is an uplifted fault block bounded by faults, and the Stanley Basin is a depressed fault block called a graben, filled with glacial outwash. Joints, cracks in the granite rock, are close together. A major fault runs along the eastern base of the Sawtooths. The jointing made it easy for the glaciers to break off and carry away the rock, leaving only narrow ridges between them. Water from snow and rain then froze in the cracks, breaking off more rock until only jagged knife-edges were left. The pale gray and beige granitic rock of the western, northern, and southern Sawtooths is part of the 88-million-year-old Idaho batholith. The rock in the east-central section is pink or

28

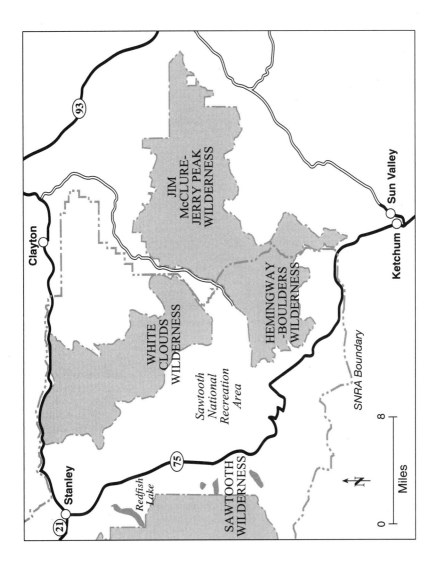

peach and it is part of the 44-million-year-old Sawtooth batholith. A batholith is molten rock that pushed up and cooled underground into granitic rock, rather than erupting from a volcano or rift as lava and then exposed by erosion.

WHITE CLOUD AND BOULDER MOUNTAINS

The 20-mile-long band of white rock giving the White Clouds their name is limestone and related rock from the Paleozoic Era more than 250 million years ago. Much of the white rock has been changed by contact with molten granite to a type of rock called calc-silicate, simi-

The White Cloud Peaks from the Strawberry Basin overlook

lar to marble, but containing silicate minerals as well as carbonate. Other types and colors of Paleozoic metamorphic and sedimentary rocks form a highly mineralized belt, which is 8 miles wide by 38 miles long and runs north-south through the center of the area. It contains major deposits of zinc, fluorite, and low grade gold and molybdenum. At the lower elevations in the eastern and southern part of the White Clouds, the vast volcanism of the Challis volcanics has left rhyolite, basalt lava, and volcanic ash. The Challis volcanics are about the same age, 44 million years old, as the Sawtooth batholith. When first deposited they covered half of Idaho. In places, mudflows in these volcanics formed lakes. Sullivan and Jimmy Smith lakes in the White Clouds are examples of lakes formed this way. There are outcrops of Challis volcanics and Paleozoic sedimentary and metamorphic rock in the Boulder Mountains as well.

PLANTS AND ANIMALS

PLANTS, TREES, AND SHRUBS

Plants, shrubs, and trees in the SNRA change with elevation, rock, soil, and exposure to the sun. The lower slopes and valleys contain big sagebrush (Artemsia tridentata), grasses like Idaho fescue and bluebunch wheatgrass, and patches of lodgepole pine, Douglas fir, and subalpine fir. Huckleberries, which have red leaves in the autumn, often grow under the Douglas fir. The foothills of the White Clouds show the vegetation differences between north-facing and south-facing slopes with open areas on the south slopes and Douglas fir on the north slopes.

Along the streams, grow aspens and willows, with snowberry and elk sedge under the aspen. (Sedges are similar to grasses but their stems are triangular instead of round and their flower parts are more tufted.) The large wet meadows fill with the bright blue blossoms of the camas in late June and early July. Other common wildflowers in wet areas are elephants' head and white wyethia. Where it is drier, sulphur plant, scarlet gilia, paintbrush, sego lily, and littleleaf penstemon grow. On the western side of the Sawtooths near Atlanta and Grandjean, the elevation is low enough for ponderosa pine. Shrubs associated with this pine are snowberry, ninebark, serviceberry, and chokecherry.

Most glacial moraines in the Sawtooths, such as those around Redfish Lake, are covered with lodgepole pine. Higher up, especially where it has been glaciated, subalpine fir, Douglas fir, snowberry, mountain alder, elk sedge, and grouse whortleberry grow, and groves of aspens and lodgepole mark old burns. (Grouse whortleberry, common here, is a low-growing relative of the huckleberry with tiny pale green leaves and miniature red berries.) The most varied vegetation occurs around lakes in the cirque basins. Subalpine fir, Englemann spruce, elk sedge, alpine bentgrass, alpine willow, grouse whortleberry, western ledum (Labrador or trapper's tea), and red mountain heath (mountain heather) all grow here. So do Kalmia (a tiny bog laurel), shooting star, mountain or explorer's gentian, and mountain bluebell.

Near timberline, at around 10,000 feet, whitebark pine and an occa-

Mountain goats

Hiking at Twin Lakes

sional limber pine replace the other trees. Whitebark pine has five needles and the dark-purple pitchy cones do not open when the seeds
ripen, unlike the cones of most pines. Here are subalpine sagebrush,
elk sedge, Idaho fescue and sheep fescue. Wildflowers include a mountain sorrel, white mountain heath, and alpine buttercup.

Rare plants here include the endemic White Clouds milk-vetch,
found only in the White Clouds. (Endemic means that this is the only
place in the world where the plant grows.) This ground-hugging plant
has gray hairy compound leaves and whitish-yellow irregular flowers.

Evening primrose

Other places with unusual vegetation are the fens, areas of peat similar to bogs, in Sawtooth Valley. These fens are watered by streams and precipitation rather than groundwater like bogs. One of their rare plants, a sundew, has tiny reddish leaves with hairs bearing sticky secretions around the edges. With the sticky secretions, it traps insects and digests them.

THE MOUNTAIN PINE BEETLE AND DOUGLAS FIR BEETLE EPIDEMICS

Many of the lodgepole and whitebark pines in the SNRA have died as the result of a mountain pine beetle epidemic. The dead trees first turn red when their needles die. When the dead needles fall off, the trees just look gray and aren't as noticeable. The beetle, Dendroctonus ponderosae, also kills the Western white pine found in northern Idaho. The beetles produce one generation a year, with adults flying to new trees in July and August. The female beetles attack the trees after mating, digging holes in which to lay their eggs. The larvae then eat tunnels in the bark, killing the tree. By the time a tree dies, it has developed white growths on its trunk that look like popcorn or little white mushrooms. Treating trees with pesticide or beetle pheromones to prevent attacks is too expensive to be practical for more than the occasional tree. Thinning the trees helps some. The main cause of the epidemic is the prolonged drought of the last few years that has weakened the trees. Mountain pine beetle epidemics are a natural part of the forest, just as fire is, and occur in cycles.

Many of the older Douglas firs have been killed by the Douglas fir beetle, also due to the drought. This beetle usually kills only trees that are more than 12 inches in diameter. Red orange dust at the base of the tree from the larvae's boring shows that a tree has been attacked,

WILDLIFE

Most of the wildlife and birds occur in several different vegetation

33

Golden mantle ground squirrel

types. A few like the mountain goat, are limited to particular elevations. Others, like the bighorn sheep, live at various elevations, but are found only in areas with rocks and cliffs. More common wildlife includes pronghorn antelope, elk, black bear, cougar, bobcat, mule deer, coyote, beaver, and muskrat. There are a few wolves and wolverines. Smaller animals include squirrels, mice, shrews, pikas, chipmunks, gophers, badgers, porcupines, rabbits, raccoons, otters, foxes, martens, weasels, and skunks. Rainbow, eastern brook, cutthroat, bull trout and California golden trout, and steelhead are found in the waters of the SNRA. There were two runs of chinook salmon and one of sockeye, in the Salmon River and Redfish and Alturas creeks, but most of the salmon returning here now are hatchery fish. Kokanee, a small landlocked salmon, occurs in the larger lakes, especially Redfish. The nearby fish hatchery is raising sockeye and chinook to try to reestablish the runs, but the genetic stock from hatcheries is less diverse than the original.

BIRDS

Birds include ducks, Canadian geese, owls, and three forest grouse: ruffed, blue, and Franklin. Other birds are robins, woodpeckers, sparrows, chickadees, warblers, juncos, bluebirds, magpies, hawks, thrushes, ospreys, snipe, killdeer, siskins, golden eagle, dipper, and water pipit. The dipper is unusual because this small dark gray bird runs underwater to look for insects.

It builds spherical nests of strands of moss with a hole in one side.

One of the most beautiful birds is Idaho's state bird, the mountain bluebird, because the males are a brilliant turquoise.

THREATENED AND ENDANGERED SPECIES

Two species listed as endangered by the federal government live here, the peregrine falcon and the sockeye salmon, although the wild form of the sockeye is nearly extinct. The Canadian lynx is endangered but hasn't bee seen in the SNRA. The gray wolf vanished many years ago, but has been reintroduced, so a few now live in the SNRA. Other Threatened species in the SNRA are the bald eagle and chinook salmon. The grizzly bear vanished from here in the 1940s, but grizzlies in eastern Idaho have been expanding their ranges, so it is possible they will get to the SNRA eventually. Wolves were reintroduced into the Frank Church Wilderness in 1995 and 1996 and some have moved from there into the SNRA. .

None of Idaho's federally endangered plants are found in the SNRA. The plants this book refers to as rare are listed in other categories: as candidates for listing by the federal government, as sensitive species by the Forest Service and Bureau of Land Management, and as sensitive species by the Idaho Native Plant Society.

ACTIVITIES

Commercial activities are few, and most today are based on recreation, such as lodges, stores, guest ranches, and outfitters. The number of cattle and sheep that use summer ranges here is strictly limited. Logging is mostly restricted to post and pole sales and firewood cutting.

Recreation predominates. Hunting and fishing are permitted in accordance with Idaho fish and game laws. The Idaho Fish and Game Department stocks some of the streams and lakes. To find out which have been stocked recently, consult the Idaho Department of Fish and Game website. Fishing is usually better in the White Clouds than in the Sawtooths because the minerals in the types of rock found dissolve more easily, releasing nutrients to nourish the invertebrates the fish eat.

Hiking, backpacking, and horseback riding and horse packing are popular forms of trail travel, even in the non-wilderness areas. Some of the non-wilderness trails are open to mountain bikers and motorcyclists. Travel plan maps that are available at Forest Service offices show which uses are allowed on trails and roads. Trails that are open to motorcycles or mountain bikes vary in the skills required to ride them safely. It is a good idea to consult with SNRA rangers before your trip.

This guidebook describes trails suitable for hikers, mountain bikers, ATVers, motorcyclists, backpackers, and horseback riders without designating the uses. It also includes cross-country routes only for hiking. A section in the appendix lists roads and trails good for mountain biking.

Sailing, water skiing, motorboating, and canoeing are popular on the lakes, and whitewater rafting and kayaking take place on the Salmon River below Stanley. The rafting and kayaking there are regulated to protect spawning salmon. On the lakes, people waterski, wake board, and even scuba-dive, although the water is so cold wet suits are usually worn. Most sunbathers enjoying the beaches at the lakes swim only a little because of the cold water. In winter, snowmobiling and cross-country skiing are the main activities. The SNRA headquarters has information on the locations and conditions of groomed snowmobile and cross-country ski trails. Backcountry outfitters lead cross-country ski treks where the guests stay in yurts. In winter Stanley residents have a curling rink.

BACKCOUNTRY TRAVEL

Most trails have register boxes at or near the beginning. All hikers and riders should register so that their presence and destination will be known if problems arise. Registering also helps the Forest Service keep the trails used by the most people in good condition. The sheets or permit cards from the registers are collected only occasionally, so ALWAYS let someone know where you are going and when you'll be back. Most register boxes for trails leading into the wildernesses hold wilderness permits for you to fill out — put one section in the box, and carry one part with you. Locations of the register boxes are not given here because the Forest Service changes them from time to time. Usually the box is at or near the beginning of a trail or at a wilderness boundary.

Horseback riders near Redfish Lake (photo by Carla Fuller)

36

Because conditions change with weather and season it is wise to check with one of the SNRA offices before a trip. Snow or high water can block some trails before July 15, and it is likely to snow any time after September 15. It can snow in the middle of the summer, but it usually doesn't. September and October weather can be beautiful even though cold (15 to 25 degrees) at night. Most trails are open from July 10 through October 15, but the times they open and close vary greatly and it can snow 8 inches in one night as early as September. Trails that open earlier or later than most are listed in the Guide to Trips in the Appendix. A few hikes described are on primitive roads or jeep trails because the destinations are worth hiking to even if some people drive there.

There is no attempt to mention every hazard along the trails. Weather, water, snow, road and trail conditions change, sometimes in only a few minutes. Also, individuals vary in their ability to follow poorly marked trails, drive rough roads, and withstand steep climbs or heat and cold. When in doubt, .about a hazard, consider safety first.

HORSE TRAVEL

When traveling by horse, use gentle horses trained to carry people or packs on narrow trails and to stand quietly when hobbled or picketed. The training should be done before they are taken into the mountains. The horses should also be conditioned by regular exercise before the trip, and they should be used to each other.

Usually, the high passes are not safe for horse travel until after the first week of August. Trying to cross with stock before the trails are bare of snow is hazardous and causes erosion. In unsafe conditions, lead horses across the problem spot, or turn back. Always use caution in passing hikers. Be aware there may be llamas or pack goats on the trail and be ready for them in case their handlers are not aware they need to get them out of your way.

Please tie stock near campsites only when loading and never for longer than one hour. Otherwise use the designated tie area if there is one. Tying stock within 300 feet of streams, springs, or lakes is prohibited. This helps keep bacteria out of the water and helps protect fragile stream banks and lake shores. Where there is no stock tie area, tie horses to highlines strung between sturdy trees over rocky ground. Or horses can be picketed. Picketing a horse to a log is safer and better for the grass than using a picket pin. It is best to picket only one or two horses, and hobble the rest. Whether tied, picketed, or hobbled, avoid leaving stock alone for more than a few hours. Before leaving camp refill any holes the horses may have caused and spread out manure.

Grazing within 200 yards of lakes is prohibited to prevent damage to the lakeshore meadows. It takes many years for this damage to be erased because plants at high altitudes have a very short growing season. Your stock will have much less impact on soils and vegetation if you camp at lower elevations, and take day trips to the high lakes. You can also reduce your impact by using backpacking foods and lightweight gear so that fewer horses are needed.

It is a good practice to carry as much feed as will be needed, but bringing hay into the wildernesses is not allowed. All feed carried into the rest of the SNRA (and into any public land) must be certified free of noxious weed seeds. Some outfitters have found alfalfa cubes are the most satisfactory feed to carry for their horses. The cubes are cheaper than pellets and keep the horses from chewing poles and trees as they tend to do when fed pellets.

LLAMAS

A few outfitters offer llama trips but llama use hasn't yet become widespread in Idaho. Most llama outfitters will not rent animals without a wrangler. Information on sources of llamas is available from the Idaho Outfitters and Guides Association. Learning to use llamas requires practice, and the llamas used for packing should have already been trained by their owner to halter, lead, and walk on trails carrying packs. Llamas are so smart, success with them is easier if you can convince them you are smarter than they are. They don't like going uphill very well, but they will go if you keep insisting. They are fun to use for packing and are easier for the inexperienced to manage than are mules or horses. When using llamas, it is important to remember horses are afraid of them. Someone should walk ahead of the llama handlers so if a horse party appears the llamas can be led off the trail before the horses see them and spook. If you forget to do this, you could cause a disaster.

PACK GOATS

Some people have begun to use domestic goats as pack animals. They cost less than llamas, and don't have to be led. However, the goats must travel with their owners for them to work well. When they are very small, they bond to their owner as though he or she were their mother, so they tend to wander if their owner isn't with them. Therefore, those with pack goats must plan to take the goats with them on any day hikes from camp. When camping with pack goats, be sensitive to the needs of future campers, and if the goats have left any manure in the campsite, even if it is scattered, rake it up and dispose of it away from camp. At present there are no pack goat outfitters in this area. Remember, too, to send someone ahead of the goats so if you meet a horse party you can get the goats off the trail.

OUTFITTERS

When planning and preparing for a backpacking trip, you may find it impossible for your family to carry everything needed to be safe, comfortable, and well fed. To help carry enough, families, especially those with young children, may want to arrange with an outfitter for horses, mules, or llamas or guides on foot to carry their gear. The wrangler and animals can accompany you for the entire trip, or the packer can carry your gear in and come back and get it in a few days. You can arrange to either ride or walk to your base camp. This arrangement is called spot-packing and is less expensive than a guided trip. To obtain a list of packers and outfitters contact the Idaho Outfitters and Guides Association. (address in the appendix.)

Llama packer in the Sawtooth Wilderness

MOUNTAIN BIKING

When riding a mountain bike, you need to take precautions for your safety and that of other trail users. Always ride in control. Sound the bell or horn or call out at corners to warn of your presence. Yield to hikers and horseback riders. Be sure horses, mules, or llamas hear you coming and hear you talk so they know you are a person. To let horses pass, move your bike off the trail on the downhill side if possible. Stay on designated roads and trails and avoid riding during and after rain and on boggy sections. When riding on the highway to complete a loop trip, ride single file. Stay as close to the edge of the road as possible and watch constantly for traffic.

Most bicycle injuries are from lack of control, not from collisions. Always wear a bicycle helmet, preferably with a hard outside shell and foam-padded interior. Gloves, long pants, and a long-sleeved shirt are also important. To prevent catching your pant legs in the chain or gears, tuck them into your socks or wear gaiters.

Ride carefully, looking ahead to anticipate hazards. Practice riding on gentle, smooth surfaces, to develop the skill needed on steep, uneven slopes. It is vital to practice skidding on gentle, even slopes so you can control a skid on loose rocks or rough ground. It is also important to brake before a curve, not within it.

In case of an emergency, carry the same 12 essentials as for hiking, plus bicycle tools, pump, and a tire patch kit. To be sure your gear stays dry, put it in plastic bags inside the bicycle bags. Use rear mounted bags; handlebar bags make control of the bicycle difficult.

Mountain bikes are prohibited in the wildernesses. In other sections of the SNRA, they are allowed on most, but not all trails and roads. Remember that they are NOT allowed off-trail. Some trails and trail sections are too steep or rocky to be safe for mountain bikes. When in doubt, it is safest to walk your bike. A list of possible mountain bike rides is in the appendix.

PREVENTING THE SPREAD OF NOXIOUS WEEDS

In recent years, noxious weeds have begun to spread into SNRA with increased visitor use. Noxious weeds are invasive, non-native species that spread rapidly, choking out native plants. You can obtain booklets identifying noxious weeds at Forest Service offices. Some of the worst offenders here are dalmatian toad flax, yellow toadflax, skeleton weed and several species of knapweed.

Here are some general rules to follow to prevent the spread of noxious weeds. You can help prevent their spread by washing the undersides and tires of your car, your boot soles and any of your camping equipment like tents that contacts the ground.

1. If taking stock into any public land, use certified weed-free feed and bedding, and brush animals before and after backcountry trips.

2. Check clothing and equipment for weed seeds before and after trips. If needed, sponge off or wash any suspect clothing or equipment.

3. Wash vehicles before and after each trip.

4. Avoid traveling through or camping in weed-infested areas.

5. Camp only at existing campsites and stay on established roads and trails.

6. Pull any noxious weeds you can identify and bag and pack out seed-producing parts.

SAFE HIKING

Hiking unaccustomed distances will exhaust you unless you are in good physical condition. If you are not, it can be dangerous. To get into condition for hiking, have a physical exam and then exercise vigorously for several weeks before any long hike or backpacking trip. The exercise should be something which strengthens the heart and lungs, such as bicycling, running, swimming, or walking up and down hills. Because keeping your balance is vital on trails, add balance exercises to your routine, such as standing on one leg for several seconds without hanging onto anything, alternating legs and doing several each day. .

Hiking will also be difficult if you forget to allow time to adjust to the higher altitude. The lower the elevation of your home, the more time you will need to acclimatize. If you don't allow enough time, you can get the severe headache and nausea of altitude sickness. Life-threatening pulmonary or cerebral edema can occur from too rapid an ascent to high altitudes. Spending one to three days at the trailhead elevation before starting a hike will help prevent altitude sickness, but full adjustment can take as long as three weeks. Because the altitudes

Crossing the North Fork of Baron Creek

in the SNRA are moderate, altitude sickness is less of a problem here than it is in higher mountains.

To avoid causing problems with your heart when hiking, take your pulse occasionally. Taking the pulse for five seconds and multiplying by 12 is accurate enough. If the rate climbs above your maximum rate (200 less your age) stop and rest immediately until it drops to your resting heart rate and then hike slower. To help keep the rate at a safe level, stop and rest for 10 minutes every half hour.

Avoid hiking alone. It is much safer to hike with others, not alone, because if an accident happens someone will be there to get you unstuck, treat you for shock or bleeding, cover you up, and go for help. A solo hiker who is injured on a cross-country hike might not be found before death. Those who insist on going alone anyway should take a survival kit, emergency locator like SPOT, plenty of water and warm clothes, and stick to well-traveled routes. There is no cell service! A solo hiker should carry a lightweight sleeping bag even on a day hike to help prevent hypothermia at night if he or she is hurt. They should also let someone know exactly where they plan to go and exactly when they plan to return and not deviate from their plan.

One of the most dangerous hazards on trails is crossing creeks. Unless a bridge is mentioned in the hike description, hikers should

41

plan on wading creeks or crossing on stones or fallen logs. Most references to footlogs have been removed from this edition because logs often wash away in spring runoff. You have to plan on fording and be pleasantly surprised if there is a log. Before July 15, some of the fords are dangerous or impassable. In wet years, creek crossings will be hazardous even longer, and children, seniors, and the inexperienced may have problems even in late summer. There are only about 30 trail bridges in the whole SNRA and ten of these are on the Harriman Trail. There are, however, many places where planking covers boggy areas to prevent erosion.

To cross a creek safely, unfasten the waist belt of your pack, so it won't hold you underwater if you fall. People have drowned in the SNRA when held underwater by their packs. Keep your boots on to protect your feet and to prevent slipping. Sandals don't give enough ankle support on the mostly rocky stream beds. The safest places to wade are shallow, gravelly areas. Wading is safer than walking on slippery wet logs or rocks. When wading, face upstream, and move diagonally, using a stick for balance. A sturdy walking stick acts as a third leg. Move only one of your three "legs" at a time. To prevent blisters, dry out your boots with a towel and change to dry socks on the other side of the creek.

Old mines have dangerous shafts and tunnels. Plan your trip to avoid them. If you must pass any, keep away and watch children carefully.

In addition, avoid burned areas especially on windy days. Burned trees can fall at any time, but are more likely to fall on windy days. Mud slides are another danger in burned areas because the soil doesn't hold water well.

SAFETY FOR ALL WILDERNESS TRAVELERS

It can snow in the SNRA any day of the year, but hypothermia can occur when it is only rainy or windy. Hypothermia, or the dangerous loss of body heat, is probably the greatest danger in these mountains and can occur in temperatures as high as 50 degrees F. Wind can make the effective temperature much lower than what the thermometer shows. This effect is called wind chill. Hypothermia can cause death in minutes.

To prevent hypothermia, keep dry and warm. Put on rain gear when it first starts to rain. Under the rain gear, wear clothes that stay warm when wet, such as fleece, pile, or wool. If it is raining hard, most waterproof, breathable pants and jackets will leak, so you need a coated nylon poncho on top of them. (Plastic ponchos tear too easily.) To prevent a large heat loss from your head, wear a wool or fleece hat that covers your ears. Use several light layers of clothing so you can remove layers to prevent sweating, because damp clothing adds to your heat loss. To protect against wind, the outside layer should be tightly-woven fabric. To help your clothing keep you warm, eat often to help maintain body heat.

If it is impossible to stay dry and warm, it is best to make camp and build a fire. To be able to make camp on a day hike, carry a tarp, tube tent, or aluminized plastic space blanket. When backpacking, a nylon tent with a waterproof floor and separate rain fly gives the best protection against rain, wind, and snow. To build a fire in these conditions, besides matches or a lighter, you need a reliable firestarter, such as previously gathered lumps of pitch, or cardboard strips held together by paraffin.

To recognize hypothermia, check for persistent shivering. A shivering person should get out of the wind and rain, change into dry clothes, drink hot liquids, and climb into a warm sleeping bag. If the person has waited too long to do this, and he or she is only semi-conscious, very gently remove clothing and place him or her into a sleeping bag with another person. That person should also be nude because skin-to-skin contact transfers body heat most effectively. In severe hypothermia like this, any exertion, rough handling, or attempts at rapid rewarming can cause death because the condition affects the heart. Horse parties should be aware that horses can get hypothermia, and to prevent it, horses need to be sheltered from wind and protected from cold.

Another hazard is the clear mountain water. In the last several years a protozoan, Giardia lamblia, has come into the area. It can cause severe diarrhea and painful stomach cramps beginning six days to three weeks after exposure. The only way to be sure the water is safe to drink is to boil it for at least five minutes, or filter it with a water filter. Therefore, a water filter or kettle is essential. Don't rely on getting water from a spring. The spring can merely be the outflow of a creek that is running higher up and can still be contaminated.

There are few animal hazards. The main ones are ticks and mosquitoes. The common larger ticks inhabit the brush all over the SNRA from May until mid-July. Only a few of them carry Rocky Mountain Spotted Fever and tularemia. The minute tick that carries Lyme disease is rare here. During the early-summer weeks, all backcountry travelers should inspect themselves for ticks at least twice a day. To urge a tick to back out, put insect repellent or white gas on it, or cover it with oil or grease. Or you can try to pull the tick out with tweezers very slowly, so it will relax its grip. If part of it remains under the skin, it can cause serious infection. Therefore, if bitten by a tick, check with your doctor after your hike.

Since mosquitoes now carry West Nile Virus, always wear insect repellent, and reapply it several times a day. Also, use a bug-proof tent.

It is unwise to feed, disturb, or approach wild animals. Deer can kick with their razor-sharp hooves. Chipmunks and ground squirrels sometimes carry bubonic plague. Any animal may bite if fed by hand, and handouts make animals dependent on humans and unable to survive winter. Black bears are seldom a problem here, but the SNRA has 150 to 200 of them. They are commonest in the brushy canyons on the west side of the Sawtooths. In these areas, it is wise to avoid smelly food like bacon, and to hang food at night on a tree limb 10 feet from the ground and 6 feet out from the tree trunk. Even if you don't hang your food, protect it at all times from chipmunks and ground squirrels because they can crawl into your pack and tear into the food in seconds. If bitten by a bat get to a doctor as soon as possible because it might have rabies, and rabies is fatal unless shots are given right away.

THE TWELVE ESSENTIALS

For safety, even on a day trip, every backcountry traveler needs to carry the following essentials:

1. Extra clothes — wear or carry all of these: long pants, a sweater or fleece pullover, an insulated jacket, a rain jacket, rain pants, a coated nylon poncho, a wool or fleece hat, and wool gloves or mittens.

2. Extra food beyond the needs of the trip.

3. Pocket knife.

4. Waterproof matches or a full butane lighter (take both, or two packets of matches stored in different places in case you lose one). Waterproof matches and most kitchen matches won't light in the field unless struck on the abrasive strip on their box, so be sure to take the strip.

5. Firestarter — the purchased stick, jelly or paraffin type, or make some at home from paraffin and corrugated cardboard (melt paraffin ONLY in a double boiler), or gather pitch in the forest before the trip.

6. First aid kit, including prescription pain medication for use in case of an accident. Each person in the party should make sure they carry any emergency medicine that has been prescribed for them, such as a bee sting kit or asthma inhaler.

7. Flashlight or headlamp — be sure it works and has extra bulbs and batteries.

8. Topographic maps — know how to interpret them. GPS units are useful but they can stop working, so you need a map and compass, too.

9. Sunglasses — if it snows, traveling over snow without eye protection can cause a severe headache and even snowblindness. Long term exposure to sun hastens the development of macular degeneration, a leading cause of blindness.

10. Compass - know to use it.

11. Full water bottles and a water filter, or pan for boiling water.

12. Emergency shelter — a space blanket, tube tent, or tarp.

A couple of new items may be useful, depending on whether you want to carry the extra weight. The miniature two-way radios may help keep track of party members. If you have a GPS unit and know how to use it, it can give useful information such as how much farther it is to your destination. Here there are so many definite landmarks, that it is not difficult to follow progress on a topographic map. At present, there is no cell phone service in the area except right in Stanley and Ketchum

MAPS

Topographic maps may be obtained from some engineering supply and backpacking stores, or online. They are essential for trail and off-trail travel. The index of US Geological Survey topographic maps for Idaho will help you decide which maps to order. You can look at the index and maps to see which ones to buy or copy at university libraries. The topographic maps for each hike in this book are listed at the top of the description. Standard US Geological Survey topographic maps are 7^1/$_2$ minute with 40-foot contour levels in a scale of 1 inch to

24,000 feet. The old 15-minute maps (with 80-foot contours) are obsolete. You can also get topographic maps by purchasing a CD-rom for Idaho made by the National Geographic. The cost is about $100. Or you can subscribe to an online service, such as mytopo.com, and print out maps. However some online maps don't show trails.

Topographic maps omit apostrophes in place names, so this book does, also. Less-detailed maps of the Sawtooth, Boise, and Salmon-Challis national forests can help you find and follow access roads. They can be purchased at main offices for each national forest and are available with a plastic coating. The new maps of the Sawtooth National Forest show which trails in the SNRA are open and which are closed to motorized travel.

Topographic maps, or printouts, will last longer if they are carried in a large Ziploc bag or covered with adhesive plastic film. To cover them, place a piece of clear adhesive-backed vinyl shelf paper that is the same size as the map on a table, with the backing side up. Peel off the paper backing, and place the map on top of the sticky vinyl surface, with the printed side down. Then trim off any unwanted edges, and fold the map so the plastic side is out.

GPS READINGS

Those who know how to use GPS to keep track of their progress over the ground can use their GPS to make a route or track between points they mark called "waypoints" on their units. Then on the way back they can retrace their route from waypoint to waypoint. However, for safety, GPS users need also carry the backup system of topographic maps and compass — and knowledge of how to use them. To make this backup system work if it's needed, the traveler must keep track of progress on the map as he or she goes.

GPS units don't always work well with U.S. Geological Survey topographic maps because the default reference point for GPS units, called the datum, is not the same as that used by the US Geological Survey maps. The difference is only 1/8 to 1/4 inch,

To make things even more confusing, there are two main grids used with the USGS maps (and dozens of other map grids in the world.) Grids are lines dividing the globe and maps into sections. The two main ones used on the USGS maps are Latitude - Longitude, stated in degrees, and UTM (Universal Transverse Mercator), a metric system. Most GPS units can be set to give the coordinates of a location in either system.

Discussion of how to use a GPS unit is beyond the scope of this book although GPS readings, taken in WGS 84, are listed for all the trailheads.

EMERGENCIES

Before setting out, be sure someone in your party has had a course in first aid and take along a copy of an up-to-date first aid book. In giving first aid, make sure the person is breathing. If they are not, apply CPR (cardio-pulmonary resuscitation). Then stop any bleeding, and treat for shock, (the possibly fatal drop in blood pressure resulting

The road to the Upper Hell Roaring trailhead

from an injury). Shock can kill even when the injury itself won't. For this reason, do not let an injured person try to sit up or stand until you are sure they feel well enough to do so.

If the victim is unable to walk but not seriously hurt, and the party is large, the least expensive alternative is to carry him or her out. A makeshift litter for carrying someone out can be made from two poles and a sleeping bag. Rip the stitching out at the foot of the bag, insert the poles lengthwise, and tie the person on top of the bag securely. For warmth, jackets or other sleeping bags can be wrapped and tied around the victim. However, a person with a suspected neck or back injury should not be moved by amateurs. A helicopter is available for emergencies, but is extremely expensive, (unless you are a member of Life Flight, which costs $35 a year), and helicopter use must be approved by the Forest Supervisor in Twin Falls.

When going for help, leave one person with the victim and send two people out if possible. To avoid mixups when you reach help, write down the information on the injury and your requests for help and hand it to the authorities. Those who go for help should call 911 when they reach a landline phone. At present there is no cell service in the SNRA except right in the Stanley area or sometimes on mountaintops.

The northernmost part of the Sawtooth Wilderness is in Boise County and Idaho City is its county seat. The southwest part of the Sawtooth Wilderness is in Elmore County (Mountain Home). The northern section of the White Clouds is in Custer County (Challis), and the Boulder Mountains and the southern section of the White

Typical "Idaho freeway"

Clouds are in Blaine County (Hailey). An emergency clinic with its own ambulance is at Stanley. The nearest hospital is at Ketchum. Calling 911 will get you the nearest help.

The emergency of getting lost seldom happens if you know how to use a topographic map and compass. These mountains have many recognizable landmarks that show on a topographic map and will guide you back to the trail or a road. Even if you rely on a GPS unit for reaching your destination, you should carry a map and compass. Satellites can be jammed or signals blocked by terrain or clouds, making your GPS unit fail.

If confused, sit down and orient the topographic map with landmarks using your compass. To do this, set the compass on the map and adjust it and the map so the needle points north, parallels the side edges of the map, and points to the top of the map. Now turn the map with the compass on it so the needle points to 19 degrees east of north. (This 19 degrees, called the angle of magnetic declination, is the difference between the direction of the north magnetic pole and the true north pole here. The magnetic declination varies with location.) When you have turned the needle to 19 degrees east of north, north on the compass points north in your surroundings and on the map.

On topographic maps, dark-brown contour lines show 200-foot differences in elevation, and the light brown lines 40-foot differences. A few topographic maps have different scales and contour intervals.) Close-together lines designate cliffs and far apart lines show flat areas.

If you are unable to match the map to the landmarks, , or if it is evening, make camp and build a fire if fire restrictions are not in effect. The fire can signal others where you are, but keep the fire small to avoid a forest fire. Setting up camp and keeping the fire going will help you avoid panic. Panic can cause you to make poor decisions that can be fatal.

LEAVE NO TRACE TRAVEL

People in wild areas have no excuse for poor backcountry manners. An informal code of behavior directs respect for other travelers. When meeting a horse party, stand quietly on the downhill side of the trail while they pass. If you are downhill from the trail and a horse stumbles, it can recover its footing by stepping uphill without stepping on you. If you have llamas with you and meet horses, get the llamas off the trail and out of sight before the horses spook.

Please burn or carry out all trash. Trash includes aluminum foil which won't burn and, when placed in a fire, releases toxins. A former SNRA ranger, Mose Shrum used to say: "Put them in your litter bag and make the rangers smile." Rangers and volunteers carry out hundreds of pounds of trash every year. Every hour of trash collecting is one hour less they spend on trail maintenance like cutting big logs that are hard to climb over. If you find other people's trash, carry it out. Try to leave the land the way you found it, or, if possible, better.

Some of the code for wild country behavior is law. Burying trash or garbage is illegal. It is also illegal to remove or collect any natural objects except berries and mushrooms and, with an Idaho license, fish and game in season. It is against the law to remove prehistoric and historical artifacts. . These objects are part of our heritage, and heavy fines and jail await those who remove them.

Taking shortcuts between trail switchbacks is also illegal. It causes erosion and washouts. No one wants to have their taxes used to repair this kind of erosion. To prevent erosion when traveling in trailless areas, keep off paths and game trails. Instead, walk on rocks whenever possible, and spread out your party. Wait until muddy trails dry before traveling them.

Good wilderness manners require portable stoves for cooking instead of fires. Wood fires scar the earth and rocks, sterilize the soil, and require chopping up dead trees that house animals and birds. Where fires are allowed and you need one for warmth, use an existing fire ring, or dig a hole for the fire and cover the ashes with dirt after they are cold. In the wildernesses, fires must be built in a fire pan or on a fire blanket and the cold ashes scattered. Cutting GREEN trees or branches is prohibited throughout the SNRA and within the Sawtooth Wilderness, cutting DEAD trees and branches is also illegal.

Please obey signs closing some campsites so the trampled vegetation will grow back and the trees roots will recover. Camping within 100 feet of main trails is prohibited in the Sawtooth Wilderness.

Please keep dogs out of lakes and streams and bury their waste. Collapsible nylon bowls are available for water and your trowel makes a handy pooper-scooper. Avoid letting your dog annoy other campers or harass wildlife — the wildlife could be a porcupine. In the Sawtooth Wilderness, dogs must be leashed during the summer months.

Respect for the land means choosing your campsite to avoid damaging vegetation. Camping in meadows harms the grass and trenching tents kills it. The growing season in mountains is very short, so the grass grows back very slowly. To avoid damaging high lake basins, camp in the canyons below them, and day hike to the lakes. Camping lower down gives an easier trip, fewer other campers, and fewer mosquitoes.

The code also includes respect for others. Camp far enough away from other campers that they can't see you or your tent from their campsite. Avoid making loud noises that disturb wildlife and other people.

When rain threatens to flood your tent, use rocks rather than trenches to divert water. A tent "footprint" UNDER your tent or a tarp or poncho laid INSIDE it will help keep gear dry. (A "footprint" is a waterproof groundcloth that is the same size and shape as your tent floor.) A tarp under your tent that extends out from its sides will collect water and funnel it under the floor. Before leaving, be sure to replace any rocks you have moved.

No one wants detergent foam in drinking water or old noodles at the edge of the lake. Wash dishes, bathe, and do laundry at least 150 feet away from lakes and streams. Use biodegradable soap, and as little of it as possible. Your washpan can be a cook pot, a folding plastic pan, or even a large plastic bag. Strain dishwater, and dump it at least 100 feet away from lakes, streams, and campsites. Burn or carry out the food particles strained from the water. Use a pan for cleaning and rinsing fish, and burn or carry out the fish entrails.

Keeping water clean requires proper disposal of human waste. For a toilet, dig a hole six to eight inches deep at least 100 feet from lakes, streams, springs, or campsites, and cover it with earth after use. Latrines can be dug for large groups, but should be long, shallow trenches at least 300 feet from water. To prevent swarms of flies, the latrine should be partly covered after each use and completely covered before leaving camp. Since animals will dig up toilet paper and scatter it, put your used toilet paper in double plastic bags and carry it out. The best way to keep the landscape clean and sweet smelling is to use the new single-use bags for human waste for your toilet and carry them out in your backpack.

PLANNING YOUR TRIP

To help you plan, the beginning of each hike description lists the round trip from the nearest trailhead, highest point reached, elevation gained, elevation lost (the return climb) if any, time to allow on foot, topographic maps, and access roads. It also gives some of the trails that join the one described and the name of the trailhead if it has one. It also includes the GPS reading at the trailhead, and a description of the destination labeled "what you'll see." For the hikes which begin at a trail junction that is far from a trailhead, an additional line says: "**This one-way section:** x miles, y feet gain." For through trips, the mileages given are also one-way. In each description and in the Guide to Trips in the Appendix, the routes are rated according to difficulty. Hikes with large elevation gains seem much longer than their mileage. Plan at least an hour to climb 1,000 feet plus an hour for every 2 miles of distance. If you forget to do this, you may think, as some hikers have that the miles here are "Fuller miles" and not accurate. You also have to figure more time and more fatigue if you are still getting in shape. If you hiked a trail twenty years ago, by now trail gremlins have stretched it and it will seem much longer and harder.

Cross-country hikes take much longer so allow extra time to find the way, climb steep slopes, and thread your way through and around downed timber. Some cross-country hikes are not described as separate hikes, but instead brief directions are given for the route in the trail description for the nearest trail. The author has hiked to almost all these places, but their names are informal. These hikes are listed in the appendix with their access trails.

A few definitions may help you understand the hike descriptions. Talus means loose boulders and rocks with no dirt between. A rock bench is a large rounded or flat place of solid rock. Switchback and hairpin mean the trail doubles back on itself. The term cairn refers to a small pile of rocks marking the route. Transfer camp means a trailhead with a campground located beside it. Blazes are cutouts in the bark of trees. They are shaped like upside-down exclamation points and are used to mark the official trails. Posted refers to private property having "no trespassing" signs at its boundaries, and there is some posted private property in the SNRA near a few of the trails.

The mileages in this book may not agree with Forest Service signs, but all mileages have been checked against Forest Service trail logs and the author's experience in hiking the trail. Mileages for trails never logged have been calculated with a map measuring instrument, taking into account switchbacks not shown on the maps. Landmarks may have changed or disappeared due to natural causes or trail rerouting.

In planning, consider the access roads as well as the trails. As trails and roads are rerouted and upgraded, mileages may change Road mileages are only approximate because odometer readings vary by a few tenths of a mile each time you drive a road — even in the same car. Different cars vary even more. The access roads are described as paved, gravel, dirt, and primitive. The gravel roads here are surfaced with gravel mixed with dirt. Dirt and primitive roads may become impassable after rain or snow. Most primitive roads require a vehicle with a high clearance and may be open only part of the summer due to mud, snow, or washouts. On these roads, 4-wheel drive helps, especially if it rains or snows. Expect to drive less than ten miles an hour on primitive roads or get a flat tire.

At Redfish Lake, you can take the lodge shuttle boat to the Inlet Transfer Camp at the upper end of the lake. Prices keep going up, but in 2016 the price for a round trip for adults was $16. The shuttle starts at 7:00 a.m. and it will take you any time there are four or more people waiting. However, when you pay for your ride, you need to sign up for one of the scheduled pickups (usually noon, 3, 5, and 7:00 p.m.) if you want a ride back. Your pickup doesn't have to be the same day. Of course, you can walk back the 5 miles along the ridge above the lake instead.

To avoid crowds consider going into the Sawtooths from the west or exploring the White Cloud or Boulder Mountains. The west side of the Sawtooths has one third as many visitors as the east. Trails to lakes are longer, but the canyons are more beautiful. Another way to avoid crowds is to take trips on weekdays or in September.

REGULATIONS IN THE WILDERNESSES

You are responsible for following the regulations for the wilderness in the SNRA in which you are traveling. Camping and any campfires must be at least 200 feet from lakes, streams or springs in any of these wildernesses. In the Sawtooth Wilderness where and when campfires are allowed they must be contained in fire pans or fire blankets. Party size is limited to ten people and the number of stock to 20.

In the While Cloud and Hemingway-Boulder wildernesses, campfires are prohibited at lakes over 9,000 feet in elevation. Party size is limited to 20 and the number of stock to 25. Regulations for the Jim McClure-Jerry Peak Wilderness are still being decided by the Salmon-Challis National Forest.

YOUR RESPONSIBILITY

Since there may be no one nearby to help in an emergency, travelers must take responsibility for themselves. You need to use common sense and not rely on the advice of anyone else, even a friend, a ranger, or a guidebook writer. Also, learn as many wilderness skills as possible before your trip and always let someone know exactly where you

51

are going and when you'll be back. It is a good idea not to hike alone.

You don't need axes, hunting knives, or guns in the backcountry. With today's stoves and backpacking food, these things are more of a danger than a help except for hunters.

Another hazard is swimming in cold back country water. To prevent falls in camp, use light-colored tent guylines or mark them with white or bright-colored tape. To prevent falls, wear boots and use trekking poles.

Not every hazard is described here. Weather, water, snow, and other road and trail conditions change over time, sometimes in only a few minutes. Also, individuals vary in their ability to follow poorly marked trails, drive rough roads, and withstand steep climbs or heat and cold. When in doubt, always turn back or make camp.

TRAILS IN THE SAWTOOTH MOUNTAINS

Finger of Fate

TRAILS IN THE SAWTOOTH MOUNTAINS

The Sawtooths barricade the west side of two small valleys that meet in the 63-person village of Stanley, This settlement is 60 miles north of Sun Valley. The cliffs, towers , and snowbanks create a jagged wall like that of the Tetons but only half as high. The pink Sawtooth granite offers solid walls for climbers. In June the meadows of Stanley Basin spread carpets of cobalt blue camas and pink shooting stars. Roads reach some of the glacial lakes on the east side of the range, such as Pettit and Redfish. Redfish is named for two fish that turn red when they spawn in it. The small kokanee, a landlocked salmon, live in nearby streams and lakes. The two-foot long sockeye salmon swim 900 miles from the ocean to spawn here, the longest such journey of any fish in the world. It is an endangered species.

When my husband Wayne took me to see the Sawtooths from Galena Summit and Alturas Lake on our honeymoon, I had to be polite and say the wooded hills were beautiful. I found out later forest fire smoke had hidden their summits that day. Only after we moved to Boise and I saw giant photos of the Sawtooths in Falk's ID store did I realize how beautiful they are and asked Wayne to take me and our toddler son Doug camping there. One August Saturday at noon we found a space in a campground at Redfish. There are no vacant spaces there on Saturdays now.

ALTURAS LAKE AREA

MILL GULCH

Round trip: 4 miles
Elevation gain: 800 feet
Highest point: 8,380 feet
Map: Frenchman Creek
Trailhead GPS: N 43 49 50.2, W 114 49 24.8
Difficulty: Expert
Time: 6 hours
Access: On Idaho 75 drive 1.4 miles south of Smiley Creek Lodge and turn west on the road to Vienna. Drive 4.1 miles through meadows and forest to a bridge to the left (south) side of the creek. Just before the bridge turn right on a two track road into a meadow with campsites.

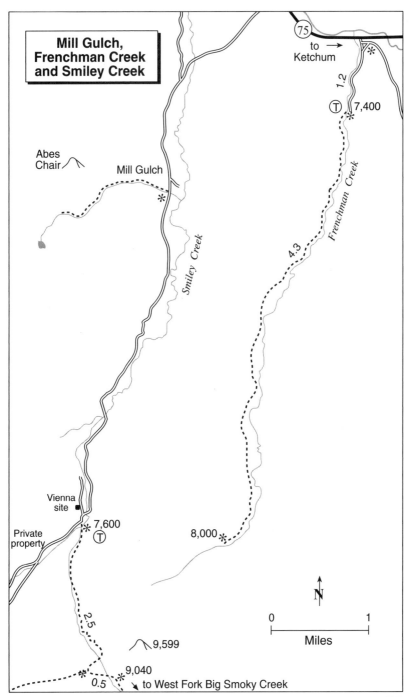

**Mill Gulch,
Frenchman Creek
and Smiley Creek**

75

to →
Ketchum

1.2

Ⓣ ✳ 7,400

Frenchman Creek

Abes
Chair

Mill Gulch

✳

Smiley Creek

4.3

Vienna
site

✳ 7,600
Ⓣ

Private
property

8,000 ✳

N

0   1

Miles

2.5

9,599

✳ 9,040
✳
0.5 ↘ to West Fork Big Smoky Creek

What you'll see: A hidden waterfall, the division between white granite and gray volcanic rock, and rust-colored towers make this trail unusual. It peters out after about two miles. Where it led originally is uncertain: up the canyon to see the views or to lush meadows at its head or to a tiny lake on the far side of the headwall are possibilities.

Directions: On the far side of the meadow, look for a no motor vehicle sign, where the trail begins. At 0 .2 mile this trail goes over to Mill Creek in an open area, then begins climbing in woods. At 0.5 mile the trail is well above the creek's gorge with the waterfall below. Here the rock on the far side of the creek is dark gray, but on the trail side the rock is small white granite boulders. Soon you see the rust-colored towers of the north canyon wall. In the next half mile there is much downed timber.

At about one mile, the trail comes out on sagebrush slopes above thick willows along the creek. Here the tread becomes faint. The trail crosses a couple of streams that were still running in mid-September of a dry year.

After the second one of these streams, the trail deteriorates into disconnected game paths, which are hard to follow. The topographic map shows the trail ending at 2 miles. Another 1.5 miles of cross country travel brings you to the lush meadows at the head of the canyon.

2.

FRENCHMAN CREEK

Round trip: 10.6 miles from where the road joins Highway 75 about 2 miles south of Smiley Creek Lodge to the end of the road; connects with an overgrown jeep trail, closed to motor vehicles, that leads to mine diggings

Elevation gain: 640 feet **Highest point:** 8,000 feet
Maps: Alturas Lake, Frenchman Creek
GPS at beginning: 43 53.040, 114 50.567
Difficulty: easy to moderate; time: 3 1/2 to 6 hours
Access: At a sign for Frenchman Creek 26.3 miles south of Stanley (34.7 miles north of Ketchum), turn south off Idaho 75 onto the Frenchman Creek Road (077). There are two roads that join in 200 yards. Although traffic is light, you need to watch constantly for vehicles. It is probably best to drive the first mile to avoid traffic from people who camp along the road in that section. In early summer, the road is gated before the bridge at 1 mile to all until the road is dry. Where a couple of logging roads branch off, keep to the most well-worn track. The road winds through lodgepole forest, then crosses an open grassy bench at 1 mile and a bridge at 1.2 miles (7,400 feet.) The hike mileage begins at the highway.

What you'll see: This road makes a pleasant conditioning hike or mountain bike ride in June and July, when cinquefoil, avens, elephant's head, and forget-me-not color the meadows. The track passes under the grayish-orange rock towers of an unnamed mountain that resembles a stegosaurus. At a large meadow halfway up the canyon, you can look ahead to four peaks, one with a 400-foot black face. Looking back down the canyon, Castle Peak appears through a gap in the wooded ridges. In early summer, snow stripes the gray, making the peak resemble a pile of sticks.

Directions: Beyond the bridge .3 mile, the road parallels a meadow fenced with logs to enclose a trout study area. From here, ahead on the right are the jagged fins of the stegosaurus mountain.

At 2.5 miles an avalanche trough scores the opposite canyon wall. At 2.8 miles, the meadows widen to 200 yards below a big talus slope. At 3.5 miles, three small ponds on the creek hide in the willows. this is the place where you can look back through a gap and see Castle Peak's serrated top.

At 4.2 miles the road climbs 100 feet into the forest, then descends to another meadow. At 4.8 miles you pass an old ore-loading platform that is off to the right. Beyond here the surface becomes so bumpy you need a high wheelbase or 4-wheel drive vehicle. At 5.5 miles, the road comes to a wooded campsite at the edge of the creek at 8,000 feet. Here a no motorized vehicles sign warns you not to drive across the creek. The road stays on this side of the creek and soon is blocked off by boulders. There are traces of it continuing up the canyon wall to mine diggings shown on the topographic map but the route is overgrown and impassable

3.

SMILEY CREEK TRAIL

Round trip: 8 miles from Vienna to the divide between Smiley Creek and the West Fork of Big Smoky Creek; connects with trails down those creeks.

Elevation gain: 1,440 feet **Highest point:** 9,040 feet

Map: Frenchman Creek

Trailhead GPS: 43 48.843, 114 49.796

Difficulty: moderate; time: 5 hours

Access: Turn south off Idaho 75 onto the dirt Smiley Creek Road (195), 25.6 miles south of Stanley (35.4 miles north of Ketchum) and drive 6.4 miles to a big parking area that is lined with white boulders. This is the trailhead for the Smiley Creek Trail, which is sometimes called the West Fork of Big Smoky Creek Trail, because that is where it goes. The trailhead is .2 mile before the site of Vienna, which has little or no historic remnants. That .2 mile is on the old road, and at that point you have to ford the creek to reach the single track trail.

What you'll see: In 1892, a fire in the Silver King Mine led to the end of mining at Vienna and 20,000 cords of wood for mine timbers were left cut and stacked in the canyon. Many of the timbers are still there beside the trail across the creek from the old parking area, and there is an old boiler up the road a few yards from it. The one cabin that used to stand near the trailhead is gone. North of the trail, red and orange outcrops sprout from an orange peak. A granite ridge holds jointed pillars on the divide between Smiley Creek and the West Fork of Big Smoky Creek. (From the parking area, the road continues for 1.2 miles before it is blocked by private property that is posted because of mining dangers. At this fence, a trail leads to the right (north) uphill over a divide into the canyon of Johnson Creek, a tributary of the Ross Fork of the Boise River.)

Vienna started in 1878, when Levi Smiley and T.B. Mulkey discovered and staked claims on a quartz vein at the head of Smiley Creek. Three settlement started as a result: Vienna on Smiley Creek, Sawtooth City on Beaver Creek, and Eureka in Alturas Lake Creek Canyon. In 1880, the owners of the Pilgrim Mine at Sawtooth City built a toll road over Galena Summit to connect the mines with the road down the Big Wood River to Ketchum.

The Vienna Mine was the largest in Smiley Creek Canyon, but there were others. By 1882, 50 buildings stood in Vienna, including 14 saloons and a sawmill. A 20-stamp mill duplicated the General Custer Mill at Custer northeast of Stanley.

Directions: On the other side of the ford (7,600 feet), the trail passes a 100-yard long pile of mine timbers at .2 mile. Then it climbs through lodgepole pines, and beside timber piles and the ruins of cabins. The second mile has many more switchbacks and stays on the east side of the creek longer than is shown on the topographic map.

At 1.5 miles, the trail zigzags up a grassy hillside, crosses Smiley Creek at 2.2 miles and passes through a meadow below small cliffs. A junction with the Emma Creek and West Fork of Big Smoky Creek trails is on a divide above the canyon of Emma Creek at 2.5 miles. From this divide, the Emma Creek Trail goes southwest 5.5 miles to a road up the South Fork of the Boise River. Follow the West Fork Trail east up a forested slope to a second divide at 3 miles (9,040 feet). On its other side is the West Fork of Big Smoky Creek.

This divide provides access via a trail south down the West Fork of Big Smoky Creek and up Helen Creek to Snowslide and Paradise Lakes, 7 miles from the trailhead.

Landslide on Alpine Creek trail

4.

ALPINE CREEK LAKES

Round trip: 7.6 miles to the west lake, 10.4 miles to the north lakes; 6.2 miles to the end of the trail where the west and north canyons join.

Elevation gain: 500 feet to end of the trail, 1,442 feet to the west lake, 2,087 feet to the north lakes

Highest point: 9,167 feet at the north lakes

Map: Snowyside Peak

Trailhead GPS: 43 53.848, 114 54.223

Difficulty: expert; routes to the lakes from the end of the trail are cross-country; time: 7 hours for the west lake, 8 hours for the north lakes

Access: From Stanley, drive south 20.9 miles (north of Ketchum 40.1 miles) on Idaho 75 to the Alturas Lake Road (205). Turn left (west) on

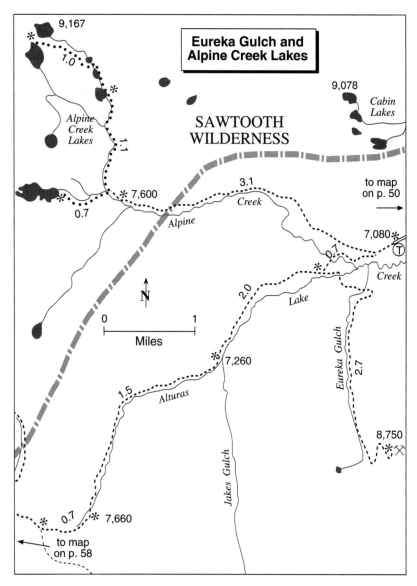

Eureka Gulch and Alpine Creek Lakes

9,167

1.0

Alpine Creek Lakes

SAWTOOTH WILDERNESS

9,078

Cabin Lakes

1.1

7,600

3.1

Creek

0.7

Alpine

7,080

T

0.7

Creek

N

Lake

2.0

0   1

Miles

Eureka Gulch

2.7

7,260

1.5   Alturas

Jakes Gulch

8,750

0.7   7,660

to map on p. 50 →

← to map on p. 58

the paved road and drive along the north side of the lake, passing a turnoff for the Inlet Campground and day use area at 5 miles. Continue past the end of the pavement at 5.4 miles to the trailhead at 6.4 miles.

What you'll see: Several wild and lonely lakes in rugged country are scattered beyond the end of the maintained trail in Alpine Creek

Canyon above Alturas Lake. The largest and closest lake is in the west canyon of Alpine Creek, but reaching it requires a climbing beside a waterfall. At the lower end of the lake, a cracked gray monolith stands guard over two tree-masted islands. At the upper end, a jumble of granite peaks hides.satellite lakes. Four more lakes are strung along the north canyon of Alpine Creek. A sawtoothed wall divides them from Alice Lake. Note that the whole Alpine Creek drainage is closed to stock and to campfires.

Directions: Park at the trailhead (7,080 feet), and start up the trail, which goes up Alturas Creek. In 150 yards, turn off to the right onto the Alpine Creek Trail. At 1 mile, it passes a rock knoll and drops into a sagebrush basin. From here, there is a fine view of the jagged north wall of the canyon and the peaks at its head. This mile makes a fine walk by itself. The trail continues through sagebrush and strips of trees. At 1.7 miles, it comes out on a recent landslide of white gravel, rocks, and pieces of trees. Just beyond is a campsite in the woods. From here, the trail ascends the canyon through forest and over granite benches. It stays out of the canyon bottom at first, then drops to edge another landslide. At 2.5 miles, it crosses above another landslide on a sagebrush hillside, then re-enters woods and fords a side creek. It reaches the main creek (7,580 feet) again 3.1 miles and 500 feet above the trailhead. Here the official trail ends. The cross-country routes up the west and north canyons to the lakes are challenging.

To reach the large lake in the west canyon, go up the main creek 20 yards, then cross it on logs or rocks. The underwater rocks here are slippery. Then zigzag up a wooded ridge, and cut northwest toward the outlet of the lake and the waterfall. At 3.2 miles, 200 feet above the crossing, is a rolling grassy area with a view of the waterfall.

Keep left (south) of the creek and climb over ledges and through willows beside the falls. A handhold may be needed. The lake (8,522-feet) is 3.8 miles from the trailhead. There are several good campsites on three peninsulas on the south shore and near the outlet on the north shore.

To reach the lakes in the north canyon from the end of the official trail at 3.1 miles, go up the creek on the right (east) for 100 yards. Then follow a line of oval blazes that turn up away from the creek. There are downed trees here that are hard to climb over. At 3.5 miles, return to the creek and go along it, continuing through a rolling meadow dotted with subalpine firs to the 8,523-foot lake at 4.2 miles.

Circle this lake on the east, and go along a stream to a narrow pond at 4.4 miles, staying east of the lake, stream, and pond. At the upper end of the pond, cross the creek to the west. Well west of the creek, climb between rounded ledges past two more ponds to an unnamed lake at 9,167 feet at 5.2 miles. From here, another unnamed lake is .1 mile to the southwest at 9,050 feet. Snowyside Peak may be climbed with caution from the saddle above Lake 9,167 by hiking and scrambling. Between the two lakes is a good campsite.

5.

EUREKA GULCH

Round trip: 6.8 miles from the Alturas Creek trailhead to the site of the Ruby Mine
    Elevation gain: 1,720 feet
    Highest point: 8,800 feet
    Maps: Snowyside Peak, Marshall Peak
    Trailhead GPS: 43 53.848, 114 54.223
    Difficulty: moderate; time: 6 hours
    Access: From Ketchum, drive south of Stanley 20.9 miles (north of Ketchum 40.1 miles) on Idaho 75 to the paved Alturas Lake Road (205). Turn left (west) and drive along the north side of the lake. Continue past the end of the pavement to the trailhead at 6.4 miles, .2 mile before Alpine Creek.

What you'll see: The hike to the mining village of Eureka is worth taking even though little is left from the mining days. There is a wonderful view of the pointed peaks and cliffs of Alpine Creek Canyon and the row of pleated cliffs of the mountains behind it. At the head of Alturas Canyon, perch two peaks shaped like chessmen. The trail follows a former jeep trail and is very rocky, so hikers need to be careful.

Directions: At the signed turnoff for the Alpine Creek Trail 150 yards beyond the trailhead keep straight ahead on the trail up Alturas Creek. At .5 mile the trail crosses Alpine Creek on a foot bridge. At .7 mile, turn left (downstream) onto the old Alturas Creek Road at a sign for Eureka. In .1 mile, turn right (south) on the old road to Eureka and ford Alturas Creek Boots are needed because most of the former jeep trail is covered with loose rocks. It is not in the wilderness, but because of the rocks, mountain bikers will find this trail tedious.

The track heads south through the woods, then east across a flat sagebrush area to a ford of the creek in Eureka Gulch at 1.2 mile. Water may cover the road beyond the ford. The jeep trail then curves west and climbs over rocks up a long switchback through the forest. At 1.5 miles it curves south into the canyon of Eureka Gulch and continues climbing. At an open avalanche area at 2.0 miles, it has climbed 500 feet. From here you begin to get a view of Alpine Creek Canyon. The trail goes back into the forest and then into another open area at 2.4 miles.

After more trees, the track comes out in the open again between sagebrush and subalpine firs. At 2.9 miles, the trail curves left and climbs steeply. At 3.1 miles, it switches back to the right (southeast) where an old jeep trail goes off to the north. The main track continues climbing to a junction at 3.4 miles (8,750 feet). Here hikers will find huge logs, some of which have been shaped by axe. Take time to look

Hiking Mattingly Creek Canyon

up the canyon of Alpine Creek. The track that goes straight ahead goes to a patented mining claim. That means it is private property. Instead take the track to the left, which goes uphill to the collapsed tunnel of the Ruby Mine at 3.5 miles. From here, you can look across Eureka Gulch and almost see a small pond that perches on the side of the canyon.

6.

MATTINGLY CREEK DIVIDE

Round trip: 12.4 miles from the Alturas Creek trailhead to the divide; connects with trail down Mattingly Creek to the Middle Fork of the Boise River
Elevation gain: 1,736 feet
Highest point: 8,816 feet
Maps: Snowyside Peak, Marshall Peak
Trailhead GPS: 43 53.848, 114 54.223
Difficulty: strenuous; time: 6 to 8 hours
Access: Turn left (west) from Idaho 75 on the paved Alturas Lake Road (205), 20.9 miles south of Stanley (40.1 miles north of Ketchum). Drive to the lake and along its north shore. Continue past the end of the pavement to the trailhead at 6.4 miles.

What you'll see: At Mattingly Creek Divide, across a meadow of bunch grasses and wildflowers, jagged peaks crowd the canyon wall. Four rock towers, one brick red and the others gray, peer over a gap like giant chessmen. Hikers seldom climb to the divide, although mountain bikers and motorcyclists sometimes ride to the wilderness boundary located here.
Directions: At 150 yards when the Alpine Creek Trail turns off, keep straight ahead on the Alturas Creek Trail to the bridge over Alpine Creek at .5 mile. Beyond the bridge, the way is level through the forest to a junction with the Eureka Gulch Trail at .7 mile. This track goes 2.8 miles with a 1,580-foot elevation gain to the old mines of Eureka. From the Eureka junction, the main trail winds up Alturas Canyon over rocks and through forest to the former end of the road at Jakes Gulch (7,260 feet) at 2.2 miles.
Beyond here, the trail at first shows that it once was a rough wagon road to mines at the head of the canyon. It reaches an open sagebrush area at 2.9 miles. From 2.9 miles to a ford of Alturas Lake Creek at 4.9 miles (7,680 feet), the trail runs through sagebrush and meadows, crossing six intermittent streams on the way.
At 4.9 miles, ford the creek to the left (south) side. Beyond the ford is a campsite. In the next 1.2 miles, the trail climbs 1,200 feet through thick forest. At 5.2 miles, it crosses a side stream. The creek then runs below the trail in a 40-foot ravine. Note that the first intersecting trail

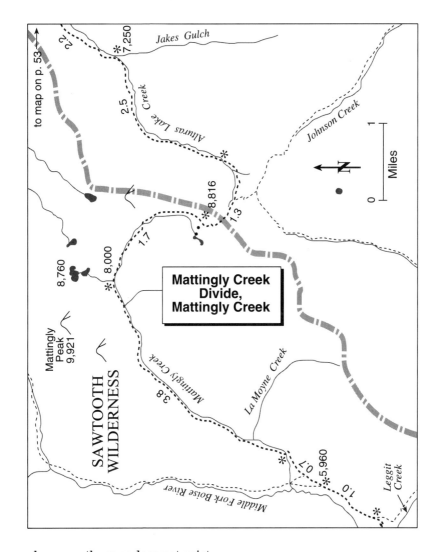

shown on the map does not exist.

At 5.6 miles (8,200 feet), a .5-mile side trail leads to a junction of the Johnson Creek and North Fork of the Ross Fork trails. This Johnson Creek Trail (another Johnson Creek Trail is near Graham) goes 7.6 miles with a 2,055-foot descent to the Ross Fork of the Boise River Jeep Trail.

Beyond this junction, the Mattingly Divide Trail continues to the head of the canyon where it returns to the right side of the creek at 5.9 miles. Then it climbs a hill to the summit (8,816 feet) at 6.2 miles, where it enters the Sawtooth Wilderness.

The divide and the trail from it down Mattingly Creek gives cross-country access to three lakes. One is at the head of the south fork of Alpine Creek and the others are two small lakes on the side of Mattingly Peak. There are also a couple of ponds .2 mile southwest of the divide. The trail down Mattingly Creek drops 2,866 feet in 6.2 miles to the Middle Fork of the Boise River Trail. This junction is 4.5 miles above the east end of the Powerplant Campground at Atlanta.

7.

MATTINGLY CREEK

This one-way section: 6.2 miles from the divide to the Middle Fork of the Boise River trail

Round trip: 24.4 miles from the Alturas trailhead to the Middle Fork Boise River Trail

Elevation gain: 1,736 feet; elevation loss: 2,856 feet **Highest point:** 8,816 feet

Maps: Snowyside Peak, Marshall Peak, Mt. Everly, Atlanta East

Trailhead GPS: 43 53.848, 114 54.223

Difficulty: strenuous; time: 3 to 4 days

Access: Following directions for Mattingly Creek Divide, hike 6.2 miles from the Alturas Creek Trailhead near Alturas Lake to the divide.

What you'll see: Mattingly Creek Canyon is as beautiful as Redfish Canyon but is seldom traveled. The canyon is lined with the typical sawteeth and pleated peaks of the Sawtooths: Mattingly Peak, and others unnamed. In late July the upper meadows are blue, red, yellow, and lavender with penstemon, paintbrush, sulphur plant, and subalpine daisy. The logistics of arranging a car shuttle to Atlanta, which is 47 miles from a paved road, is the reason the canyon is seldom traveled. However, you can see most of it on a three- or four-day trip from Alturas Lake. The hike mileage given here begins at the divide.

Directions: Before descending the creek from the divide, which is 6.2 miles from the Alturas trailhead, you may wish to make a side trip to three tiny lakes (no campsites) These lakes are .2- to .3 mile cross-country west of the divide. Campsites are in the trees on the east side of the divide.

From the grassy divide, the Mattingly Creek Trail plunges down, with a view of cliffs ahead on the canyon wall. Within .5 mile, the ground flattens and you cross to the right side of a small creek in a meadow and come out of the woods into an open area of flowers. At .7 mile, the trail crosses to the left (west) side of Mattingly Creek. Gray cliffs and knolls appear on the right, and the trail stays level through a long wet meadow. At 1.4 miles confusing fords end on the right (east) side of the creek. The trail stays on that side for the next several miles.

Beyond these fords, the trail drops through boulders and over slabs. It passes grassy and mossy places and at 1.7 miles (8,000 feet) crosses a side creek that comes down from two trailless lakes on the north canyon wall. It is possible to climb along this stream over boulders to these lakes. It is probably easier to reach them by descending another 200 feet and 3/4 mile on the main trail and then go up to the lakes. Both routes have been hiked by two of the author's friends.

Below this stream crossing, the trail remains steep and rocky as it descends in the open. At 2.2 miles is a large meadow. At the far end is a campsite with a view of the mountain wall. Beyond the campsite at 2.4 miles, the trail fords the stream to the left (west) side for 200 yards. It may do this only to access a large flat area of forest, where there are possible campsites. It fords back right away. From this second crossing, you look up at triangular towers.

Beyond here, the creek runs in a gorge 20 feet deep. The trail now alternates forest on steep hillsides with open areas of rocks, grasses, and wildflowers. At a grassy area at 2.8 miles, a tongue of talus in the creek bottom points up the canyon. The canyon wall on the other side is open with a big cave in the cliffs. The trail is still steep.

At 3.2 miles, where the grade flattens, the creek runs over granite in a little waterfall, and below it you'll find space for one tent. Beyond here the trail levels some but still has steep stretches. At 4 miles, you come out opposite a side canyon with a waterfall. The trail crosses 200 yards of boulders, and at 5 miles has a view up wooded LaMoyne Creek on the other side of Mattingly Creek. Past more boulders, the trail appears to branch. Take the downhill branch into a steep ravine where, in alders, it fords the creek to the left (southeast) side at 5.5 miles. This ford is swift and deep in late July with no logs to cross on.

The temperature will be warmer now, for you have descended 2,000 feet, and in mid-summer, it can be more than 90 degrees. Ponderosa pines join the forest beyond the ford. The trail climbs onto a wooded hillside and goes along it with narrow tread. Back up the creek is the pleated face of Mattingly Peak. As the trail rounds a corner, you can look up and down the Middle Fork at the canyon walls.

The grade lessens before a junction at 5.5 miles with a short cut on a gentle grassy slope. to the Middle Fork of the Boise There are campsites on the grass near the junction. This is the first possible campsite since the little waterfall back up Mattingly Creek.

The junction with the Mattingly Creek Trail to the Middle Fork trail is at 6.2miles. (5,960 feet) From here, it is 4.5 more miles to the east end of the Powerplant Campground at Atlanta.

The First Cabin Lake

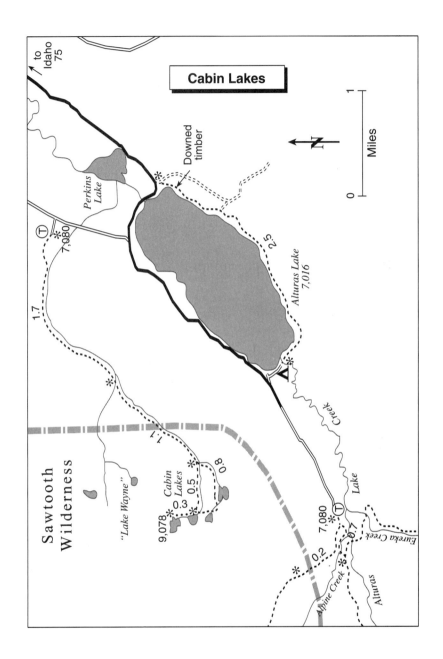

Cabin Lakes

to Idaho 75

Perkins Lake

Downed timber

Alturas Lake
7,016

2.5

N

Miles

Sawtooth Wilderness

"Lake Wayne"

Cabin Lakes

9,078

0.3

0.5

0.8

1.1

1.7

7,080

7,080

Alturas Lake

Eureka Creek

Alpine Creek

Creek

0.2

0.7

8.

CABIN LAKES

Round trip: 7.5 miles from the Cabin Creek trailhead near Alturas Lake to the lower, upper, and twin lakes
    Elevation gain: 1,998 feet **Highest point:** 9,078 feet
    Maps: Alturas Lake, Snowyside Peak
    Trailhead GPS: 43 56.221, 114 51.292
    Difficulty: strenuous; time: 7 to 8 hours
    Access: On Idaho 75, about 10 miles south of Stanley at Milepost 170, turn west on the rough gravel Cabin Creek Road. At .8 mile it crosses Alturas Creek. At 1 mile turn left (south) on road 207. At 2.5 miles turn right (west) on a primitive road, and drive .2 mile to a parking area. Note that the Cabin Creek Road no longer goes through to Alturas Lake.

What you'll see: From the trail you see the sandy crest of McDonald Peak, sprinkled with pines, and the canyon above the five small Cabin Lakes. At the first and deepest lake, a rippling waterfall and a knoll of cracked gray cliffs plunge into aquamarine water. On a granite shelf, the highest lake sprawls off-trail among rocky peninsulas, flowered turf, and golden sand. A lower lake has two lobes divided by a ten-foot wide channel.

Directions: From the Cabin Lakes trailhead, 7,080 feet, the trail climbs northwest through trees and up a sagebrush hillside. It then goes west along a steep hillside above the creek.

At .8 mile, woods and open grassy areas begin to alternate. At 1.7 miles, the trail climbs a side creek for 200 yards before fording it. Here intrepid hikers can climb along that creek cross-country to two unnamed lakes under a shoulder of Mt. McDonald, but the route is steep and rough.

From the ford, the trail continues to climb and cross streams. At 2.8 miles, beyond a grassy basin and a ford of a side creek, it approaches the main creek and becomes faint. (Here a route to the twin lakes turns off to the left. Returning by that trail allows a loop trip of 1.3 miles.) Follow the main trail over granite ledges up the right (north) side of the main creek. It climbs ledges through trees to the first lake (8,811 feet) at 3.3 miles where it ends. To reach the 9,073-foot upper lake go .2 mile around the east side of the first lake and turn northeast up a gully that is to the right of the creek between the lakes.

Alice Lake (photo by Chris Fuller)

PETTIT LAKE AREA

9.

ALICE LAKE

Round trip: 10.8 miles from Pettit Lake hikers' trailhead; connects with the trail to Toxaway Lake

Elevation gain: 1,600 feet **Highest point:** 8,596 feet

Maps: Alturas Lake, Snowyside Peak

Trailhead GPS: 43 59.059, 114 52.314

Difficulty: strenuous; time: 8 hours

Access: From Idaho 75, 18 miles south of Stanley (43 miles north of Ketchum) turn left (west) on the gravel Pettit Lake Road (208). Go 1.6 miles to a four-way junction. Turn right (north), cross a bridge, keep left where the Yellow Belly Road (365) turns off to the right, and drive .5 mile to the Tin Cup hikers' transfer camp.

What you'll see: The gnarled lodgepoles and subalpine firs on the granite peninsulas at Alice Lake seem arranged by a supernatural landscape gardener. Two ponds just below the lake huddle close to the pale peach wall of El Capitan. At the upper end of the blue-green lake,

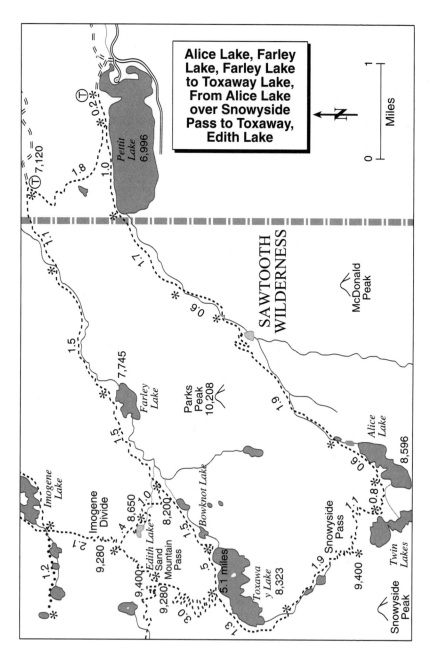

Alice Lake, Farley Lake, Farley Lake to Toxaway Lake, From Alice Lake over Snowyside Pass to Toxaway, Edith Lake

Miles

SAWTOOTH WILDERNESS

McDonald Peak

Pettit Lake 6,996

7,120

0.2

1.8

1.0

1.1

1.7

0.6

1.5

7,745

Farley Lake

Parks Peak 10,208

0.9

Alice Lake 8,596

0.9

0.8

1.7

Imogene Lake

Imogene Divide

8,650

1.0

8,200

Bowknot Lake

Edith Lake

Sand Mountain Pass

Snowyside Pass

9,280

.4

1.5

.5

1.9

9,400

Twin Lakes

1.2

9,400

9,280

3.0

5.1 miles

Toxaway Lake 8,323

1.3

2.1

Snowyside Peak

a row of dragon peaks parades.

Directions: The trail starts out through trees and sagebrush to a view of Pettit Lake (6,996 feet). then goes along above the shore. At .2

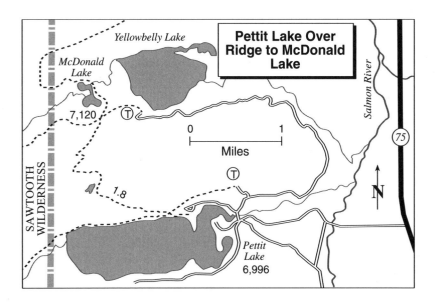

Pettit Lake Over Ridge to McDonald Lake

mile, a side trail leads 1.8 miles and 524 feet over a ridge to the Toxaway Lake Trail. This cutoff trail allows a loop trip from Pettit Lake to Alice and Toxaway lakes.

The Alice Lake Trail leaves Pettit Lake at 1.2 miles and continues level through Douglas and subalpine firs, huckleberry and grouse whortleberry for .6 mile before beginning to climb. At 2.8 miles, it goes along above a gorge, and at 2.9 miles fords the creek to the east side. This deep crossing is difficult for hikers until at least midsummer. At 3.5 miles, the trail fords back to the right (west) of the creek. Here the canyon opens out, revealing a split in the granite walls. The trail zigzags up through brush and then small rocks. In the canyon bottom is a meadow that 40 years ago was a log-strewn pond

After a big switchback it goes over bigger rocks with a drop off below. It fords back to the left side of the creek at 4.1 miles. From here you can look back across the canyon at flat-topped towers that used to have mountain goats. The next half mile is in the shade. The trail crosses back to the right side at 4.3 miles in a flat crossing. Then the trail enters a gorge and switchbacks up a knoll. Above a waterfall at 4.8 miles, the trail returns to the east (left) side on a bridge and levels out.

At 5.1 miles, the trail goes back to the west (right) side of the creek just before the first of two blue-green ponds. Above them the summit of El Capitan points south like a flame in wind. Alice Lake (8,596 feet) appears at 5.4 miles. The trail goes along the shore and over a knoll to a peninsula at 6 miles where it turns right (north) to go on to Twin Lakes. Avoid the overused campsites on this peninsula. To avoid crowds, camp on the off-trail side of the lake. To reach that side, turn left before Alice Lake on a path along the upper end of the second pond. That path crosses the lake's outlet to the off-trail side of the lake. From the off-trail side it is an easy cross-country side trip to one or

more of the ponds above the upper (south) end of the lake.
Alice Lake is heavily used. For a true wilderness experience, choose another area. Remember that campfires are prohibited in the Alice-Toxaway drainage. Bring sneakers or plenty of dry socks for the first three creek crossings.

*10.

FROM PETTIT LAKE OVER THE RIDGE TO MCDONALD LAKE

Round trip: 4 miles
Elevation gain: 500 feet **Highest point:** 7,520 feet
Elevation loss (return climb): 444 feet
Maps: Alturas Lake, Snowyside Peak
Trailhead GPS: N 43 59.059' W 114 52.314'
Difficulty: easy **Time:** 6 hours
Access: From Idaho 75, 18 miles south of Stanley (43 miles north of Ketchum) turn west onto gravel Forest Road 208. Drive 1.5 miles to a 4-way intersection. Turn right here, cross a bridge, and keep left where a road to Yellow Belly Lake goes off to the right. Drive 0.5 more to the Tin Cup Hikers Transfer Camp.

What you'll see: A pond on top of the ridge has a beautiful view of Parks Peak that is especially good in early summer when snow is still on it. The grassy shores of McDonald Lake rise to the slanted cliffs of Parks Peak on the left and the pointed top of Imogene Peak on the right.
Directions: From the transfer camp, start out on the main trail to Alice Lake. At .2 mile a side trail turns north (right) towards Yellow Belly Lake. Turn here and climb the steep slope, which is mostly in the open with arrow leaf balsamroot in bloom in June. The trail is gravelly and will be slippery on the way back. At .3 mile the trail goes into forest, with a couple of open areas before it reaches the top of the ridge at 1 mile. Here, the pond is off to the left (west). Beyond the pond, the trail descends through lodgepole forest in switchbacks to a junction at 1.8 miles with the main trail from Yellow Belly Lake to Farley and Toxaway. From the junction take the side trail .2 mile to McDonald Lake.

11.

FROM ALICE LAKE OVER SNOWYSIDE PASS TO TOXAWAY LAKE

This one-way section: 5.1 miles, 804-foot gain, 1,000-foot loss from Alice to Toxaway
Connects with the trail to Twin Lakes and at Toxaway, trails to Edna and Farley Lakes
Round trip: part of the 18-mile Alice-Toxaway loop trip from Pettit Lake
Elevation gain: 2,404 feet **Highest point:** 9,400 feet
Map: Snowyside Peak
Trailhead GPS: 43 59.059, 114 52.314
Difficulty: strenuous; time: 3 hours for this section; 3 days for the whole loop
Access: Following directions for Alice Lake, hike 6 miles to the place on its shore where the trail turns uphill toward Twin Lakes.

What you'll see: The trail up Snowyside Pass from Alice Lake first passes high above Twin Lakes,which are divided by a strip of pines and firs on granite outcrops. The two-headed dragon peak is closer now, and two peninsulas in the lower lake reach out toward it. From the upper lake, talus and flower-filled slopes sweep up to the slabs, cliffs and snowbanks of Snowyside Peak. From the Snowyside Pass, Twin Lakes resemble sapphires inlaid in a gray granite brooch.
Directions: This hike description begins .6 mile from the lower end of 8,596-foot Alice Lake where the trail turns uphill toward Twin Lakes. From the turnoff at Alice Lake (6 miles and a 1,600-foot climb from the trailhead) the trail ascends west along the creek between Alice and Twin Lakes to a little grassy valley. Here it turns right (east) and makes a big switchback up a rocky slope inhabited by pikas. Well above Twin Lakes at .8 mile, a side trail turns off to the left to them. It descends about 100 feet to the narrow strip of land between the lakes. A path leads along the shores in both directions and there are several good campsites.
The trail over Snowyside Pass is different from what is shown on the topographic map. Halfway around Upper Twin Lake and well above it, the trail heads north into a meadow with a pond. Then it switchbacks four times before the 9,400-foot pass which is at 1.9 miles. In years with normal snow, this pass may not be open to stock until the first week in August. Hikers can travel it sooner, but the snow on the north side is hazardous. To avoid danger and erosion and to avoid damaging the soils, wait until the snow melts and the trail has dried out.
On the far side, the trail descends 14 zigzags over rocks, turf, and mountain heather to two turquoise ponds. The first pond is at 3.2

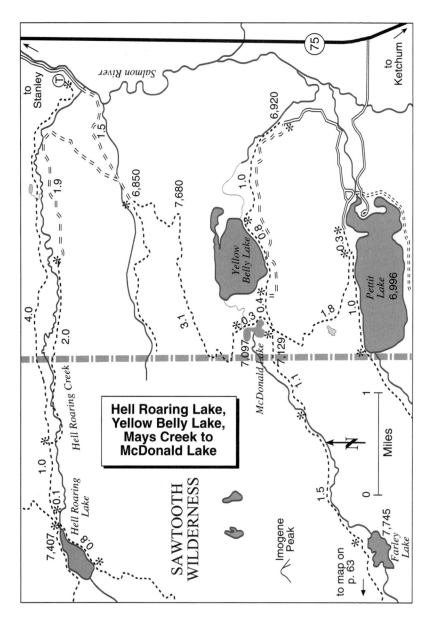

Hell Roaring Lake,
Yellow Belly Lake,
Mays Creek to
McDonald Lake

miles. At the second pond, the trail descends to the shore across from an inlet that, in midsummer, flows through the white flowers of parrot's beak.

Below this pond, the trail runs beside the stream as it slides over granite to a third tiny pond. Then it switchbacks down through boulders and subalpine firs making more switchbacks than shown. At 3.8

miles, it crosses the creek on logs below a waterslide, and at 4 miles, passes a campsite just above Toxaway Lake.

The trail goes along the north side of the lake on granite benches, crossing side streams. From here, the White Clouds and the scalloped gray wall of Parks Peak are visible . A junction with the trail to Sand Mountain Pass is at 5.1 miles (8,400 feet) above a peninsula of rock benches and tiny trees.

At times, small landslides make the trail on the pass unsafe for horses. So if you are planning to take horses over the pass, check with the SNRA first.

12.

YELLOW BELLY LAKE

Round trip: 2 miles from a parking area part way up a primitive road to Yellow Belly Lake to the lower end of the lake; connects with the trail from Yellow Belly to Farley and Toxaway lakes

Elevation gain: 240 feet **Highest point:** 7,076 feet

Maps: Alturas Lake, Obsidian, Snowyside Peak

Trailhead GPS: 43 59.707, 114 50.957

Difficulty: easy; time: 2 hours

Access: From Idaho 75, 18 miles south of Stanley (43 miles north of Ketchum), turn left (west) on the gravel Pettit Lake Road (208). Go 1.6 miles to a 4-way intersection. Turn right (north) on road 355 and cross a bridge over the outlet. On the other side of the bridge, turn right (north) again on a road to the Tin Cup horse transfer camp. (Don't keep straight ahead to the hikers' transfer camp.) At .5 mile, keep straight ahead (east) where a road turns left to the horse transfer camp. Continue on the dirt road to where it splits at 1.6 miles at a sign and parking for the Yellow Belly Trail.

What you'll see: This can be an excellent hike for families with small children, because the trail is easy, little used and pretty. However, in the winter of 2015-16 three dozen trees fell in this one mile, so it is best to wait until they are cleared before hiking it. Most hikers going beyond Yellow Belly hike over the ridge from Pettit Lake or drive the 4-wheel drive road. This trail first goes to the lower end of the lake and then along the shore to the main trailhead at the upper end, The lake has gentle shores covered with grouse whortleberry, Labrador tea, and lodgepole pine. From the lower end, you can look west across the blue-green water to the pointed summit of Imogene Peak and the jumbled helmet of Parks Peak. If you continue along the lake shore, you can also see the white peaks of the White Clouds across Sawtooth Valley.

Directions: From the undeveloped trailhead (6,920 feet), the trail climbs northwest along the outlet of Yellow Belly Lake. At .4 mile it comes near the road for a few feet. Then the trail leaves the creek and climbs up and down over small knolls in woods. At .7 mile, it crosses an old road to a campsite. Continue straight ahead on the trail as it goes level in lodgepoles, at a distance from the outlet. At 1 mile, the trail curves over to the outlet and then back along the lake shore (7,076 feet). You can stop anywhere or continue on the trail to the head of the lake at 1.8 miles where it intersects the 4-wheel drive road. From here, a trail leads west to Toxaway Lake in 6.5 miles.

13.

FARLEY LAKE

Round trip: 6 miles from the trailhead at the upper end of Yellow Belly Lake to the lower end of the lake; trail continues to Toxaway Lake where it connects with trails to Alice and Edna lakes

Elevation gain: 724 feet **Highest point:** 7,800 feet

Maps: Snowyside Peak

Trail beginning GPS: 43 59.795, 114 52.796

Difficulty: easy; time: 5 hours

Access: From Idaho 75, 18 miles south of Stanley (43 miles north of Ketchum) turn left (west) on the gravel Pettit Lake Road (208). Go 1.6 miles to a four-way intersection. Turn right (north) on road 355 and cross a bridge over the outlet. On the other side of the bridge, turn right (north) again on a road to the Tin Cup horse transfer camp. At .5 mile, keep straight ahead (east) where a road turns off to the horse camp. Continue on the primitive, rocky road to a signed trailhead at the west end of Yellow Belly Lake, 3.3 miles from the bridge.

What you'll see: Three granite islands, one with a crew of trees, sail the teal blue water of Farley Lake below the furrowed cliffs of Parks Peak. From these cliffs, white ribbons of water plunge into the clear depths. Across the lake from the cliffs and falls, avalanche chutes clogged with tiny firs gouge the sides of an unnamed orange mountain, sometimes called Imogene. Just below the lake, the creek thunders into a meadow between rock. jaws.

Directions: Don't try to take a passenger car up the Yellow Belly Lake Road to the trailhead. The road is full of football-sized rocks. A high wheelbase is essential, and early in the summer and when it rains, you need 4-wheel drive too. You can instead begin the hike on the Yellow Belly Lake Trail at its trailhead, which is 1.6 miles up the Yellow Belly Road. This trail reaches the parking area at the end of the 4-wheel drive road at 1.8 miles. Or you can walk the Alice Lake Trail from Pettit Lake and, at .2 mile, take a cutoff trail over a 524-foot forested ridge. This 1.8-mile-long trail meets the Yellow Belly Lake Trail .4 mile above Yellow Belly Lake.

Farley Lake

From the west end of Yellow Belly Lake (7,076 feet) the trail runs through sagebrush flats, lodgepole forest, and an old burn to the Mays Creek and McDonald Lake Junction at .4 mile. Here a side trail leads north .2 mile to 7,097-foot McDonald Lake, a shallow green lake in marsh grass and young trees. It has an excellent view of Parks and Imogene peaks and Mt. McDonald. From this lake, the side trail continues 3.2 miles over a ridge to the Mays Creek Road. Back on the main trail, the cutoff trail from Pettit Lake comes in 100 yards beyond the McDonald Lake junction.

The main trail continues through lodgepoles with a few ups and downs to a ford of the outlet of Farley Lake at 1.5 miles. This crossing can be difficult or impassable in early summer, especially in wet years. On the other side, the trail switchbacks uphill in forest. At 2.3 miles, it runs beside cascades and around 10-foot boulders that have fallen from three orange towers on the wall above. There is a rocky meadow with small trees at 2.5 miles. Above it to the south is a waterfall. The trail now climbs a granite bench in rocky switchbacks. From the switchbacks you can see the White Clouds and Castle Peak to the east. Now the route descends past an old avalanche area of big dead logs to an overlook of the lake (7,745-feet) at 3 miles. Here a path turns down to campsites. There are also sites on a peninsula at 3.3 miles, and more sites off-trail at the upper end of the lake. No campfires are allowed in the entire drainage of Farley and Toxaway lakes.

14.

TOXAWAY LAKE

Round trip: 12 miles to the lower end of the lake from Yellow Belly Lake; connects with trails to Alice Lake and Sand Mountain Pass
Elevation gain: 1,247 feet **Highest point:** 8,400 feet
Map: Snowyside Peak
Trailhead GPS: 43 59.795, 114 52.796
Difficulty: strenuous; time: 8 hours
Access: Following directions for Farley Lake, hike 3 miles from Yel-

79

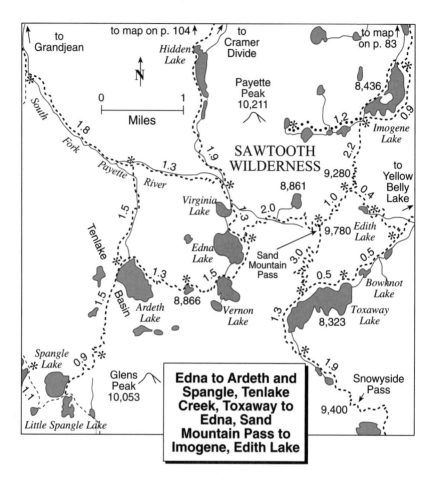

to map on p. 104

Edna to Ardeth and Spangle, Tenlake Creek, Toxaway to Edna, Sand Mountain Pass to Imogene, Edith Lake

low Belly Lake to the lower end of Farley Lake.

What you'll see: Granite peninsulas scallop the flower-embroidered shores of mile-long Toxaway Lake, the longest backcountry lake in the Sawtooths. Drowned peninsulas, decked with lodgepoles and subalpine firs, create islands. Above the west end of the blue-green lake, Snowyside Peak resembles a dinosaur with a pointed head and a tooth-like spine at its neck. South of the dinosaur, an unnamed, gray and orange peak borders the lake.

Directions: Begin by hiking to Farley Lake from Yellow Belly or Pettit Lake, following the directions under Farley Lake. Then take the trail along that lake, which runs well above its shore across rocks and among aspens, sagebrush, and subalpine firs. At .3 mile, it passes a tiny pond in the rocks. Beyond the lake, it continues, climbing gently through sagebrush and aspens. You cross a little stream that enters the

Edna Lake

main creek at a U-shaped curve a few feet from the trail. At .6 mile, there is a big meadow below a talus slope. The trail climbs a steep rocky slope, across talus, to cross the outlet of Edith Lake at 1.1 miles. At 1.5 miles is a junction with the Edith Lake Trail.

Beyond this junction .2 mile, the main trail passes a narrow pond with a good view of Parks Peak and an unnamed peak above Toxaway. Beyond the pond, the creek slides over glacier-polished granite in a little waterfall. The trail edges a small marshy pond before passing Bowknot Lake in a grassy glade at 2 miles. Two peninsulas almost cut this marshy lake in two below a peak shaped like the end of a house. The trail then climbs steeply through lodgepoles, subalpine firs, and granite benches to the lower end of Toxaway Lake (8,323 feet) at 3 miles. Staying 50 vertical feet above the north shore, it goes half way along the lake to a junction at 3.5 miles with the trail to Sand Mountain Pass. (Sand Mountain Pass gives access to Edna Lake to the west and Imogene Lake to the east and connects with the Edith Lake Trail above Edith Lake.) There are many campsites on the peninsulas on both sides of Toxaway.

If you camp at Toxaway, you can day hike to Edith Lake, over Sand Mountain Pass, to Snowyside Pass and Twin Lakes, and to three off-trail lakes near the lower end of Toxaway. To reach these two tiny lakes and a higher, unnamed lake at 8,723 feet, cross Toxaway's outlet on a log jam and climb east between the granite benches. The tiny lakes are relatively easy to reach as they are less than 100 feet above Toxaway. To reach the highest of the three lakes, stay above the two tiny lakes and go around the north end of the ridge that separates the lake from Toxaway. Then it will be easy to drop a few feet into the canyon the lake is in and walk up the creek to it. This lake is right under Parks Peak and

81

could be called Parks Peak Lake. Above it, two pointed peaks lead a parade of jagged teeth along a talus ridge that faces the lake's turquoise water.

15.

EDITH LAKE

This one-way section: 1.4 miles from the Toxaway Lake Trail to the junction with the trail to Imogene Divide above the lake, 750-foot elevation gain

Round trip: 11.2 miles from Yellow Belly Lake, Connects with a trail to Sand Mountain Pass and the Imogene Divide

Elevation gain: 1,874 feet **Highest point:** 8,950 feet at the junction with the Imogene Divide Trail

Map: Snowyside Peak

Trailhead GPS at Yellow Belly Lake: 43 59.795, 114 52.796

Difficulty: strenuous; time: 9 hours

Access: Following directions under Farley and Toxaway Lakes, hike the trail to Toxaway Lake to its junction with the Edith Lake trail.

What you'll see: Northwest of little Edith Lake, the fluted cliffs of a sharp-pointed orange peak stairstep down to the Imogene Divide. On the south side of the lake, high white granite slabs slide into bluegreen water.

Directions: From the Edith Lake Junction (8,200 feet), the trail to the lake switchbacks up through outcrops on the south side of the outlet with glacial scratches marking the smooth granite. At .5 mile, the trail crosses to the north side of the outlet and goes through 200 yards of talus. At .8 mile you step across the creek to the south side by going from slab to slab at the lower end of a little pool. A few feet below the lake (8,650-feet) at 1 mile, the trail crosses back to the north side of the creek. It goes around the northeast side of the lake over granite benches and talus and through forest, passing near a miniature pond at 1.2 miles. The trail wanders up a slope of grass and rocks and climbs the right side of a tiny creek that, in August, flows through a cloud of yellow arnica. It reaches a little pond in the rocks and the junction (8,950 feet) at 1.4 miles with the trail leading from Sand Mountain Pass over the Imogene Divide to Imogene Lake.

No stock is allowed in the Edith Lake Basin. Also, campsites at the lake may be closed to allow them to recover from overuse.

16.

TOXAWAY LAKE TO EDNA LAKE

This one-way section: 5 miles, 880-foot elevation gain, 876-foot elevation loss

Round trip: 22.6 miles from Yellow Belly Lake; connects with trails to Spangle Lakes and the South Fork of the Payette River

Elevation gain: 2,204 feet

Elevation loss (return climb): 876 feet **Highest point:** 9,280 feet

Map: Snowyside Peak

Trailhead GPS: 43 59.795, 114 52.796

Difficulty: strenuous; time: 2 to 3 days

Access: Following directions for Farley Lake and Farley to Toxaway Lake, hike to Toxaway Lake and along the lake to the junction at 8,400 feet with the trail to Sand Mountain Pass. This junction is 6.5 miles from the trailhead at the upper end of Yellow Belly Lake.

What you'll see: Mountains with delicate points and smooth sides ring Edna Lake. Between them to the north, the canyon of the South Fork of the Payette River drops away, giving an end-of-the-world effect. The wide expanse of blue water and groves of firs and pines are relaxing. From the trail, the prongs of North and South Raker stand out in the distance. The climb from Toxaway to Sand Mountain Pass gives a wonderful view of the dragon-like back of Snowyside Peak. As you descend from the pass to the lake, you pass a pond, sometimes called Rendezvous Lake. It gleams in a meadow of tiny firs below a gabled, orange mountain.

Directions: From the junction at Toxaway Lake (8,400 feet), the rocky trail climbs slopes of grass, sprinkled with boulders, granite benches, and tiny firs. The switchbacks are as long as .2 mile and only a few are on the map. Higher up, the slope steepens and becomes talus. Here the trail switchbacks east through trees and then west again. Next it switchbacks east again for .5 mile, crosses a sandy gully, and circles the south side of a ridge of rock and sand. At 3 miles, it drops to the notch called Sand Mountain Pass (9,280 feet). From the pass, the trail to the Imogene Divide turns off to the north, and with steep, and rocky tread climbs to an unnamed pass at 9,400 feet in .3 mile, but that is not your route.

Back at Sand Mountain Pass, the trail down to Edna Lake zigzags west through whitebark pines to the edge of the meadow surrounding Rendezvous Lake (8,861 feet) at 3.7 miles. Then it descends grassy slopes along a creek and crosses the outlet of the lake at 4.2 miles. A junction with the trails to Ardeth Lake and Grandjean is at 5 miles in tiny firs just above Edna Lake (8,404 feet). Campsites may be reached from either trail.

Sand Mountain Pass is usually snow-covered until mid-July or early August. To avoid danger and to avoid causing erosion, wait until the snow melts before traveling it.

17.

EDNA LAKE TO ARDETH AND SPANGLE LAKES

This one-way section: 5.2 miles, 1,186-foot elevation gain, 1,005-foot elevation loss

Round trip: 29 miles from the trailhead at Yellow Belly Lake via Edith Lake to Spangle Lakes; connects with trails down the Middle Fork of the Boise and South Fork of the Payette

Elevation gain: 3,390 feet **Highest point:** 8,866

Elevation loss (return climb): 1,881 feet

Maps: Snowyside Peak, Mt. Everly

Trailhead GPS: 43 59.795, 114 52.796

Difficulty: strenuous; time: 3 to 4 days

Access: The shortest way to reach Edna Lake, where this hike description begins, is to hike 9.3 miles from Yellow Belly Lake by way of Edith Lake. (Directions for this route are found in Farley Lake to Toxaway Lake, Edith Lake, and Toxaway to Edna Lakes.)

What you'll see: Spangle Lake is round, deep, and dark blue, but Little Spangle is the opposite: sprawling, shallow, and olive green. At dawn here, under a ridge of short gray cliffs, white granite slabs and islands spangle the water with reflections. Below the divide between Ardeth and Spangle Lakes the lakes of Tenlake Basin shine like scraps of sapphire. Above the divide, gray granite boulders and benches climb to the summit of Glens Peak.

Directions: From the junction (8,480 feet) above the east shore of Edna Lake, take the trail toward Ardeth Lake. It goes south above the shore and climbs to Vernon Lake at .5 mile. Here carved granite rises to the crumbled cliffs of a triangular peak. There are campsites on the east shore of the lake and near the inlet. A side trail goes south around the lake to a pond above it.

Take the main trail around the north side of Vernon Lake. The trail crosses the outlet on logs, and then at .8 mile, it crosses the creek from Summit Lake. The trail zigzags through woods, returns to the north side of the creek, and arrives at Summit Lake at 1.5 miles. At the west end of the lake, the ground rises to the 8,866-foot summit of the divide between Edna and Ardeth, a point 464 feet above Edna Lake.

Now the trail drops 638 feet in switchbacks over loose rocks and through trees to 8,228-foot Ardeth Lake at 2.4 miles. At 2.7 miles, it fords the outlet of Ardeth Lake to reach a junction at 2.8 miles with the Tenlake Creek Trail. A good campsite is west of this junction and others are off-trail to the southwest.

From here, the trail to Spangle Lakes climbs the side of a ridge to a meadow and pond at 3.1 miles. Then it switchbacks in rocks to the 8,952-foot divide at 4.3 miles. This divide is 724 feet above Ardeth Lake. From it, you can climb Glens Peak (10,053 feet) cross-country over large boulders. The view from this peak is worth the effort.

From the Ardeth-Spangle Divide, the trail drops 367 feet to a meadow on the east side of Spangle Lake (.8,585-feet.) Then it goes along the shore to a junction with the Middle Fork of the Boise River and Benedict Creek trails at 5.2 miles. There are plenty of campsites around both Spangle Lakes, but mosquitoes can be bad in wet years, especially at Little Spangle. It takes most people at least two days to reach Spangle Lakes on foot, whichever way they go.

18.

SAND MOUNTAIN PASS TO IMOGENE LAKE

This one-way section: 4.1 miles, 450-foot elevation gain, 1,294-foot elevation loss

Round trip: 25 miles from the upper end of Yellow Belly Lake to the lower end of Imogene; connects with trails to Edna and Hell Roaring lakes

Elevation gain: 2,654 feet **Highest point:** 9,400 feet at an unnamed pass .3 mile toward the Imogene Divide from Sand Mountain Pass.

Elevation loss (return climb): 1,294 feet

Map: Snowyside Peak

Trailhead GPS: 43 59.795, 114 52.796

Difficulty: strenuous; time: 3 to 4 days

Access: Following directions for Farley to Toxaway, and Toxaway to Edna lakes, hike to the junction of the Edna Lake and Imogene Divide trails on Sand Mountain Pass.

What you'll see: Next to a pleated orange ridge, the Imogene Divide overlooks a dozen switchbacks in gray talus. Below them, white granite peninsulas edge sapphire blue Imogene Lake. From the high point, the gap of Imogene Divide is visible to the north, the dragon back of Snowyside Peak and crags of Parks Peak to the south, the hand and fingers of the Rakers peaks to the west, and craggy Payette Peak to the north.

Directions: From the junction (9,280 feet) on Sand Mountain Pass, the steep, narrow, and rocky trail toward Imogene Lake zigzags to an unnamed pass at 9,400 feet at .3 mile. Then it switchbacks down through talus, scree, and whitebark pines to a meadow at .6 mile. Although the ground is flat here. It is too marshy for camping. The trail climbs over a low ridge to a tiny pond in the grass at 1 mile where

85

it joins the trail from Edith Lake at 8,950 feet.

Next the trail to Imogene climbs 330 feet up a sandy slope, dotted with whitebark pines, to Imogene Divide (9,280-feet) at 1.9 miles. On the north side the trail switchbacks down into timber, reaching a stream at 2.8 miles. At 3.2 miles, beside a marsh, the inlet of the 8,336-foot lake meets a trail around its west side. There are several campsites on both sides of the lake.

Take the main trail along the east side of the lake past three peninsulas with campsites. From here, ribbed, jagged mountains near Mt. Cramer are seen down the canyon below the lake. The trail joins the one from the other side of the lake just below the lower end of the lake 4.1 miles from Sand Mountain Pass.

Sand Mountain Pass and the Imogene Divide are usually blocked by snow until early August. To avoid danger and to avoid damaging fragile soils, wait until the snow melts to go over them.

HELL ROARING AREA

19.

MAYS CREEK TRAIL TO MCDONALD LAKE

Round trip: 6.8 miles from the Mays Creek Road; connects with the trail to Toxaway Lake from Yellow Belly Lake

Elevation gain: 830 feet **Highest point:** 7,680 feet

Elevation loss (return climb): 583 feet

Maps: Mt. Cramer, Obsidian, Snowyside Peak

GPS at parking before the steep, rocky section of the Mays Creek Road: 44 14.879, 114 27.338 (Road will be closed to vehicles about here in 2011.)

Difficulty: moderate; time: 5 hours

Access: On Idaho 75, turn left (west) 13.8 miles south of Stanley (47.2 miles north of Ketchum) onto the Decker Flat Road (210). After crossing a bridge over the Salmon River at .3 mile, turn left (south) on road 315 to where that road turns to a jeep trail at 1.6 miles. Take the left branch (the Mays Creek Road 037) and park where the road goes up a steep hill full of rocks.

What you'll see: The Mays Creek Trail is a pleasant, shady walk with veiled glimpses of peaks. This trail leads over a ridge from Mays Creek to McDonald Lake. Shaped like a melted hourglass, the lake is surrounded by marsh grass, willows, huckleberries, lodgepole pines, and shrubby cinquefoil. Up the canyon unnamed peaks loom, and

Hell Roaring Lake

across the canyon a sphinx-like shoulder of Mt. McDonald peers over a ridge. The trail links the Yellow Belly and Hell Roaring Creek Trails, making loop trips possible, but it is on neither the topographic nor the Sawtooth National Forest map.

Directions: Park at the bottom of the steep hill (at 6,850 feet). The hike mileage is measured from here. Walk up the rocky road. In 300 yards it splits. Turn left on an old 2-wheel track and walk up it.

The trail winds up the side of a wooded ridge to its crest at .8 mile. Here it turns right (west) and climbs gently along the ridge top. At 2.3 miles at a high point (7,680 feet), it drops off the ridge. First it goes straight down, then switchbacks on grassy shelves. The trail descends to the shore of McDonald Lake (7,097 feet) and follows it east to the outlet which it fords at 3.1 miles into a lodgepole forest. It then goes south to a junction with the Yellow Belly Trail at 3.4 miles, .4 mile above Yellow Belly Lake.

20.

HELL ROARING LAKE

Round trip: 10 miles from the lower trailhead at the road bridge over Hell Roaring Creek; 6 miles from the upper trailhead; connects with trails to Redfish and Imogene lakes.

Elevation gain: 607 feet from lower trailhead, 250 feet from upper
Highest point: 7,407 feet

Map: Mt. Cramer

GPS: 44 01.535, 114 50.567 upper: 44 01.683' 114 53.728

Difficulty: easy to moderate; time: 4 to 7 hours, depending on which trailhead you choose

Access: From Idaho 75, turn left (west) 13.8 miles south of Stanley (47.2 miles north of Ketchum) on the Decker Flat Road (210). In .3 mile it crosses the Salmon River on a bridge. Turn left (south) on road 315 and drive .3 mile to the lower trailhead. There is space for only four cars to park near the sign, so you may need park near the Salmon River bridge.

If you have 4-wheel drive and a high wheelbase you can drive 1.5 miles farther to a junction with the Mays Creek Road, turn right (still road 315) and drive 1.9 miles up the jeep trail to a parking area just before the wilderness boundary. Beginning there, one mile of the old jeep road is now a pack trail. By way of a foot log it joins the trail from the lower trailhead at about its 3-mile point, which is 2 miles from the upper trailhead. The jeep trail is maintained to a very low standard, so can damage even high-wheelbase four-wheel-drive vehicles.

What you'll see: This shady trail climbs along the white water of

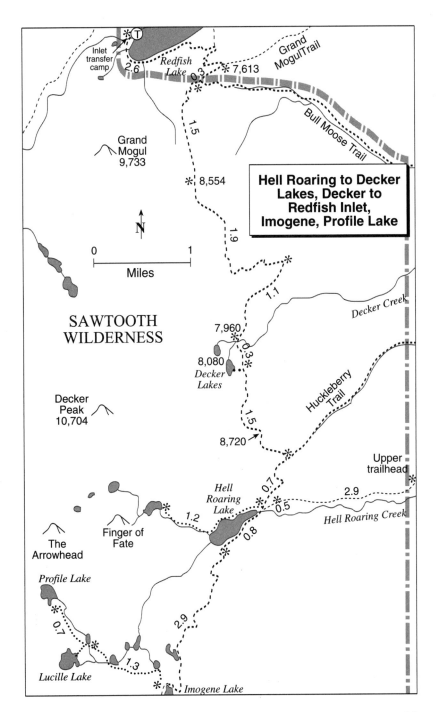

Inlet transfer camp

(T)

2.6

Redfish Lake

0.3 ✳ 7,613

Grand Mogul Trail

Bull Moose Trail

Grand Mogul 9,733

1.5

✳ 8,554

Hell Roaring to Decker Lakes, Decker to Redfish Inlet, Imogene, Profile Lake

N

0   1

Miles

1.9

1.1

SAWTOOTH WILDERNESS

Decker Creek

7,960 ✳

0.3 ✳

8,080 *Decker Lakes*

Huckleberry Trail

Decker Peak 10,704

1.5

8,720 →

Upper trailhead ✳

Hell Roaring Lake

0.7

0.5

2.9

The Arrowhead

Finger of Fate

1.2

0.8

Hell Roaring Creek

Profile Lake

2.9

0.7

1.3

Lucille Lake

✳ *Imogene Lake*

89

Hell Roaring Creek and then ambles through woods carpeted with red-berried grouse whortleberry. Silvered logs and lime-green marsh grass enclose the lower end of the blue-green lake. Behind the upper end, the slanting 800-foot Finger of Fate points at the sky. To the left of it, an accordion-pleated headwall leads to the slabs and talus of Mt. Cramer. To the right of the finger, granite gnomes bear the fanciful names of The Arrowhead and The Birthday Cake. The trail is often dusty and has little water except in the first 1.5 miles where it is close to the creek.

Directions: From the lower trailhead (6,800 feet) near the Salmon River .3 mile east of Hell Roaring Creek, the trail angles over to the creek, climbing as it goes. Then it runs parallel to the creek in lodge-poles and pale-orange boulders capped with black and gray lichen. Next it turns away from the creek and winds along parallel to it. At .5 mile it returns 150 yards to the creek. This first section goes through a recent burn.

At .7 mile, the ground flattens, and the creek meanders in hairpin curves. Here the trail winds alongside little hills covered with boulders. Off to the right at 1.5 miles is the lower end of a pond set in apricot boulders. For a view of peaks reflected in the pond, go around to its upper end. The trail continues through flat lodgepole woods, intersecting with the spur trail from the 4-wheel drive road at 3 miles.

From the junction with the spur trail, the main trail leads through a lodgepole pine forest, past a couple of meadows. It crosses an intermittent stream at 4.8 miles. At 4.9 miles is a junction with a trail to Redfish Lake just above Hell Roaring Lake (7,407 feet). It is another .1 mile to the flattened, double footlog over the lake's outlet.

For the best view of the Finger of Fate and the surrounding mountains cross the footlog. There are several campsites on both sides of the lake.

From the upper end of the lake, you can take a side trip to an unnamed lake under the Finger of Fate. To do this, leave the main trail before the foot log over the outlet at 5 miles and follow the right (north) shore of the lake to an inlet at the west corner of the lake. (In late summer it is possible to leave the main trail at the upper end of the lake, cross the creek from Imogene and some marshes, and find the correct inlet on the side of the lake.) Go up the right (north) side of this inlet 1.2 miles to the lake (8,200 feet.) The unnamed lake is 4.2 miles from the upper trailhead and 800 feet above Hell Roaring Lake.

*21.

HUCKLEBERRY CREEK

Round trip: 8 miles
Elevation gain: 1,441 feet **Highest point:** 8,116 feet

90

Maps: Obsidian, Mt. Cramer
Trailhead GPS: GPS: N 44 03' 30.2', W 114 51' 52.4'
Difficulty: Expert; Time: 7 hours to junction with Hell Roaring - Redfish trail
　　Access: To reach the Huckleberry Creek Trail turn left (west) on the Hell Roaring — Decker Flat road 14.8 miles south of Stanley across Idaho 75 from the Sawtooth Work Center. At 0.2 mile the road crosses a bridge over the Salmon River. Here turn right on the Decker Flat Road (210). The other branch goes to the Hell Roaring and Mays Creek trailheads. Go north on the Decker Flat Road. (210) The road splits and the left branch curves away from the river. Stay on the right branch. Go 2.3 miles to an unmarked two track road that turns 90 degrees to the left. Drive 0.8 mile to a gate, where another two track turns right 90 degrees. Park here and crawl under the fence. There is no sign.

　　What you'll see: This trail gives you good views of the high peaks of the White Clouds at the beginning and from a meadow part way up. The reason to take it is for a challenge and to avoid other hikers. In early summer before the upper Hell Roaring trailhead is open, it is a passable route of only 5.7 miles to Hell Roaring Lake in contrast to the 5 miles from the lower trailhead. If your destination is Decker Lakes this trail is shorter than going by Hell Roaring. However the trail has not been maintained for many years and it is an adventure to even find it according to trails manager Jay Dorr.
　　Directions: Once through the fence, go straight (west) for about 200 yards. Then look to the northwest to a log framework about .5 mile away. Head toward it across the pasture, which is often flooded with irrigation water. There is no path there, The framework spans a deep irrigation canal, more like a pond. Climb along and over the framework. Beyond it, there is still no path. Walk west and cross Huckleberry Creek, which is only three feet wide and a foot deep. Beyond it is a stream to cross as well. At the base of the hill on the west, look for paths parallel to it. The topographic map shows open areas below the hillside, but it is partly timbered grass and bushes. The paths connect into a trail at about 1.0 mile. It is hard to follow because of downed timber.
　　The trail climbs west in woods and at about 2 miles in an open area you can look out at the White Clouds through trees. This is the only place except at the beginning that there is much of a view. The trail becomes faint but just go southwest and find it again in the forest. At 3 miles it crosses to the northwest side of the creek and back again at 3.2 miles. After another crossing of the creek, the way becomes gentler and at 4 miles joins the main trail from Hell Roaring Lake to Redfish. This junction (8,200 feet) is 1.5 miles from the turnoff for the cross-country route to Decker Lake and 0.7 mile from Hell Roaring Lake.

91

22.

HELL ROARING LAKE TO DECKER CREEK AND LAKES

This one-way section: 2.4 miles, 1,360-foot elevation gain, 680-foot elevation loss
Round trip: 14 miles from the lower trailhead; connects with trails to Imogene and Redfish lakes
Elevation gain: 1,560 feet
Elevation loss (return climb): 680 ft. **Highest point:** 8,720 feet
Map: Mt. Cramer
Lower trailhead GPS: 44 01.535, 114 50.524
Difficulty: strenuous, with .3 mile cross-country; time: 8 hours
Access: Following directions for Hell Roaring Lake, hike from the upper trailhead 3 miles to the junction just before that lake.

What you'll see: Below the crinkled walls and sloping snowfields of Decker Peak, sheets of white granite embrace a flock of blue tarns. The true summit is the 10,704-foot peak 1.3 miles southwest of the Decker Peak marked on the topographic map. The lowest of these tarns, the two Decker Lakes, are just west of the trail from Hell Roaring to Redfish.

Directions: Hell Roaring Lake (7,407 feet) is a 3.0 mile walk and 250-foot climb from the new end of the 4-wheel drive road, and a 5 mile hike and 607-foot climb up the trail from the lower trailhead. Turn right (north) at the junction .1 mile before the lower end of the lake.

From this junction, the trail toward Decker Creek and Redfish Lake switchbacks northeast in woods. At .7 mile, it meets the Huckleberry Creek Trail. This trail, which has come 3.8 miles with a 1,430-foot elevation gain from Decker Flat continues toward Redfish over the 8,720-foot crest of the ridge at 1 mile, 1,360 feet above Hell Roaring Lake. From the north side of the ridge, the snowy face of Decker Peak appears through the trees. At 1.5 miles, the trail turns north and drops down a ravine along a stream which is often dry.

To reach Decker Lakes, continue to where the ground flattens at 2.2 miles. Leave the trail and climb west .2 mile cross-country to the largest lake (8,080 feet). Decker Creek is not a good route to the lake because the slope is steep and has downed timber. To reach the smaller, upper lake, circle the larger lake on either side and cut northwest .1 mile. On the main trail, Decker Creek is .3 mile north of the turnoff to the lakes.

Try to do this hike in early summer, as later on, the lakes have little water. The best campsites are along the trail at Decker Creek, not at the lakes. There is no water between Hell Roaring and Decker Lakes.

92

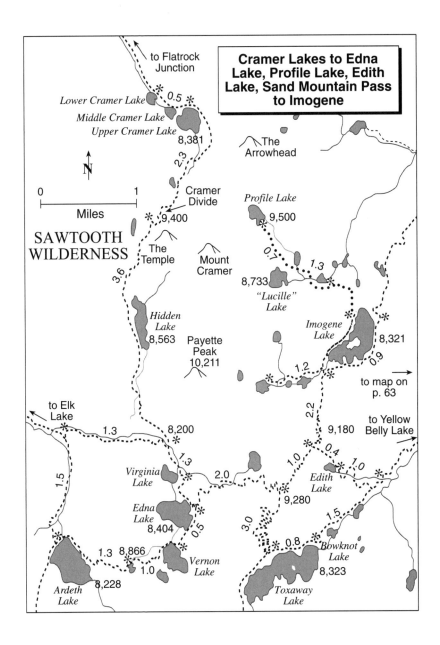

to Flatrock Junction

Cramer Lakes to Edna Lake, Profile Lake, Edith Lake, Sand Mountain Pass to Imogene

0.5

Lower Cramer Lake
Middle Cramer Lake
Upper Cramer Lake
8,381

The Arrowhead

N

0   1

Miles

SAWTOOTH WILDERNESS

2.3

Cramer Divide
9,400

Profile Lake
9,500

0.7   1.3

8,733

"Lucille" Lake

3.6

The Temple

Mount Cramer

Imogene Lake
8,321

Hidden Lake
8,563

Payette Peak
10,211

1.2   0.9

to map on p. 63

to Elk Lake

1.3   8,200

2.2

9,180

to Yellow Belly Lake

1.3

Virginia Lake

2.0

1.0   0.4   1.0

Edith Lake
9,280

1.5

Edna Lake
8,404

0.5

3.0

1.5

1.3   8,866

1.0

Vernon Lake

0.8   Bowknot Lake
8,323

Ardeth Lake   8,228

Toxaway Lake

93

23.

DECKER CREEK TO REDFISH INLET TRANSFER CAMP

This one-way section: 7.4 miles from Decker Creek to the Redfish Inlet Transfer Camp, 794-foot elevation gain, 2,207-foot elevation loss

Through trip from the lower Hell Roaring Creek Trailhead: 14.4 miles; connects with trails to Imogene, Bench, Alpine, and Cramer lakes.

Elevation gain: 2,354 feet
Elevation loss: 2,967 feet
Highest point: 8,554 feet
Map: Mt. Cramer
Trailhead GPS: 44 01.535, 114 50.977
Difficulty: strenuous; time: 9 hours, plus time to set up a car shuttle and take the boat from Redfish Inlet back to the lodge by pre-arrangement.

Access: Following directions for Hell Roaring Lake and Hell Roaring to Decker Lakes, hike to Decker Creek, 2.5 miles from Hell Roaring Lake.

What you'll see: From this trail, lodgepole pines screen the pale shapes of the White Clouds and the immense turquoise of Redfish Lake. From the descent to the lake, you get a good view of the fractured beige wall of Mt. Heyburn, which is the first of the peaks that make up the walls of Redfish Canyon. It has avalanche chutes like great claw marks.

Directions: From Decker Creek (7,960 feet), the trail climbs north, drops northeast, and then climbs sharply. At a 90-degree bend at 1.1 miles, an old, now impassable trail to Decker Flat goes off to the right. At 1.4 miles, the main trail turns left (west) up the center of a ridge with a view of the White Clouds near the top.

At 2.2 miles, the trail switches north with glimpses of Redfish and Little Redfish. Then it drops 200 feet to the head of a stream and climbs along another ridge at 2.6 miles. It runs north along the center of this ridge to its 8,554-foot high point at 3 miles. From here, Mt. Heyburn is ahead and the Grand Mogul on the left. From the ridge at 4 miles, you look down on Redfish Lake and see to the north the fangs of Cabin Creek Peak in the Salmon River Mountains.

At 4.5 miles, the Bull Moose Trail goes off 4.5 miles to Decker Flat with a 1,020-foot elevation loss. Then from a low point in the ridge at 4.8 miles, a trail called the Grand Mogul Trail (see Hike 24) heads northeast 4.8 miles to Sockeye Campground (near the lower end of Redfish) with a 1,060-foot elevation loss. At this junction, if you have arranged for a boat ride or are prepared for the 5-mile walk around the lake, take the trail to the left (northwest) toward Redfish Inlet. This trail zigzags

Lucille Lake

down the side of the ridge and along the shore.

At 7.1 miles the trail drops to the lake and disappears in the sand for 50 yards before it returns to forest. At high water, you must wade or take a path through the brush here. Next the trail bridges a creek, then climbs 150 feet to meet a side trail to the Lily Pond at 7.3 miles (labeled Lily Lake on the topo map). The pond is .2 mile up this path and has a beautiful view of Mt. Heyburn.

From the Lily Pond junction, the main trail descends to the shore and crosses a bridge over Redfish Creek. Then it goes through a pole fence and through the transfer camp (6,547 feet) at 7.4 miles. (It is 5 more miles and a 973-foot climb around the lake to the road from here.)

24.

IMOGENE LAKE

Round trip: 16.6 miles from the lower Hell Roaring trailhead; connects with Imogene Divide trail
Elevation gain: 1,636 feet
Highest point: 8,436 feet
Maps: Mt. Cramer, Snowyside Peak
Trailhead GPS: 44 01.535, 114 50.524
Difficulty: strenuous; time: 8 hours
Access: Following directions for Hell Roaring Lake, hike 4.7 miles to the lower end of Hell Roaring Lake from the lower trailhead.

What you'll see: The arms of Imogene Lake turn one of its high granite peninsulas to an island in early summer. Above the upper end of the lake, a chain of little lakes skips up a hanging valley in grass and wildflowers. Above, a shoulder of Payette Peak holds fluted cliffs. On the east side of the lake, orange needles climb a wall of unnamed mountains. These little lakes, Imogene Divide, the unnamed lake sometimes called Lucille, and Profile Lake are beautiful side trips from Imogene.

Directions: From the lower end of Hell Roaring Lake (7,407 feet), hike along its left (southeast) shore on the main trail. At the head of the lake at .8 mile, the trail switchbacks up ledges and through forest across the canyon from crinkled cliffs. From here to Imogene, the trail is different from what is shown on the map. Between 1.6 and 2 miles it goes along an open hillside amid young trees.

At 2.1 miles, the trail circles the left side of a small pond that is not shown on the map. It edges another pond full of lilies at 2.6 miles. At 2.7 miles, it is on the east side of a larger pond where the pleated cliffs of the canyon of Profile Lake are visible. At 3.5 miles, the trail crosses logs to the west side of Imogene's outlet, then goes along the right side of another lily pond. At 3.6 miles, it crosses the outlet again to the east before arriving at the 8,436-foot lake at 3.7 miles.

To make a side trip to the chain of tiny lakes at the head of Imogene, follow the main trail along the left (east) side of the lake to a meadow at 4.5 miles where that trail meets the one around the west side. Turn right (north) onto this unofficial trail and ford the inlet to its north side. Just before a bridge over a stream, turn left (southwest) up the inlet. Climb granite ledges, passing a waterfall, to the first lake, Esther.

The coves of this shallow lake sprawl between grassy patches and granite benches. Here you look up the canyon to roof-like Payette Peak. To reach the higher lakes, go around the right (north) side of the first lake to a tiny lake in the grass. Continue up the inlet, over ledges and benches to the third lake which features turquoise water, and huge sawteeth on the ridge above. Follow the stream to the highest lake at 8,950 feet, 1.2 miles and a 520-foot climb above Imogene. For directions for reaching the large unnamed lake (8,733 feet), sometimes called Lucille, northwest of the lower end of Imogene, see the following hike description for Profile Lake.

25.

PROFILE LAKE

This one-way section: 2 miles, 1,224-foot elevation gain, 160-foot loss from Imogene Lake

Round trip: 20.8 miles from the lower Hell Roaring Creek trailhead to Profile Lake

Elevation gain: 2,700 feet **Highest point:** 9,500 feet

Elevation loss (return climb): 240 feet

Side trip to Lucille Lake: additional .2 mile one-way

Maps: Mt. Cramer, Snowyside Peak

Lower Hell Roaring trailhead GPS: 44 01.535; 114 50.524

Difficulty: expert; cross-country for this section; time: 12 hours or 2 days

Access: Following directions for Hell Roaring and Imogene Lakes, hike 8.4 miles from the lower Hell Roaring trailhead to the lower end of Imogene Lake. (Imogene is 6.7 miles from the upper trailhead.)

What you'll see: Northwest of Imogene Lake, great granite triangles overshadow the unnamed 8,733-foot lake, sometimes called Lucille. To the right (west) of this wall, orange ledges stairstep to the summit talus of Mt. Cramer. Above Lucille 700 feet in a bowl of rocks, Profile Lake takes the shape of a bust of George Washington. The creek connecting these lakes tumbles in waterfalls.

Directions: From the lower end of Imogene Lake (8,436 feet), take the unofficial trail around the west side of the lake and across the outlet to the narrow bay at its northwest corner. Just before the bay turn right (northwest) down a granite-walled gully to a round pond (8,400 feet.) Walk around the south side of the pond. Then head west over low granite outcrops (not the creek) to a second pond (8,300 feet) at .8 mile. Ford its outlet 100 to 150 yards below the pond where it spreads over flat granite. Or go around its south side and ford the inlet. Then climb rock benches along the right (north) side of the inlet. When the inlet splits, continue up the right side of the stream that drains Profile Lake, not up the outlet of Lucille, which runs in a gorge. At 1.3 miles, cross the creek on logs below a narrow pond (8,680 feet). From this pond, climb southwest about 60 vertical feet in .2 mile to Lucille Lake at 8,733 feet, 1.5 miles from Imogene.

To continue to Profile Lake, return to the lower end of the narrow pond. Staying to the left (west) of the creek, go up a series of grass-filled gaps in the granite ledges. At 1.8 miles (.5 mile from the narrow pond) is a tiny, rocky pond. Above the tiny pond climb steep talus above the gorge and turn left (west) away from the creek and up gentler ledges to the top of a granite ridge. From it, descend to the 9,500-foot lake at 2 miles. This cross-country hike to Lucille and Profile lakes is challenging, and it is easy to lose the way. Avoid camping at either to avoid causing damage.

To climb Mt. Cramer, return to the granite ridge above Profile Lake and follow it west over slabs and boulders. When it steepens, go up the right side of a rectangular snowbank which is prominent much of the summer. Then follow the southeast ridge of the peak to the summit. It is .8 mile and a 1,216-foot hike from Profile Lake to the summit of Mt. Cramer.

*26.

BULL MOOSE TRAIL

Through trip: 7.3 miles from trailhead to Redfish Inlet
Elevation gain: 1,019 feet **Highest point:** 7,640 feet
Elevation loss: 1,093 feet
Maps: Mt. Cramer, Obsidian
Trailhead GPS: N 44 04' 62.6", W 114 54' 08.1"
Difficulty: moderate Time: 6 hours
Access: Turn left (west) on the Hell Roaring ñ Decker Flat road 14.8 miles south of Stanley. At 0.2 mile the road crosses a bridge over the Salmon River. Just beyond it turn right on the Decker Flat Road. The other branch goes to the Hell Roaring and Mays Creek trailhead. Go north on the Decker Flat Road. (210) The road splits. Stay on the right branch through sagebrush-covered Decker Flat to a bridge over Huckleberry Creek at 4.2 miles and a trail sign.

What you'll see: From a meadow half way up this trail is a beauti-

The Lily Pond

ful view of Mt. Heyburn with its wall looking flattened. Near the high point you can look out over the turquoise water of Redfish. This trail is little used and hard to follow in places.

Directions: From the bridge, take the signed trail along the north side of the creek. Much of this first section borders the north side of a research natural area that preserves a fen, where sphagnum moss grows with rare plants. The trail runs along the base of a partly open hillside, then crosses a creek to its south side. Soon it turns 90 degrees to the right in thick, tall grass. Next it climbs a steep hillside and at about 3 miles comes out on a long, dry meadow with sagebrush. Beyond it is a bigger meadow with a fine view of Mt. Heyburn and the Grand Mogul. This is a pleasant destination for a short hike. The trail continues to the Redfish Ridge trail. This allows you to take a through hike to the Inlet Transfer Camp and by arrangement ride the shuttle boat to the lodge. Beyond the meadow the trail climbs through grouse whortleberry, lodgepoles, and boulders to the top of a ridge to join the trail between Hell Roaring and Redfish. To reach the transfer camp from here, turn east for 0.2 mile, then turn north down to the lake and along its upper end.

REDFISH LAKE AREA

27.

GRAND MOGUL TRAIL

Through trip: Begins at Redfish Inlet Transfer Camp and goes 7,4 miles to Sockeye Campground; requires boat shuttle or 5-mile hike to reach the Inlet Transfer Camp; connects with trail south to Decker and Hell Roaring Lakes and trails along the west side of Redfish and up Redfish Canyon. New connecting trails around Redfish and to Stanley are in the planning process.

Elevation gain: 1,053 feet **Highest point:** 7,600 feet
Maps: Mt. Cramer, Stanley
Trailhead GPS (at Inlet Transfer Camp): 44 05.987, 114 57.264
Difficulty: Moderate; time: 5 hours
Access: Drive 4.3 miles south of Stanley (56.7 miles north of Ketchum) to the paved Redfish Lake Road (214.) Turn left (west) and go 2 miles to a junction for the lodge. Turn right and continue to the lodge at 2.3 miles. If you want to make your hike a through trip, you need to take a second car to the boat launch on the left side of the lake. Then drive back to the lodge and take the shuttle boat to the Inlet Transfer Camp at the upper end of the lake. The shuttle boat cost $16 per adult for a round trip in 2016. The boat goes up the lake any time after 7 AM

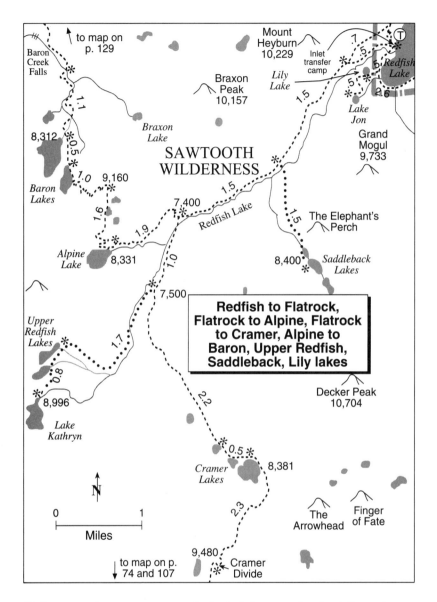

to map on p. 129

Baron Creek Falls

Mount Heyburn 10,229

Inlet transfer camp

Lily Lake

Redfish Lake

8,312

Braxon Peak 10,157

Braxon Lake

Lake Jon

SAWTOOTH WILDERNESS

Grand Mogul 9,733

9,160

Baron Lakes

7,400

Redfish Lake

The Elephant's Perch

Alpine Lake   8,331

8,400   Saddleback Lakes

7,500

Redfish to Flatrock, Flatrock to Alpine, Flatrock to Cramer, Alpine to Baron, Upper Redfish, Saddleback, Lily lakes

Upper Redfish Lakes

Decker Peak 10,704

8,996

Lake Kathryn

N

0   1

Miles

Cramer Lakes   8,381

The Arrowhead   Finger of Fate

9,480   Cramer Divide

to map on p. 74 and 107

if there are four or more people, but picks up only at set times (noon, 3, 5, and 7) and only by advance arrangement.

What you'll see: This trail along the east side of Redfish gives wonderful views of the pointed summits that make up the Grand Mogul, the pleated wall of Mt. Heyburn, the great tooth of Thompson Peak (the highest peak in the Sawtooths) Because it is 2.5 miles farther by this trail to the Inlet Transfer Camp at the head of the lake than it is by the trail on the west side of the lake, it is little used, so you will see few people. Taking the boat ride at the beginning of the hike gives you more time to enjoy all that you see. You won't have to rush to make your boat pickup time.

Directions: To reach the trail from the boat landing at the Inlet Transfer Camp (6,547 feet), walk through the campground and turn left at the restrooms. Follow a trail that goes through an opening in the campground and across a footbridge over Redfish Creek. From here, that trail goes along in the forest parallel to the shore through undeveloped campsites. It passes cliffs and begins to climb. At .3 mile, it reaches the junction for the Lily Pond. Then it goes downhill toward the lake and fords the outlet of a higher pond (Lake Jon). At .4 mile, the trail drops to the shore and runs along the beach. Except in late summer of dry years, this section is underwater. A path leads uphill above the shore past this section and crosses another little creek before returning to the shore in willows and alders. The trail crosses tiny streams, one on a plank bridge, at .7 mile. Just before the trail starts climbing the ridge at 1 mile, there is a little beach with a good view.

The trail switchbacks up the wooded ridge, so that by the time it reaches the top it has climbed 1,060 feet. It doesn't reach the ridge top (7,600 feet) until 2.6 miles, where there is a junction with the trail south to Hell Roaring Lake.

Turn left (northeast) on the trail along the ridge top. After .2 mile, it enters an open area where snowbrush is covered with sprays of white flowers in July. From this open area, you can look back and see three or four of the pointed towers of the Grand Mogul close by. The trail returns to the forest, which is mostly Douglas fir, and winds along up and down past big granite boulders. Beyond the junction 1 mile, you get a fine view up Redfish Canyon and of Mt. Heyburn and its neighbors across the lake. The trail descends 60 feet to a junction at 4.4 miles with the Redfish Ridge trail, which descends a ridge 3.5 miles to Decker Flat.

The main trail climbs to the top of the ridge, then it descends its right side with a view of the White Clouds. The route continues along the ridge and then curves around a knoll at 5.3 miles. Here you can climb the knoll for another view of Redfish and its peaks.

Now the trail goes downhill, along the ridge and along the side of it. Soon switchbacks begin and there are more than on the map. Some sections are steep, so take care. When switchbacks end at 7 miles, the trail wanders level in lodgepoles and willows to the trailhead at 7.4 miles in the Sockeye Campground. Parking in the campground or at the nearby boat landing both require a fee.

You can use the Grand Mogul Trail to ride a mountain bike around Redfish Lake, for the trail doesn't cross the Sawtooth Wilderness boundary even though it meets it a couple of times. However, the trail is rough enough to make you walk your bike in a few places. You would finish your ride on the trail along the west side of the lake, which has a lot of foot traffic.

102

Fishhook Creek Meadow

28.

THE LILY POND (LILY LAKE)

Round trip from Redfish Inlet transfer camp: 1 mile; .2 mile more for waterfall
Elevation gain: 100 feet **Highest point:** 6,960 feet
Map: Mt. Cramer
Trailhead GPS: 44 05.987, 114 57.264
Difficulty: easy; time: 2 hours plus boat ride
Access: Drive 4.3 miles south of Stanley (56.7 miles north of Ketchum) and take the paved Redfish road (214) to the lodge. From there take the boat shuttle or hike the 5-mile trail along the lake to the Inlet Transfer Camp.

What you'll see: Peach-colored cliffs of Mt. Heyburn create a 2,800-foot wall above the Lily Pond. The green, heart-shaped leaves of yellow pond lily cover its green water. In season, cup-shaped yellow blossoms decorate each leaf. The hike is a short walk suitable for almost anyone

103

who is willing to pay to ride the boat shuttle ($16 round trip in 2016 for adults), but a foot-high ledge may hinder some.

Directions: The boat shuttle runs any time four people want to go to the end of the lake, but return trips take place at set times. You must arrange your pickup time before hand. From the boat landing (6,547 feet), walk through the campground and turn left at the restroom on a trail through a gate in the fence. It goes over Redfish Creek on a foot-bridge and then along the south shore between undeveloped campsites and a steep hillside. After .3 mile, a sign points you to the right uphill .2 mile to the Lily Pond (6,750 feet). Watch small children carefully on the ledge at the lower end of the pond. From the pond, you can hike around its left side and up the creek for .2 mile to a waterfall. Be very careful not to tumble off the edge. In .2 mile of bushwhacking, you can reach a second waterfall.

*29.

UNNAMED LAKE 7,100 (LAKE JON)

Round trip: 2 miles
Elevation gain: 553 feet **Highest point:** 7,100 feet
Map: Mt. Cramer
Trailhead GPS: 44 05.987, 114 57.264
Difficulty: cross-country Time: 4 hours plus boat ride
Access: Drive 4.3 miles south of Stanley (56.7 miles north of Ketchum) and take the paved Redfish road to the lodge, Hake the boat shuttle or hike 5 miles along the lake to the Inlet Transfer Camp. Then hike .3 mile to the Lily Pond.

What you'll see: This small pond gives a wonderful view of the flat face of Mt. Heyburn and the towers and ravines of the Grand Mogul. Surrounded by granite knolls and grassy shores, its water reflects lodgepoles and a few cottonwood trees. It has no official name but the family of Jon Francis, a young man who died while climbing down the Grand Mogul alone, has put up an unauthorized sign in his memory. Perhaps it will remind visitors of the dangers of these mountains.

Directions: From about half way between the Lily Pond and the waterfall go northwest through the forest and up granite benches until you hear the rushing water of a creek south of Redfish Creek Then turn south and go over ledges and through shrubs to that creek, which drains Lake Jon. Now climb the ledges through the alders and willows that line this creek. Persist and you will reach the lake. The creek starts below the lake, not at its lower end most of the summer.

30.

FISHHOOK CREEK MEADOW

Round trip: 4.4 miles; trail continues another mile to crossing of side creek
Elevation gain: 242 feet **Highest point:** 6,800 feet
Map: Stanley
Trailhead GPS: 44 08.884, 114 55.205
Difficulty: easy; time: 3 hours
Access: On Idaho 75, turn left (south) 4.3 miles south of Stanley (56.7 miles north of Ketchum) on the paved Redfish Lake Road (214). To reach the backpackers parking lot (6,558 feet) where this hike begins, keep straight ahead at a junction 1.9 miles from the highway. The parking lot is on the right .1 mile beyond the junction.

What you'll see: Pale aqua and crystal Fishhook Creek meanders through a large meadow at the destination of this hike. The creek flows under high grassy banks and widens into beaver ponds. At the head of the meadow, an old beaver dam holds in the largest pond. The pointed towers of Mt. Heyburn jut above the left side of the meadow. To the right of Mt. Heyburn, the double black hump of Horstmann Peak crouches like a black cat. North of the meadow, a ridge of square teeth leads toward the shoulders of Thompson Peak. Between these mountains at the head of the canyon, you can see the umbrella-tent of Mt. Ebert.

Directions: From the backpackers parking lot, cross the lodge road to a hiker sign, and trail leading west up Fishhook Creek. The trail climbs along a sagebrush hillside to the right of and paralleling the creek. When the trail levels out, a trail from the Redfish Corrals comes in from the right.

At a junction at .3 mile. the trail along the west side of Redfish begins. It crosses Fishhook Creek on a bridge, climbs the ridge and goes along it 5 miles to the Inlet Transfer Camp.

At this junction, continue straight ahead, through fir and lodgepoles and fallen logs. At .8 mile keep straight ahead where a trail turns north to climb 480 feet in .6 mile to the Alpine Way Trail. By this route, Marshall Lake is 4.7 miles. At 1.5 miles, the Fishhook Creek Trail turns right (northwest) away from the creek through the trees. Then it curves left along the base of a steep ridge. At 2.2 miles (6,800 feet) is the meadow. The largest beaver pond is .1 mile farther.

The trail continues past the pond through forest and over fallen logs to the crossing at 3.1 miles of the outlet of Thompson Cirque Lake. Experts can continue cross-country up the canyon of Fishhook Creek 4 more miles to the Stephens Lakes. This is a difficult and treacherous route due to downed timber, quicksand, and a long stretch of talus blocks.

On the Alpine Way (photo by Mike Hall)

31.

THE ALPINE WAY FROM REDFISH TO MARSHALL LAKE AND IRON CREEK

Through trip from the backpackers parking lot at Redfish to the Iron Creek trailhead: 12.3 miles. Round trip to Marshall Lake: 9.4 miles

Elevation gain: 2,382 feet **Highest point:** 8,040 feet
Elevation loss (return climb): 1,180 feet
Maps: Stanley, Stanley Lake;
Trailhead GPS: 44 08.884, 114 55.205
Difficulty: strenuous; time: 2 days
Access: On Idaho 75, turn left (south) 4.3 miles south of Stanley (56.7 miles north of Ketchum) on the paved Redfish Lake Road (214). At a junction at 1.9 miles keep straight ahead to the backpackers parking lot (6,558 feet)

What you'll see: Near the beginning of the Alpine Way Trail, the towers of Mt. Heyburn and the black face and nose of Horstmann Peak soar ahead. Just off the trail, at 4.6 miles, tiny Marshall Lake nestles under cliffs laced with waterfalls. The lodgepoles and subalpine firs edging the shallow green lake blur the stripes of Williams Peak above. Farther along the trail, Goat Falls tumbles in steps, each short burst split into ribbons by boulders.

Directions: The Alpine Way Trail begins .6 mile up a spur road from Idaho 75 near the ranger station, but the spur road requires high clearance. And is .7 miles longer than by way of the cutoff from the Fishhook Creek Trail .8 mile up it. From the Fishhook Creek Trail, turn right (north) at a sign for Marshall Lake. Then hike .5 mile (480 feet climb) to the top of a ridge where the Alpine Way Trail joins 1.3 miles from the backpackers lot. (This junction is 2 miles from the Alpine Way trailhead near Highway 75.) If you decide to begin at the Alpine Way trailhead (GPS: 44 10.421, 114 55.309), add .7 mile to the distances given here.

From the ridge top junction, the trail goes west along the ridge. Paths lead to a fine view of peaks at the head of Fishhook Creek. The view is a good destination for a morning or evening walk from Redfish.

For more than the next mile, the trail is in the open within a few steps of this view. At 2.5 miles, it returns to forest. It steepens at 3.3 miles and at 3.8 miles turns right (north) north toward the White Clouds across the valley. (This corner is where a side trip to Thompson Cirque Lake begins.).

Continue on the Alpine Way Trail to a high point (8,040 feet) on an open, grassy slope. The trail then descends through woods and at 4.6 miles, joins a .1 mile spur trail to 7,715-foot Marshall Lake. On the main trail you cross the outlet of Marshall Lake on logs at 4.7 miles.

Beyond here, the trail goes down Marshall Lake`s outlet, then northwest downhill through dense lodgepoles. At 7.6 miles (6,900 feet), an former jeep trail comes in from Meadow Creek. Access to it from roads is blocked by posted private property.

From here, the main trail turns west along the side of a ridge. At 8.5 miles, it drops to ford Goat Creek which can be difficult in early summer. Next it switchbacks up a wooded hillside to an unsigned junction (7,400 feet) at 9.3 miles. From here, a well-worn path leads south .4 mile to Goat Falls. From this junction, it is 3 miles to the Iron Creek trailhead and 10.8 miles to Stanley Lake. For a description of this route, see Goat Lake and The Alpine Way Trail from Iron Creek to Stanley Lake.

Water on this hike is available at the creek crossings and Marshall Lake and the only good campsites are at the lake.

*32.

THOMPSON CIRQUE (PROFILE) LAKE

Round trip: 10 miles

Trail to Bench Lakes from Inlet Transfer Camp

Elevation gain: 2,475 feet **Highest point:** 9,033 feet
Maps: Stanley, Stanley Lake
Trailhead GPS: N 44 08.884 W 114 55.205
Difficulty: Expert; 1.2 miles is cross-country **Time:** 10 to 12 hours
Access: 4.3 miles south of Stanley on Idaho 75, turn west on the Redfish Lake Road (214) and keep straight ahead at a junction at 1.9 miles to the Backpackers Parking Lot.

What you'll see: This deep blue lake is surrounded by boulders, ledges, and cliffs with no trees or grassy spots. A narrow slanting snowbank gives the face of Thompson Peak a smirk. Near the lower end of the lake an outcrop resembling an African mask is probably why locals call this lake Profile. Dave Lee, the first chief wilderness ranger in the SNRA, called it Thompson Cirque Lake.

Directions: The first part of the hike is the trail from the Backpackers Parking Lot at Redfish to the Marshall Lake junction on the Fishhook Creek Trail, then up that trail towards Marshall Lake.

Where this trail turns north 3.8 miles, The elevation at this corner is 8,000 feet, 1,500 feet above the parking lot. Here you have 1,000 feet to go in 1.2 miles on a rough climbers' route. The reason to put this route in the book is that most people who climb Thompson use it to access the climb.

To follow this route, from the trail corner, go west off trail 100 yards through forest to a grassy hillside and climb it 400 vertical feet. Then curve left across a very steep hillside that has a few rock outcrops blocking the way. If you can get across the first rock outcrop using your hands you can do the other three or four. Trekking poles get in the way on the outcrops, but help on the rest of the route. About .7 mile from where you turned off the trail is a large plant and rock filled ravine. Go up it for 200 yards, then cross to the south side, and climb into a grassy basin.

From here go southwest up the side of the basin toward the lake. At 1.2 miles from the trail corner you reach rocky benches that overlook the lake. The shores are steep rock and the only campsites are a tiny ones near the outlet. It is also possible to camp higher up at a pond just below the saddle between Thompson and Williams. This route although difficult is easier than cutting over to a pond below the lake and climbing straight up the talus from it. (The pond is sometimes called Yurt Lake.)

33.

BENCH LAKES

Round trip to second lake: 7.8 miles, add 1 mile cross-country one-way and 863 feet gain for the other three lakes; connects with trail to the Inlet Transfer Camp

Elevation gain: 1,202 feet **Highest point:** 7,760 feet at second lake, 8,623 feet at fifth lake

Maps: Stanley, Mt. Cramer

Trailhead GPS: 44 08.884, 114 55.205

Difficulty: moderate; expert cross-country for upper lakes; time: 6 hours; add 3 hours for higher lakes

Access: On Idaho 75, turn left (south) 4.3 miles south of Stanley (56.7 miles north of Ketchum) on the paved Redfish Lake Road (214). To reach the backpackers parking lot (6,558 feet) where this hike begins, keep straight ahead at a junction 1.9 miles from the highway and go .1 mile more,

What you'll see: This hike brings close the pleats and notches of the 1,000-foot face of Mt. Heyburn. In early summer, snow fills the chimneys between its orange and gray towers. Each of the blue-green lakes comes nearer to this face, until, at the fifth lake, you can see chockstones caught in the chimneys. From the trail, you see the clear blue water of Redfish Lake extending to the beginning of Redfish Canyon. On both sides of the canyon, rows of spiked peaks march in a vast parade.

Directions: From the backpackers parking lot (6,558 feet), walk west across the paved lodge road to find the trail at a hiker sign. At .3 mile, turn left (south) on the trail that goes around the lake to Redfish Canyon. It bridges Fishhook Creek, then zigzags through forest onto the ridge, which is a glacial moraine. Beyond a stream at 1.2 miles, the trail overlooks the lake and follows the crest of this moraine. There is no water. On the north side of the ridge at 3.1 miles, turn right (north) on the side trail to Bench Lakes.

The trail to the lakes switchbacks up to the grassy edge of the first lake at 3.7 miles. Across it to the north, four sharp-pointed peaks peer over a wooded ridge. The official trail ends at the second lake, at 3.9 miles (7,760 feet), which nestles below Mt. Heyburn.

There is no trail to the upper three lakes, and reaching them is challenging. There are two possible routes. The best one circles the left (south) shore of the second lake, crosses its inlet, and climbs along the right (north) side of it through downed timber to the tiny third lake at 4.5 miles. To reach the fourth lake, it is easiest to go half way around the right (north) side of the third, and then climb west up a little valley to a talus slope. Turn left (south) here and ascend a gentle gully to a low ridge just above the fourth lake. Going directly from the second lake to the fourth is more difficult than this route because of steep, rocky slopes. To continue to the fifth lake, go around the fourth lake on the right (north) and cross its inlet. Then climb a little ridge left (south) of this inlet to the lake (8,623 feet) at 5.3 miles. Avoid camping at the upper lakes to protect the fragile timberline plants.

Back where the Bench Lakes Trail turns off the main trail, the Redfish-Baron Lakes Trail continues high above Redfish Lake into Redfish Canyon. Beyond the Bench Lakes Junction 1.5 miles, a branch trail drops .5 mile to the Inlet Transfer Camp at the upper end of Redfish Lake. You can use the boat shuttle and this trail to shorten the distance to the lakes by 1 mile.

To find this branch trail, at the transfer camp, follow the trail that goes from the boat dock into the campground. At the restroom turn right uphill onto the main trail up Redfish Canyon. In a few yards the signed branch trail turns right. It connects with the trail around Redfish along its north shore 1.5 miles from the Bench Lakes junction.

34.

REDFISH INLET TO FLATROCK JUNCTION

Round trip: 7 miles from Redfish Inlet Transfer Camp to meet trails to Alpine and Cramer lakes
Elevation gain: 853 feet **Highest point:** 7,400 feet
Maps: Mt. Cramer, Warbonnet Peak
Trailhead GPS: 44 06.003, 114 57.172
Difficulty: easy; time: 5 hours
Access: Take the boat from Redfish Lake Lodge to the Inlet Transfer Camp. To reach the lodge, turn left (west) on the paved Redfish Lake Road (214) 4.3 miles south of Stanley (56.7 miles north of Ketchum). At a junction at 1.9 miles, turn right to the lodge and boat dock.

What you'll see: Jagged peaks fringed with delicate spires line both sides of Redfish Canyon. Between the peaks, lakes hide in hanging valleys cut off by an ancient glacier. Deep blue Redfish Lake, enclosed by glacial moraines, meets this canyon below the jumbled points of the Grand Mogul and the fluted cliffs of Mt. Heyburn. The orange Saddleback on the southeast wall of the canyon, at 2 miles. It is one of the most dramatic peaks in the canyon because it looks like an oversized saddle, complete with horn. At Flatrock Junction, the trails to Alpine and Cramer Lakes diverge and Redfish Creek slides in shining sheets over white granite. This hike gives you the essence of the Sawtooths with little effort. Even a boat ride to the trailhead at the upper end of the lake is scenic.

Directions: After your boat ride to the Inlet Transfer Camp at 6,547 feet take the trail through the campground. Turn right at the restroom and walk up the trail past a cutoff to the trail to the lodge. Stay on the main trail, which climbs through woods and across open grassy slopes to another junction with the trail from the lodge at .5 mile. Turn left on the main trail.

The main trail continues up the canyon, alternating open areas with trees and giving views of the lake, beginning at 1.2 miles. At 1.4 miles, the trail crosses a side creek. Statue-like towers on the canyon wall and enormous boulders create an area some call "Garden of the Giants" at 1.6 miles. At 2 miles, the trail crosses another creek, which is the unmarked turnoff for cross-country routes to Saddleback Lakes. And

111

Braxon Peak.

The trail up Redfish Canyon continues in trees, over rock benches, and beside cascades to Flatrock Junction (7,400 feet) at 3.5 miles. There are campsites and picnic spots a few yards farther up the creek on the Cramer Lakes Trail.

35.

SADDLEBACK LAKES

Round trip: 7 miles, from Redfish Inlet Transfer Camp to the middle lake, upper lake is .5 mile farther
Elevation gain: 1,803 feet **Highest point:** 8,400 feet at the upper lake
Map: Mt. Cramer
Trailhead GPS at Inlet Transfer Camp: 44 06.003, 114 57.172
Difficulty: expert: half is cross-country; time: 8 hours
Access: On Idaho 75, turn left (west) 4.3 miles south of Stanley (56.7 miles north of Ketchum) on the paved Redfish road (214). At a junction at 1.9 miles, keep straight ahead to the backpackers parking lot Walk .5 mile to the lodge and take the boat shuttle to the Inlet Transfer Camp or hike 5 miles to it.

What you'll see: The top of the Saddleback resembles a saddle for giants complete with saddle horn. From its summit, an orange granite wall plunges 1,300 feet into the lowest turquoise lake. Climbers call this face The Elephant's Perch. Across the lakes from this wall , are narrow, blunt-topped triangles of dark rock, called Goat Perch and Eagle Perch. Above the highest lake, teeth of Decker Peak peer over a striped ridge.

Directions: From the transfer camp, take the trail up Redfish Canyon that leads to Flatrock Junction. It climbs through woods and across open grassy slopes to a junction with the main trail from the lodge at .5 mile. The joined trails continue up the canyon, alternating open areas with trees and giving views of the lake, beginning at 1.2 miles. At 1.4 miles, the trail crosses a side creek. Statue-like towers on the canyon wall and enormous boulders create an area unofficially called "Garden of the Giants' at 1.6 miles.

Where the trail up Redfish Canyon fords the stream coming from Braxon Peak at 2 miles, a path leads 200 yards down to Redfish Creek. Take this path, and cross the creek (at 7,200 feet) on a complex of logs in a section where the creek spreads out in wide, thin sheets over smooth, peach-colored granite. Although the water is shallow, it is very swift if you try to wade it. The logs are safer. The old route from a campsite .2 mile farther up the trail is no longer recommended because the log jam has washed away and willows and alders have overgrown it.

Once you cross Redfish Creek at the wide, smooth place, go 100 yards into the forest. Turn right (southwest) and go up the creek at a distance from it. In .2 mile, after an open, grassy area, turn left (south) and climb over rock benches. Be sure not to go too far up Redfish Creek before making this turn because the outlet of Saddleback Lakes flows in a gorge of downed timber.

In 200 yards, the route comes to a belt of steep rock across the middle of sloping granite. To get over the belt angle to the left between rock benches then switchback to the right. After this, the route runs along the right side of a stretch of 30-foot cliffs that form a wall for 400 yards. Then follow lesser cliffs through forest and beside big boulders. At 1 mile, you come out on talus and gravel and look up at the face of the Elephant's Perch. Cut left up the steep, gravelly slope toward the face, squeezing past boulders and trees. You see the lake's outlet in the canyon below. Now go along the right side of another, shorter set of cliffs for 200 yards, toward the cascading outlet.

When the cascade flattens at 1.2 miles, cross the creek to the right (west) side and follow it up. At 1.3 miles, a sliver of a pond is below and across it The Elephant's Perch. At 1.5 miles are the flat granite benches at the lower end of the first lake (8,350 feet), 3.5 miles from Redfish Inlet Transfer Camp. There are campsites at the lower end and around the lake to the right, but avoid camping in the fragile lake basin if possible.

To reach the higher lake, go around the right (west) side of the lower lake. This lake (8,400 feet), 2 miles from the trail, is enclosed by sentinels of Decker Peak.

36.

FLATROCK JUNCTION TO CRAMER LAKES

This one-way section: 3.7 miles, 981-foot elevation gain from Flatrock Junction to the upper lake

Round trip: 14.4 miles from Redfish Inlet Transfer Camp to the upper lake; connects with the trail over Cramer Divide

Elevation gain: 1,834 feet **Highest point:** 8,381 feet at Upper Cramer Lake

Maps: Mt. Cramer, Warbonnet Peak

Trailhead GPS at Inlet Transfer Camp: 44 06.003, 114 57.172

Difficulty: strenuous; time: 10 hours from Redfish Inlet Transfer Camp or 2 days

Access: Following directions for Redfish Inlet to Flatrock Junction, hike 3.5 miles from the Inlet Transfer Camp to that junction.

What you'll see: At Upper Cramer Lake, above a meadow sprinkled with wildflowers, a giant arrowhead thrusts out of the mountain wall. The outlet of the lake thunders into the water of the middle lake in a

Upper Cramer Lake

short, wide waterfall. Above the lakes, the 800-foot face of Mt. Cramer and the needled ridge of The Temple edge the cirque leading to Cramer Divide.

Directions: From Flatrock Junction (7,400 feet), the trail to Cramer Lakes first fords 25-foot Redfish Creek. This ford can be impassable in early summer for hikers and remains treacherous all year. Beyond the ford, the trail goes level through woods for .8 mile. It then curves southeast and climbs along the side of the canyon. From 1.5 to 2 miles the trail switchbacks, then levels in a forest that veils Elk and Reward Peaks to the southwest. At 2.5 miles, the trail continues to climb along the canyon wall, crossing small side streams. It crosses another side stream at 3 miles and at 3.2 miles reaches Lower Cramer Lake (8,320 feet). The trail continues on the left (northeast) side of the lakes to the middle lake at 3.5 miles and the upper lake (8,381 feet) at 3.7 miles. Several campsites are at all three lakes. From the upper lake the trail heads through wildflower meadows, boulders and ledges toward Cramer Divide.

37.

CRAMER LAKES TO EDNA LAKE

This one-way section: 7.5 miles, 1,303-foot elevation gain, 1,280-foot loss from Upper Cramer Lake

Round trip: 29.4 miles from Redfish Inlet Transfer Camp to Edna Lake via Cramer Lakes; connects with trails to Toxaway and Spangle lakes

Elevation gain: 3,137 feet **Highest point:** 9,480 feet

Elevation loss (return climb): 1,280 feet

Maps: Mt. Cramer, Warbonnet Peak, Snowyside Peak

Trailhead GPS at Inlet Transfer Camp: 44 06.003, 114 57.172

Difficulty: strenuous; time: 4 days

Access: Following directions for Redfish Inlet to Flatrock Junction and Flatrock Junction to Cramer Lakes, hike 7.2 miles from the Inlet Transfer Camp to Upper Cramer Lake.

What you'll see: From Cramer Divide, rows of peaks lead in every direction beginning with the splinters of The Temple which march east to the sliced-off summit of Mt. Cramer. This ridge continues east to Sevy Peak and The Arrowhead, a rock resembling the tip of an arrow sticking out of the mountain. South of the divide, rocks and wildflowers edge the crystal water of Hidden Lake which drains into a narrow pond in a marsh. From the pond, granite benches and ledges soar east to the wide triangle of Payette Peak.

Directions: Cramer Divide is usually blocked by snow until early to mid-August. To avoid danger and to prevent damage, wait until the snow melts before traveling the trail.

Above Upper Cramer Lake (8,321 feet), the trail climbs granite benches, crosses a creek at .7 mile and the outlet of a pond at 1.3 miles. It switchbacks past a smaller pond in rocks and zigzags up talus below cliffs to the divide (9,480 feet) at 2.3 miles.

On the other side, it drops south in whitebark pines along a ridge, overlooking a narrow blue pond. Then it zigzags to a crossing of the inlet in a meadow at 3.3 miles. The trail continues down grassy slopes to the shore of Hidden Lake (8,563 feet) at 4 miles. It then edges the west shore of the lake and the narrow pond below it. At 4.9 miles, it crosses the outlet of the lake and descends through forest and angles over to ford the South Fork of the Payette River at 8,200 feet. On the south side of the river is a junction with a trail down the river to Elk Lake and Grandjean and up the river to Virginia and Edna lakes. This junction is 5.9 miles from Upper Cramer Lake.

To reach Edna Lake from here, go up the South Fork Trail, which fords the river to the east at 6.4 miles and a creek coming from Sand Mountain Pass at 6.5 miles. It passes Virginia Lake, a shallow lake in grass and woods, at 6.6 miles. Then the trail climbs 200 feet to the lower end of Edna Lake at 6.9 miles.

38.

FLATROCK JUNCTION TO ALPINE LAKE:

This one-way section: 1.9 miles, 931-foot elevation gain from Flatrock Junction to lake
Round trip: 10.8 miles from Redfish Inlet Transfer Camp; connects with a trail to Baron Lakes
Elevation gain: 1,784 feet
Highest point: 8,331 feet
Map: Warbonnet Peak
Trailhead GPS at Inlet Transfer Camp: 44 06.003, 114 57.172
Difficulty: strenuous; time: 8 hours
Access: Following directions for Redfish Inlet to Flatrock Junction hike 3.5 miles from the Inlet Transfer Camp to that junction.

What you'll see: On the west side of Alpine Lake, furrowed cliffs unite in a pointed granite mountain. On the other three sides of the lake, lodgepole pines and subalpine firs decorate granite benches. Above the benches to the northeast, spires peek over a ridge.
Directions: At Flatrock Junction (7,400 feet), the left branch of the trail goes to Cramer Lakes. Take the right (west) branch toward Alpine Lake. This trail switchbacks up 931 feet, through grass, and brush and up cliffs, crossing back and forth over a stream. At .7 mile, it passes cliffs sprinkled with trees. It levels out at 1.6 miles, fords an inlet, and at 1.9 miles, reaches the lake (8,331 feet). Campsites on the trail side of the lake are overused, so try the upper end or across the outlet. Remember campfires are not allowed within 200 feet of Alpine Lake.

39.

ALPINE LAKE TO BARON LAKES

This one-way section: 3.1 miles from Alpine Lake to the lower end of Baron Lake, 829-foot elevation gain, 848-foot elevation loss
Round trip: 17 miles from Redfish Inlet Transfer Camp; connects with trail to Grandjean.
Elevation gain: 2,613 feet **Highest point:** 9,160 feet
Elevation loss (return climb): 848 feet
Map: Warbonnet Peak

116

Difficulty: strenuous; time: 2 - 3 days

Access: Following directions for Redfish Inlet to Flatrock Junction and Flatrock Junction to Alpine Lake, hike 5.4 miles from the Inlet Transfer Camp to Alpine Lake.

What you'll see: The trail from Alpine Lake to Baron Lakes crests at Baron Divide. Here peaks, crags, and serrated ridges stretch in every direction into blue haze. Below, Baron Lakes perch in a hanging valley at the head of the South Fork of the Payette River. On the left, slender, cone-shaped towers on the face of Monte Verita overhang the lakes. To the right of this peak is a ridge topped with sawteeth. At the north end of it, Big Baron Spire raises a pinnacle resembling the tip of a bent thumb.

Directions: From the north side of Alpine Lake (8,331 feet), take the trail to the divide which makes four, 300-yard switchbacks in woods and then climbs the outlet of three ponds. At .7 mile, the trail edges the west side of the first pond, then goes north toward the other ponds.

At 1.3 miles, it turns southwest and zigzags west up rocks to the 9,160-foot divide at 1.6 miles. On the other side, the trail hairpins down through ledges, talus and whitebark pines to the rocky edge of Upper Baron Lake, (8,505 feet) at 2.6 miles. It continues along the edge of the lake where, at 2.8 miles, a path turns off to some campsites. Then it descends in woods to Baron Lake (8,312 feet) at 3.1 miles. The best campsites are off-trail northeast of Upper Baron Lake and at the lower end of Baron Lake. Baron Divide is usually blocked by snow until mid-July or early August. To avoid danger and to avoid damaging the soils, wait until the snow melts from before traveling the trail.

40.

UPPER REDFISH LAKES

This one-way section: 2.5 miles, 1,496-foot elevation gain from Cramer Lakes trail to highest lake,

Round trip: 14 miles from Redfish Inlet Transfer Camp;

Elevation gain: 2,449 feet **Highest point:** 8,996 feet

Maps: Mt. Cramer, Warbonnet Peak; trailhead GPS at Inlet Transfer Camp: 44 06.003, 114 57.172

Difficulty: expert; 5 of the 14 miles are cross-country; time: 10 hours or 2 days

Access: Following directions for Redfish Lake to Flatrock Junction and Flatrock Junction to Cramer Lakes, hike 3.5 miles to Flatrock Junction from the Inlet Transfer Camp and 1 mile above it on the Cramer Lakes trail.

What you'll see: Snowfields splash the 800-foot charcoal gray saw-teeth of Elk Peak above the three Upper Redfish Lakes. Rock needles

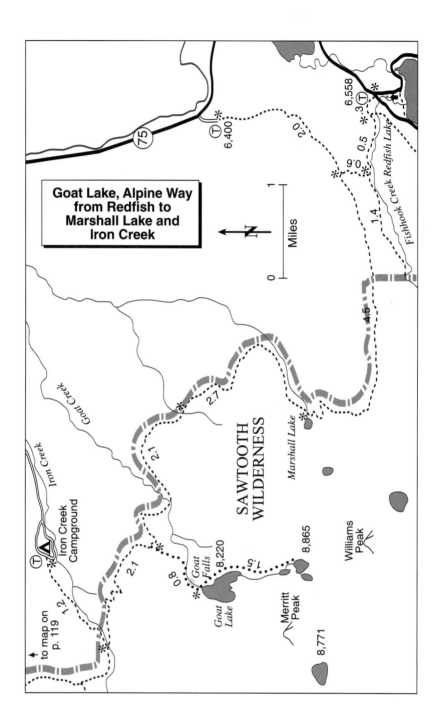

Goat Lake, Alpine Way
from Redfish to
Marshall Lake and
Iron Creek

Miles

SAWTOOTH
WILDERNESS

Fishhook Creek Redfish Lake

Marshall Lake

Goat Creek

Iron Creek

Iron Creek
Campground

to map on
p. 119

Goat
Falls

Goat
Lake

Merritt
Peak

Williams
Peak

8,865

8,220

8,771

6,558

6,400

0.2

0.3

0.5

0.6

1.4

4.5

2.7

2.1

1.5

2.1

0.8

1.2

75

guard the ridge between this peak and the talus cap of Reward Peak. These peaks and needles, white granite knolls, turquoise water, and whitebark pines swollen with burls decorate the upper lake, Lake Kathryn. The two lower lakes, set between trees, granite outcrops, and flower-splashed meadows, have a different backdrop. On the northeast, pickets of an orange mountain fence in the aqua water of the twin lakes. This is a challenging hike and it is easy to get lost or find yourself climbing cliffs.

Directions: To find the lakes, hike 1 mile up the Cramer Lakes trail from Flatrock Junction. Then, where the trail jogs uphill to the left at 7,500 feet, leave it. This point is 4.5 miles from the Inlet Transfer Camp. Descend to Redfish Lake Creek and follow it for .6 mile through dense forest, downed timber, and bogs. Then cross the creek on logs to the right (west) side while the ground is still level.

Climb along the creek to where the outlet of Cramer Lakes joins it, at .8 mile. Just before this point, where the banks steepen, climb west here 100 yards onto a little ridge and follow it. At 1 mile, the creek divides again into three sections. Climb along the right (north) side of the right branch, which is running west. At 1.2 miles, the canyon gets even steeper, and your branch of the creek splits again into outlets for the two lower lakes, but only one is on the map.

Keep to the right (northeast) of BOTH streams and walk up between granite ledges, but AVOID cliffs on the right. This route is easier than going through the brush between the streams. Each time the creek splits, keep to the right of all branches of it. The stream runs through a series of cascades before the granite becomes flat at 1.5 miles. At 1.7 miles is the lower lake (8,663 feet). Go left (south) around the lower lake and cut across a strip of land to the middle lake at 2 miles. If possible avoid camping in the fragile lake basin to prevent damaging it.

The upper lake, Lake Kathryn, can be reached from the lower end of the middle lake by scrambling south .5 mile up a 300-foot ridge. To find this route, cross the outlet of the lake and circle the ridge to the left of it until you can climb between granite benches to its top. Then follow the flattened summit of the ridge until you can descend to the lake (8,996 feet) near its outlet at 2.5 miles.

IRON CREEK AREA

41.

ALPINE, SAWTOOTH, AND MCGOWN LAKES

Round trip: 10 miles from the Iron Creek trailhead to the junction with a trail to McGown Lakes at the upper end of Sawtooth Lake; connects with a trail down the North Fork of Baron Creek to the South

Fork of the Payette River.

Elevation gain: 1,720 feet **Highest point:** 8,430 feet

Side trip to McGown Lakes: add 1.5 miles one-way and 330-foot elevation gain, 255-foot loss

Map: Stanley Lake

Trailhead GPS: 44 11.925, 115 00.816

Difficulty: strenuous; time: 8 to 9 hours

Access: On State Idaho 21, 2.5 miles north of Stanley, turn left (west) on the gravel Iron Creek Road (619) and drive 3.2 miles to a transfer camp.

What you'll see: Above the lower end of Sawtooth Lake, the largest lake in the Sawtooth Wilderness, sculptured granite curves from the shore to the cap-like summit of Mt. Regan. From the trail to McGown Lakes, the twisted rust and silver trunks of dead whitebark pines frame this peak and the immense sapphire of the lake. A mile before the lake, the cracked cliffs of Alpine Peak fall to two orange peninsulas which pierce the lime and blue-green water of Alpine Lake. From the trail between the lakes, two hills in the distance to the east resemble potatoes, one with its jacket on, and in early summer, the other opened and topped with sour cream and chives. This trail is heavily used. For a true wilderness experience, choose another. No campfires are allowed here.

Directions: The trail begins at 6,710 feet in a flat lodgepole forest. In a few yards it skirts the right side of a meadow, and then climbs away from the creek along the side of a ridge. At about .5 mile, the trail returns to the creek for a few yards. Here you can see heaps of rounded rocks that came down with a flood in 2010.

Next the trail climbs a rise, curves around a 15-foot boulder, and winds to a junction with the southern branch of the Alpine Way Trail at 1.2 miles. This branch goes south to Marshall Lake and to a trailhead near the Stanley Ranger Station. From this junction, stay on the Iron Creek Trail, which edges the right side of a meadow. At 1.8 miles, the north branch of the Alpine Way Trail turns off to Stanley Lake. To the south, up a side canyon, is a sliced-off dome.

Continue on the Iron Creek Trail, which angles up the side of the ridge and makes four switchbacks. At 2.9 miles, it fords Iron Creek to a wildflower meadow. Then it makes 12 switchbacks up a forested ridge to a junction at 3.9 miles with a .1-mile trail to Alpine Lake (7,823 feet).

Above Alpine Lake, the main trail has been blasted out of the granite benches and the trail surface is sharp rocks. At 4.5 miles, it flattens, bridges a stream, and switchbacks up the headwall to a pond at 4.8 miles, where there are campsites. (The only campsites at Sawtooth Lake itself are small and overused.) The trail crosses the outlet of Sawtooth Lake and back again on logs to the left (east) side. It reaches a junction a few yards from the edge of the lake (8,480 feet) at 5 miles. No campfires are allowed within 200 yards of Alpine and Sawtooth lakes. The right (west) branch goes 1.5 miles with a 330-foot elevation gain and 255 foot loss to McGown Lakes.

For a good view of Sawtooth Lake, take the left (south) branch past a snow pond to a grassy area at 5.2 miles. From here it is .6 mile to the south end of the lake, where a pond sits in flowers under the wall of Mount Regan. Below this pond .7 mile at the head of the North Fork of Baron Creek, are two more ponds, which have a couple of small campsites.

You may want to retrace your steps to the head of the lake and climb to McGown Lakes, which are set in gray talus. The main reason for taking this side trip is the excellent view of Sawtooth Lake from above.

42.

GOAT FALLS AND LAKE

Round trip: 6.6 miles from the Iron Creek trailhead to the falls; 7.6 miles to the lake

Elevation gain: 870 feet; 1,590 feet for lake **Highest point:** 7,400 feet at falls; 8,220 feet at lake

Elevation loss (return climb): 80 feet

Map: Stanley Lake

Trailhead GPS: 44 11.925, 115 00.816

Difficulty: expert; the .5 mile route up the falls is slippery cross-country; time: 5 to 6 hours

Access: On Idaho 21, 2.5 miles north of Stanley, turn left (west) on the gravel Iron Creek Road (619) and drive 3.2 miles to the transfer camp.

What you'll see: Goat Falls tumbles in fluffy cascades toward an inky green pond, which is also fed by two other high waterfalls. At Goat Lake, two small permanent snowbanks with aquamarine edges spit chunks of ice into the lake. These snowbanks hang above the teal blue water at the base of a 1,800-foot wall. On the wall, rock towers thrust out of the cliffs like gigantic divers ready to plunge. On the other three sides of the lake, shorter cliffs enclose shallower turquoise water. Strands of a braided waterfall weave through lime green grass into the upper end. Behind the falls, the tip of Thompson Peak is made up of rounded spires.

Climbing to Goat Lake from the falls is the most dangerous hike in this book. Since the first editions of the book, the steep slopes beside the waterfall have deteriorated. Walking it now is like climbing a steep roof on ball bearings. Going up the cliffs may be easier.

Directions: From the Iron Creek trailhead, at 6,710 feet (see Sawtooth Lake), take the Iron Creek Trail to the junction at 1.2 miles (7,000 feet) with the south branch of the Alpine Way Trail.

Turn left on that trail and cross Iron Creek on small, logs or wade. The trail goes through woods, then at 1.6 miles turns east and bridges a stream. Next it turns south and switchbacks up the northeast side of

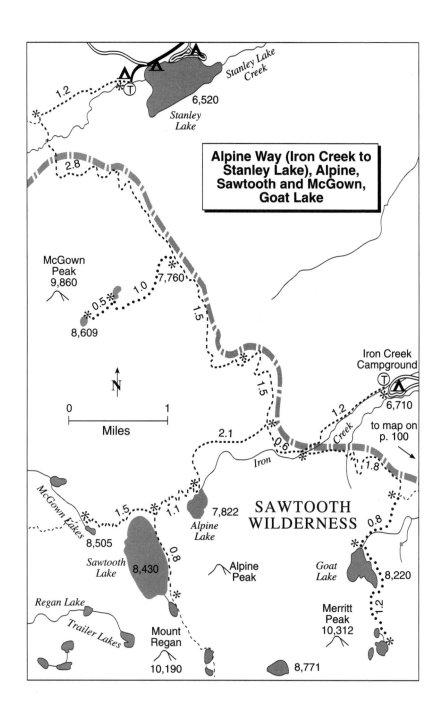

Stanley Lake Creek

1.2

6,520

Stanley Lake

Alpine Way (Iron Creek to Stanley Lake), Alpine, Sawtooth and McGown, Goat Lake

2.8

McGown Peak
9,860

1.0
0.5
7,760
8,609

1.5

Iron Creek Campground

N

0   1
Miles

1.5

1.2

6,710

2.1

0.6

Iron Creek

to map on
p. 100

1.8

McGown Lakes

1.5
1.1
7,822

Alpine Lake

SAWTOOTH
WILDERNESS

0.8

8,505

0.8

Goat Lake

8,220

Sawtooth Lake
8,430

Alpine Peak

Regan Lake

Trailer Lakes

Mount Regan
10,190

0.8

Merritt Peak
10,312

1.2

8,771

the alder-filled ravine. From here you can sometimes look out at upper Iron Creek. At the head of the ravine at 2 miles, the trail turns northeast up the side of a ridge and rounds the end of it.

At 3 miles, at an unmarked junction, peaks behind Goat Lake are visible. Here the main Alpine Way Trail turns east downhill, but is much less worn than the non-system path to the falls. Take the path toward the falls. It goes through two open areas. The second one contains a dry stream bed and a triangular tower of gray cliffs above it. The treacherous ballbearing slopes rise above this open area. Continue to the base of the falls at 3.4 miles.

To reach the lake, turn up beside the falls and cautiously scramble up the ledges and cliffs. The first 300 feet are the steepest. At the top of the falls, follow the creek and then edge away from it among boulders. At 3.6 miles, to avoid enormous boulders, cross the creek to the left on a complex of logs or on rocks. Early in the summer, you may need to cross farther up or not at all. Climb along the left side of the creek through forest and over granite outcrops to the 8,220-foot lake at 3.8 miles.

This hike is recommended for expert adults only because of the slippery climb and the dropoffs at the lake. Campfires are not allowed within 200 feet of Goat Lake, and camping is discouraged in the fragile lake basin. There is little space for it.

To reach the upper lakes, go around the east side of the lake to the upper end, climbing between the benches and then dropping to the shore. From the end of the lake, aim for a rock ramp leading to a 150-foot high bench on the near (east) side of the two inlets. To get onto the ramp you must scramble up a ten-foot cliff. Climb the ramp to the top of the bench and go along it until you can descend onto the elongated snowfield shown on the map. Walk up the snowfield past the first tiny lake, which is set in talus, to the largest of the upper lakes (8,865 feet). It is 645 feet and 1.2 miles above Goat Lake. A dark knoll separates this lake from a teardrop-shaped lake west of it.

43.

THE ALPINE WAY FROM IRON CREEK TO STANLEY LAKE

This one-way section: 6.4 miles, 1,090-foot elevation gain, 1,200-foot elevation loss from the Iron Creek trail to the Stanley Lake Creek trail; add 2.6 miles to go from trailhead to trailhead; additional 1.5 miles one-way and 849-foot elevation gain to see off-trail lakes

Through trip: 8.8 miles from the Iron Creek trailhead; connects with trails to Sawtooth Lake and Trail Creek Lakes.

Elevation gain: 1,530 feet **Highest point:** 7,760 feet

Elevation loss (return climb): 1,720 feet

Map: Stanley Lake; Iron Creek

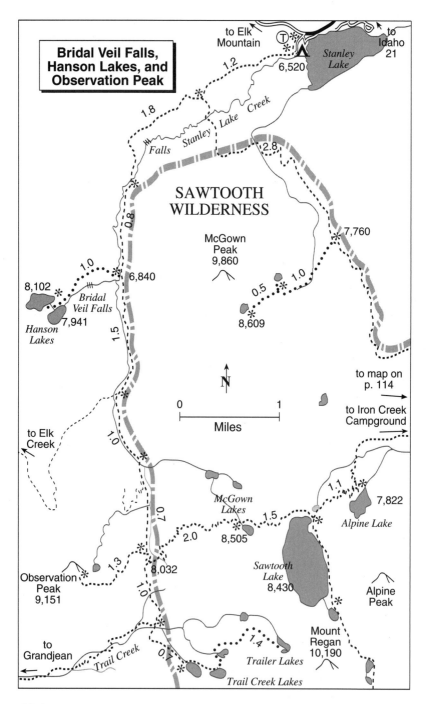

Bridal Veil Falls,
Hanson Lakes, and
Observation Peak

to Elk
Mountain

to
Idaho
21

Stanley
Lake

6,520

1.2

1.8

Stanley Lake Creek

Falls

2.8

SAWTOOTH
WILDERNESS

McGown
Peak
9,860

7,760

0.8

1.0

6,840

8,102

Bridal
Veil Falls

7,941

0.5

1.0

8,609

Hanson
Lakes

1.5

N

to map on
p. 114

to Iron Creek
Campground

to Elk
Creek

0
1

Miles

1.0

McGown
Lakes

1.1

7,822

0.7

2.0

1.5

Alpine Lake

1.3

8,505

Observation
Peak
9,151

8,032

Sawtooth
Lake
8,430

Alpine
Peak

to
Grandjean

Trail Creek

0.7

1.4

Mount
Regan
10,190

Trailer Lakes

Trail Creek Lakes

Trailhead GPS: 44 11.925, 115 00.816

Difficulty: cross-country for experts for lakes; time: 7 hours for the trail, 3 hours more to for lakes

Access: On Idaho 21, 2.5 miles north of Stanley turn left (west) on the gravel Iron Creek Road (619) and drive 3.2 miles to the Iron Creek Transfer Camp. Then hike 1.8 miles to the North Alpine Way Trail.

What you'll see: This section of the Alpine Way crosses side canyons lined with spires, crags, and waterfalls and passes below the double points of McGown Peak, the mountain above Stanley Lake. From the high point of the trail, a cross-country hike reaches two tiny lakes in a sawtoothed canyon. On the east, the lake is guarded by a granite gargoyle. A narrow flower-strewn moraine borders the upper lake.

Directions: This hike description begins at the junction of the Iron Creek Trail with the North Alpine Way Trail 1.8 miles from the Iron Creek trailhead and its mileage has been figured from there. The Alpine Way then angles up the side of a grassy ridge to a flat summit at .5 mile. Then it switchbacks down in the trees, crosses a small creek, and goes over Crooked Creek (6,920 feet) on logs at 1.5 miles. It skirts the base of the mountain in woods and sandy areas. At 2.5 miles, it fords a stream in a gorge, then climbs s to a saddle (7,760 feet), the high point of the trail, at 3 miles.

To reach the off-trail lakes, turn southwest here at a ridge. Go along the east side of the ridge to a notch at .3 mile where the ridge smooths out enough to follow the top of it. At .5 mile, the ridge ends in a cirque. Climb the headwall of the cirque along the creek mostly on the left side past a waterfall. At the top, continue to a shallow pond shown as a marsh on the map and turn right (north). Climb through a gap between hills to the lower lake (8,575 feet) at 1 mile. To reach the upper lake (8,609 feet) 1.5 miles from the trail, return to the marsh and walk past a second pond to the head of the valley.

From the high point, the trail on to Stanley Lake descends a ridge in trees with a view of the towers of McGown Peak. It switchbacks down toward Stanley Lake Creek and at 4.5 miles, crosses a side creek on logs or rocks, then descends the left side of that creek in lodgepoles. At 5 miles, as the ground flattens, the trail turns right (north) toward Stanley Lake Creek, which it fords at 5.5 miles. This ford may be hazardous in early summer.

At 5.8 miles, the trail intersects the Stanley Lake Creek Trail, 1.2 miles above a handicapped only parking area at Stanley Lake (6,513 feet). From this parking area it is .2 mile more, mostly along the road, to the trailhead which has parking for everyone.

125

STANLEY LAKE AREA

44.

BRIDALVEIL FALLS AND HANSON LAKES

Round trip: 8 miles to the falls from the Stanley Lake trailhead; 9.6 miles to the lakes; connects with trails to Trail Creek Lakes, Observation Peak, and Grandjean.

Elevation gain: 320 feet to the falls, 1,582 feet to the highest lake
Highest point: 8,102 feet

Map: Stanley Lake

Trailhead GPS: 44 14.658, 115 03.948

Difficulty: moderate to falls, expert for lakes; time: 4 hours for falls, 7 hours for lakes

Access: On Idaho 21 drive northwest of Stanley for 5 miles. Turn left (west) on the paved Stanley Lake Road (456) and go 4.3 miles to the trailhead parking at the beginning of the Elk Mountain Road (649). The trail leads .2 mile along the dirt Inlet Campground Road past beaver ponds to the handicapped parking. Hike mileage is figured from this parking. If you don't have a handicapped sticker for your car, you can drop off your party at the handicapped parking, drive .2 mile back to the trailhead and walk the .2 mile extra.

What you'll see: Bridalveil Falls puffs out at the top, then plunges in a veil of lacy water. Beside the falls, grow red paintbrush, magenta mimulus, and pale blue bluebells in a bride's bouquet. Higher up, a double-humped monolith, textured by fractures, overlooks the deep turquoise water of the two Hanson Lakes. A natural earth dam stabilized by firs keeps the upper lake from tumbling into the lower. The route to Hanson Lakes is steep and slippery and it is easy to get onto the hazardous slope beside the waterfall. Avoid camping in the fragile lake basin.

Directions: Where the trail begins at the disabled parking at the Inlet Campground at 6,520 feet, go west through the gate and follow a wide track through willows near the creek. At .5 mile from the gate, the trail turns right (northwest) into a big meadow. After the meadow on the north and crossing streams, it enters forest. The first mile of this trail has been raised to allow early summer use when the wildflowers are in bloom but the meadows are wet. At 1.2 miles the north end of the Alpine Way Trail turns off to the south. Keep straight ahead to the west through trees and more small meadows.

At 2.3 miles, the trail curves across and up a sharp rise in the canyon floor. Then it turns straight up the canyon again. Here you can walk northeast .2 mile to see Lady Face Falls.

At 3 miles, the trail fords Stanley Lake Creek to the left (east) side.

126

The footlogs here are underwater in early summer. To see Bridalveil Falls continue along the trail to a sandy place (6,840 feet) at 3.8 miles. Here, turn off toward the creek and ford it to the west side. Once across, go southwest .2 mile for a view of the falls at 4 miles. In doing so, avoid the dangerous sandy slope to the right of the falls, and DO NOT try to climb it to the lakes.

To reach the lakes safely, back at the ford notice three vertical sandy ridges leading up the canyon wall to the right (north) of the waterfall. To the right of them, a strip of brush parallels the ribs. Zigzag up the right (north) side of this steep, brushy area, skirting the forest. When the steepness lessens, cut left to a small creek. Cross this creek and contour across the hillside to a small flat meadow. Traverse a rocky slope and plunge through willows past mossy springs to the outlet of the lakes.

Turn right (southwest) along the outlet to the lower lake (7,941 feet), .7 mile from the ford. Go around the lake on its right (north) side and then up its inlet to the upper lake (8,102 feet), 1 mile from the ford. For safety on the return, be sure to turn left (north) across the slope .2 mile below the lower lake BEFORE the slope plunges down beside the waterfall.

45.

ELK MEADOW

Round trip: 5 miles from the Elk Mountain trailhead; connects with trail to Elizabeth Lake
Elevation gain: 120 feet **Highest point:** 6,760 feet
Elevation loss (return climb): 40 feet
Map: Elk Meadow
Trailhead GPS: 44 15.545, 115 02,767
Difficulty: easy; time: 3 hours
Access: On Idaho 21, 8.1 miles northwest of Stanley, turn left (west) on the gravel Elk Meadows Road (614). At a junction at .3 mile, turn left and drive to a parking loop at the end of the road at 1.7 miles.

What you'll see: From the vast green bogs of Elk Meadow, views of McGown Peak and the canyon wall of upper Elk Creek entice hikers. Elk Meadow makes a pleasant day hike, especially in late June when the wildflowers are at their best. This trail to Elk Meadow is a mile longer than the one from the Elk Mountain Road (649), but avoids a 240-foot climb on the way back.

Directions: From the loop parking area (6,675 feet) where the old Elk Meadows Road is closed by boulders, a connecting trail leads down across the creek on a footbridge. On the other side it intersects the Elk Mountain bike trail. Turn right (west) here and follow this trail,

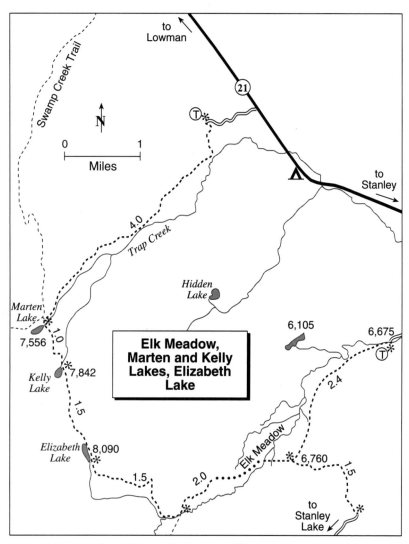

toward the meadow (not on the topographic map.)

At 2.2 miles, the trail crosses a tongue of meadow, then returns to forest. At 2.4 miles, it joins the Elizabeth Lake Trail at 6,760 feet. (Note that this trail from the Elk Mountain Road is only 1.5 miles long, so it is a shorter way to reach Elk Meadow.) Beyond the junction, the trail on the topographic map across the meadow does not exist. Walk cross-country across the meadow and look for the trail up Elk Creek on the other (west) side and then the branch of that trail that goes to Elizabeth Lake. Or you can just walk out in the meadow to see the wildflowers and the view up the canyon.

Taking a side trip to the unnamed marshy green lake (6,105 feet) northwest of Elk Creek and 1.5 miles from the road is no longer recommended because the old Elk Meadow Road that used to lead within .3 mile of it has been obliterated.

46.

OBSERVATION PEAK

This one-way section: 4.5 miles, 2,311-foot elevation gain from Bridalveil Falls
Round trip: 16.6 miles from the Stanley Lake trailhead; connects with trails to Trail Creek and McGown lakes
Elevation gain: 2,631 feet **Highest point:** 9,151 feet
Map: Stanley Lake
Trailhead parking GPS: 44 14.658, 115 03.948
Difficulty: strenuous; time: 2 days
Access: On Idaho 21, 5 miles north of Stanley, turn west on the paved Stanley Lake Road (456) and drive 4.3 miles to the trailhead parking at the beginning of the Elk Mountain Road (649). Park here and walk .2 mile along the dirt Inlet Campground road to the beginning of the trail. Following directions to Bridalveil Falls and Hanson Lakes, hike 3.8 miles up the Stanley Lake Creek Trail to the path to the falls.

What you'll see: From this sandy hill above the Trail Creek - Stanley Lake Creek Divide, the jagged spires of the Sawtooth Range stretch southeast, becoming bluer with distance, to the needles of North and South Raker on the skyline. Across the canyon, dark cliffs sweep to the rounded top of Mt. Regan. Near it, Warbonnet, resembles a dark blue wave rushing east. To the north, the view includes the rounded mountains above Elk Creek, and the serrated wall of McGown Peak.
Directions: From where the path to Bridalveil Falls turns off (at 6,840 feet) 3.8 miles from Stanley Lake, The trail up Stanley Lake Creek crosses an open area below the cliffs of McGown Peak, then continues in woods. A campsite is at .7 mile beside a side stream flowing through sand. At 1.5 miles, a trail is supposed to turn off to the right (west) to Elk Creek Summit. It climbs 1,520 feet and descends 1,780 feet in 9.5 sketchy miles to join the Elk Meadow trail.
Continue on the Stanley Lake Creek Trail. At 2 miles, it threads a narrow meadow below a wall of boulders and cliffs and passes a campsite. Just beyond the meadow, it fords the creek to the right (west) side. At 2.5 miles, the old road to the Greenback Mine turns to the right up the canyon wall. From this junction, the trail continues south up the creek well above it. At 3.2 miles is the Trail Creek - Stanley Lake Creek Divide (8,032 feet). You can camp here, but there is no water.
On the divide is a 4-way junction. To the left (east) a trail goes 2 miles to McGown and Sawtooth Lakes. McGown Lakes are 2 miles

toward Sawtooth Lake. The trail straight ahead descends 1 mile to the Trail Creek Lakes Junction with a 451-foot elevation loss and then goes on down Trail Creek to Grandjean (see Trail Creek Lakes). To the right (west) is a trail up Observation Peak. It climbs 1,119 feet in 1.3 miles up a sandy hillside sprinkled with whitebark pines to a gentle summit at 4.5 miles.

To see the site of the Greenback Mine on the return, descend north from Observation Peak .7 mile cross-country to a round pond. Follow its outlet .5 mile to a boggy meadow and then the old road to the mine from Stanley Lake Creek. The mine is 200 yards up the road, but the only thing left to see is a shaft. To return to the trail, descend the steep road switchbacks for .7 mile. This 1.4 mile route saves .6 mile over the trail, but the cross-country hiking along the pond's outlet is rough. The forest near the divide with Trail Creek burned in the 2006 Trailhead Fire.

47.

MARTEN AND KELLY LAKES

Round trip: 10 miles from the Trap Creek trailhead; connects with trails to Elizabeth Lake and Idaho 21 at Bench Creek near Banner Summit.

Elevation gain: 979 feet **Highest point:** 7,842 feet
Elevation loss (return climb): 40 feet
Maps: Elk Meadow, Banner Summit
Trailhead GPS: 44 15.697, 115 07.183
Difficulty: moderate; time: 7 hours
Access: On Idaho 21, 8.5 miles north of Stanley, turn left (west) on a dirt road (627) at a sign for Marten Lake. Drive through a usually dry creek at .3 mile. Continuing up through rocks to the beginning of the trail at .7 mile may require 4-wheel drive for a few yards.

What you'll see: Tree-dotted cliffs and peaks of rounded triangles back Marten and Kelly Lakes. Marsh grass edges Marten Lake and red mountain heath and Labrador tea surround Kelly Lake. The trail gives a view to the east across Stanley Basin of the striped ramparts of Cabin Creek Peak in the Frank Church Wilderness. Few hike to Marten and Kelly lakes because they are north of the main rocky mass of the Sawtooths. The stillness may be broken only by the sighing of pines or cry of a Clark's nutcracker.

Directions: The trail leads south from the dirt road, beginning at 6,863 feet in lodgepole pines. At .5 mile, are snow ponds. At 1 mile I a tiny, marshy lake gives a view of the peaks ahead. At 2.5 miles, the trail climbs along the base of an open hillside. In woods at 3.5 miles, it crosses sections of Trap Creek, the largest on a bridge. At 4 miles is

Marten Lake (7,556 feet), which has several campsites.

Just before the lake is a junction with a signed trail to the right (north). This trail splits in a few yards into the Bench Creek and Swamp Creek trails. The Bench Creek Trail goes west 5.4 miles to Idaho 21 near the Bull Trout Lake Road (100), with a 644-foot climb and 1,280-foot descent. The Swamp Creek Trail goes 6 miles north with a 910-foot elevation loss to Idaho 21 just south of the Thatcher Creek Campground

The trail from Marten to Kelly Lake crosses the outlet of Marten Lake on a log, then wanders over a ridge through subalpine firs to a stream crossing at 4.5 miles. It rounds the east end of the ridge and turns south to the lake (7,842 feet) at 5 miles. Campsites are limited. The trail continues beyond Kelly Lake 1.5 miles with a 491-foot elevation gain and 243-foot elevation loss to Elizabeth Lake.

Marten Lake

48.

ELIZABETH LAKE

Round trip: 10 miles from the Elk Mountain Road above Stanley Lake; connects with the trail to Marten and Kelly lakes from Trap Creek.

Elevation gain: 1,410 feet **Highest point:** 8,090 feet

Elevation loss (return climb): 360 feet

Maps: Banner Summit, Elk Meadow

Trailhead GPS: 44 17.283, 115 04.296

Difficulty: expert; time: 8 hours

Access: On Idaho 21, 5 miles north of Stanley turn left (west) onto the paved Stanley Lake Road (456). Drive 4.3 miles to a junction with the road up Elk Mountain (649). Turn right and drive up that road to an undeveloped trailhead at 6.1 miles.

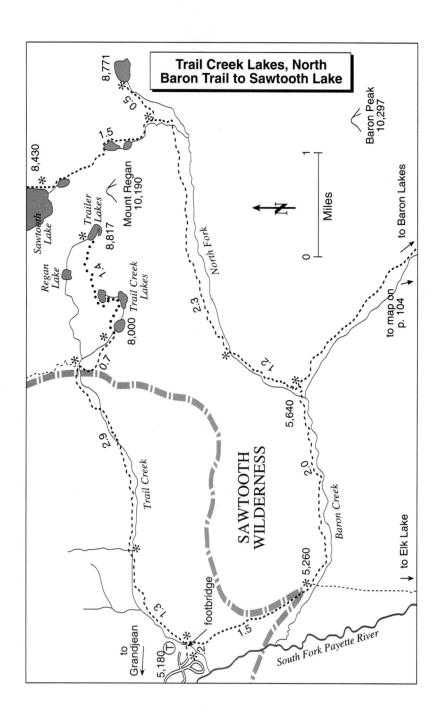

Trail Creek Lakes, North Baron Trail to Sawtooth Lake

8,771

0.5

1.5

8,430

Sawtooth Lake

Trailer Lakes

Mount Regan 10,190

8,817

Regan Lake

1.4

Trail Creek Lakes

8,000

0.7

North Fork

2.3

Baron Peak 10,297

1

Miles

N

0

to Baron Lakes

to map on p. 104

5,640

0.?

2.9

Trail Creek

2.0

Baron Creek

5,260

to Elk Lake

SAWTOOTH WILDERNESS

1.3

footbridge

1.5

to Grandjean

5,180

T

.2

South Fork Payette River

132

What you'll see: This little lake of marshy edges and green water hides behind lodgepole pines and subalpine firs and under ridges of crumbled granite. Beyond it, two small jagged peaks cling to the wall of Elk Creek Canyon. Just before the lake, McGown Peak and the White Clouds can be seen in the distance. On the way to the lake, the creeks and bogs of Elk Meadow make it difficult to find the way. So this trail is best for late summer.

Directions: From the trailhead, at 6,960 feet, the trail goes north over a small ridge and west down to the edge of Elk Meadow at 1.5 miles where it disappears near a signed junction with the Elk Mountain Loop Trail. Although the topographic map shows a trail across Elk Meadow, there is no trail tread.

After going west across the meadow, you'll need a compass and topographic map or GPS to find the trail up Elk Creek again. First, go west over to Elk Creek and ford it at 2 miles. The ford is deep and swift.

Beyond the ford, cut over toward the woods and willows, crossing two or three side creeks on the way. The trail should appear along the edge of the forest at 3 miles. It is on the west side of the meadow near its upper end. In the woods the trail to Elizabeth Lake turns off to the right just before a ford of Elk Creek at 3.5 miles. A trail used to continue across that ford and up Elk Creek 6 miles to Elk Creek Summit with a 1,780-foot climb, and then go 3.5 more miles down to the Stanley Lake Creek Trail but there is little trace of it now.

The Elizabeth Lake Trail goes along the right (north) side of Elk Creek and then a side creek. Avoid cow paths before the trail starts to climb. At 3.8 miles, it climbs straight up the wooded hillside. It turns away from the creek at 4 miles.

At 4.8 miles the trail crosses a branch of the outlet to the left (west) side. It goes west up a steep ridge and then follows the top of it. At 5 miles, an unsigned path drops left (west) 100 yards to the lake (8,090 feet). The main trail continues 1.5 miles with a 243-foot climb and 491-foot elevation loss to Kelly Lake.

GRANDJEAN AREA

49.

TRAIL CREEK LAKES

Round trip: 10.2 miles from the Grandjean trailhead to the first lake; other lakes are cross-country; connects with Stanley Lake Creek and Sawtooth Lake trails

Elevation gain: 2,820 feet to first lake **Highest point:** 8,000 feet at first lake, 8,817 feet at Trailer Lakes.

Side trip to the Trailer Lakes: 1.4 miles one-way and 880 feet addi-

133

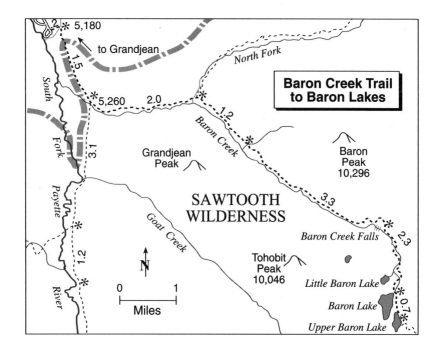

**Baron Creek Trail
to Baron Lakes**

to Grandjean

North Fork

Baro̅n Creek

South Fork Payette River

5,180

5,260 2.0

1.5

3.1

1.2

Grandjean Peak

Goat Creek

SAWTOOTH
WILDERNESS

1.2

Baron Peak
10,296

3.3

Tohobit Peak
10,046

Baron Creek Falls

2.3

Little Baron Lake

Baron Lake

Upper Baron Lake

0.7

N

0   1

Miles

tional elevation gain

Maps: Grandjean, Stanley Lake

Trailhead GPS: 44 08.956, 115 09.046

Difficulty: strenuous; expert for the cross-country route to upper lakes and Trailer Lakes; time: 9 hours for the first lake, 4 hours more for the Trailer Lakes

Access: On Idaho 21, 37.1 miles northwest of Stanley, turn left (east) on gravel Grandjean Road (524). Drive 7.1miles to the trailhead in the campground. There are separate trailheads for hikers and horses. The road to the horse trailhead turns left off the main road .2 mile before the hikers' trailhead.

What you'll see: The lowest Trail Creek Lake reflects a dark triangular peak with hunched shoulders. At the peak's base, a tilted slab touches the blue-green water with one corner. The inlet cascades down a flower-dusted notch. Cliffs of the triangular peak hang over the second lake, but a grassy peninsula and talus soften its shore. Granite knolls, whitebark pines, marsh grass and Labrador tea wreathe the dark green third lake below the jagged teeth of a peak roofed with sloping slabs.

Regan and Trailer lakes are near the third lake. Above round green Regan Lake, peach talus climbs to cliffs scribbled with stripes. The lower of the two Trailer Lakes is fish-shaped with a talus eye. Above it, pale orange cliffs sweep to the lumpy summit of Mt. Regan. Avoid camping in the fragile lake basin of the upper lakes. The entire Trail

Lowest Trail Creek Lake

Creek drainage burned in the 2006 Trailhead Fire, so you'll see a forest recovering from fire

Directions: Note that the trail climbs 2,820 feet to the first lake and there is no shade, so take it easy. Park in the hikers parking area 7 miles from the highway unless you have horses with you.

From the trailhead (5,180 feet) on the east side of the campground, the trail leads through woods to a bridge over Trail Creek. At a junction on the other side at .2 mile, turn left (north) on the Trail Creek Trail. It switchbacks up a sagebrush hillside, then follows the creek on a steep, grassy slope across from rock towers.

At 1 mile, the trail hairpins away from the creek and returns to it through brush at 1.2 miles. It crosses to the left (north) side of the creek at 1.5 miles. This ford is dangerous in early summer. Now the trail makes a big switchback up a talus slope, and at 1.7 miles returns. At 2.4 miles, it zigzags up a brushy slope, where it is often washed-out At 2.9 miles, it fords the creek to the south.

Now the trail makes 16 switchbacks up to 200 yards long in climbing 320 feet up granite ledges. At 3.3 miles, it runs along the ravine of the creek and crosses it back to the left (north) at 3.5 miles. At 3.9 miles, after the creek splits, it crosses the north branch of the creek to the right (east) side. The next section has another 20 switchbacks, climbing 300 feet in .5 mile.

The sign for the Trail Creek Lakes turnoff is at 4.4 miles (7,581 feet). 9The main trail climbs 451 feet in 1 mile to the Trail Creek - Stanley

135

Baron Lake from its outlet

Lake Creek Divide.) Turn right on the lakes trail, which crosses Trail Creek in mud and goes up a hillside. It climbs the right (west) side of the outlet of the first lake, skirting talus where pikas live. The first lake (8,000 feet) is at 5.1 miles. Campsites are at its lower end and around the side of it.

There is no trail to the upper lakes. To reach them, go around the north shore of the lake and climb east up a ravine to the left of granite benches. In a dry creek bed, turn right (south) cross-country to the lower end of the second lake (8,225 feet), .5 mile from the first lake.

To reach the third lake (8,245 feet), go half way along the north side of the second lake. Then turn left (north) and walk past a pond to the lake at .7 mile.

To get to Trailer Lakes, circle the third Trail Creek Lake on the north. The steeper route climbs the inlet in a gully of tiny trees. From this gully, continue up a slot in the rocks to the flat sand and granite benches near the smallest, highest lake (8,860 feet), which is .1 mile above the large, fish-shaped lake (8,817 feet).

To follow the second route, head north from the north side of the third Trail Creek Lake for 200 yards up a little canyon. Turn east and go between granite knolls to a low saddle (8,600 feet), 1.4 miles from the lowest lake. Regan Lake is .2 mile below to the north. To reach the Trailer Lakes from here, go east above cliffs along the side of the ridge.

136

50.

BARON CREEK TRAIL TO BARON LAKES

Round trip: 22.4 miles from Grandjean to the upper lake; connects
with the trail over Baron Divide to Alpine Lake and Redfish Canyon
Elevation gain: 3,325 feet **Highest point:** 8,505 feet
Maps: Grandjean, Stanley Lake, Warbonnet Peak
Trailhead GPS: 44 08.956, 115 09.046
Difficulty: strenuous; time: 2 to 3 days
Access: From Idaho 21, 37.2 miles west of Stanley (20.8 miles east of
Lowman), turn (east) on the gravel Grandjean Road (524) and drive 7.1
miles to the trailhead in the Grandjean Campground.

What you'll see: The trail from Grandjean to Baron Lakes ascends
a canyon shadowed with spires and lacy with waterfalls. At Baron
Lakes, the face of Monte Verita resembles organ pipes. The ridge connecting this peak with a shoulder of hidden Warbonnet Peak holds a
row of tilting spires. To the northwest, the summit of Big Baron Spire
resembles a bent thumb. Below the lakes, Baron Peak forms a sawtooth
wall.

Directions: Beginning at the end of the campground at 5,180 feet,
the trail bridges Trail Creek to a junction at .2 mile with the trail to
Trail Creek Lakes. Stay on the level South Fork of the Payette River
Trail, under lodgepole and ponderosa pines.

At 1.7 miles, turn left (east) on the Baron Creek Trail, which climbs
along the left (north) side of Baron Creek through forest and brush
below granite cliffs. At 3.6 miles, it fords the North Fork of Baron
Creek, where a slanting log allows a precarious crossing. Fording here
is dangerous. Crossing on the log requires care. Be sure to undo the
waist belt of your pack. Once a woman who didn't do this drowned
here. There is a campsite on the far side, where at 3.7 miles, the North
Fork of Baron Creek Trail turns off to Sawtooth Lake.

As the trail continues up the canyon, you can see on the right (east),
the folded face of Grandjean Peak. At 4.9 miles, the trail fords Moolack
Creek. It comes close to Baron Creek at 5.5 miles at a campsite marked
by a trailside boulder. Past this in an open grassy area, the grade steepens. At 6.8 miles, a waterfall tumbles from Tohobit Peak on the east.

Switchbacks begin opposite another falls at 7.5 miles. They climb
1,000 feet in 1 mile, mostly over rocks to a view of Baron Creek Falls.
Above the falls at 8.5 miles is a small campsite at the edge of a grassy
slope.

The trail bridges Baron Creek at 9 miles to the west side. The main
trail has three more creek crossings (at 9.5, 10 miles, and 10.4 miles) but
no more bridges. The last ford is just below the lower end of 8,312-foot

137

Baron Lake at 10.5 miles. The best campsites are near the outlet. The trail then zigzags through forest up a ridge to 8,505-foot Upper Baron Lake at 11.2 miles. The best campsites here are off-trail northeast of its lower end in a tiny valley with a pond.

Side trips from the lakes include Little Baron Lake and an unnamed lake on the side of Monte Verita. To reach Little Baron Lake, from the lower end of Baron Lake climb through a notch in the ridge and descend 200 feet in forest.

For the unnamed lake, sometimes called Cirque Lake, go around Baron Lake along the east shore crossing the outlet of Upper Baron Lake (not shown on the map) and the inlet draining the small lake on the side of Monte Verita. Climb the inlet over grassy slopes and granite benches to the lake (9,020 feet) 1.2 miles from the lower end of Baron Lake and 708 feet above it.

51.

NORTH BARON TRAIL FROM BARON CREEK TO SAWTOOTH LAKE

This one-way section: 6 miles, 2,819-foot elevation gain, 59-foot elevation loss; connects with the Iron Creek Trail to Sawtooth Lake
Round trip: 19.4 miles from Grandjean to Sawtooth Lake
Elevation gain: 3,309 feet **Highest point:** 8,489 feet
Elevation loss (return climb): 59 feet
Maps: Grandjean, Stanley Lake
Trailhead GPS: 44 08.956, 115 09.046
Difficulty: strenuous; time: 2 to 3 days
Access: Following the directions for Baron Creek Trail to Baron Lakes, hike the Baron Creek Trail from Grandjean to the junction with the North Fork of Baron Creek Trail at 3.7 miles, just beyond a difficult crossing of that creek.

What you'll see: This trail climbs the canyon of the North Fork of Baron Creek between pleated granite walls trimmed with pinnacles. As it ascends the headwall, orange stripes across the canyon etch the charcoal pleats of a 1,500-foot face. From the top of this climb, it is a short cross-country hike to a round turquoise lake in a bowl of scalloped cliffs. Back on the trail after this side trip, you soon pass three aquamarine ponds in talus and wildflowers under the orange cliffs of Mt. Regan. Around a corner, the high rounded point of this peak hangs over the ponds and sapphire blue Sawtooth Lake.
Directions: From the junction (5,640 feet) with the Baron Creek Trail, 3.7 miles from Grandjean, the North Baron Trail switchbacks up through grass , brush and Douglas firs. In your planning, remember that you have to ford the North Fork of Baron Creek to reach this junc-

138

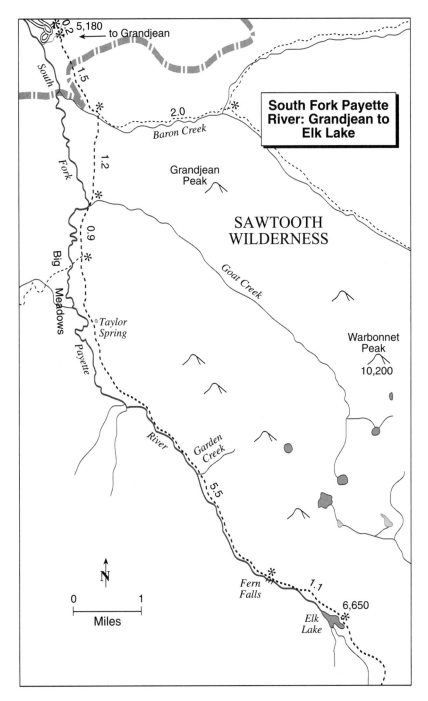

South Fork Payette River: Grandjean to Elk Lake

5,180

← to Grandjean

0.2

1.5

South

2.0

Baron Creek

1.2

Fork

Grandjean Peak

SAWTOOTH WILDERNESS

0.9

Big

Goat Creek

Meadows

Taylor Spring

Warbonnet Peak

10,200

Payette

River

Garden Creek

5.5

N

0   1

Miles

Fern Falls

1.1

6,650

Elk Lake

139

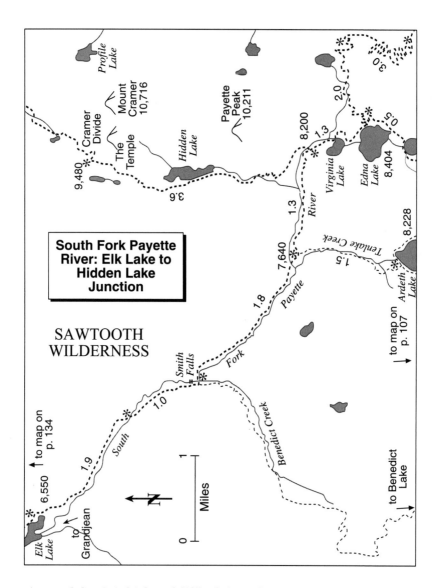

South Fork Payette
River: Elk Lake to
Hidden Lake
Junction

SAWTOOTH
WILDERNESS

tion, and that it is high and difficult in early summer The 2,800-foot elevation gain on this trail makes using it as part of a loop including Sawtooth Lake difficult, unless you go to Sawtooth Lake first.

At 1.2 miles, the trail fords the North Fork to the left (north) side. In early summer, it is best to pick your way across the log pile just above the ford. Even on logs, the crossing is hazardous for hikers until late summer.

Once across, the trail switchbacks through brush and rock, then alders, willows, and cottonwoods. At 3 miles, it crosses open slopes of

140

grass, tiny firs, and sagebrush, scree and talus At 4 miles is a ford to the right (east) side. This crossing can also be difficult in early summer.

Now the trail hairpins up the wall of the hanging valley containing Sawtooth Lake. It crosses back and forth over a white quartz outcrop. When the trail levels, at 4.5 miles, before the first of two ponds in the woods, hikers can take a cross-country side trip northeast to the 8,771-foot round lake under Merritt Peak.

To take this side trip, go toward the outlet of that lake keeping just below the edge of the talus, but above a gorge. For the last 200 yards, scramble along ledges beside the creek. At the lake, which is .5 mile and 600-feet above the trail, you must climb out of the stream bed to the right to avoid cliffs.

From the turnoff for the side trip, the main trail continues .2 mile to the first pond, which has campsites, the first since Baron Creek. It then threads wildflowers and talus to two larger ponds at 4.7 and 5 miles. There are campsites on the wooded knoll between these ponds. Above the upper pond (8,271 feet), the trail zigzags through rocks to its high point opposite still another pond (8,489 feet) in the grass right under Mt. Regan. Then it drops to the shore of Sawtooth Lake (8,430 feet) at 6 miles. From here, it goes .8 mile along the east shore to the Iron Creek Trail (see Alpine, Sawtooth and McGown Lakes).

52.

SOUTH FORK PAYETTE RIVER: GRANDJEAN TO ELK LAKE

Round trip: 20.8 miles to where the trail nears the lake shore; connects with the trail up the South Fork of the Payette River
Elevation gain: 1,470 feet **Highest point:** 6,650 feet
Maps: Grandjean, Edaho Mountain, Warbonnet Peak
Trailhead GPS: 44 08.956, 115 09.046
Difficulty: strenuous; time: 2 to 3 days
Access: On Idaho 21, 37.2 miles northwest of Stanley (20.8 miles from Lowman), turn left (east) on the gravel Grandjean Road (524), and drive 7.1 miles to the Grandjean Campground.

What you'll see: Along the way to Elk Lake, Taylor Spring bubbles from emerald moss at the side of Big Meadows. These meadows unfurl five miles of green velvet along the South Fork of the Payette. Farther up the river at Elk Lake, a fir forest crowds lime green marsh grass. Behind the lake, the fractured north wall of the canyon faces rock ridges bristling with trees.

Directions: From the campground (5,180 feet), the trail bridges Trail Creek at .2 mile, then passes a turnoff for Trail Creek Lakes. The

141

trail up the South Fork continues mostly level through trees and grassy areas.

At 1.7 miles, the Baron Creek Trail turns off to the east. Continue south on the river trail. Right away it fords Baron Creek, which is split into several channels. On the south side of the first channel, the trail angles to the right. It is marked with rock cairns directing you to better crossings of the new side channels before turning back to the existing trail. Baron Creek is expected to shift location more in the future.

At 2.5 miles, the trail has been diverted to an old mining road for .4 mile, to make the ford of Goat Creek at 2.9 miles easier. Both Baron and Goat Creeks are deep and rushing all summer. The bridges that once were here were removed when they became unsafe. In early summer and until midsummer in wet years, these fords are dangerous. When crossing them any time, always unfasten your pack belt and use sturdy shoes, not sandals.

At 3.8 miles, a trail turns off to the right (west) up the North Fork of the Boise River. This trail first crosses the South Fork of the Payette in a 120-foot ford that is dangerous for hikers all summer. It then goes 11.8 miles up a ridge and down the North Fork of the Boise to meet the Bayhouse Trail 1 mile from the 4-wheel drive Graham Road. There is a 2,271-foot climb and 1,656-foot elevation loss. Most of the forest along this trail burned in 1994.

Continue on the South Fork Trail to Taylor Spring at 5 miles. It is only 140 feet higher than Grandjean. There are several campsites. (The site and grave of Deadman's Cabin are .9 mile south of the spring.)

At 6.5 miles, the trail begins to climb. Below Garden Creek at 8 miles are waterfalls and a campsite. There are sometimes washouts above here. There are many switchbacks in brush, but none are shown on the map. A campsite is off-trail in a grassy area toward the river. Fern Falls at 9.3 miles is two short waterfalls. At 10.4 miles, the trail comes close to Elk Lake, (6,650 feet) halfway along it. There is one campsite earlier, down a path to the lake at 11 miles, but the more attractive sites lie at the upper end of the lake at 12 miles.

53.

SOUTH FORK PAYETTE RIVER: ELK LAKE TO HIDDEN LAKE JUNCTION

This one-way section: 6 miles, 1,550-foot elevation gain from Elk Lake

Round trip: 35.2 miles from Grandjean; connects with trails to Cramer and Edna lakes

Elevation gain: 3,020 feet **Highest point:** 8,200 feet

Maps: Warbonnet Peak, Mt. Everly, Snowyside Peak

Trailhead GPS: 44 08.956, 115 09.046

Difficulty: strenuous; time: 3 to 4 days

Ardeth Lake

Access: Using the directions for South Fork of the Payette River Trail: Grandjean to Elk Lake, hike 11.6 miles to the point where the trail comes close to Elk Lake halfway along it.

What you'll see: Along the South Fork of the Payette River above Elk Lake, glacier-polished rocks glide up to the spires and turrets of the canyon walls and of each side canyon. Just below Benedict Creek, the river foams in a cascade known as Smith Falls. In this trail section, the route fords Benedict Creek once and the river three times.

Directions: Above Elk Lake (6,650 feet), the trail climbs through woods to a 120-foot ford of the river to the right (south) side at 1.9 miles. This ford is usually only one to two feet deep, but is dangerous and may be impassable in June. Beyond the ford, the trail climbs along the river, passing Smith Falls, just before a junction with the Benedict Creek Trail at 2.9 miles. That trail gains 960 feet in 3.5 miles to a junction with the Queens River Trail below Benedict Lake.

The South Fork Trail next crosses Benedict Creek, and then the river to the left (north) and climbs more steeply. This ford and the Benedict Creek one are hazardous in early summer. At Tenlake Creek, at 4.7 miles, the trail fords the South Fork again to the south side and a junction (7,640) with the Tenlake Creek Trail. (The Tenlake Creek Trail climbs 588 feet in 1.5 miles to Ardeth Lake.)

Between this junction and the Hidden Lake Junction, the trail switchbacks up 600 feet through lodgepoles and grouse whortleberry. At the junction, at 6 miles (8,200 feet), trails turn north to Hidden Lake and south to Edna Lake. From Elk Lake to this junction, water can be

143

obtained only from the river.

54

TENLAKE CREEK TRAIL TO ARDETH LAKE

This one-way section: 1.5 miles, 588-foot elevation gain from the South Fork of the Payette River
Round trip: 35.6 miles from Grandjean; connects with the trail to Spangle Lakes
Elevation gain: 3,048 feet **Highest point:** 8,228 feet
Map: Mt. Everly
Trailhead GPS: 44 08.956, 115 09.046
Difficulty: strenuous; time: 3 to 5 days
Access: Using directions for South Fork Payette River: Grandjean to Elk Lake and Elk Lake to Hidden Lake junction, hike 16.3 miles to Tenlake Creek (7,640 feet).

What you'll see: This trail leads to Ardeth Lake, a .5 mile-long blue lake set below the wide triangle of Glens Peak in a basin containing ten lakes. The topmost cliffs of this peak peer at Ardeth Lake over a 600-foot shelf of solid granite. Two slanting chimneys, usually snow-filled, divide the sides of the shelf into three leaning cylindrical towers.
Directions: From the junction (7,640 feet) on the South Fork of the Payette River Trail, the Tenlake Creek Trail ascends that creek through thick forest, and at .2 mile fords it to the right (west). At 1.2 miles, just below Ardeth Lake, it returns to the left side of the creek. These fords have deep, rushing water and are hazardous in early summer. The trail joins the trail from Edna to Spangle Lakes in woods near campsites at the lower end of Ardeth Lake (8,228 feet), which is 1.5 miles up Tenlake Creek from the South Fork of the Payette.

GRAHAM AREA

55

BAYHOUSE AND JOHNSON CREEK TRAILS

Round trip: 13.2 miles from the Graham trailhead to the junction

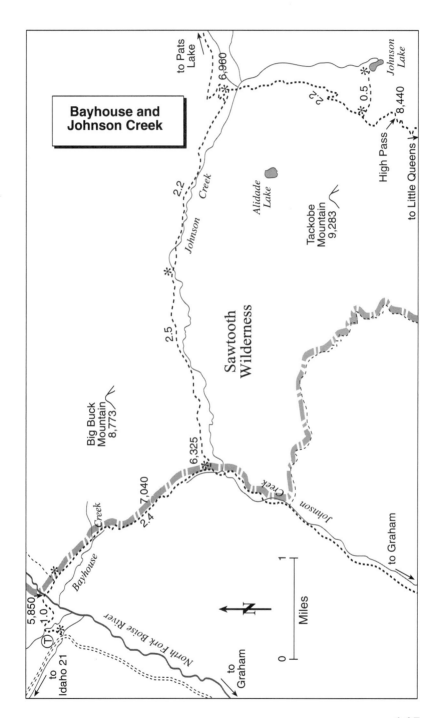

Bayhouse and
Johnson Creek

to Pats
Lake

6,960

Johnson
Lake

2.2

0.5

8,440

High Pass

to Little Queens

Johnson Creek

2.2

Alidade
Lake

Tackobe
Mountain
9,283

Sawtooth
Wilderness

2.5

Big Buck
Mountain
8,773

6,325

Johnson Creek

to Graham

Bayhouse Creek

7,040

2.4

Miles

N

1

0

5,850

1.0

to
Idaho 21

North Fork Boise River

to
Graham

145

with the trail from High Pass to Pats Lake; add 10 miles round trip if the Graham Road is closed at its summit as it sometimes is. Connects with Little Queens and Queens River trails.

Elevation gain: 1,780 feet **Highest point:** 7,040 feet
Elevation loss (return climb): 720 feet
Maps: Swanholm Peak, Nahneke Mountain
Trailhead GPS: 43 59.551, 115 15.560
Difficulty: strenuous; time: 3 to 4 days; this route gives difficult access to the Sawtooth Wilderness
Access: From Idaho 21, at the Edna Creek Campground 18 miles northeast of Idaho City drive to the Graham trailhead on a rough, primitive road (312) that requires 4-wheel drive. Be sure to inquire at the Idaho City Ranger District (208-392-6684) for road conditions before traveling it. (This road is not under SNRA management, so the SNRA won't have the latest information.) Those who travel beyond the summit of this road do so at their own risk.

What you'll see: From the summit of the Graham Road, the splintered panorama of the entire Sawtooth range outlines the horizon. This road is for the brave, since it is rocky, steep, and hangs above deep canyons. From the road, the Bayhouse Trail climbs through a burned fir forest over a ridge and down through sparse sagebrush to the Johnson Creek Trail. The trail meanders with the creek in and out of meadows and the remains of lodgepole groves below the granite spurs of Big Buck Mountain. By these two trails, the Graham Road used to provide the shortest access to Pats Lake (10.5 miles), but that road and trail go through a lot of dead timber from a 1994 fire. These trails provide an opportunity to observe how a forest regenerates after fire. Remember burned snags can fall without warning, especially on windy days. Several years ago, the author saw one fall at the Johnson Creek Campground on a calm August day.
Directions: To reach Graham, drive 18 miles northwest of Idaho City on Idaho 21 to the Edna Creek Campground. Turn right here and go 4.2 miles to the Graham Road (312). Turn left (north) on that road. At a summit 13.3 miles from the turnoff, the road looks down on the 1,000-foot deep canyon of Jackson Creek. The track skirts the canyon wall to a junction with a 2.3 mile side road to Jackson Peak Lookout at 14.6 miles.

From this point on, the Graham Road is suitable only for 4-wheel drive vehicles with high clearance. The road drops 300 feet into Trapper Flat at 15.6 miles. Then it climbs the Crooked River to a view of the Sawtooths at 21 miles (8,080 feet). At 22.4 miles, the road reaches a summit . In the next five miles, it descends 2,000 feet with some sharp turns into the canyon of Silver Creek. At 25.9 miles, the road fords Little Silver Creek.

At 27.4 miles, (31.6 miles from Idaho 21), a short side road to the Graham trailhead turns left off the main road. There are level campsites and a toilet along the side road, but no tables. The main road continues another 4.4 miles, passing the foundations of the Graham Mill and going through the Graham Bridge Campground at 29.7 miles on the

146

way. The old Graham Bridge washed out several years ago, so to continue beyond this campground you must use 4-wheel drive LOW to ford the river to the old guard station at 28.4 miles and the Johnson Creek Campground at 31.8 miles.

The level trail from the Graham trailhead (5,904 feet), which is sometimes called the Silver Creek trailhead, fords Cow Creek at .2 mile and the North Fork of the Boise River (5,850 feet) at .8 mile. The river crossing is difficult and dangerous in early summer. A trail turns up the North Fork of the Boise at 1 mile. It climbs 1,656 feet and descends 2,271 feet in 11.8 miles to meet the South Fork of the Payette River Trail across a dangerous ford 3.8 miles above Grandjean.

At the junction with the North Fork of the Boise Trail, take the Bayhouse Creek Trail to the right, southeast up 1,140 feet along the boundary of the Sawtooth Wilderness and SNRA. At 1.9 miles, it crosses a branch of Bayhouse Creek. It reaches a summit, (7,040 feet) at 2.5 miles, with a view of the lower end of Johnson Creek Canyon. Then it drops 720 feet over an open slope to a junction (6,320 feet) at 3.4 miles with the Johnson Creek Trail, a poor trail which has come 5 miles and 700 feet from near the Johnson Creek Campground with four fords of the creek. If you want to do some hiking from the Johnson Creek Campground, fording Johnson Creek just above its confluence with Silver Creek at the campground, hiking down the creek, and going up to the lakes on the side of Swanholm Peak. is a better option. (These trails are not in the Sawtooth Wilderness or the SNRA.)

At the junction with the Bayhouse Trail, 3.4 miles from the Graham trailhead, turn left (east) up the Johnson Creek Trail, which enters the wilderness. At 5.9 miles, it fords the creek in a meadow. At the other end of the meadow, at 6.2 miles, it fords back again to the north side of the creek. Up the canyon, the horns of two peaks form a headwall behind Azure and Rock Island Lakes. The trail goes gently along the canyon bottom, and at 7.8 miles begins to climb. At 8.1 miles, it joins the Pats Lake Trail. There are several campsites along the canyon, but the only safe ones are those sites well away from burned trees. In late summer, there is water only in Johnson Creek, and in a year with little snow it dries up beyond the first ford in late summer.

QUEENS RIVER AREA

56.

QUEENS RIVER CANYON TO PATS LAKE JUNCTION

This one-way section: 12.4 miles from trailhead to junction with the trail over Pats Lake Divide

Round trip: 24.8 miles; connects with the trail down Benedict Creek

147

to the South Fork Payette
Elevation gain: 3,080 feet **Highest point:** 8,280 feet
Maps: Atlanta West, Atlanta East, Mt. Everly
Trailhead GPS: 40 50.552, 115 11.074
Difficulty: strenuous; time: 3 days
Access: To reach the trailhead, on Idaho 21, 18 miles northeast of Idaho City, turn right (east) at the Edna Creek Campground onto a gravel road, (384), which goes along Willow Creek and then down Little Owl Creek. At 14.8 miles, turn left (west) on Road 327 up the North Fork of the Boise River. At 21.3 miles, keep right when a road to the Deer Park Guard Station goes off to the left. Your road descends Swanholm Creek. At 26.7 miles, turn left (east) at a four-way intersection onto the gravel Middle Fork of the Boise River Road (268) and drive to the Queens River Road (206) at 37.5 miles. (This road is 4.5 miles west of Atlanta.) Here, turn left (north) and drive 2.3 miles on the narrow, rocky road to a transfer camp. The Queens River Road continues beyond the parking area to a small campground. Be sure to check on the road conditions before starting for Atlanta or the Queens River. (There is an alternate route to Atlanta, the James Creek Road from Rocky Bar near Featherville (076) but it is narrow and steep and can require 4-wheel drive. It is nicknamed the Boiler Grade.)

What you'll see: Cracked gray cliffs 1,000 feet high line the canyon of the Big Queens River from its mouth to the Pats Lake Junction. The first five miles go through the remnants of a ponderosa pine forest that burned in 2014. Higher up the trail traverses open grass, brush, and rocks with views of fluted peaks ahead. Beyond Nanny Creek, streams pour down the side of the canyon and make bogs on the trail. Near the head of the canyon, you can hike 1-mile cross-country to an unnamed lake with a dagger-shaped tongue of grass at the inlet. Farther up the trail at the Pats Lake Junction, the river begins as a stream babbling down from ponds through a rocky meadow under the gray granite hat of Mt. Everly.

Directions: From the parking area, the trail begins as an old road, closed to motor vehicles, which drops left (north) to cross the Queens River on a bridge (5,200 feet) in 200 yards. At .2 mile, the trail splits into the Queens River and Little Queens River trails.

From this junction, the right hand trail up the Queens River climbs more gradually. This trail wanders through burned forest, crossing side creeks at 1.4 and 2 miles under the high cliffs of the canyon wall. At 2.6 miles the Joe Daley Trail goes off to the south over a ridge to primitive roads leading to Atlanta, but it is hard to find the turnoff and that whole trail burned in 2014. Many washouts occurred after the fire, but the trail through the washouts has been marked with cairns except at the Atlanta end of Joe Daley.

At 3 miles in early summer a side creek overflows the Queens River Trail. At 3.3 miles, the trail fords the river to the right (south), in two sections. This crossing and the next two are dangerous in early summer. Later in the summer the first two can be confusing but the fords are marked with cairns.

148

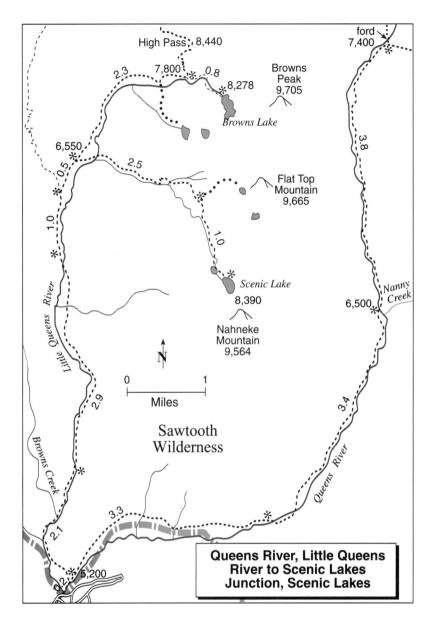

High Pass 8,440
7,800
2.3
0.8
8,278
Browns Peak
9,705
Browns Lake
ford 7,400
6,550
0.5
2.5
1.0
Flat Top Mountain
9,665
3.8
1.0
Scenic Lake
8,390
Nanny Creek
Nahneke Mountain
9,564
6,500
Little Queens River
2.9
Browns Creek
N
0   1
Miles
Sawtooth Wilderness
3.4
Queens River
3.3
2.1
0.2
5,200

Queens River, Little Queens River to Scenic Lakes Junction, Scenic Lakes

Once across the first ford, the trail ascends away from the river into brush below the canyon wall. At 3.8 miles, it goes over a side creek, and at a campsite, it returns to the river and fords back to the left (northwest) side of the river. Soon an open, brushy area extends upstream for 3 miles. On the with waterfalls hiding in the cliffs above. Just before Nanny Creek, the trail returns to forest then crosses the river in sev-

149

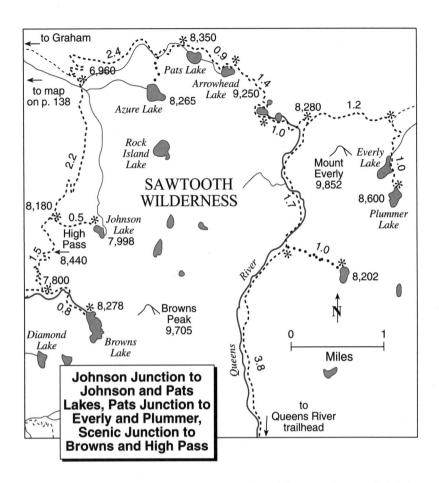

to Graham

2.4

6,960

*8,350

0.9

Pats Lake

Arrowhead
Lake 9,250

1.4

to map
on p. 138

Azure Lake

8,265

8,280

1.2

2.2

Rock
Island
Lake

SAWTOOTH
WILDERNESS

River

Mount
Everly
9,852

Everly
Lake

1.0

8,180

0.5

Johnson
Lake
7,998

8,600

Plummer
Lake

High
Pass
8,440

1.5

1.0

8,202

7,800

0.8

8,278

Browns
Peak
9,705

N

Diamond
Lake

Browns
Lake

Queens

0   1

Miles

3.8

**Johnson Junction to
Johnson and Pats
Lakes, Pats Junction to
Everly and Plummer,
Scenic Junction to
Browns and High Pass**

to
Queens River
trailhead

eral sections at 6.9 miles (6,500 feet) to a flat with campsites on the right (east) side of the river.

Beyond here, the trail is in open grass and rocks with ledges above. The grassy and wooded flats at 8 miles have campsites. Now there are several side streams and only patches of woods. At 9.6 miles, the trail jogs 90 degrees to the right (east) for 100 yards, then continues up the canyon. At 10.7 miles, it fords the creek to the left (west) side at 7,400 feet. Before the ford you can go off to the right to an unnamed lake (8,200 feet).

To make this side trip, wind west up the ridge, then continue along above the gorge of the lake's outlet until the ground flattens in a grassy area below talus at .7 mile. Here cut left (northeast) across the outlet and climb along near it. West of a tiny pond, return to the south side of the creek, and then climb along the west shore of the lake to a campsite in trees 1 mile from the main trail.

Fifty yards beyond the turnoff for this side trip, the trail fords the river at 7,360 feet, and then climbs through a meadow with little trail

150

tread. Beyond the meadow, the trail is can be hard to find. Gradually it returns to the river, then switchbacks in the open.

At 11.6 miles, the trail crosses back over the now six-foot river to the right (north) and angles along a ridge with black and white striped cliffs across the canyon. At 12.3 miles, the trail returns to the left (west) side of the creek, and joins the Pats Lake Trail at 12.4 miles (8,280 feet).

57.

PATS LAKE JUNCTION TO EVERLY AND PLUMMER LAKES

This one-way section: 2.2 miles, 684-foot elevation gain, 352-foot elevation loss

Round trip: 29.2 miles from the Queens River trailhead; connects with a trail to Pats Lake and one down Benedict Creek to the South Fork of the Payette

Elevation gain: 3,764 feet **Highest point:** 8,640 feet

Elevation loss (return climb): 352 feet

Map: Mt. Everly

Trailhead GPS: 40 50.552, 115 11.074

Difficulty: strenuous; time: 3 days

Access: Following directions for Queens River Canyon to Pats Lake Junction, hike 12.4 miles from the Queens River Transfer Camp to that junction.

What you'll see: The trail to Everly and Plummer Lakes runs below the double hump of the dark gray north face of Mt. Everly. On the south side of the mountain, cliffs and ledges plunge to the lakes' white granite benches and turquoise water. On the east side of Plummer Lake, cliffs rise 700 feet to two triangular peaks. Even though the lakes are only .2 mile apart, Everly Lake drains into a tributary of the Payette River, and Plummer Lake empties into a tributary of the Boise River.

Directions: From the junction with the Pats Lake Trail at 8,280 feet, take the Queens River Trail east up through a grassy basin and forest. It passes through two meadows on the way to an 8,592-foot divide at .7 mile with a view of the face of Mt. Everly. After a grassy flat, it drops through trees to a triangle of trails at 1.2 miles (8,240 feet). The triangle is the junction to the lakes. From here, the Queens River Trail drops to the Benedict Creek Trail in .9 mile with a 360-foot descent. At

151

A pond with Mount Everly from Pats Lake Pass

the triangle turn off onto the side trail, which fords a small creek to a meadow, then winds through trees and outcrops up the side of the outlet. It crosses the outlet on rocks just below Everly Lake (8,628 feet) at 1.7 miles.

The trail goes along the left (east) side of the lake below granite benches to campsites. From these, a path leads east to a tiny pond, then south between benches to the north end of Plummer Lake (8,600 feet) at 2.2 miles.

58.

PATS LAKE JUNCTION TO PATS LAKE

This one-way section: 3.3 miles, 970-foot elevation gain, 840-foot elevation loss

Round trip: 31.4 miles from the Queens River trailhead; connects with trails to Graham and the Little Queens River.

Elevation gain: 4,050 feet **Highest point:** 9,250 feet

Map: Mt. Everly; Queens River
Trailhead GPS: 40 50.552, 115 11.074
Difficulty: strenuous; time: 3 to 4 days
Access: Following directions for Queens River Canyon to Pats Lake Junction, hike 12.4 miles from the Queens River Transfer Camp to that junction.

What you'll see: The trail to Pats Lake from the Queens River hairpins 400 feet up the canyon wall in less than a mile. Along the way, two ponds hug the grass like blue mirrors on green velvet. At the larger pond, granite hills frame the elephant shape of Mt. Everly across the canyon. Taking turns throughout the summer, buttercups, shooting stars, and gentians carpet the grass. From the divide, you see the misty canyon of the Queens River on one side and the blue ovals of Arrowhead and Pats lakes on the other.

Directions: The divide between the Queens River and Pats Lake is one of the last to open in the summer. To avoid danger and damage, wait until the snow has melted before traveling the trail.

From the Pats Lake Junction (8,280 feet), 12.4 miles and a 3,080-foot climb up the Queens River, the trail climbs through woods and rock benches to the first pond at .7 mile. A second, larger pond is in turf at 1 mile. At 1.2 miles, the trail passes above a third tiny pond set in granite benches. Camping at the ponds is scenic but uncomfortable because of lumpy turf. Next, the trail passes left of a tiny pond in a grassy basin; then switchbacks up granite ledges to 9,250 feet and drops into a notch (9,200 feet) at 1.7 miles. The trail hairpins down 200 feet over slabs and talus .3 mile to another tiny pond. At 2.4 miles from the junction is Arrowhead Lake (8,770 feet) with a few, small campsites.

The trail zigzags down through ledges and trees to Pats Lake at 8,350 feet and then circles its north side. At the lower end at 3.3 miles, a path goes 100 yards to shoreline campsites. Below Pats Lake, the trail goes through a 1994 burn.

59.

LITTLE QUEENS RIVER TO SCENIC LAKES JUNCTION

Round trip: 13.4 miles from the Queens River trailhead
Elevation gain: 1,360 feet **Highest point:** 6,560 feet
Maps: Atlanta West, Nahneke Mountain
Trailhead GPS: 40 50.552, 115 11.074
Difficulty: strenuous; time: 9 hours
Access: To reach the trailhead, drive 18 miles northwest of Idaho City on Idaho 21 to the Edna Creek Campground. Turn right (east) here onto a gravel road (384), traveling along Willow Creek and Little Owl Creek. At 14.8 miles, turn left (west) on Road 327 up the North Fork

of the Boise River. At 21.3 miles, keep right when a road to the Deer Park Guard Station goes left. Now 327 descends Swanholm Creek. At 26.7 miles, turn left (east) at a four-way intersection onto the Middle Fork of the Boise River Road (268) and drive to the Queens River Road (206) at 37.5 miles. (This road is 4.5 miles west of Atlanta.) Here, turn left (north) and drive 2.3 miles on the narrow, rocky road to the trailhead and a small campground.

There are signs for Atlanta on the approach, but on the way back you'll need to use road numbers. Be sure to check on road conditions before starting for Atlanta or the Queens River. (An alternate route to Atlanta, the James Creek Road (126) from Rocky Bar near Featherville, often requires 4-wheel drive.)

What you'll see: The Little Queens River trail used to make a beautiful early summer walk through a rainbow of wildflowers beside the vanilla-scented trunks of ponderosa pines. Above, Douglas firs feathered the canyon walls. In 2014, the whole drainage of the Little Queens burned, so if you go into the area be sure to consult with the SNRA trails managers first for conditions and safety precautions. The trail follows an old wagon road for the first three miles. Here, rusted pieces of mining machinery give the feeling of stepping back in time.

Directions: From the junction (5,200 feet) of the Queens and Little Queens River trails .2 mile from the trailhead, take the left (west) branch of the trail up the Little Queens River in an open, burned forest of Douglas fir and ponderosa pine. The trail bridges the river to the west at 1.1 miles. Then it runs along the base of a steep hillside, and crosses Browns Creek at 1.7 miles. At 1.8 miles are cabin ruins in sagebrush across the river from an old dangerous mine tunnel. At 2.3 miles, the trail fords the river back to the right (east) in two sections.

A log cabin remnant used to be at 3 miles in a grassy area across from mine diggings. Beyond here, the trail climbs away from the creek in forest for 2 miles. In this section, it crosses Scott Creek at 3.9 miles, Tripod Creek at 4.7 miles, and Fezip Creek at 5 miles. At 5.2 miles, it fords back to the left (west) side of the river. In late summer, hikers can cross on rocks, but in early summer this crossing will be difficult.

At 6.2 miles is a junction with the Neinmeyer Creek Trail, which goes 7.6 miles to meet the Johnson Creek Trail .6 mile south of the Bayhouse Trail Junction. The Little Queens trail goes along the edge of a beaver pond and reaches the junction (6,550 feet) with the side trail to Scenic Lakes at 6.7 miles.

60.

SCENIC LAKES

This one-way section: 3.5 miles, 1,840-foot elevation gain from the

Little Queens River; connects with a route to Flat Top Lakes
Round trip: 20.4 miles from the Queens River trailhead
Elevation gain: 3,190 feet
Highest point: 8,390 feet
Map: Nahneke Mountain
Trailhead GPS: 40 50.552, 115 11.074
Difficulty: strenuous; time: 3 days
Access: Following directions for Little Queens River to Scenic Lakes Junction, hike 6.7 miles up the Little Queens River

What you'll see: On a dark gray face overhanging the small lake below Scenic Lake, two dark gray rock layers form a V. The thinner layer ends in an arrowhead. Above Scenic Lake itself, a curved line of dark brown decorates the cliffs. Two more dark layers, round and weathered, resemble gigantic brown candles. This trail is in the Little Queens drainage so burned in 2014.

Directions: From the Scenic Lakes junction (6,550 feet), the side trail to the lakes fords the 75-foot wide Little Queens River at .2 mile. This crossing is hazardous in early summer and in wet years until late summer. Beyond it, the trail winds above the canyon of Scenic Creek in alternate forest and open grass. At 1 mile, it zigzags through brush, with a view of a waterfall. At 1.7 miles, a sign warns that horse travel is not recommended because the steep route is difficult for horses and the area is fragile.

Here the trail is a foot path that climbs straight up in grass and brush with a view of towers to the left, then cuts to the right below cliffs. Next it zigzags up the right side of the cliffs, and at 2.1 miles angles along the canyon wall. The trail descends left of an orange and white outcrop and circles to the right of a pond to a junction with a line of blazes (no path) to Flat Top Lakes at 2.5 miles. This route climbs 800 feet in .7 mile to the first Flat Top Lake.

Continue on the Scenic Lakes Trail across a boggy meadow, over a granite outcrop, and along the center of the first of three large meadows. Beyond this meadow, the route is on the left of the creek between it and granite ledges. In the second, meadow, the trail tread disappears, and then reappears at a cairn on an outcrop halfway along the meadow. Now the trail follows the creek next to ledges. After crossing the third, smaller meadow, it fords the creek at 3.2 miles to the right (west). The smaller, unnamed lake, where the official trail ends, is at 3.4 miles. A few small campsites are nearby.

To reach the upper lake, ford both branches of the outlet and go along the left (east) edge of the small lake below a granite knoll. At the far end of the lake, climb over grass and rocks and through woods to Scenic Lake, 8,390 feet, at 3.5 miles. Two small rocky campsites are on benches near the outlet.

61.

SCENIC LAKES JUNCTION TO BROWNS LAKE, HIGH PASS, AND JOHNSON LAKE JUNCTION

This one-way section: 3.8 miles, 1,880-foot gain, 260-foot loss from the Scenic Lakes junction
Round trip: 21 miles from the Queens River trailhead; connects with trails to Pats Lake and to the Graham trailhead
Elevation gain: 3,240 **Highest point:** 8,440 feet
Elevation loss (return climb): 260 feet
Side trip to Browns Lake: add .8 mile and 478 feet elevation gain
Map: Nahneke Mountain
Trailhead GPS: 40 50.552, 115 11.074
Difficulty: strenuous; time: 3 days

What you'll see: The whole drainage of the Little Queens River burned in 2014 including this section. On the east side of the Little Queens River near its headwaters, are towers on the crinkled wall of Browns Peak. Across Browns Lake from this wall, tiers of cliffs follow the shapes of the benches edging the lake. Near the lower end, a white island resembles a sea monster. In the distance north of High Pass, the orange and charcoal needles of North and South Raker Peaks stick up like the points of giant quill pens. Between the pass and the peaks, dead trees like toothpicks cover the drainage of Johnson Creek, which burned in the 1994 Rabbit Creek Fire.

Directions: Above the Scenic Lakes Junction, the Little Queens River Trail runs in open brush and scattered snags, crosses three side streams, and curves east. At 1.7 miles, it is in a grassy basin with sub-alpine firs. Where it switchbacks left (north) at 1.8 miles, you can leave the main trail and take a .9-mile route to Diamond Lake, fording the river and then climbing 640 feet. Beyond this unmarked junction, it is .5 mile to the Browns Lake Junction (7,800 feet) at 2.3 miles.

The side trail to Browns Lake climbs east on the north side of its outlet over open slopes and through forest. At .4 mile, it crosses the outlet to the right (south) in alders. It runs along the base of granite benches and up between them to a meadow with campsites in the trees. At .8 mile is the lake (8,278 feet). Campsites are on the west shore and at the outlet.

From the Browns Lake Junction, the main trail to High Pass switchbacks up sandy slopes between lodgepoles to the 8,440-foot pass at 3.3 miles. From here, you can look back at the canyon walls of the Little Queens River, and the gray peaks around Browns Lake , and ahead at the Rakers.

On the other side, the trail switchbacks twice and continues northwest. Below is the small pond shown on the map. At 3.6 miles, the trail curves right in woods to an unsigned junction (8,180 feet) at 3.8 miles with the .5-mile side trail to Johnson Lake.

62.

JOHNSON LAKE JUNCTION TO JOHNSON LAKE AND PATS LAKE

This one-way section: 4.6 miles, 1,390-foot gain, 1,220-foot loss from Johnson Lake Junction
Round trip: 30.2 miles from the Queens River trailhead via the Little Queens River trail; connects with the trail over Pats Lake Pass to the Queens River and with the trail down to Graham.
Elevation gain: 4,630 feet **Highest point:** 8,350 feet
Elevation loss (return climb): 1,480 feet
Side trip to Johnson Lake: add .5 mile one-way and 182 feet return climb
Maps: Nahneke Mountain, Mt. Everly
Trailhead GPS: 40 50.552, 115 11.074
Difficulty: strenuous; time: 4 to 5 days
Access: From the Queens River Transfer Camp hike 10.5 miles up the Little Queens River over High Pass to the Johnson Lake Junction.

What you'll see: A gigantic granite breast swells above the upper end of shallow Johnson Lake. To the right of it, a second, smaller peak echoes that silhouette. Huckleberries and Labrador tea surround the misty green lake, which contains two granite islands. One is large and plumed with firs and the other is tiny and rocky.
Directions: From the Johnson Lake Junction (8,180 feet), which is 200 yards into the woods on the north side of High Pass, follow the blazed side trail east to a crossing of a pond's outlet. The trail wanders through lodgepoles, then drops to the lower end of the 7,998-foot lake near a campsite, .5 mile from the main trail. From a marsh .3 east of the lake, experts can continue .7 mile cross-country to The Hole and Glacier Lake.

In reaching Pats Lake from the Johnson Lake Junction, take the main trail north down through burned forest. It crosses an avalanche area, and at .5 mile, makes two switchbacks above a grassy area At .8 mile, is a glimpse of a small green pond. It runs down the outlet of the pond, then descends through grass, flowers, and remnants of forest to a ford of Johnson Creek at 2.1 miles (6,960 feet). At 2.2 miles, the trail joins the trail that goes down Johnson and Bayhouse creeks to Graham.

Above this junction the trail to Pats Lake switchbacks up open slopes with views up Johnson Creek toward High Pass and down the creek toward Graham. At 2.8 miles, it runs along the side of the ridge

157

into an old burn. It crosses to the south bank of the creek at 3.9 miles. At 4 miles, the trail is below talus blocks which pour down from a notch on the skyline. These blocks mark a .5-mile, 400-foot cross-country route for experts to Azure Lake. Just beyond this point, the trail fords the creek back to the north in a meadow.

The route to Azure Lake (8,265 feet) goes up along the edge of ledges just to the right (west) of the talus. From the notch on the skyline, descend a narrow ridge to the lower end of the lake where a granite peninsula shelters a campsite. Climbing directly from Pats Lake to Azure Lake is not recommended because of cliffs.

From the Azure Lake turn off, the main trail fords the creek, then climbs between rock ledges. It crosses the twice more before a path leads to the lower end of Pats Lake (8,350 feet) at 4.6 miles.

ATLANTA AREA

63.

MIDDLE FORK BOISE RIVER: POWERPLANT CAMPGROUND TO ROCK CREEK

Round trip: 17 miles from Powerplant Campground to the junction with the side trail to Timpa Lake; connects with the trail up the Middle Fork to Spangle Lakes and the trail up Mattingly Creek

Elevation gain: 960 feet **Highest point:** 6,400 feet

Maps: Atlanta East, Mt. Everly

Trailhead GPS: 43 48.757, 115 06.132

Difficulty: strenuous; time: 10 hours or 2 days

Access: To reach the trailhead, on Idaho 21, 18 miles north of Idaho City, turn right (east) at the Edna Creek Campground. Take this gravel road (384) along Willow Creek and down Little Owl Creek. At 14.8 miles, turn left (west) on Road 327, which goes up the North Fork of the Boise River. At 21.3 miles, keep right when a road to the Deer Park Guard Station turns left. Road 327 descends Swanholm Creek to a four-way intersection at 26.7 miles. Here, turn left (east) onto the gravel. Middle Fork of the Boise River Road (268) and drive to Atlanta, which is 42 miles from the highway. On the way in, signs show the way, but on the way back only road numbers direct you .It's best to check road conditions before starting out. At Atlanta, follow signs east for 1.5 miles to Powerplant Campground. (An alternate route to Atlanta, the James Creek Road from Rocky Bar near Featherville is steep and often requires 4-wheel drive.)

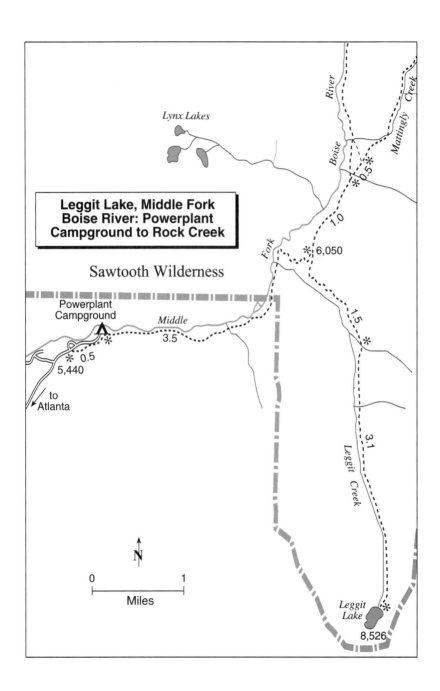

Lynx Lakes

River

Boise

Mattingly Creek

Leggit Lake, Middle Fork Boise River: Powerplant Campground to Rock Creek

Sawtooth Wilderness

Fork

0.5

1.0

* 6,050

1.5

*

Powerplant Campground

Middle

3.5

* 0.5
5,440

to
Atlanta

3.1
Leggit Creek

N

0   1
Miles

Leggit Lake
8,526 *

Atlanta school

What you'll see: The road to the trailhead wanders through the weathered town of Atlanta. The town nestles in lodgepole pines and aspens below Greylock Peak, a cliff-faced giant with a stubble of pines and rock towers. Some of the old buildings have collapsed. Others have been refurbished and are still used as bars, homes, cabins, and small stores. Modern cabins hide in the forests above. From Powerplant Campground, the trail up the Middle Fork of the Boise leads through forest. From the colorful undergrowth of flowers, fluffy grass, and bushes, you look up at spires, cliffs, and teeth on the canyon wall.

Directions: Just before Powerplant Campground (5,440 feet) is a meadow with a trail sign, circular drive and horse loading area. The trail begins to the right (south) of the road here. You can save .5 mile by driving to the end of the campground. Do not park there unless you want to pay for camping. The trail passes 100 feet southeast of the end of the campground. An old road that goes along the river from here for a few hundred yards is not the trail. The hike mileage given here is figured from the trailhead parking and sign, not from the far end of the campground.

The trail begins by climbing 80 feet, and then descending to a large grassy area. At 2 miles, it fords Grays Creek. Beyond here, it runs along a steep hillside, and at 2.8 miles fords Leggit Creek among small rounded rocks. Then it switchbacks uphill, curves around a knoll, and

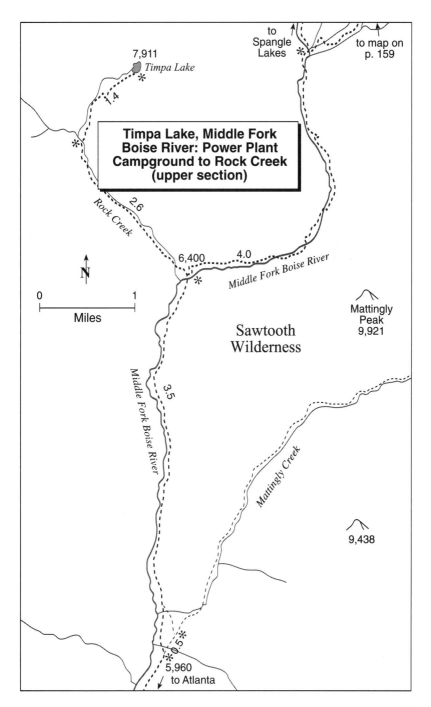

to
Spangle
Lakes

to map on
p. 159

7,911
Timpa Lake

1.4

Timpa Lake, Middle Fork
Boise River: Power Plant
Campground to Rock Creek
(upper section)

Rock Creek

2.6

N

0   1
Miles

6,400   4.0

Middle Fork Boise River

Mattingly
Peak
9,921

Sawtooth
Wilderness

Middle Fork Boise River

3.5

Mattingly Creek

9,438

5,960
to Atlanta

.5

crosses a level park-like area under ponderosa pines. At 3 miles, the trail switchbacks 200 feet up a steep grassy hillside. At 3.5 miles it reaches the Leggit Lake Junction (6,060 feet), which has a fine view of the canyon. Beyond here, the trail wanders up and down over grassy slopes until the first of two side trails leading to the Mattingly Creek Trail comes in at 4.5 miles. From here that trail leads 12.2 miles with a 2,856-foot elevation gain and 1,786-foot elevation loss to the Alturas trailhead, At the junction with the Mattingly Creek Trail, a high knoll of solid rock appears ahead.

Beyond the junction .1 mile, the Middle Fork Trail crosses Corral Creek in a grassy flat with a view of a dark rock hill, 100 feet high, that rises between the two branches of the Mattingly Creek Trail. At 5 miles, the second branch comes in and the Middle Fork Trail fords Mattingly Creek, which can be difficult in early summer.

It is 3.5 miles more through forest to a ford (6,400 feet) to the north side of the river just beyond its confluence with Rock Creek. There are campsites nearby. The ford, 8.5 miles from Powerplant Campground, is rushing, and dangerous in early summer. Across the ford is a junction in a wide grassy area with the trail up Rock Creek to Timpa Lake. From here, the main trail continues on up the river 6 miles to Spangle Lakes in a 2,185-foot climb.

64.

LEGGIT LAKE

This one-way section: 4.6 miles, 2,466-foot gain from the Middle Fork Boise River Trail

Round trip: 16.2 miles from Powerplant Campground at Atlanta
Elevation gain: 3,086 feet **Highest point:** 8,526 feet
Map: Atlanta East
GPS where trail passes far end of campground: 43 48.939, 115 06.134
Difficulty: strenuous; time: 12 hours or 2-3 days
Access: Following directions for Middle Fork Boise River: Powerplant Campground to Rock Creek, hike 3.5 miles to the Leggit Lake Junction.

What you'll see: On the way up Leggit Creek, a 1,000-foot dark gray cliff reminds hikers of walls in Yosemite. Five-hundred-foot ridges hold Leggit Lake in a rocky cup high in the sky. It is surrounded by miniature dark gray peaks.

Directions: From the Leggit Lake junction (6,060 feet), on a knoll 400 feet above the Middle Fork Canyon, the trail angles steeply up the canyon of Leggit Creek. Beyond a large campsite at 1.5 miles, the trail goes south toward Leggit Creek. At this curve, avoid an old road that leads up the left wall of the canyon to a prospect. The trail tread may be indistinct here. At 1.8 miles, the trail enters a gravelly area that is opposite the immense black cliff. Beyond the gravel, it crosses a side stream. At 3 miles, the forest gives way to rocks, grass, flowers and tiny subalpine firs.

At 4.1 miles, the trail becomes steep, rocky, and sketchy. At 4.4 miles, it goes left (east) of the creek to avoid cliffs and disappears. After a few yards it reappears, then climbs the scree past scattered trees and over a ridge to the lake (8,526 feet) at 4.6 miles. A few small campsites are at the lower end. On this trail, water is available at two side streams and from the creek.

65.

TIMPA LAKE

This one-way section: 4 miles, 1,511-foot gain from the Middle Fork of the Boise River

Round trip: 25 miles from Powerplant Campground at Atlanta

Elevation gain: 2,471 feet

Highest point: 7,911 feet

Maps: Atlanta East, Mt. Everly

Trailhead GPS at the upstream end of Powerplant Campground: 43 48.939, 115 06.134

Difficulty: strenuous; time: 3 days

Access: Following directions for Middle Fork Boise River: Powerplant Campground to Rock Creek, hike 8.5 miles up the river to Rock Creek.

What you'll see: Turf and marsh grass border the shallow blue-green water of Timpa Lake. On the west are talus and ledges that lead to an elephant-shaped ridge. Across the canyon below the lake, a ridge sweeps up into a house-like gable. At the head of Rock Creek, Chickadee, Surprise, Confusion, and Low Pass lakes hide off-trail behind wooded knolls and rock ridges.

Directions: On the Middle Fork of the Boise when you reach the Rock Creek junction (6,400 feet), turn off onto that trail, which fords Rock Creek to the left (west) side at .2 mile. This ford can be dangerous at high water and because of rocks is difficult or dangerous all summer even for stock. From it, the trail zigzags up the canyon beside cascades and pools of the creek . At 1.3 miles, it passes a huge boulder pile and becomes more gradual. It fords the creek back to the east at 2.6 miles where a collection of logs may help you cross. Above this crossing, the trail leaves Rock Creek and zigzags up the canyon of Timpa Creek, then goes straight along the side of the canyon to a sudden ending 50 vertical feet above the lake (7,911 feet) at 4 miles. Water is available at the creek crossings and lake.

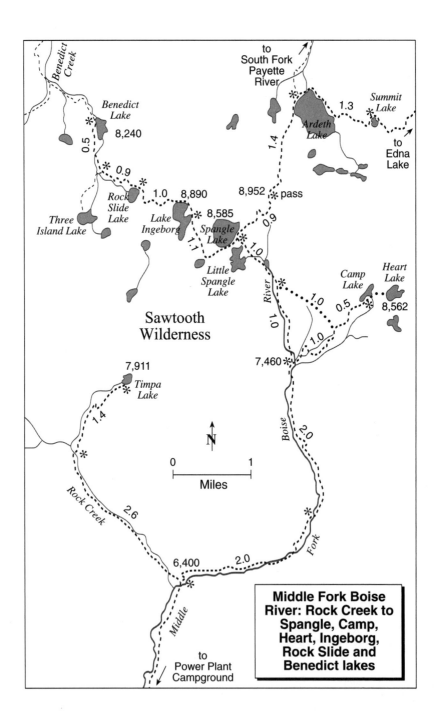

Benedict Creek

to
South Fork
Payette
River

Benedict
Lake
8,240

Ardeth
Lake

1.3

Summit
Lake

0.5

to
Edna
Lake

0.9

1.4

Rock
Slide
Lake

1.0   8,890

8,952   pass

Three
Island Lake

Lake
Ingeborg

8,585

0.9

1.1

Spangle
Lake

1.0

Little
Spangle
Lake

River

Camp
Lake

Heart
Lake

Sawtooth
Wilderness

1.0

0.5

8,562

1.0

1.0

7,460

7,911

Timpa
Lake

Boise

2.0

1.4

N

0   1

Miles

Rock Creek

2.6

Fork

6,400   2.0

Middle

to
Power Plant
Campground

**Middle Fork Boise
River: Rock Creek to
Spangle, Camp,
Heart, Ingeborg,
Rock Slide and
Benedict lakes**

66.

MIDDLE FORK BOISE RIVER: ROCK CREEK TO SPANGLE LAKES

This one-way section: 6 miles, 2,185-foot elevation gain from the Timpa Lake junction

Round trip: 29 miles from Powerplant Campground at Atlanta; connects with trails to Camp Lake and to Edna Lake and the South Fork of the Payette River

Elevation gain: 3,145 feet **Highest point:** 8,585 feet

Maps: Mt. Everly, Atlanta East

Trailhead GPS at upstream end Powerplant Campground: 43 48.939, 115 06.134

Difficulty: strenuous; time: 4 days

Access: Following directions for Middle Fork Boise River: Powerplant Campground to Rock Creek, hike 8.5 miles to Rock Creek.

What you'll see: In this section of the canyon, Mattingly Peak resembles a dark gray bucket decorated with triangular spires. As the trail passes under scalloped cliffs, wildflowers abound, from delphinium to grass of Parnassus. From Spangle Lakes, Snowyside Peak resembles a dinosaur, with a spine at the neck, a square head with ears, and gullies between its ribs.

Directions: This hike description starts at the junction with the Rock Creek Trail (6,400 feet) to Timpa Lake. It is 8.5 miles and a 960-foot climb from Powerplant Campground. Just before the junction, you must ford the river in two sections. These fords are difficult or hazardous for hikers in early summer and dangerous for pack stock all summer.

From the junction, the Middle Fork Trail goes east along the river through snowbrush. At 1.1 miles, it crosses to the right (south) bank of the river. It enters woods, goes through a side creek, and at 1.5 miles returns to the left (north) side of the river. Then it climbs 100 feet under dark gray cliffs. In the next half mile the river curves north, so a crossing to the right side of the river at 2 miles is to the east side.

Now it enters a grassy field with small trees where a talus-covered mountain is ahead on the left. It jumps two side streams here, passes a pond on the river, and crosses to the left (west) bank just before a junction with the Flytrip Creek Trail (7,460 feet) at 4 miles. This trail gives access to Camp and Heart Lakes (See Hike 68).

At 4.2 miles, the main Middle Fork trail crosses back to the right (east) side of the river. It zigzags up granite benches, then switchbacks along a ridge.

At the top of the switchbacks, hikers from Spangle Lakes can turn off on a cross-country shortcut to Camp Lake. At 5.5 miles, the trail crosses the river to the left (west) side at the end of a marsh. It reaches the northern tip of Little Spangle Lake at 5.9 miles. At 6 miles, on the shore of Spangle Lake (8,585 feet), is a junction with a trail leading east to Ardeth Lake and west to Ingeborg, Rock Slide and Benedict lakes.

67.

INGEBORG, ROCK SLIDE AND BENEDICT LAKES

This one-way section: 3.5 miles, 365-foot elevation gain, 710-foot loss from Spangle lakes

Round trip: 36 miles from Powerplant Campground at Atlanta; connects with trails to the Queens and the South Fork of the Payette rivers

Elevation gain: 3,700 feet **Highest point:** 8,950 feet

Elevation loss (return climb): 2,536 feet

Map: Mt. Everly

Trailhead GPS at upstream end Powerplant Campground: 43 48.939, 115 06.134

Difficulty: strenuous; time: 5 days

Access: Hike to Spangle Lakes from Yellow Belly Lake (14.5 miles, 3,390-foot elevation gain) or from Atlanta (14.5 miles, 3,145-foot elevation gain).

What you'll see: A scalloped ridge of crumbling granite lines the west side of Lake Ingeborg and continues down the canyon of Benedict Creek, where a single scallop drops boulders into Rock Slide Lake. Farther down, Benedict Lake and its meadows are trapped between granite benches. From the trail between Ingeborg and Rock Slide Lakes, the orange and black fangs of the Raker Peaks stand out ahead. One of these peaks resembles the end of a foot, with a big toe and three little toes.

Directions: The trail to Ingeborg from Spangle Lake first fords the stream between Spangle (8,585 feet) and Little Spangle. Next it switchbacks up the side of the canyon to a pond under a row of cliffs at .6 mile. Here the trail turns north over a low saddle and drops 60 feet to Lake Ingeborg (8,890 feet, 1.1 miles). It goes along the right shore of the lake near campsites, then descends past a marsh to Rock Slide Lake (8,668 feet) at 2.1 miles. This lake is so small it has few campsites. The trail descends to a pond and junction with a trail to Three Island Lake at 3 miles. (That trail climbs 200 feet in .6 mile to the lake.)

Below this junction, the main trail keeps dropping, crosses the creek and zigzags down to the shore of 8,240-foot Benedict Lake at 3.5 miles, where there are several campsites. It continues down Benedict Creek 4.6 miles to the South Fork of the Payette River in a 1,060-foot descent.

166

68.

CAMP AND HEART LAKES

This one-way section: 1.8 miles, 1,102-foot elevation gain from the Middle Fork Boise River

Round trip: 28.6 miles from Powerplant Campground

Elevation gain: 3,122 feet

Highest point: 8,562 feet

Maps: Mt. Everly, Snowyside Peak

Trailhead GPS at the upstream end of Powerplant Campground: 43 48.939, 115 06.134

Difficulty: strenuous; time: 4 days

Access: Following directions for Middle Fork of the Boise River Trail: Powerplant Campground to Rock Creek and Rock Creek to Spangle Lakes, hike 12.5 miles to the junction with the trail up Flytrip Creek to Camp Lake.

What you'll see: At the head of Flytrip Creek, narrow Camp Lake extends from a meadow like blue toothpaste from a green tube. Over a wooded ridge from it, lurks the orange dinosaur of Snowyside Peak. On the other side of the ridge, Heart Lake, edged with granite and Labrador tea, faces this monster. To the south, low ridges divide Heart Lake from P.S. Lake and a matching dinosaur.

Directions: To reach the Flytrip Creek Trail, which leads to Camp Lake, hike up the Middle Fork of the Boise River from Atlanta 12.5 miles in a 2,020-foot climb or hike 2 miles down the river from Spangle Lakes. There is a large campsite at the junction (7,460 feet).

The Flytrip Trail fords the river to the east side, and then ascends the side of the canyon in woods. It crosses an unnamed creek three times before two small ponds appear at 1 mile. The lake (8,520 feet) is at 1.5 miles. Heart Lake (8,562 feet) is .3 mile to the east by cross-country travel. Both lakes have small campsites.

The Flytrip Creek Trail climbs more than 1,000 feet and begins 1,125 feet lower than Spangle Lakes, so from Spangle Lakes, it is less work to take a cross-country shortcut to Camp Lake. To do this, hike down the Middle Fork of the Boise for 1 mile below Spangle Lakes. Just before the steep switchbacks start, turn east off trail and drop to a marsh. From this marsh, go southeast to a larger marsh and cut across at that level, avoiding talus slopes, to two small ponds that are on the trail .5 mile below Camp Lake The cross-country part of this hike is 1 mile long and saves 1.3 miles and 600 feet of elevation gain.

Stanley

THE SALMON RIVER MOUNTAINS

This vast range of mountains surrounding the main part of the Salmon River is mostly in the Frank-Church-River of No Return Wilderness, The land varies from the wooded hills of Chamberlain Basin to the giant fins of Fishfin Ridge in the Bighorn Crags. This wilderness is well known for its white water rafting on the main and middle forks of the salmon river. The hike written up here just gives you an introduction to the area. This wilderness can be reached from Stanley and Challis on the south, Cascade and McCall on the west, and Salmon on the east. It is also known for its fishing, hunting, hot springs and the 19 airstrips that provide back country access, In most of the area the main footprints you'll see are those of elk and deer.

My first time in the Frank Church Wilderness it was still the Idaho Primitive Area. On the 6th day our raft bounced and plunged through acres of white water at the bottom of a gorge so deep we could see only a little of the sky. It was like being at the bottom of a kettle.

168

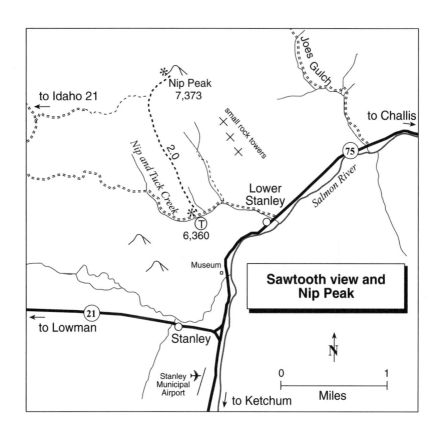

LOWER STANLEY AREA

69.

SAWTOOTH VIEW AND NIP PEAK

Round trip: 4 miles
Elevation gain: 1,013 feet **Highest point:** 7,373 feet
Map: Stanley, Basin Butte
Trail beginning GPS: 44 13.988, 114 56.022
Difficulty: easy, but slippery footing; the route is a non-system jeep road; time: 4 hours
Access: In Lower Stanley, 2.5 miles past the junction of Idaho 21

View from the trail to Nip Peak

with Idaho 75, turn left (north) on the unsigned Nip and Tuck Road (633) and drive .8 mile to where a steep jeep road goes off to the right. This turnoff is .2 mile past a parking area, stream, and path leading right (east), which mark the beginning of a cross-country hike.

What you'll see: A half mile up a little ridge that this jeep trail climbs you get a superb view of the northern end of the Sawtooths from Mt. Heyburn to McGown Peak. The view is most dramatic in June when snow accents the pleats in the mountain wall.

Directions: Because the route is not an official road, it is possible it will someday be removed.

Until it is, or is converted to a hiking trail, it is an easy way to see an excellent view of the northern Sawtooths. It is much easier than walking cross-country on the adjacent hills or up a nearby creek. Although this jeep or ATV track was probably created many years ago, it is an example of the problems the Forest Service has with off-road motor vehicle travel. Motorized travel is not allowed off official roads because it causes unsightly scarring and erosion that destroy native plants and silt up the rivers, killing fish.

To begin the hike, walk up the jeep trail until it comes to a little saddle. It gradually curves left as it goes. Because it is so steep at and near the bottom, to prevent erosion and a fall, walk your own zigzag path off to the side until it becomes more gentle. From the top of a little ridge

170

there is a superb view of the northern end of the Sawtooths from Heyburn to Mt. Regan. The track continues and descends to a saddle. Beyond the saddle, another jeep track comes up from Nip and Tuck Road below, and joins. From the junction, the track climbs straight up through sagebrush, where again it is safer to walk your own zigzag path. As it becomes less steep, the route goes through woods to the summit of Nip Peak (7,373 feet). You can recognize the summit by a triangular wooden box that was used years ago by the US Geological Survey to help determine the elevation.

Part way back, you can cut down cross-country from the higher saddle into the canyon of a creek and follow it down to a short unofficial trail to the better parking .2 mile nearer town. This path begins just below where the drainage divides at a tailings pile. Up the side canyon here are fanciful rock towers.

TRAILS IN THE WHITE CLOUD MOUNTAINS

Scree Lake in the White Cloud Mountains

TRAILS IN THE WHITE CLOUD MOUNTAINS

In Sawtooth Valley, south of Stanley, hills of sagebrush and Douglas fir give only glimpses to the east of the high peaks of the White Clouds. Some of these peaks are of a creamy white rock. A ridge of them runs north and south for 20 miles, ending on the south in the Castle Peak, 11,815, the highest peak in the range, which is half white on the west side. Most of the White Clouds are 1,000 feet higher than the Sawtooths and so get snow earlier and keep it later, Most of the peaks here can be scrambled up without ropes in contrast to the technical climbs required in the Sawtooths.

A endemic plant (one that grows nowhere else in the world) grows here, the White Cloud milkvetch, a member of the pea family with pale yellow flowers daubed with purple. It is an alpine plant found at elevations around 10,000 feet, such as on Railroad Ridge. On this rounded ridge a few 1200-year-old whitebark pines still grow, but many of the whitebarks here have died from mountain pine beetle. Any loop trips in the White Clouds require some cross-country travel. There are fewer lakes here than in the Sawtooths but they have better fishing. That's because the rock has more nutrients. You are more likely to see mountain goats and bighorn sheep than in the Sawtooths.

I first went into the White Clouds in 1969, the summer after Wayne and our oldest son Doug had built the shell of our summer cabin on Forest Service land in the Sawtooths. We were lucky to get a cabin permit for the Forest Service no longer creates new areas or new permits. Existing cabins are allowed to remain but at much higher fees. I had all five of my children with me that day in 1969. Our youngest, Stuart, was only two. I drove up the Fourth of July Creek Road as the ranger recommended, and scared myself because it was so steep and rutted and full of rocks the size of Jack-o-lanterns. The road has been improved since then. We didn't find 4th of July Lake on that trip. The Forest Service map didn't show the trail in the right place and the only topographic nap was Bear Valley 1896. The US Geological Survey was working on making modern topographical maps for Idaho the but hadn't gotten very far by then.

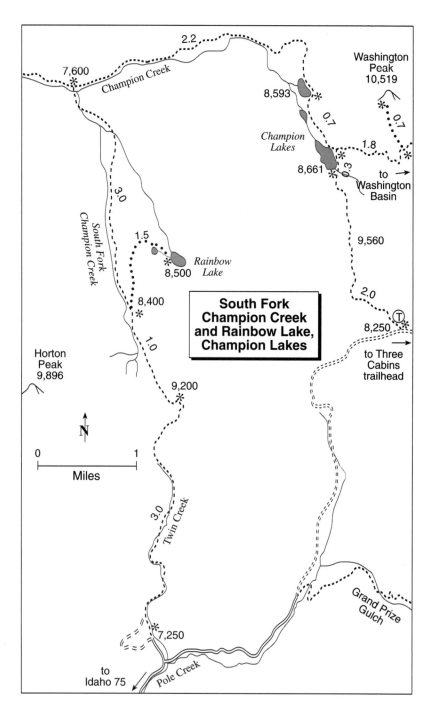

South Fork Champion Creek and Rainbow Lake, Champion Lakes

7,600

2.2

Champion Creek

Washington Peak
10,519

8,593

Champion Lakes

0.7

0.7

1.8

8,661

0.3

to → Washington Basin

9,560

3.0

South Fork Champion Creek

1.5

8,500

Rainbow Lake

8,400

1.0

2.0

8,250

T

to Three Cabins trailhead

Horton Peak
9,896

9,200

N

0   1

Miles

3.0

Twin Creek

Grand Prize Gulch

7,250

to Idaho 75

Pole Creek

174

GERMANIA CREEK AREA

70.

SOUTH FORK CHAMPION CREEK AND RAINBOW LAKE

Round trip: 11 miles from the Twin Creek - South Fork Champion Creek trailhead; connects with the Champion Creek Trail
Elevation gain: 2,155 feet **Highest point:** 9,200 feet
Elevation loss (return climb): 905 feet
Map: Horton Peak
Trailhead GPS: 43 55.770, 114 43.363
Difficulty: expert because trail disappears often; time: 11 hours or 2 days
Access: From Idaho 75, 24.5 miles south of Stanley (36.4 miles north of Ketchum), turn right (east) on the gravel Pole Creek-Germania Creek Road (194). Go 2.3 miles to a junction with the Valley Road. Keep right here on road 197. At 4.5 miles, turn left (north) onto a dirt road leading to the South Fork Champion Creek Trail. Drive .5 mile to an unmarked trailhead where the road makes a 90-degree left turn. The trailhead sign is before where the spur road climbs a steep hill to the left (west).

What you'll see: The trail gives a fine view to the south of the Boulder Mountains and of a 700-foot high fluted wall east of Horton Peak. The Twin Creek - South Fork Champion Creek divide provides a scenic destination for a day hike. Beyond it on the side of the South Fork Champion Creek Canyon, Rainbow Lake lies on a bench. Above the lake, a curved rock that is striped rust, white and yellow resembles a rainbow. On the topographic map, a small pond is labeled Rainbow Lake, but the lake is east of this pond, where a marsh is shown on the map. The lake is marshy around the edges and stagnant in late summer, but is much larger and deeper than the pond.
Directions: From the trailhead (7,250 feet), the trail goes up the narrow canyon of Twin Creek in dense forest, staying left (west) of the creek for the first .3 mile. It crosses to the east side, goes 50 feet above the stream then returns to the west side at .5 mile.
In the next .3 mile, the trail crosses the small creek five more times. Sometimes it runs through narrow jaws of rock and disappears. The canyon then opens out into a grassy basin where the trail, now on the right side, dwindles. It goes along a grassy shelf above the creek, then drops to the creek and fords it to the left (south) just beyond where the creek curves left and then right at 1 mile.
Because of the downed timber, it is easier to stay on the right side of

175

the creek in sagebrush and pick up the trail again where it crosses back to the right at 1.2 miles. There are two more crossings which are not shown on the topographic map. The trail returns to the west side in a narrow meadow, where the canyon becomes open and the tread fades. At 1.6 miles, it crosses to the right side of the creek and enters forest.

The trail now is on the right (east) of the creek, but disappears often At the end of the meadow at 2 miles, it fords back and forth, then becomes obvious as the forest closes in at 2.1 miles. Around 2.4 miles, there are three more fords and the trail ends up on the left (west) side of the creek.

As the canyon bends, the trail curves right and disappears in trees. At 2.8 miles, it cuts northeast out of the canyon, climbing 300 feet up a grass and sagebrush slope to a 9,200-foot saddle at 3 miles.

From the top, the wooded summit and sagebrush sides of Horton Peak are to the west. From beyond the saddle to the north, a big fluted cliff east of Horton Peak can be seen.

At 3.5 miles, the trail passes to the right of a small wooded knoll, then comes out on open hillsides with a view of a big flat meadow, to which it descends. On the return it is difficult to find where the trail leaves the meadow so before you go down into it memorize a landmark on the trail that you can find coming back up on your return.

The trail stays in trees on the right of the meadow, and then passes a campsite. The meadow and makes a good destination for a hike or overnight trip because it is lush, wild, and remote.

Those who wish to go on to Rainbow Lake should leave the trail just beyond the north end of the meadow at 4 miles (8,400 feet) opposite some white cliffs on the other side of the canyon. (The trail continues 3 more miles down the South Fork to Champion Creek with an elevation loss of 800 feet.)

To reach Rainbow Lake, climb north off the trail up the side of the canyon. Walk north cross country to a notch between two wooded hills. The notch (8,600 feet) is .8 mile from the meadow, and a hill 8,681 feet on the topographic map is north of it.

Now descend to a tea-colored pond below to the east (8,495 feet) 1 mile from the trail. As you go, look back and memorize a landmark on the trail. The pond is shadowed by wooded granite cliffs. Now go east-southeast through forest to the pale green lake (8,500 feet), which is in marsh grass 1.5 miles from the trail and 5.5 miles from the trailhead

71.

CHAMPION LAKES

Round trip: 6 miles from the Champion Lakes trailhead near Pole Creek Summit; connects with trails to Washington Basin and Champion Creek

176

Elevation gain: 1,310 feet **Highest point:** 9,560 feet
Elevation loss (return climb): 967 feet
Maps: Horton Peak, Washington Peak
Trailhead GPS: 43 58.541, 114 40.265
Difficulty: strenuous: time: 6 hours
Access: From Idaho 75, 24.5 miles south of Stanley (36.4 miles north of Ketchum), turn right (east) on the gravel Pole Creek-Germania Creek Road (194). At a junction at 2.3 miles keep right on road 197 and go east to Pole Creek Summit at 9.2 miles. The road becomes primitive at Grand Prize Gulch at 6.5 miles. Descend the other side of the summit to a grassy hillside at 11.3 miles. (The last 4 miles of the road are rough, rocky and muddy but passable for passenger cars.) At 10.2 miles, turn left (north) on a short spur road, park, and walk uphill to the beginning the trail. You can also reach Champion Lakes, in 8 miles, from the Fourth of July Creek Road by way of the cutoff trail that leads to Champion Creek and up it. The forest along that trail and up Champion Creek burned in the 2005 Valley Road Fire).

What you'll see: South of the divide on the trail, are views of pink and charcoal gray crags in the Boulder Mountains. To the north, the blue-green ovals of Champion Lakes sit in a basin of woods, rocks, and meadows west of the pearl gray scree of Washington Peak. Mats of pink algae float in the upper lake in late summer. On the west side of the lower lake, a gray and white mountain ends in a wall of towers. This trail is closed to mountain bikes and horse use is discouraged because of its steepness.
Directions: From the trailhead (8,250 feet), the trail crosses a stream, and then a creek. It climbs north along the west side of this creek amid bluebells in midsummer. At .3 mile, it crosses back and forth several times. At .7 mile, it turns right (north) leaves the creek, and climbs a steep slope of grass and sand to a 9,560-foot divide at 1.2 miles.
On the other side, the trail descends over loose rock and angles down steep scree into a gully of firs. Below the gully, it crosses a dry flat area at 1.5 miles and climbs an 80-foot wooded ridge. Next it drops 300 feet, passes a pond and a meadow to the first lake, (8,661 feet) at 2 miles.
The official trail crosses the inlet in a meadow and goes around the east side of the lake. It passes some campsites. Halfway around the lake, at 2.3 miles, a trail turns east to go 1.8 miles with a 1,419-foot climb and 700-foot descent over the shoulder of Washington Peak to Washington Basin.
The Champion Lakes trail continues through boggy meadows to the lower lake (8,593 feet) at 3 miles. The best camping is at the upper end. A third small lake is 200 yards to the west halfway between the two larger lakes. Below the lower lake, the trail descends Champion Creek 5 miles with a 1,493-foot elevation loss to a junction with the Champion Creek cutoff. The cutoff leads 3 miles with a 450-foot elevation gain and 250-foot elevation loss to the Fourth of July Creek Road.

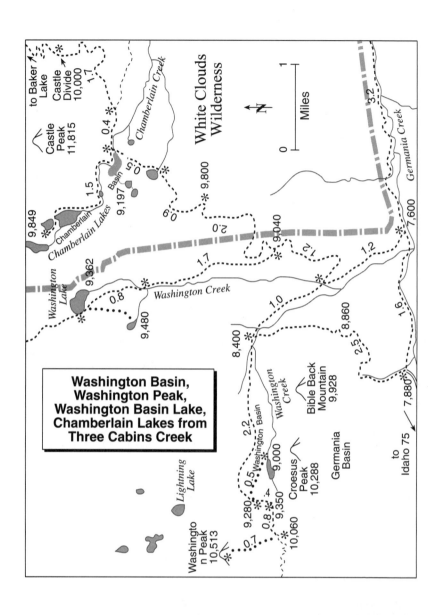

Map labels:

to Baker Lake
Castle Divide 10,000
1.7
Castle Peak 11,815
Chamberlain Creek
0.4
White Clouds Wilderness
0.5
9,800
1.5
Chamberlain Basin 9,197
0.9
N
Miles
0 1
3.2
Germania Creek
9,849
Chamberlain Lakes
2.0
9,040
7,600
9,362
1.7
1.2
1.2
Washington Lake
0.8
Washington Creek
9,480
1.0
1.6
8,400
8,860
2.5
Washington Creek
Bible Back Mountain 9,928
7,880
2.2
Washington Basin
Lightning Lake
Croesus Peak 10,288
Germania Basin
to Idaho 75
2.2
0.5
9,000
9,280
.4
9,350
0.8
Washington Peak 10,513
0.7
10,060

Washington Basin, Washington Peak, Washington Basin Lake, Chamberlain Lakes from Three Cabins Creek

72.

WASHINGTON BASIN

Round trip: 9.6 miles from the Three Cabins Creek trailhead on

Washington Peak (Photo by Dottie Greenwood)

Germania Creek; connects with trails to Chamberlain Basin and Champion Lakes.

Elevation gain: 1,900 feet **Highest point:** 9,380 feet

Elevation loss (return climb): 400 feet

Maps: Horton Peak, Galena Peak, Washington Peak, Boulder Chain Lakes

Jeep trail beginning GPS: 43 58.760, 114 38.009

Difficulty: strenuous; time: 8 hours

Access: From Idaho 75, 24.5 miles south of Stanley (36.4 miles north of Ketchum), turn right on the Pole Creek- Germania Creek Road (194). Keep straight ahead on road 197 where the Valley Road turns north at 2.3 miles. Drive 6.5 miles on gravel and 7.5 miles on a primitive road over Pole Creek Summit to the Three Cabins Creek trailhead at 12.1 miles. The trail to Washington Basin is a jeep trail that begins at this point.

What you'll see: The white and dark red stripes of Croesus Peak, hang above the old cabin and mines of Washington Basin. Deep-cut grooves and an "X" in the stripes accent the wall. On the east, this wall merges with the gray, caramel, and cream-colored rock of Bible Back Mountain. On the west the wall curves into the pale gray of Washington Peak. From the head of the basin, the pleated face of Castle Peak forms a distant backdrop to a narrow green lake in the rocks below. The historical diggings and buildings are on private property, so please treat them with respect.

Directions: This hike is on a steep jeep trail. The basin is so inter-

179

esting, it is worth hiking there if you don't have 4-wheel drive. In early summer or wet weather, leave ordinary passenger cars before the second ford on the Pole Creek Road .2 mile below the Three Cabins Creek trailhead (7,880 feet). The first 300 yards of the jeep trail is covered with football and basketball-sized rocks.

At .6 mile, the jeep trail switchbacks to the right, leaves the boulders, and climbs steep forest to an 8,800-foot summit at 1.5 miles. Then it drops to a ford (8,400 feet) of Washington Creek, at 2.5 miles, that requires 4 wheel drive low. Here, a one mile-long trail down Washington Creek to the Chamberlain Lakes Trail and a trail to upper Washington Creek begin. Beyond the ford, the jeep trail climbs through forest with bridges at 2.6 and 2.7 miles. At 3.5 miles the slope lessens opposite the colorful wall of Bible Back Mountain and Croesus Peak. Several old mines, and cabin ruins are at 3.8 miles. Just beyond the ruins, a branch road leads right to mines and the main road fords a small creek that is usually dry and crosses open grassy slopes.

At 4.3 miles, it fords another creek, then passes a branch road that leads a few yards to a seasonal pond and the site of an old mill. This creek marks the turnoff for the small lake in Washington Basin. You can walk around the pond to see mill timbers, a mine shaft, and an old boiler. The main road climbs on past ruins of log cabins and a track at 4.6 miles leading left to the remnants of the Black Rock Mine.

Continue on the steep main road, passing a junction with a trail to Champion Lakes at 4.7 miles (9,360 feet). This trail climbs 700 feet over the side of Washington Peak, and down 1,419 feet to Upper Champion Lake in 2 miles. From the junction, follow the road down to the ruins of the highest cabin beside a meadow at 4.8 miles. This meadow was once a lake formed by an earthen dam. There is no trace of the trail shown on the topographic map as leading south up the mountain wall from this meadow.

The dam may have been built by a black miner, George Z. Blackmon, who lived in the basin from the 1880s into the 1930s. Blackman Peak above Fourth of July Creek was named for him, although the name was misspelled. The US Bureau of Geographic Names has recently corrected the spelling. His middle name has been wrongly reported as Washington and people have said Washington Peak and lake were named for him.

73.

WASHINGTON BASIN LAKE

This one-way section: .5 mile, 280-foot elevation loss from the jeep trail at the tailings pond
Round trip: 9.8 miles from the Three Cabins Creek trailhead
Elevation gain: 1,800 feet **Highest point:** 9,280 feet
Elevation loss (return climb): 680 feet

180

Map: Washington Peak
GPS at beginning of jeep trail 43 58.877, 114 38.009
Difficulty: easy if you drive to the basin; strenuous if you walk from Three Cabins Creek, Time: 2 hours from basin; 9 hours from Three Cabins Creek
Access: Following directions for Washington Basin, hike or drive in 4-wheel drive 4.4 miles from the Three Cabins Creek trailhead to the place where the jeep trail crosses the outlet of the intermittent pond.

What you'll see: This small, narrow lake is set against the swirled and cream-colored cliffs of Croesus Peak, with a view of gold and cream-splashed Bible Back Mountain in the distance. The willow-filled meadow at the upper end and another higher meadow provide havens for wildlife.
Directions: This hike begins at the outlet of the part-year pond (9,280 feet) at 4.3 miles. Park beside the spur road that leads toward the pond. Look for an old jeep trail going downhill on the right (south) side of the outlet and walk down it. The track crosses to the left side of the usually dry creek in 150 yards. At 300 yards, you can look over at the long orange rock piles of the former Black Rock Mine. The track angles down the canyon toward Bible Back Mountain and splits at .4 mile. You can take the right branch out into a meadow where it ends and then climb over a little ridge to the upper end of the lake, or you can follow the road until it is opposite the lower end of the lake and cut over to it at .5 mile.

74.

WASHINGTON PEAK

This one-way section: 1.5 miles, 1,200-foot elevation gain, 42-foot elevation loss
Round trip: 12.4 miles from the Three Cabins Creek trailhead
Elevation gain: 3,100 feet **Highest point:** 10,519 feet
Elevation loss (return climb): 442 feet
Map: Washington Peak
GPS at Three Cabins Creek trailhead where the jeep trail begins 43 58.877, 114 38.009
Difficulty: moderate from the basin; time: 3.5 hours
Access: Following directions for Washington Basin, hike or drive in 4-wheel drive 4.7 miles from the Three Cabins Creek trailhead to the junction of the Washington Basin Jeep Trail with the trail to Champion Lakes.

What you'll see: If you stop and look east as you climb the knife-edged ridge of Washington Peak, you'll see the pleated face of Castle Peak and its white shoulder. To the west below are the dark blue eyes of Champion Lakes. To the south is the face of Croesus Peak, swirled

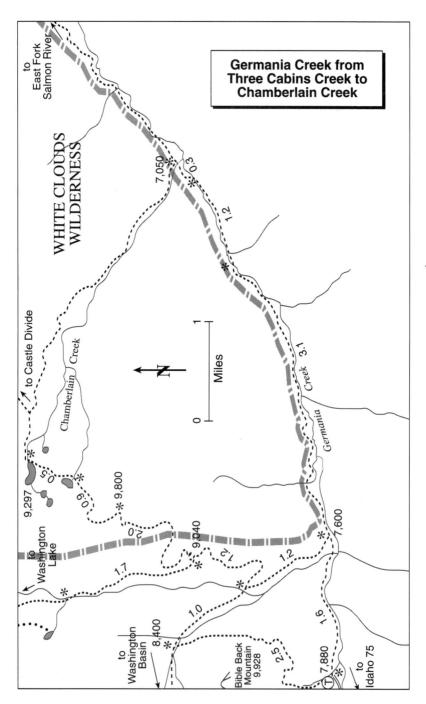

Germania Creek from Three Cabins Creek to Chamberlain Creek

to East Fork Salmon River

WHITE CLOUDS WILDERNESS

7,050

0.3

1.2

to Castle Divide

Chamberlain Creek

Germania Creek

3.1

1

Miles

N

0

9,297

0.5

0.6

9,800

2.0

9,040

1.2

7,600

to Washington Lake

1.7

1.2

1.2

1.0

8,400

Washington Basin

Bible Back Mountain 9,928

2.5

1.6

7,880

T

to Idaho 75

with orange, cream, and dark red. From the top of Washington Peak, you can look down on Heart Lake and the other Six Lakes.

Directions: This route begins at the junction of the Washington Basin jeep trail at 4.7 miles with the trail to Champion Lakes. Park where the road levels out at 4.8 miles. Then walk back up to the trail sign (9,360 feet). The trail goes straight uphill through gravel amid scattered subalpine firs and whitebark pines. At .3 mile it curves back and forth and steepens. Here you begin to get views of Croesus Peak and Castle Peak. At .5 mile the trail switchbacks to the left and angles along the hillside to a 10,050-foot divide at .8 mile. From here, the trail plunges 1.2 miles to Upper Champion Lake with a 1,419-foot elevation loss.

From the divide a path leads along the sharp crest of the ridge .7 mile north to the summit of Washington Peak. It drops off on either side, so be careful.

75.

GERMANIA CREEK TRAIL: THREE CABINS TO CHAMBERLAIN CREEK

Round trip: 12.6 miles from Three Cabins Creek to the junction with Chamberlain Creek trail; (The Germania Creek Trail continues down Germania Creek to the East Fork of the Salmon River; connects with Chamberlain Creek and Bowery Cutoff trails.

Elevation gain: 380 feet
Elevation loss (return climb): 1,210 feet
Highest point: 7,880 feet
Maps: Horton Peak, Galena Peak, Boulder Chain Lakes
Trailhead GPS: 43 58.877, 114 38.400
Difficulty: strenuous; time: 8 hours
Access: From Idaho 75, 24.5 miles south of Stanley (36.4 miles north of Ketchum), turn right (east) onto the gravel Pole Creek- Germania Creek Road (194). Keep straight ahead on road 197 at a junction with the Valley Road at 2.3 miles. At 6.5 miles the surface becomes primitive. Continue over Pole Creek Summit to the Three Cabins Creek trailhead at 12.1 miles

What you'll see: In this canyon, Germania Creek changes from a tiny mountain stream to a large creek roaring through gorges and curving beside meadows. Scalloped charcoal-gray cliffs overlook the canyon, especially at Chamberlain Creek. As the trail descends, the trees change from lodgepole and spruce to Douglas fir and cottonwood.

Directions: At the Three Cabins Creek Trailhead, 12.1 miles up the Pole Creek - Germania Creek Road (197), the road turns left (north) and becomes the Washington Basin Jeep Trail. At this turn, the Germania Creek Trail takes off to the right (east). (7,820 feet). Within 100 yards, it fords a side stream called Three Cabins Creek.

183

Lowest Chamberlain Lake

At .8 mile, Deer Creek joins from the opposite side of the canyon. The trail climbs through sagebrush across from a double-humped mountain at 1.2 miles. Then it drops 100 feet through trees to cross Washington Creek at 1.5 miles (7,600 feet). In .1 mile is a junction with a trail up Washington Creek. That leads to a trail to Chamberlain Lakes, which are 5.3 miles from here. Driving the Washington Basin Jeep Trail to a ford of Washington Creek shortens the distance by 1.8 miles.

Continuing down Germania Creek, the main trail climbs onto a sagebrush hillside and goes over a knoll at 2.2 miles. Then it drops to cross Jack Creek at 2.5 miles on rocks to another sagebrush hillside. At 3 miles, it descends to a mile-long meadow, passes clumps of trees and almost disappears in grass and willows at the edge of the creek at 3.5 miles. At 3.8 miles, it skirts rock ledges close to the creek, and at 4 miles, is in woods again. The trail runs along a gravel bar and climbs a bank. Across from a rock outcrop, it drops to ford the creek to the right (south) side at 4.7 miles.

For the next mile, the trail goes through a thick Douglas fir forest below dark gray cliffs. It is treacherous where the trail climbs and descends a rocky bluff at 5.5 miles. The trail goes through level woods, beside mossy outcrops and through a narrow slot between cliffs to a meadow.

The trail climbs a steep bank at a sign for the Bowery Cutoff at 6 miles and then disappears in the meadow. The route to Bowery Guard Station leads 4.5 miles in a 1,660-foot climb and 2,000-foot descent. It is narrow, eroded, and steep.

Those continuing down Germania Creek to the East Fork of the Salmon River or planning to take the Chamberlain Creek trail to Chamberlain Lakes need to ford Germania Creek in this meadow. The easiest crossing is at the upper end of the meadow where the creek widens over gravel. In early summer, this ford is dangerous. Across the canyon, cliffs tower above Chamberlain Creek

Once across Germania Creek, paths form a trail on a sagebrush hillside. Gray rock knolls hide a waterfall on the creek below. At 6. 2 miles, the trail fords Chamberlain Creek (7,050 feet). On the other side, a little-used trail leads left (north) up Chamberlain Creek. This trail climbs 2,190 feet in 3.7 miles to the Castle Divide Trail .4 mile east of the lowest Chamberlain Lake. About 2.4 miles up it is a view of Chamberlain Falls. There are more switchbacks on the trail than are shown on the topographic map. Reaching the lakes by this trail is 3 miles longer than the route up Washington Creek. From this junction, the Germania Creek Trail descends 440 feet in 5 miles of sagebrush, firs, aspens and rock knolls to the East Fork of the Salmon River Road.

76.

CHAMBERLAIN LAKES FROM THREE CABINS CREEK

Round trip: 13.8 miles to the first lake, 14.8 miles to the second (lowest lake), 1.5 more miles one-way for three upper lakes; connects with trail over Castle Divide to Little Boulder Creek
Elevation gain: 2,200 feet, additional 652 feet for upper lakes. **Highest point:** 9,800 feet
Elevation loss (return climb): 800 feet
Maps: Horton Peak, Washington Peak, Galena Peak, Boulder Chain Lakes
Trailhead GPS: 43 58.877, 114 38.009
Difficulty: strenuous; time: 11 hours or 2 days
Access: From Idaho 75, 24.5 miles south of Stanley (36.4 miles north of Ketchum), turn right (east) on the gravel Pole Creek-Germania Creek Road (194). At a junction at 2.3 miles keep right on road 197 and go east over Pole Creek Summit at 9.2 miles. (The road becomes primitive at Grand Prize Gulch at 6.5 miles.) Continue to the Three Cabins Creek trailhead at 12.1 miles.

What you'll see: The 2,500-foot wall of Castle Peak, cut with avalanche chutes, hangs above the blue-green lakes in Chamberlain Basin. From a 9,800-foot divide on the trail, a grassy basin, sprinkled with trees and the lakes, rolls toward this pinnacle-topped wall, which is white on the right side.

On one side of the lowest Chamberlain Lake is a double-humped white mountain with gray stripes. On the other is the magnificent wall of Castle Peak. A gully in the peak's white side branches into three. The left (west) of these is the route for scrambling up the peak. Hummocks of turf, covered with wildflowers, surround the turquoise water of the first of three upper lakes. Above it, a maze of orange needles hides the white part of Castle Peak.

Directions: From the Three Cabins Creek Trailhead (7,880 feet) descend the Germania Creek Trail for 1.6 miles. Here, just beyond a crossing of Washington Creek (7,600 feet), turn left on a trail up that creek, which climbs 1.2 miles to a junction. From it one trail goes to Chamberlain Lakes and one goes 1 mile to the Washington Basin Jeep Trail.

From the junction, the trail to Chamberlain Lakes makes a .2 mile switchback to the right and then turns back to the left toward ledges. It makes a shorter switchback to the right and then left among small hills to a junction (9,040 feet) with a trail from Washington and Fourth of July lakes at 4 miles.

The trail on to Chamberlain Lakes switchbacks up a ridge, goes along the side of it, and then straight uphill for .5 mile. It zigzags left and then right to a 9,800-foot saddle at 6 miles that has the view of Castle Peak with its white shoulder. From here the trail drops through talus, scree and wildflowers and then follows a tiny inlet down to the first lake (9,280 feet) at 6.9 miles. This lake has campsites in trees at the lower end.

Below the lake, the route crosses two meadows to the lowest lake (9,197 feet) near its outlet at 7.4 miles. This point is 5.6 miles from the ford on the Washington Basin Jeep Trail. Campsites are off-trail on the south shore. At the outlet is a junction with the trail over Castle Divide. From here, it is 6.4 miles and an 800-foot climb and 1,840-foot descent to the Little Boulder Creek Trail where it joins the trail to the Boulder Chain Lakes.

To continue to the upper Chamberlain Lakes from the junction with the Castle Divide Trail, follow a path around the north side of the lowest lake. Then go through woods into a meadow with a large campsite on the left. Next, cross the creek and climb the right (east) side of a ravine lined with white rocks. Above this is a round green pond in the trees. From the pond, follow the stream between the lakes on the right (east) side to the long turquoise lake (9,477 feet). Campsites are on the east shore. Just above the north end of the large lake is a small round lake. The highest lake (9,849 feet), 1.5 miles from the lowest one, can be reached from the round lake by climbing a gully to the left (west) of the cliffs above it.

77.

HORTON PEAK

Round trip: 6.2 miles
Elevation gain: 2,746 feet
Maps: Alturas Lake, Horton Peak
Trailhead GPS: 43 57.435, 114 46.906
Difficulty: strenuous; time: 6 hours
Access: From Idaho 75, 15.3 miles south of Stanley (45.6 miles north of Ketchum) turn right (east) on the Valley Road (194) and drive south 4.6 miles. Then turn left onto a spur road (459) signed Horton Peak and go 1.1 miles to its end in an aspen grove. Passenger cars can drive this mile with caution.

What you'll see: Horton Peak gives a relief-map view of Alturas, Perkins, Pettit, and Yellow Belly lakes and a 360-degree panorama of mountains. The mountains include the whole Sawtooth range, the pink and gray summits of the Salmon River Mountains, and Castle Peak and the white peaks of the White Clouds. From here Castle Peak resembles an immense lampshade, etched with gullies and snow streaks. From the lookout, you look down on a tiny turquoise sliver of lake at the head of Lost Creek. You need to carry all your water for the climb because there aren't any creeks or springs along the trail.

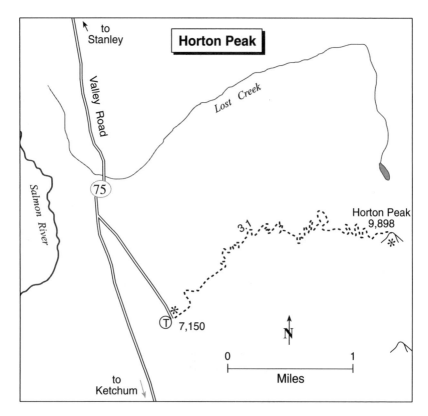

Directions: The first 1.5 miles of the trail have no shade, and the total climb is nearly 3,000 feet in 3 miles, so an early start will help. Only a "no motor vehicles" sign marks the beginning of the trail (7,150 feet). The trail heads northeast through an aspen grove and then sagebrush and grass. At .2 mile, it zigzags back and forth, past outcrops.

At .5 mile, the trail reaches the crest of the ridge and follows it up on the right (southeast) beside more outcrops. At 1 mile is a long switchback to the north into a patch of forest. The end of the switchback gives an excellent view of Alturas Lake and the Salmon River. At 1.4 miles, the trail enters a Douglas fir forest, still on the ridge crest. From 1.8 to 2.2 miles, the trail is in open sagebrush above the last of the aspens. At 2.3 miles, it starts crossing back and forth over a dry creek bed, once again in forest, now of lodgepole pine. It stays in the forest the rest of the way, but the trees thin out and change to subalpine firs and whitebark pines.

At 2.5 miles is a ridge top like a false summit and the trail goes straight along it . The next section climbs 500 feet in .3 mile. At 2.9 miles, the grade flattens out again in a notch. Then it climbs a rocky slope 100 vertical feet to the lookout (9,898 feet) at 3.1 miles. The lookout was built in 1938 and has not been used since 1970, except in emergencies. It is a historic building, so please treat it with respect.

188

FOURTH OF JULY CREEK AREA

78.

CHAMPION CREEK

Round trip: 16 miles from the Champion Creek Cutoff trailhead on Fourth of July Creek; connects with a trail up the South Fork Champion Creek and a trail to Washington Basin.
Elevation gain: 1,460 feet **Elevation loss:** 480 feet
Highest point: 8,661 feet at Upper Champion Lake
Maps: Obsidian, Washington Peak
Trailhead GPS: 44 02.374, 114 45.043
Difficulty: strenuous; time: 2 to 3 days
Access: From Idaho 75, 13.8 miles south of Stanley (47.2 miles north of Ketchum) turn right (east) and go 4.7 miles on the gravel Fourth of July Creek Road (209). Turn right at a sign for the Champion Creek Trailhead and drive .1 mile to a parking area.

What you'll see: The first 3 miles of this trail were constructed to allow people to use the Champion Creek Trail to reach Champion Lakes. That trail is blocked at the lower end by posted private land. The new trail, sometimes called the Champion Creek Cutoff, has excellent views of the southern end of the Sawtooths: such as the dinosaur-like mountains behind Alice Lake. The good view is due to the hillsides burning in the 2005 Valley Road Fire. A wildflower meadow at 1 mile, a viewpoint to the south at 2 miles, and a beaver pond with iridescent Kelly green water at 3.5 miles make good destinations for day hikes and because it is little used, there is a good chance to see wildlife.
Directions: The trail is a safer, but much longer, route to Champion Lakes than the 2-mile trail from the Pole Creek-Germania Creek Road because it avoids its dangerous, slippery section.
From the trailhead (7,520 feet), the trail climbs west up a burned hillside. At .5 mile it passes below two long talus slopes of whitish rock with cliffs above. At .7 mile, it turns southwest over a ridge and at 1 mile reaches a wildflower meadow above a sagebrush slope. The view is of Mt. McDonald, Pettit Lake, and the mountains above it.
In the next mile, the trail climbs through burned snags underlain by grasses. At 1.7 miles is its high point at 7,880 feet. At 1.9 miles, it switchbacks northeast where the view includes Abe's Chair, Snowy-side Peak, and Pettit and Alturas Lakes.
At 2 miles, the trail switchbacks southwest, then crosses the remnants of an old trail. It descends to the northwest and then cuts back to the east at 2.5 miles. This mile is mostly in sagebrush and aspen. A

189

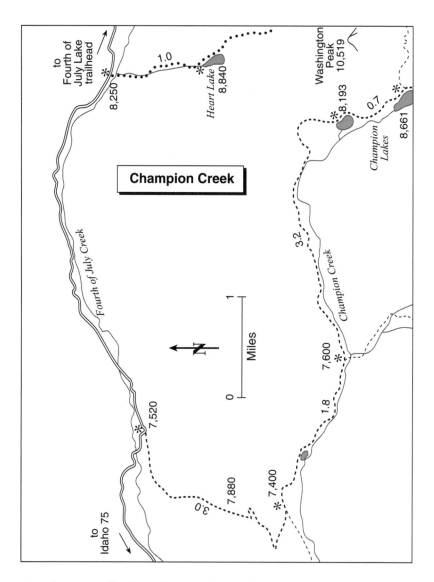

Champion Creek

to Fourth of July Lake trailhead

8,250

1.0

Heart Lake 8,840

Washington Peak 10,519

8,193

0.7

8,661

Champion Lakes

Champion Creek

3.2

7,600

1.8

Fourth of July Creek

Miles

7,520

7,880

3.0

7,400

to Idaho 75

junction at 3 miles (7,400 feet), points to the trail up the canyon and to the way you came, so that you won't get onto the old trail leading down to the former Champion Creek trailhead on private property.

The trail on up the creek stays out of the creek bottom a few feet to avoid mud, but in this first mile only wooded ridges are visible. At 3.2 miles, it descends closer to the creek. A beaver pond of one acre appears to the right of the trail at 3.5 miles. At 3.7 miles, the trail wanders through a meadow with willows, then passes beneath splintered and crumbled pink cliffs.

190

At 4.8 miles is a junction with the South Fork Champion Creek trail (7,600 feet). All you can see up that drainage are wooded ridges, that burned in 2005. Between 5.3 and 7.2 miles, the trail fords four side creeks. At 7 miles, you can look across the canyon at the wrinkled face of the 10,121 foot unnamed mountain that dominates the lower lake. At 7.9 miles is a small teardrop-shaped pond, and at 8 miles Lower Champion Lake. The upper lake is .5 mile farther. Before July 15, the last mile below the lakes is usually snow-covered and muddy. Trying to travel it then will cause damage and can be dangerous.

79.

HEART LAKE AND SIX LAKES

Round trip: 4 miles from a pullout on the Fourth of July Creek Road

Elevation gain: 1,030 feet **Highest point:** 9,240 feet

Elevation loss (return climb): 40 feet

Map: Washington Peak

Trail beginning GPS: 44 02.718, 114 40.824

Difficulty: cross-country; time: 4 hours

Access: On Idaho 75, 13.8 miles south of Stanley (47.2 miles north of Ketchum) turn right (east) on the gravel Fourth of July Creek Road (209). Drive 9 miles to an unmarked pullout .5 mile above a big campsite in the trees. Here a chocolate brown mountain looms ahead up the canyon.

What you'll see: At the upper end of Heart Lake, reflections of a charcoal-gray knoll color the green water an inky blue. Behind it, a pearl gray shoulder of Washington Peak spreads into a triangle. East of Heart Lake, the second of the six lakes huddles under a corrugated wall that bristles with gray, brown and orange needles. Below the wall, chocolate-brown boulders seem to melt into talus. The turquoise water of the highest lake mirrors whitebark pines and the gentler, gray peaks at the head of the canyon, including Washington Peak. The forest along the route burned in the 2005 Valley Road Fire, but trees around the lake didn't.

Directions: This hike crosses a difficult ford at the beginning and then climbs 600 feet in a mile over slippery slopes and through downed timber. From the pullout, descend to Fourth of July Creek and ford it (8,250 feet). This ford is hazardous in early summer and until August in wet years. Once across it, climb south up the west (right) side of the outlet of Heart Lake. At an open area, climb out of the gorge the creek runs in, onto less steep ground.

At .5 mile, descend the hillside to a flat meadow. Here, cross to the left (east) side of the creek for 150 yards and then cross back. At the lower end of a second meadow, go over to the east side of the creek again and back once more. For the last .2 mile, climb along the right (west) side of the creek through forest to the lake (8,840 feet) at 1 mile. Although the hike is short, it is not recommended for small children or the elderly because of its ford, steep slopes, and downed timber.

To reach the higher lakes, go left (east) around Heart Lake to a creek east (left) of the charcoal cliffs. Climb the meadow on the right (south) of the inlet. Where the meadow ends in talus, turn right (south) to the second lake at 1.5 miles.

Circle this lake on the right (west) along a wooded slope. At the southwest corner of the lake, climb a gully leading up the wooded knoll separating the lakes. From it, descend to a peninsula on the north edge of the highest lake (9,200 feet) at 2 miles. The other three lakes are small ponds west of the second lake.

80.

PHYLLIS LAKE

Round trip: 4.4 miles from Fourth of July Creek; connects with the route to Lightning Lake
Elevation gain: 700 feet **Highest point:** 9,240 feet
Elevation loss (return climb): 240 feet
Map: Washington Peak
Trailhead GPS: 44 02.791, 114 39.454
Difficulty: moderate; time: 6.5 hours
Access: On Idaho 75, 13.8 miles south of Stanley (47.2 miles north of Ketchum) turn right (east) on the gravel Fourth of July Creek Road (209) and drive 10.2 miles to the trailhead.

What you'll see: The last .5 mile of trail from the end of the jeep trail is a wheelchair accessible trail, but it is too steep for some wheelchair users to propel themselves up it. Phyllis Lake, a white peak with slanting brown stripes contrasts with water so green it appears to have a light inside it. From this white peak, cliffs with stripes of orange and brown extend to a burnt orange shoulder of Washington Peak. Under this summit, a rocky peninsula guards a meadow where the flowers of forget-me-nots and paintbrush color it blue or red in season.

Directions: This hike description begins at the Fourth of July Creek trailhead (8,760 feet). From the trailhead, walk up the trail .1 mile to where it crosses the Phyllis Lake Jeep Trail and turn right (south) on that trail. If you have 4-wheel drive and high clearance you can drive this track to the start of the wheelchair trail. within .5 mile of Phyllis Lake.) As you walk along the jeep trail from the junction, avoid roads downhill to the right and uphill to a mine prospect. Follow the main road down to a stream (8,980 feet) at 1.3 miles. The slopes are wooded with some open areas and many burned trees.

Across the stream, the jeep trail climbs through thick woods and

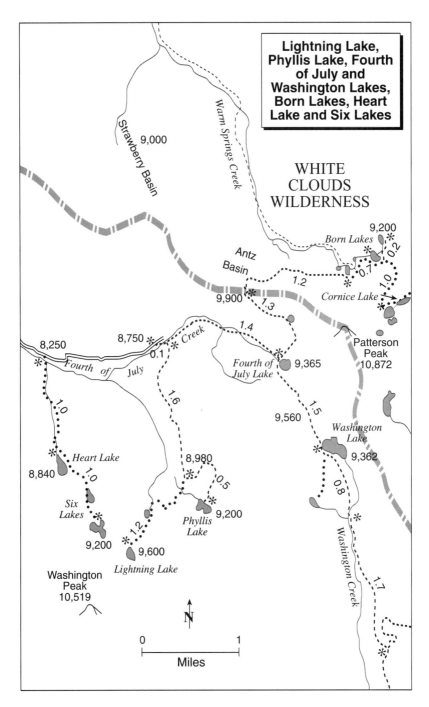

Lightning Lake, Phyllis Lake, Fourth of July and Washington Lakes, Born Lakes, Heart Lake and Six Lakes

WHITE CLOUDS WILDERNESS

Strawberry Basin

9,000

Warm Springs Creek

Antz Basin

Born Lakes 9,200

0.2

0.7

1.2

1.0

9,900

1.3

Cornice Lake

1.4

Patterson Peak 10,872

8,250

8,750

0.1

Creek

Fourth of July

Fourth of July Lake

9,365

1.5

1.0

1.6

9,560

Washington Lake

9,362

Heart Lake

8,840

1.0

8,980

0.5

0.8

Six Lakes

1.2

9,200

Phyllis Lake

9,200

9,600

Washington Creek

Lightning Lake

Washington Peak 10,519

1.7

N

0   1

Miles

193

The fifth Born Lake

over tiny streams to a junction at 1.7 miles. The right (west) fork, which used to go to mines at the head of the canyon, leads to a parking area that gives access to a route to Lightning Lake. To reach Phyllis Lake, take the left (southeast) fork of the road which ends in 300 yards. From its end, go up the wheelchair trail, which goes over a side creek on a bridge. It winds up through forest, then a meadow and a ravine and climbs over a low saddle to the lake, (9,200 feet) at 2.2 miles.

81.

LIGHTNING LAKE

This one-way section: 1.2 miles, 640-foot gain, 40-foot loss from Phyllis Lake jeep trail
Round trip: 5.8 miles (1.6 miles cross-country) from Fourth of July Creek
Elevation gain: 1,100 feet **Highest point:** 9,600 feet
Elevation loss (return climb): 240 feet
Map: Washington Peak
Trailhead GPS: 44 02.791, 114 39.454
Difficulty: moderate but slippery; partly cross-country; time: 7 hours

Access: On Idaho 75, 13.8 miles south of Stanley (47.2 miles north of Ketchum) turn right (east) on the gravel Fourth of July Creek Road (209) and drive 10.2 miles to the trailhead. Walk along the trail to where it crosses the Phyllis Lake jeep trail (053) at .1 mile and then hike up the jeep trail to a split in the track at 1.7 miles. (If you have a 4-wheel drive and high clearance, you can drive to this point and down the right fork to a parking area.)

What you'll see: A furrowed mountain and scalloped ridge enclose Lightning Lake in a cup of rocks. A few whitebark pines guard the natural dam which prevents the blue green water from spilling, but in dry years the lake shrinks to a pool in the rocks anyway. Wildflower meadows, the small green rectangle of Thunder Lake, and the pale amber saucer of a pond make the route colorful.

Directions: This hike description begins on the jeep road to Phyllis Lake where it branches (8,980 feet) 1.7 miles from the Fourth of July Creek trailhead. The left fork of the jeep road goes a few yards toward Phyllis Lake and ends where the wheelchair trail begins.

Take the right branch of the road to a gate .2 mile from the junction. A roofless log cabin that once belonged to the former resident miner, Elmer Enderlin, is nearby. Walk past the cabin, then turn right (northwest) down into a meadow.

Turn left (west) at .4 mile at the creek in the meadow and climb a stream to a bog. Circle the bog on the right (north) and go over a small ridge (9,320 feet) to the outlet of Thunder Lake. Ascend the creek on the left (east) side to little Thunder Lake (9,200 feet) at .7 mile, a lake that is unnamed on the maps. Walk along the left (east) side of it and its inlet through rocks and grass to an amber pond at 1 mile. Go right (west) around the pond and up the inlet through talus blocks to Lightning Lake (9,600 feet) at 1.2 miles.

82.

FOURTH OF JULY AND WASHINGTON LAKES

Round trip: 6 miles from Fourth of July Creek trailhead; connects with a trail to Chamberlain Lakes and route to Born (Boorn) Lakes
Elevation gain: 800 feet **Highest point:** 9,560 feet
Elevation loss (return climb): 200 feet
Maps: Washington Peak, Boulder Chain Lakes
Trailhead GPS: 44 02.791, 114 39.454
Difficulty: easy; time: 5 hours
Access: On Idaho 75, 13.8 miles south of Stanley (47.2 miles north of Ketchum) turn right (east) onto the gravel Fourth of July Creek Road (209) and go 10.2 miles to the trailhead.

What you'll see: Triangular gray cliffs flank the gray and orange face of Patterson Peak. Below the peak, wildflowers color the meadows around shallow Fourth of July Lake. Over a ridge from this lake, an orange wall of crumbled cliffs and scree turns to white at the lower end of blue-green Washington Lake. Two grassy peninsulas thrust into the water. Much of the Fourth of July Creek Canyon burned in the Valley Road Fire of 2005, and the canyon is now a garden of young aspens and tiny lodgepoles in a forest of blackened poles.

Directions: Although the road continues beyond the trailhead (8,760 feet), which has parking; no parking is allowed beyond it. The road has been improved enough since the early days of the SNRA that passenger cars can drive it. This trail is heavily used. For solitude, choose another.

The trail starts by crossing Fourth of July Creek on a bridge to the right (south) and climbing along the creek in the trees. It crosses the Phyllis Lake jeep road at .1 mile and a side creek a few yards beyond it. At .8 mile, the trail fords the main creek to the left (north) side, then a side creek at .9 mile. It goes over to the left side of another creek at 1.1 miles.

The ground flattens out in forest as you approach a junction with the trail to Antz Basin, Born (Boorn) Lakes and Warm Springs Creek at 1.5 miles. Keep straight ahead (south) here and walk over to the outlet just below the lake (9,365 feet) at 1.6 miles. There are campsites up in the trees across the outlet and on the north side of the lake.

Across the outlet, the trail to Washington Lake climbs a ridge among whitebark pines with glimpses of the Sawtooths. At the flat, sandy top of the divide (9,560 feet) at 2.6 miles is a tiny snow pond. From here, the trail descends an open slope to Washington Lake (9,362 feet) at 3 miles, crossing an inlet on the way. There are a few campsites in trees at the south end of the lake. From a pond in a meadow above the west shore of the lake, you can climb south-southwest between ledges to a tiny unnamed lake at 9,480 feet, a lake we call Second Washington.

83.

BORN (BOORN) LAKES

This one-way section: 3.4 miles, 825-foot gain, 500-foot elevation loss from a junction .1 mile below Fourth of July Lake

Round trip: 9.8 miles from Fourth of July Creek; connects with the trail down Warm Springs Creek

Elevation gain: 1,360 feet **Highest point:** 9,900 feet

Elevation loss (return climb): 500 feet

Maps: Washington Peak, Boulder Chain Lakes

Trailhead GPS: 44 02.791, 114 39.454

Difficulty: partly cross-country; time: 8 hours

Access: Following the directions for Fourth of July and Washington Lakes, hike 1.5 miles to the Born (Boorn) Lakes junction just below

Antz Basin Pass

Fourth of July Lake.

What you'll see: Talus, wildflower meadows, subalpine firs and, whitebark pines enclose the tiny ponds of the Born (Boorn) Lakes below orange and gray splintered crags. The number of lakes depends on whether you count two seasonal ones and the one at a distance from the others. The largest is only 200 yards across, so these lakes seem newborn, but they are actually named for a prospector named Boorn. Above the highest lake, a large gray pinnacle on a fractured ridge guards a ravine called the Devils Staircase. At sunset, the alpenglow paints the ridge salmon pink. On the way to these lakes, the green velvet bench of Antz Basin gives a view across Warm Springs Canyon of the White Cloud Peaks gleaming like white chalk. This entire range of mountains is called the White Clouds, but among them is a single chain known as the "White Cloud Peaks" for its color and the lack of individual names. They are mostly of white rock that is a metamorphosed limestone similar to marble but containing silica.

Directions: At the junction below Fourth of July Lake, take the left branch of the trail northeast. The other goes .1 mile to Fourth of July Lake. At .2 mile, the trail crosses a meadow where a path comes up from the lake. It continues northeast with fine views of the lake and the Sawtooths. At .3 mile, it cuts back to the northwest, and at .5 mile passes a small green pond in talus. Above the pond, the trail climbs west along the side of the ridge and zigzags to a saddle (9,900 feet) with a view of the white peaks at 1.1 miles. Here you enter the White Clouds Wilderness.

197

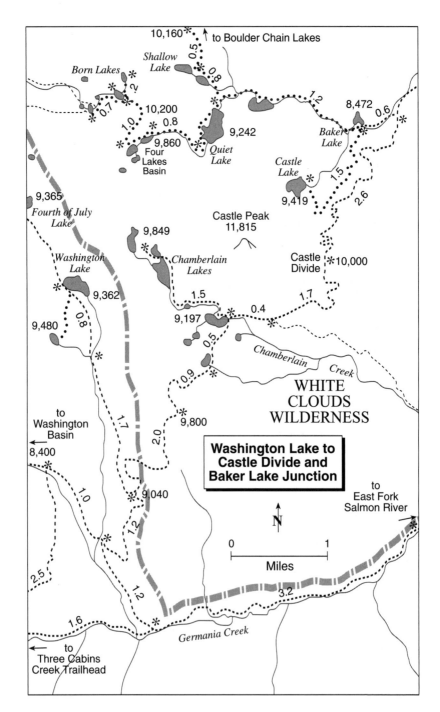

10,160 * ↑ to Boulder Chain Lakes

Shallow Lake

Born Lakes

0.5

0.8

1.2

1.2

8,472

0.6

0.7

10,200

1.0

0.8

9,242

Baker Lake

9,860
Four Lakes Basin

Quiet Lake

Castle Lake

9,419

1.5

2.6

9,365

Fourth of July Lake

Castle Peak
11,815

9,849

Washington Lake

Chamberlain Lakes

Castle Divide * 10,000

9,362

0.8

1.5

1.7

9,480

9,197

0.4

0.5

Chamberlain Creek

WHITE CLOUDS WILDERNESS

0.9

to Washington Basin

8,400

1.7

2.0

9,800

Washington Lake to Castle Divide and Baker Lake Junction

to East Fork Salmon River

9,040

N

1.0

0 ────────────── 1
Miles

1.2

2.5

1.2

3.2

1.6

Germania Creek

to Three Cabins Creek Trailhead

The trail parallels the saddle for 100 yards, then zigzags through slippery scree down to Antz Basin (9,560 feet) at 1.3 miles. The trail down into Warm Springs Canyon is no longer maintained, Instead you have to reach the Warm Springs Canyon trail from the second Born (Boorn) Lake.

Take the trail east across Antz Basin from the bottom of the zigzags to the southeast corner of the basin at 1.7 miles. It descends a gully to the northeast, then goes east across the lower edge of a talus slope. Below the talus, at the bottom of the valley, is a meadow with a pond in it, but the route keeps well above it. Continue across talus and through trees to the left (north) side of the second lake (9,420 feet) at 2.5 miles (4 miles from the trailhead).

To reach the higher lakes, go around the left side of the second lake, cross the creek between the two lakes and then climb a wooded hillside, where you will find the trail coming up Warm Springs Canyon. Climb to the third lake, which is only a little round pond in the woods and continue to the fourth lake (9,555 feet), .7 mile from the second lake. Then go north along the creek through the open and whitebark pines, for .2 mile to the fifth and highest lake (9,700 feet). This lake is set in the rocks at 3.4 miles (4.9 miles from the trailhead). To find the other four even smaller lakes, consult the map.

84.

BORN (BOORN) LAKES TO QUIET LAKE THROUGH FOUR LAKES BASIN

This one-way section: 1.8 miles, 725 feet elevation gain, 1,038 foot loss from Born (Boorn) Lakes
Round trip: 13.6 miles from the Fourth of July Creek trailhead
Elevation gain: 2,085 feet **Highest point:** 10,280 feet
Elevation loss (return climb): 1,538 feet
Maps: Washington Peak, Boulder Chain Lakes
Trailhead GPS: 44 02.791, 114 39.454
Difficulty: cross-country for experts; time: 3 to 4 days
Access: Following directions for Fourth of July and Washington Lakes and Born (Boorn) Lakes, hike 4.7 miles to the fourth Born (Boorn) Lake at 9,555 feet.

What you'll see: The off-trail pass between Born (Boorn) Lakes and Four Lakes Basin, gives a view of the crinkled ridges of Patterson Peak, the dark blue Sawtooths, and the great gabled wall of Castle Peak. At the turquoise lakes in Four Lakes Basin, the few stunted whitebark pines grow only above the lakes on talus mounds, which are warmer than the lake shores.
Directions: Cornices above Four Lakes Basin on this route can be hazardous until mid-August, but this divide is a much safer way of

199

making a loop trip in the White Clouds than the Devils Staircase.

From the east end of the fourth Born (Boorn) Lake (9,555 feet), go south up a ravine to a big grassy basin on the side of the upper canyon. From the basin, zigzag up the greener parts of the scree toward a low point on the skyline, then. descend to the large flat area (10,200 feet) shown on the map at .5 mile. To reach the lakes from here, you must first go around a big snowbank with a cornice at the southeast edge of the flat area. It is easiest to go to the right (southwest) .2 mile along a ledge above cliffs until the slope lessens enough to walk down to Emerald Lake 1 mile from the fourth Born (Boorn) Lake and then go 200 yards farther to Cornice Lake (9,860 feet). Late in the summer, you can go to the left (east) end of the cornice and then southeast to Cornice Lake. You can't drop directly to Cornice Lake from the saddle because of cliffs. The other two lakes, Rock and Glacier, are south of Emerald Lake off the route described here.

To descend to Quiet Lake, go along the north (left) side of Cornice Lake and its outlet, threading through boulders when the creek disappears. Trees and earth between the rocks begin again at 1.4 miles. At 1.6 miles, leave the outlet at a flat area at 9,400 feet and descend a ravine east-northeast to the upper end of Quiet Lake (9,242 feet) at 1.8 miles.

85.

WASHINGTON LAKE TO CASTLE DIVIDE AND BAKER LAKE JUNCTION

This one-way section: 11.8 miles, 1,835-foot elevation gain, 1,725-foot elevation loss

Round trip: 28 miles from the Fourth of July Creek trailhead; connects with the trail down Little Boulder Creek to the East Fork of the Salmon River Road and with a trail to Three Cabins Creek

Elevation gain: 2,555 feet **Highest point:** 10,000 feet

Elevation loss (return climb): 1,926 feet

Map: Boulder Chain Lakes

Trailhead GPS: 44 02.791, 114 39.454

Difficulty: strenuous; time: 3 to 4 days

Access: Following directions for Fourth of July and Washington Lakes, hike 2.6 miles to Washington Lake.

What you'll see: From Castle Divide, the view east is of Castle Peak and its white shoulders, jagged towers on Serrate Ridge, and the orange wall behind the Boulder Chain Lakes. Between Castle Peak and the divide gleam two white, pointed shoulders, etched with gray stripes.

Directions: Castle Divide is usually closed by snow until early August. To avoid danger and damage, wait until the snow melts before traveling this trail.

From the lower end of Washington Lake (9,362 feet), the trail descends to a flat meadow at .5 mile, and at .8 mile a larger meadow. Here it crosses Washington Lake Creek to the left (east). Just before this ford at .8 mile (9,040 feet), a gorge to the right (west) divides a pink hump of rock from a white hump. Up this gorge is an unnamed lake at 9,480 feet, which we call Second Washington, but it is easier to reach it from a pond just above the west side of Washington Lake. Above the ford are campsites on a knoll. In the meadow is a junction with a trail not shown on the map. This trail climbs south over a ridge to Washington Creek, and the Washington Basin Jeep Trail, at its 2.5-mile point.

Beyond the ford, the trail to Chamberlain Lakes descends through lodgepoles, sagebrush, and meadows to 8,840 feet, and then climbs the side of the canyon. It turns east to join the Livingston-Castle Divide Trail at 2.5 miles (9,040 feet).

Turn onto that trail, which climbs over 9,800-foot Chamberlain Divide and descends to the first lake at 5.2 miles and the second one at 5.7 miles (9,197 feet). The divide has an excellent view of Castle Peak as half white. For detailed directions for this section, see Chamberlain Lakes from Three Cabins Creek.

The lowest Chamberlain Lake is right under Castle Peak. From this lake, the Castle Divide Trail crosses rolling meadows to a junction (9,240 feet) at 6.1 miles with a trail down Chamberlain Creek. This sketchy, trail drops 2,180 feet in 3.7 miles to Germania Creek, meeting it 6.2 miles below Three Cabins Creek. It gives a view of Chamberlain Falls about 1.3 slippery miles below this junction.

From the Chamberlain Creek junction, the Castle Divide Trail climbs over a ridge spur in the trees and crosses meadows with a view of the Boulder Mountains. It then ascends scree and talus under red-orange rock walls. It circles to the right of a small hill marked 9,643 on the map. The trail makes a big switchback to the right and one to the left and then steepens. By the time it crosses the divide it has curved from east to north. The divide (10,000 feet) is at 7.8 miles between pink outcrops on one side and the white shoulders of Castle Peak on the other.

The trail zigzags down the north side of the divide through grass and scree to where trees begin again. It winds down to a junction (8,400 feet) at 11.4 miles with a .6 mile spur trail to Baker Lake. The round trip given for this hike is figured from Washington Lake to this junction. The Livingston-Castle Divide Trail continues to a junction with the Little Boulder Creek Trail at 12.1 miles. The mile-long section between these two junctions is covered under Baker Lake. There is no water on the trail between Chamberlain Lakes and a stream one mile north of the divide.

Old Obsidian post office

OBSIDIAN AREA

86.

THE MEADOWS ON WARM SPRINGS CREEK

Round trip: 8 miles to the meadows from Fisher Creek near the Aztec Mine, 12 miles to a view up the canyon; connects with Warm Springs Creek Trail.

Elevation gain: 267 feet
Highest point: 8,300 feet at the trailhead
Elevation loss (return climb): 717 feet
Map: Washington Peak
Trailhead GPS: 44 04.989, W 114 44.642
Difficulty: moderate to strenuous; time: 5 to 7 hours
Access: On Idaho 75, 13.1 miles south of Stanley (47.9 miles north of Ketchum), turn right (east) on the primitive Fisher Creek Road (132) and drive 5.6 miles through burned forest to the end of the road on a saddle well above the old Aztec Mine ruins.

What you'll see: More than 3 miles of wide green meadows stretch

202

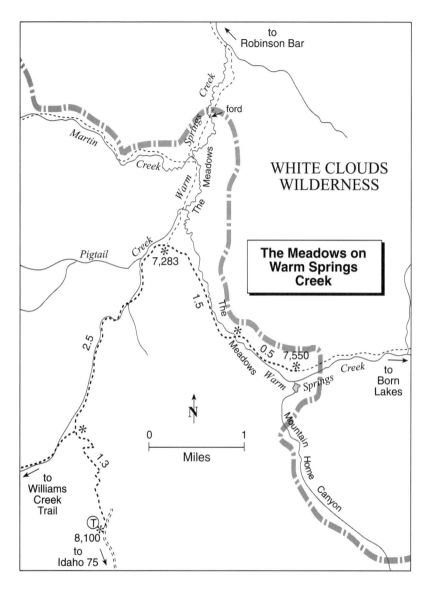

The Meadows on Warm Springs Creek

to Robinson Bar

WHITE CLOUDS WILDERNESS

ford

7,283

1.5

0.5 7,550

to Born Lakes

2.5

1.3

N

0   1
Miles

to Williams Creek Trail

T
8,100
to Idaho 75

along Warm Springs Creek halfway between the Salmon River and Born (Boorn) Lakes. Before the fire, the meadows and the wooded ridges once formed an all-green world. From the upper end of The Meadows, an open hillside above a small marshy pond gives a view of gray and white crumbly peaks of the upper canyon. The canyon above The Meadows burned in the Valley Road Fire of 2005, but the fire didn't extend to Born (Boorn) Lakes

Directions: The Fisher Creek Road and the first mile of the trail are part of a popular loop for mountain bikers, so everyone on this trail needs to watch for traffic.

The Fisher Creek Road can be very muddy early in the summer and the upper 1.5 miles are too steep and rocky for passenger cars. The Aztec Mine beyond the end of the road is historic, and on private property, so should be avoided.

From the road's end (8,300 feet), the trail switchbacks northwest along the side of a ridge to its crest. Then it drops to intersect the Pigtail Creek Trail that comes in from the west at 1.3 miles. (From here, you can reach Idaho 75 near Obsidian in 6.6 miles by way of that trail and the Williams Creek Trail.)

The main trail to The Meadows continues north through open grass, sagebrush and woods. At 2.7 miles, it circles the base of a granite knoll and fords the creek to the east, then crosses back at 3.1 miles. At 3.8 miles it splits in a Y (7,283 feet). The left (north) branch goes 11.2 miles with a 1,360-foot drop down Warm Springs Creek to a trailhead just west of the Robinson Bar Ranch. The right (south) branch leads up Warm Springs Canyon 10 miles with a 2,255-foot climb to the second Born (Boorn) Lake.

At the Y-shaped junction, turn right on the south branch and go .2 mile to The Meadows. Those eager to glimpse the upper canyon can continue south through The Meadows.

The trail comes close to the creek at 4.3 miles. At 5.1 miles, blazed posts mark the trail's route through the grasses to a creek crossing.

Ford the creek here to the east side. The crossing is .2 mile before burnt forest closes in at the upper end of The Meadows and will be difficult in early summer. The trail reappears at 5 miles and curves east with the creek. At 6 miles, it climbs 100 feet up the side of the canyon to an open area (7,550 feet). Here you can see peaks in the upper canyon and a pond below, which is across the creek from where Mountain Home Canyon enters Warm Springs Creek. There is a campsite by the creek near the pond.

87.

WILLIAMS CREEK TRAIL

Round trip: 10.5 miles from Idaho 75 near Obsidian, including 2.5 miles along the highway; it is an extra 6 mile round trip to see The Meadows. Connects with the trail to the Fisher Creek Road in a loop trip popular with mountain bikers.

Elevation gain: 1,560 feet **Highest point:** 8,200 feet
Elevation loss (return climb): 120 feet
Map: Obsidian
Trailhead GPS: 44 06.012, 114 50.977
Difficulty: moderate; time: 7 hours
Access: Park at the Williams Creek Trailhead on the east side of

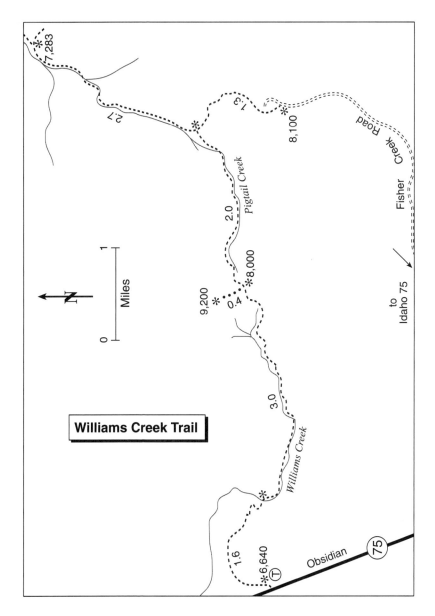

Idaho 75, 10.8 miles south of Stanley (50.1 miles north of Ketchum.)

What you'll see: A ridge above this trail gives a close view of the white section of the White Clouds. In late afternoon, when the sun shines on this side of the peaks, they resemble mountains of vanilla ice cream. The ridge also shows a panorama of the Sawtooths that emphasizes their glacial sculpture below the teeth. The gradual, shady climb is pleasant on a warm day. Because the trail starts at the highway and the summit is only 8,000 feet, this route provides a way into the White Clouds when access roads and trails are closed by snow and mud. This trail is popular with mountain bikers, so watch out for them.

Directions: At the trailhead (6,640 feet) next to the highway, keep well away from the nearby house because it is private property and be as quiet as possible so as not to disturb the residents.

The trail angles along the side of a sagebrush hill and curves at .4 mile to the right (east) into lodgepoles. At .8 mile, it turns southeast at a small meadow. It switchbacks over a 320-foot ridge and then descends 120 feet of sagebrush into a teardrop-shaped meadow at 1.5 miles. The trail crosses Williams Creek on a bridge at the lower end of this meadow at 1.6 miles (6,840 feet) at a junction with a trail from the Idaho Rocky Mountain Ranch. The Williams Creek Trail is missing from the map until it joins this trail.

Continue on the main trail, which goes east along the meadow, then at 1.8 miles, curves left (north). At 2.5 miles, it crosses to the right (south) of the creek on a culvert. Then it curves in and out of ravines across from sagebrush slopes scattered with granite outcrops. At 4.4 miles, it goes back to the left (north) side of the creek. As the trail begins to climb a sagebrush slope, an old trail joins from the left. From this slope, Mt. Heyburn is seen across the valley.

Next, the trail goes through a basin of lodgepoles on the way to a wooded 8,000-foot summit at 4.6 miles. To get views of the Sawtooths and White Clouds, leave your bike at the summit and turn left (north) on a path up a gentle ridge. The ridge becomes open and the Sawtooths appear at 4.8 miles and the White Clouds at 5 miles at 8,200 feet. Back at the summit, the trail drops 400 feet in 2 miles to the trail from Fisher Creek to The Meadows.

If you take a bike on the Williams Creek Trail and plan to make a loop, it is safer to ride UP the steep and rocky Fisher Creek Road and then ride DOWN the Williams Creek Trail.

CASINO CREEK AREA

88.

BOUNDARY CREEK TRAIL, CASINO LAKES AND BIG CASINO CREEK

Through trip: 11.8 miles from the Boundary Creek trailhead near Redfish to the Big Casino Creek trailhead on the Salmon River east of

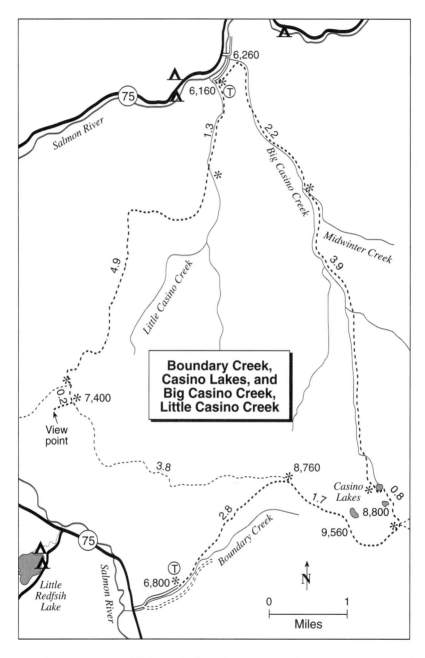

Stanley; connects with trails to Rough Creek, Little Casino Creek, and Garland lakes

Elevation gain: 2,760 feet **Highest point:** 9,560 feet

Elevation loss: 3,300 feet
Maps: Casino Lakes, East Basin Creek; Boundary Creek
Trailhead GPS: 44 08.401 114 52.061
Difficulty: strenuous; time: 10 hours
   Access: From Idaho 75, turn right (east) 5.8 miles south of Stanley (55.2 miles north of Ketchum) on road 212. Avoiding a side road to cabins, drive .8 mile to the end of the dirt road.

What you'll see: Wooded hills, talus ridges, and white granite knolls shadow the marsh grass that wreathes the three Casino Lakes. At the lower lake of the two on the trail, asters, gentians, elephant's head, and Jacob's ladder decorate a marshy garden. From the summit of the trail, the wide blue ribbon of Redfish Lake glistens below overlapping zigzags of the Sawtooths. Here, the white peaks of the White Clouds appear to the south and the pink and tan summits of the Salmon River Mountains to the north. From the lakes, the Big Casino Trail descends to the Salmon River beside the wildflowers and moss-covered rocks of a shady canyon.

Directions: Making a through trip from Boundary Creek to the Salmon River, instead of returning to Boundary Creek, avoids a 960-foot return climb. For this reason the hike is described as a through trip. From the Boundary Creek trailhead (6,800 feet), the trail winds through sagebrush, then aspen, lodgepole and Douglas fir. At .5 mile, a trail joins from cabins across the creek. Here the main trail turns north, crossing a side creek on a bridge, and then zigzagging up a ridge. An open sagebrush area at 1.3 miles used to give an excellent view of Redfish Lake and the Sawtooths, but the trees have grown enough that the view is now from off-trail.

On a saddle (8,760 feet), at 2.8 miles, at the top of the main ridge the Sunny Gulch Trail joins from the left (north). This trail goes 6 miles with a 160-foot elevation gain and a 2,400-foot loss to the edge of the Salmon River opposite the Sunny Gulch Campground, but there is no bridge. A branch stays on the ridge top to meet the Little Casino Trail in 4 miles in a confusing junction. The Little Casino trail goes 5.2 miles with a 1,200 foot elevation loss to the Casino Creek Road.

On the Boundary Creek Trail at its junction on the saddle at 2.8 miles, take the right (southeast) branch of that trail. It winds in trees on the right (west) side of the ridge through a narrow strip of grass, a dry flat, and a lush green meadow where there are springs. At 3.3 miles, it climbs onto and follows the crest of the ridge, reaching an elevation of 9,560 feet at 3.5 miles. From here, you see mountains in every direction and the highest Casino Lake below.

The trail descends to a saddle (9,560 feet) and drops to the east along a spur ridge. This ridge is sprinkled with subalpine fir, lupine, and red mountain heather. At 4.2 miles, it passes left of a large wet meadow with campsites and crosses a stream to the right (south). At 4.5 miles, just east of another saddle (9,120 feet), is a junction. (From this junction, the Garland Creek Trail joins the Rough Creek Trail in 1 mile at one of the Garland Lakes.)

From the Garland Creek junction, take the Big Casino Trail north. It crosses a stream to the west and then back to the east as it descends to the first of the marshy Casino Lakes (8,800 feet) at 4.8 miles. It continues through forest to the lowest lake (8,600 feet), bridging the inlet stream just before the lake at 5.3 miles. The trail goes around the left (west) side of the lake before descending the canyon of Big Casino Creek.

The highest lake at 9,040 feet is reached cross-country. There are two possible routes. The simplest is back at the saddle (9,560 feet) to turn off the trail and descend a gully 520 feet in .5 mile to the shore. The other is to go west .5 mile from the first lake.

Below the lowest lake, a mile of trail is now on the east (right) side of the creek with boardwalks over wet areas. The trail crosses two talus slopes at about 7 miles and goes over a side stream at 7.8 miles. At 8.5 miles, it follows a stream for .5 mile in a level lodgepole forest between Big Casino and Midwinter Creeks, crossing Midwinter Creek at 9.2 miles.

When the valley widens, two rock outcrops resemble crocodiles. At 10.8 miles, the trail fords the creek to the left (west) to the bed of an old road and follows it. The lower end of the trail leaves the creek and cuts down across the hillside for a mile to the main trailhead, at 11.8 miles at 6,260 feet for both Big and Little Casino creeks The GPS there is 44 15.169, 114 51.479. The bridge over the Salmon River to Idaho 75 at Casino Creek is .3 mile east of the trailhead and Stanley is 5.4 miles west of the bridge.

89.

LITTLE CASINO CREEK

Round trip: 10.8 miles to a viewpoint of the Sawtooths near where it connects with the Sunny Gulch Trail

Elevation gain: 1,440 feet **Highest point:** 7,440 feet

Maps: East Basin Creek, Casino Lakes, Stanley

Trailhead GPS: 44 15.134, 114 51.515

Difficulty: strenuous; time: 8 hours

Access: At the intersection of Idaho 21 and Idaho 75 in Stanley, drive east on Idaho 75 for 5.4 miles to a bridge over the Salmon River at Casino Creek. Turn right across the bridge and keep right on road 212 and drive past Casino Campground to the trailhead for both Big and Little Casino creeks.

What you'll see: This trail passes through a wildflower meadow with a view of the summit and shoulders of Thompson Peak in the Sawtooths. From here, the peak is a scalloped cap accented by a white diagonal line of snow in July. The trail leads to a superb view of the most beautiful part of the Sawtooths, including Redfish and Little Redfish Lakes, Goat Creek Falls, and Mt. Heyburn.

Directions: From the trailhead (6,160 feet), the Little Casino Trail begins as an old mining road. Walk along it past a mining claim. At .3 mile, the track crosses the creek to the right (west) side. Now the road shrinks to a single track trail. The west side of the canyon is partly sagebrush, while the east side is all forested. The creek meanders along in curlicues. At 1 mile, the trail passes another old mining claim.

At 1.3 miles, the trail crosses to the left (east) bank of the creek and then the first of three big meadow. On the opposite wall of the canyon are pale peach-colored outcrops. Halfway up the third meadow a sign points to the right to the creek, and here, at 2.3 miles, the trail crosses back to the right (west) side again.

Now the trail is rockier and begins climbs more steeply through lodgepoles and grass. On the right is a jointed gray outcrop and more peach-colored cliffs. At 3 miles, the trail crosses back over the creek to the left and there are soon more crossings. Rerouting is planned to raise the trail up onto the ridge.

The trail continues on the right (west) side of the creek as the hillside steepens in aspens and grasses. It goes along in a narrow canyon, with Little Casino Creek branching off to the left (south). The trail follows its right-hand branch, which is not the main creek. It arrives at the lower end of a round meadow at 4.5 miles. From its lower end, you can see the top of Thompson Peak.

Beyond here, the trail wanders a bit and then at 5 miles joins the Sunny Gulch Trail, which has come from Boundary Creek. Leave the trail here and walk west a few yards to see a panorama of the Sawtooths. This view is the destination of this hike.

From the junction near the viewpoint you can continue 3.8 miles south on the other branch of the Sunny Gulch Trail, following it up and down along ridges to where it joins the Boundary Creek Trail to Casino Lakes. Then you can descend the Boundary Creek Trail to its trailhead. Completing the hike that way is only .5 mile longer than returning to the Little Casino trailhead, but has 1,600 feet more elevation gain and requires a car shuttle. Do not attempt to go from the Little Casino Trail to the Salmon River across from Stanley, for the land by the river is all private property, and the trails and primitive roads on the maps don't connect to the Little Casino Trail.

ROUGH CREEK AREA

90.

ROUGH AND GARLAND LAKES

Round trip: 9 miles to Rough Lake from the Rough Creek road with 1 mile cross-country, 9 miles for the first Garland Lake; connects with the trail up Lookout Mountain

Elevation gain: 1,790 feet for Rough Lake; 1,690 feet for the first Garland Lake

Elevation loss (return): Rough Lake, 240 feet, Garland Lake, 150 feet **Highest point:** 9,160 feet

Side trip to other Garland Lakes: 2.4 miles one-way, 320-foot elevation gain, 240-foot loss

Map: Casino Lakes

Trailhead GPS: 44 13.322, 114 47.249

Difficulty: strenuous; cross-country for Rough Lake; time: 7 hours for Rough Lake, 10 hours for all the Garland Lakes

Access: Drive 9.6 miles northeast of Stanley on Idaho 75 and turn right (south) over a bridge over the Salmon River and drive 4.2 miles up the dirt Rough Creek Road (626) to the end of it.

What you'll see: Near the moss and wildflowers of Rough Lake's inlet, a round-topped 100-foot cliff falls into the blue-green water. Along the shores grow whitebark pine, subalpine fir, Labrador tea, and red mountain heather. The first Garland Lake is amber-colored and sits in a basin of grasses, swamp laurel, alpine buttercup, tiny firs, and red and white mountain heather. Water pipits, ground-nesting birds, sometimes fly along the shore to their nests in the heather. From a saddle on the trail, there is a distant view of the high White Cloud peaks.

Directions: At the trailhead (7,360 feet), an old road leads to the right to some campsites, but the trail starts out to the left (south) through woods. It fords the small creek to the right (west) at .3 mile. Then it climbs in forest and meadows with boggy stretches. At 2.2 miles is a crossing back to the left (east) side of the creek. The trail then switchbacks up a ridge and goes along it. At 3.1 miles is a turnoff at 8,520 feet for Lookout Mountain. This side trail climbs 400 feet in 2 miles to the 9,954-foot summit. From the junction you can look ahead across the canyon to the small cliffs above Rough Lake.

To reach Rough Lake, continue on the main trail, which curves right (southwest) around the head of the canyon in woods. There are several creek crossings on the way to a saddle (9,050 feet) at 4 miles. Just before the saddle, another trail to Lookout Mountain comes in from the east, but it is 1 mile longer to Lookout Mountain that way than it is by the first trail.

To reach the lake from the saddle, leave the trail and climb west up the ridge until the slope lessens at 9,160 feet. Then turn right (north) and descend 240 feet to the lake (8,880 feet) at 4.5 miles.

For the Garland Lakes, stay on the trail at the saddle, and descend it to the southwest past a pond. The first tiny Garland Lake (8,900 feet) is at 4.5 miles. (The Garland Creek Trail turns east before it. That trail descends Garland Creek 2,040 feet in 6.8 miles to the Warm Springs Creek) To reach the other lakes, continue on the same trail for .6 mile. At a four-way junction, turn left (east) onto the Martin Creek Trail. Two additional Garland Lakes are along this trail. The first (8,850 feet) is 1 mile from the junction. To reach the second (8,800 feet), turn south off the trail 1.6 miles from the junction and walk .2 mile.

211

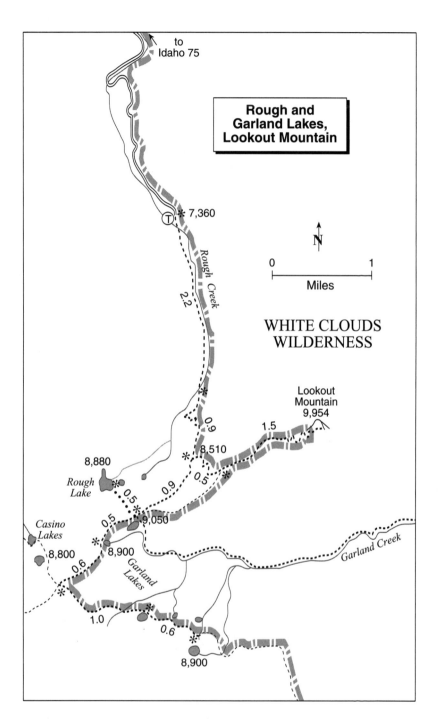

Rough and Garland Lakes, Lookout Mountain

WHITE CLOUDS WILDERNESS

to Idaho 75

7,360

Rough Creek

2.2

Lookout Mountain
9,954

1.5

0.9

8,510

0.9

8,880

Rough Lake

0.5

0.9

0.5

0.5

9,050

Casino Lakes

0.5

8,800

0.6

8,900

Garland Lakes

Garland Creek

1.0

0.6

8,900

0
Miles
1

N

Lookout Mountain

91.

LOOKOUT MOUNTAIN

Round trip: 10.2 miles; connects with the trails to Garland Lakes
Elevation gain: 2,554 feet **Highest point:** 9,954 feet
Map: Casino Lakes; trailhead GPS: 44 13.322, 114 47.249
Difficulty: strenuous; time: 9 hours
Access: Drive 9.6 miles northeast of Stanley on Idaho 75. Just beyond Basin Creek, turn right (south) on the Rough Creek Road (626), which crosses a bridge over the Salmon River. Drive 4.2 miles to the end of the dirt road.

What you'll see: The view from Lookout Mountain includes the Sawtooths, Lost River Range, the Salmon River Mountains and the white part of the White Clouds. Only in the afternoons and only on sunny days do they look white from here.
Directions: To climb Lookout Mountain, follow the directions for Rough and Garland Lakes, to the first turnoff for Lookout Mountain at 3.1 miles (8,520 feet). Take this trail, which switchbacks up past granite and lodgepoles on a very steep hillside. From it you can look north into the Salmon River Mountains. At a sandy saddle (9,040 feet) at 3.6

213

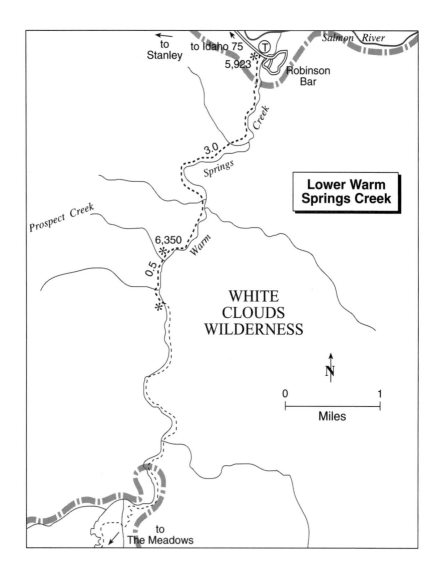

miles beside a granite outcrop another trail comes up from the south.

Follow the lookout trail northeast as it descends and then curves left along the side of a larger outcrop. It then climbs 200 feet along the side of a hill to the ridge crest at 4 miles. After another sandy saddle, it begins to switchback up the mountain with 750 feet more to climb.

Mountain bikes and motorcycles have eroded the trail into a slippery trough, so be careful. An outhouse sits just below the lookout. From it, you must climb a granite outcrop to reach the lookout at 5.1 miles. (9,954 feet).

The lookout, which was built in 1933, is painted beige with a green shingled roof. It is the standard 14-foot square wooden lookout, known as the L-4 design. Since 1972 it has been used by the Forest Service only in emergencies. Please remember that the lookout is a historic building and treat it with respect.

SUNBEAM AREA

92.

LOWER WARM SPRINGS CREEK

Round trip: 6 miles to Prospect Creek from the new trailhead; connects with the Williams Creek Trail
Elevation gain: 400 feet
Elevation loss (return climb): 80 feet **Highest point:** 6,350 feet at Prospect Creek
Map: Robinson Bar
Trailhead GPS: 44 14.888, 114 40.847
Difficulty: easy except for some steep, slippery stretches; time: 4 hours
Access: From Stanley drive east on Idaho 75 for 15 miles. Turn south on a dirt road (454) that crosses the Salmon River on a bridge to the O'Brien Campgrounds. Continue past the campgrounds to a trail sign at 1.4 miles. It is just before the locked and posted gate of Robinson Bar Ranch.

What you'll see: The lower end of Warm Springs Creek is a pleasant, shady walk. The river flows in riffles and pools through forest and beside talus slopes and sagebrush hillsides. At side canyons are glimpses of some of the peaks of the White Clouds. Beginning at about 3 miles, the canyon is recovering from the 2005 Valley Road Fire.
Directions: From the trailhead (5,923 feet) this trail first climbs a steep hillside on the west side of the creek, through Douglas firs. At the top of an outcrop is a view across the creek of Robinson Bar Ranch. Beyond this, the trail drops through talus and firs to a flat at .7 mile. After climbing around another outcrop it descends to a fir and sagebrush flat below a cliff that resembles a stone head. The trail curves west with the river and crosses a ravine into a lodgepole forest. On a sagebrush hillside is a granite outcrop with a mushroom-shaped tower. At 1.2 miles, the trail fords a stream, and descends to its shore at 1.7 miles where it bends to the east. A big pile of black rocks is across the creek, with a ridge of pointed outcrops behind it.

Next the trail climbs a hillside with talus and cliffs above., then descends to a flat lodgepole forest. At 2.2 miles it crosses a stream. The trail then goes along a steep, rocky hillside. At 2.8 miles it skirts the bottom of a 400-foot bluff where the creek curves. At 3 miles, it crosses

215

Prospect Creek. The ford of Warm Springs Creek shown on the map is a half mile farther along. At the ford, the creek is at least 20 feet wide, so in June and early July is dangerous or impassable for hikers.

From here, the trail goes 9.2 miles up the canyon with a 940-foot elevation gain. to The Meadows with another big ford of the river, and several creek crossings. From The Meadows, it is 10 more miles with a 2,350-foot climb to the second Born (Boorn) Lake.

SLATE CREEK AREA

93.

HOODOO LAKE

Round trip: 5 miles
Elevation gain: 1,727 feet **Highest point:** 8,677 feet
Map: Robinson Bar
Trailhead GPS: 44 10.460, 114 37.269
Difficulty: moderate, but the old mining road that serves as the trail varies from the route shown on the topographic map; time: 4 to 5 hours
Access: Drive northeast of Stanley on Idaho 75 for 24.1 miles to the south side of a bridge over the Salmon River and turn right on the dirt Slate Creek Road (666). It goes west along the river and at .8 mile bridges Slate Creek and comes to a T-intersection. Turn left (south) up Slate Creek, and drive to the end of the primitive road in rocks at 7.5 miles.

What you'll see: At the head of emerald-green Hoodoo Lake, a C-shaped groove often filled with snow indents a gray mountain. A burnt orange ridge bristling with rock towers goes along the east side of the lake. Common juniper, marsh grass, and shrubby cinquefoil line the shores of this lake. Its level was raised years ago by an earthen dam. To protect wildlife, the trail is not maintained. Therefore, washouts may have changed it from this description.
Directions: From the parking area (6,920 feet), the trail follows traces of the old road. The first part is a sketchy path across a landslide for 200 yards. Then the old road passes a hot spring, an old mine, and the high sandy rim of a tailings pond. Stay clear of the mine ruins. They are private property and contain mine shafts and toxic chemicals. Follow the old road around the tailings pond and ford the outlet of the lake. At .5 mile, the old road splits.

Take the right (west) fork of the old road. Avoid a spur track to the right. Head southwest on the large switchback shown on the topo-

216

Trail to Hoodoo Lake

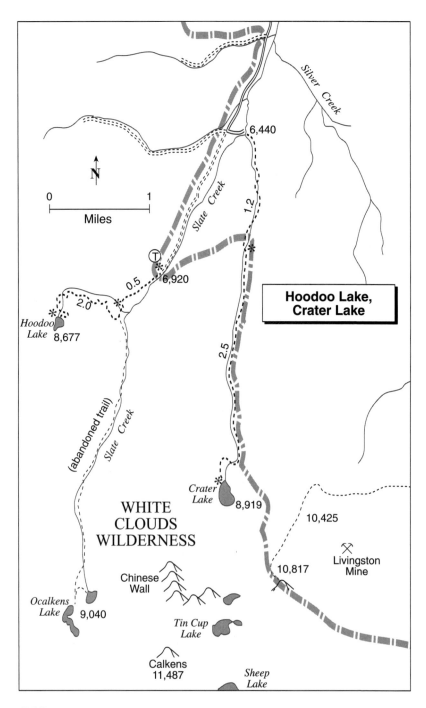

N

0   1
Miles

Silver Creek

6,440

Slate Creek

1.2

T
0.5
6,920

**Hoodoo Lake,
Crater Lake**

2.0

Hoodoo
Lake   8,677

2.5

(abandoned trail)

Slate Creek

Crater
Lake   8,919

10,425

WHITE
CLOUDS
WILDERNESS

Livingston
Mine

10,817

Ocalkens
Lake   9,040

Chinese
Wall

Tin Cup
Lake

Calkens
11,487

Sheep
Lake

218

graphic map. At .9 mile, it switches back to the right (northwest) toward the creek. At 1.2 miles, the track crosses a side branch of the creek on a culvert and curves to the right. At the next switchback, at 7,600 feet, a road goes off to the right with big fallen rocks on it. Below this switchback is a waterfall.

Avoid the rock-covered road here, and switchback to the left on the original road. It soon turns to the right, then left again. Finally, at 1.4 miles, the road turns straight up the canyon, passing to the right (north) of a talus slope at 1.5 miles. The track continues west along the side of the canyon above the creek into the trees.

At 1.8 miles, the old road switchbacks left and then right (8,200 feet). For the next half mile the route is much different from the one shown on the map. At this corner, a track goes off to the left (southeast) for 100 yards and ends. Keep to the right on the main road under a gravel bank. Where the road crosses a side creek, turn left off-trail and go up that creek. Don't take the road here because it dead ends. At about 2 miles you see a road going off to the right. Walk along it and in a few yards it switchbacks to the left and ends at the creek. Cross the creek here to the left (east) bank and climb along it on a path for 100 yards until you see the road going off to the right across the creek once more.

Follow the road to the right (west) uphill. After 150 yards, it turns back to the left and crosses the creek to the east bank again. Continue east on the old road which soon has a good view of Slate Creek Canyon. Next the route curves back to the right (west), climbing steeply. At 2.5 miles, it comes out on a little knoll above the lake (8,677 feet).

Because the old jeep road is becoming fainter each year, you need to know how to follow a route using the topographic map and a compass or take the GPS coordinates for the lake from Google Earth before the hike and using your GPS walk to them.

94.

CRATER LAKE

Round trip: 8 miles from the Slate Creek Road near the confluence of Slate and Livingston creeks

Elevation gain: 2,479 feet **Highest point:** 8,919 feet

Map: Livingston Creek

GPS at trail parking: 44 116.58, 114 36.460

Difficulty: strenuous; time: 7 hours

Access: Drive northeast of Stanley on Idaho 75 for 24.1 miles to the south side of a bridge over the Salmon River and turn right on the dirt Slate Creek Road (666), which goes west along the river. At .8 mile, the road crosses Slate Creek on a bridge and comes to a T-intersection. Here, turn left (south) on the road up Slate Creek, and drive to an unsigned four-way intersection at 5.9 miles. Turn right and park along, but not on, the old road that goes up Last Chance Creek (684). Then walk back down to the main road, cross it, and descend a side road 200 yards through private property to Slate Creek.

What you'll see: Above the gray talus and cloudy blue water of Crater Lake, three small teeth, joined at the base, block passage across a saddle. To the right of the teeth, layers of white rock, striped with dark gray, tip up at each end like a warped pile of plywood. This mountain is called the Chinese Wall. East of the lake, old mining roads slash the round gravelly end of Railroad Ridge. Out of consideration for wildlife, the trail to Crater Lake is not maintained.

Directions: After walking down to Slate Creek (6,440 feet), ford it to a trail that was once a road. After passing an old cabin follow it up the side canyon of Livingston Creek. Beyond a gate, the trail crosses that creek to the left (east) and climbs gently under Douglas firs. At .5 mile, it fords two sections of the creek to the right (west), and then returns to the east in 200 yards. Ignore old mining roads which join this track from time to time. Keep on the one nearest to the creek. At 1 mile, it fords to the west again, and returns to the left (east) at 1.2 miles.

The trail passes log cabin ruins and a side stream and levels out at 2.7 miles across from a talus slope. It reaches a basin of talus and grass at 3.5 miles. Near an old mine tunnel at the head of this basin, the trail crosses the creek again to the right (west). It now makes a .3 mile-long switchback to the north as the creek curves west. To save distance, you can turn left off the trail and climb the talus and ledges along the creek. At 4 miles, the switchback returns to the creek at a grassy area just above the gravel of the lake shore (8,919 feet).

*95.

MILL CREEK - HOLMAN CREEK LOOP

Through trip: 6 miles
Elevation gain: 1,600 feet **Highest point:** 7,400 feet
Map: Thompson Creek, Livingston Creek
Trailhead GPS: at Mill Creek N 44 * 15' 16.3", W 114* 29' 23.9""; at Holman Creek N 44* 14' 45.6", W 114* 31' 48"
Difficulty: easy time:5 ? hours
Access: From the junction of Idaho 21 and Idaho 75 in Stanley, drive 24.6 miles east on Idaho 75 to a sign for Mill Creek on the right. The sign is a half mile east of a bridge over the Salmon River. Park at the beginning of the road up Mill Creek. You can no longer drive the 1/4 mile of jeep road that leads to the trailhead.

What you'll see: This short hike has views of bare ridges with strips of timber and aspens that are gold in the fall. It also has many wildflowers early in the summer.

Directions: The trail first goes up a steep hillside to the right (west). Then it descends to Mill Creek, crosses it, and climbs along its left side, mostly in forest. At 2.2 miles it reaches a meadow with a spring. At 2.5 miles there is an unsigned split in the trail. To complete the loop, take the left (east) branch uphill 200 vertical feet to the low point in a bare ridge. A path leads on up the canyon a ways if you wish to explore it instead of, or in addition to, going over into Holman Creek. The loop trail crosses a 7,040 foot divide near a muddy pond that is not on the topographic map.

Once over the divide, the trail drops 500 feet to Holman Creek, which has many aspens .Once at Holman Creek a path goes on up the canyon if you wish to explore it. Holman Creek has many more trees along it than Mill Creek, and one Douglas fir appears to have a diameter of 12 feet. When you turn down the canyon, at about 5 miles the trail comes out into sagebrush and willows beside beaver dams. At 6 miles it meets a road that leads a few yards to the Holman Creek campground, which is 26 miles east of the Idaho 21-75 junction at Stanley. From Holman Creek it is 1.6 miles back to the Mill Creek trailhead by way of the highway.

*96.

FRENCH CREEK

Round trip: 19 miles

Elevation gain: 2,300 feet **Highest point:** 8,100 feet at junction with Big Lake Creek Trail

Maps: Clayton, Potaman Peak, Livingston Creek

Trailhead GPS: N 44 15 17.0, W 114 29 23.9

Difficulty: Strenuous Time: 3 to 4 days

Access: Because of private property at the lower end of French Creek, the trail up that creek begins on a hill across Idaho 75 from the Yankee Fork guard station. The trailhead is 28.3 miles northeast of the junction with Idaho 21 in Stanley

What you'll see: The land along French Creek at first is high bare hills with timber on the upper slopes, especially on the north facing ones. In June and July the meadows have wildflower displays and about October 1st the many aspens in the canyon are aflame. The trail gives access to Railroad Ridge, which lies 1.2 miles beyond the Big Lake Creek junction. The ridge has a far reaching view of Mt. Borah in the Lost River Range, Castle Peak in the White Clouds, and Twin Peaks in the Salmon River Mountains. This route to Railroad Ridge is much longer but gentler than walking the rough 4-wheel drive road from Livingston Mill on Big Boulder Creek.

Directions: The trail starts up the side of the hill to the south and

Old cabin on French Creek

curves around the base of it. It climbs 400 feet and then drops to the old road that comes in from the north from a ranch. On the way it passes a historic telephone pole that is enclosed by a fence. The trail goes along in sagebrush and grass and then beside French Creek on its left. Cottonwoods provide occasional shade. At 1.5 miles an old unpainted cabin stands a hundred vertical feet above the creek.

At 2 miles the trail crosses to the right side in sagebrush, willows, and forest . At 2.3 and 2.5 miles are two more creek crossings. At 3 miles Pistol Creek comes into French Creek at an angle from the left (east). Now the trail goes off to the right (west) away from French Creek and along an unnamed stream parallel to French Creek. It crosses back and forth over this creek at 3.2 and 3.5 miles and then crosses French Creek to the left side at 5 miles and begins to climb through forest. It continues mostly through forest to meet the Big Lake Creek trail from Jimmy Smith Lake at 9.5 miles. At 10.5 miles, the joined trails, as a jeep road, meet the jeep trail from Livingston Mill on top of Railroad Ridge.

CLAYTON AREA

97.

SULLIVAN LAKE

Round trip: 5 miles from Highway 75 about 30 miles east of Stanley; connects with a trail from Jimmy Smith Lake
Elevation gain: 1,730 feet **Highest point:** 6,960 feet
Elevation loss (return climb): 520 feet
Map: Potaman Peak; GPS at beginning of route: 44 14.879, 114 27.338
Difficulty: cross-country for experts because private property limits access to the old trail; time: 6 to 7 hours
Access: From Stanley, drive east along Idaho 75 toward Challis. Between the settlement of Old Sawmill Station, 29.2 miles from Stanley, and the first of two close-together bridges over the Salmon River at 30.2 miles watch for a pullout on the right (south) side of the road and park.

What you'll see: Hills covered with sagebrush and Douglas fir and decorated with a few pointed outcrops surround marshy Sullivan Lake. The route passes below striped and swirled butterscotch-colored towers. It climbs to a divide, and from it you see a red-orange monolith in the canyon of Sullivan Creek, and the cliffs of a peak named Potaman beyond it. Lack of shade and low elevation make this hike best for cool days. Because half of the lake disappears in marsh grass by late summer and the area is heavily grazed, June and early July are the best times for a visit.

Directions: Private property at the beginning of the trail means that you can't hike the trail up Sullivan Creek . Instead you must go up Corral Creek 6.5 miles and 1,540 feet from Jimmy Smith Lake. Or from Idaho 75 take this short steep route that avoids the private property.

From the pullout (5,576 feet) on the highway, walk a few yards east through the grass until you see a path going uphill to the right. Go up it onto a grass and sagebrush bench, which is above the eastern of the two intermittent creeks that are shown running into the Salmon River at a big curve. The route climbs that drainage on the east side but well above it. There are many confusing animal paths. The ascent is so steep it can challenge experts, especially on the return. Trekking poles are helpful. You just need to climb the hillside to the divide shown on the map, but you can't see the divide from the highway. To find it, climb the hill through Douglas firs, staying between a wall of butterscotch cliffs on the east and a triangular tower on the west. Once you come even with the top of the tower at .4 mile, angle up and over to the right toward the divide, which you will soon see on the skyline ahead, but it is almost another steep mile until you come out on it in the sagebrush.

From the divide, at 1.3 miles (6,760 feet) descend southeast toward aspens just above the canyon of Sullivan Creek, then turn and follow a path south along the right (west) side of the creek. It joins the trail along Sullivan Creek at 1.9 miles, at a fence that coincides with the SNRA boundary. There are few traces of the lower part of the trail down Sullivan Creek from the fence because cattle have trampled it.

Just beyond the fence, the trail to the lake crosses the creek to the left (east) side. It climbs to the left up a sagebrush hillside, then turns back to the right to the creek. The trail runs along the left side of the creek, which often dries up by late summer. Then it crosses to the right (west) side at 2.4 miles and comes out on the lake shore (6,731 feet) at 2.5 miles.

EAST FORK OF THE SALMON RIVER AREA

98.

JIMMY SMITH LAKE

Round trip: 1.2 miles from the end of the Big Lake Creek road; connects with a trail to Sullivan Lake, and to the Big Lake Creek trail to Railroad Ridge

Elevation gain: 250 feet; **Highest point:** 6,360 feet

Map: Potaman Peak

Trailhead GPS: 44 09.613, 114 23.356

Difficulty: easy; time: 1 hour

Access: From Stanley, go east 37.6 miles on Idaho 75 toward Challis to the East Fork of the Salmon River Road. Turn right (south) and drive 13.4 miles on the paved road. At a sign for Jimmy Smith Lake turn right (west) up Big Lake Creek on a gravel road (677) and drive 1.2 miles to its end.

What you'll see: This lake sprawls in fir-topped hills that are decorated with lavender cliffs and pink, purple, and orange rock. When you look down on the lake, it is a milky green, perhaps reflecting the shoreline willows, but in the distance that color changes to light blue. June or early July is the best time for the hike, when the wildflowers, such as the pale pink bitterroot, brighten the sandy soil between the sagebrush.

Directions: From the trailhead (6,150 feet), the trail starts out as an old road (not open to motor vehicles). It winds along through the sagebrush on the east side of the willows and cottonwoods lining Big Lake Creek. At .4 mile it curves into and out of a ravine, and comes out on a hilltop above the lake at .6 mile. Then it descends a few yards to the shore (6,326 feet) and continues around the right (north) side of the

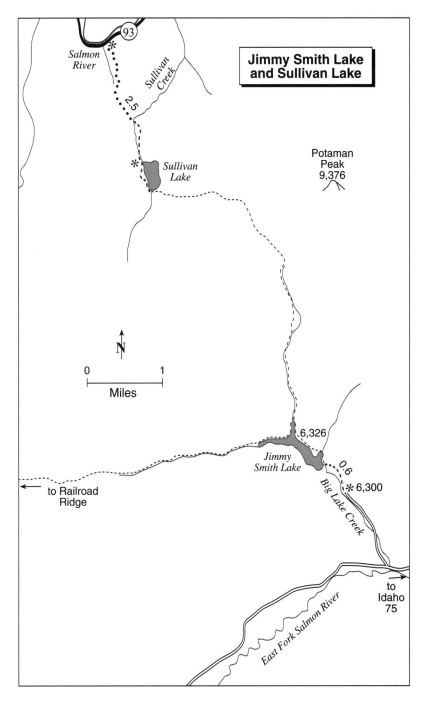

Jimmy Smith Lake and Sullivan Lake

Salmon River

93

Sullivan Creek

2.5

Sullivan Lake

Potaman Peak 9,376

N

0   1
Miles

6,326

Jimmy Smith Lake

0.6

6,300

Big Lake Creek

to Railroad Ridge

to Idaho 75

East Fork Salmon River

225

Jimmy Smith Lake

lake. The lakeshore trail leads to two more trails. One of these, the Corral Creek Trail, goes north 6.5 miles to Sullivan Lake in a 1,540-foot climb. The other, the Big Lake Creek Trail, ascends 10.5 miles in a 3,020-foot climb to the French Creek Jeep Trail on the north side of Railroad Ridge.

99.

RAILROAD RIDGE

Round trip: 12.6 miles from Livingston Mill on a jeep trail; connects with Big Lake Creek trail
Elevation gain: 3,265 feet; **Highest point:** 10,425 feet
Elevation loss (return climb): 80 feet
Map: Livingston Creek
GPS at jeep trail beginning: 44 07.991, 114 31.044
Difficulty: strenuous; time: 12 hours or 2 days if on foot
Access: On Idaho 75, 37.6 miles east of Stanley, turn right (south) on the paved East Fork of the Salmon River Road and go 18.2 miles to the junction with the Boulder Creek Road to Livingston Mill (667). Turn right (northwest) on the dirt road and drive 4.2 miles to a sign for the Big Boulder Trailhead. Here, turn left and go .2 mile unless you have 4-wheel drive and a high wheel base. If you do, you can drive part or all

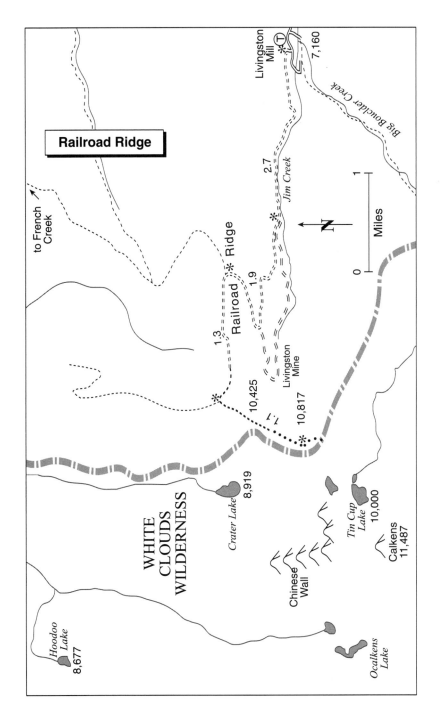

Railroad Ridge

to French Creek

7,160

Livingston Mill

Big Boulder Creek

Jim Creek

2.7

Railroad * Ridge

1.9

1.3

N

Miles

0   1

Livingston Mine

10,425

10,817

1.1

WHITE CLOUDS WILDERNESS

Crater Lake
8,919

Tin Cup Lake
10,000

Chinese Wall

Calkens
11,487

Hoodoo Lake
8,677

Ocalkens Lake

of the jeep trail (669) onto the ridge.

What you'll see: On the top of Railroad Ridge are many fragile alpine flowers, such as alpine forget-me-not and the White Clouds milk vetch, an endemic, which means it grows nowhere else in the world. In late July, various yellow flowers turn the ridge golden, and lupine accents that carpet with purple spikes. From the summit you look north onto blue Crater Lake set in a cup of gray talus. Beside this lake, the Chinese Wall is a textbook example of rock layers warped downward in the center. Looking east from the ridge, you see near Livingston Mill a layer cake of strawberry and chocolate colored rock.

Directions: On the way up Railroad Ridge, please stay away from the mine buildings and houses. They are private property and hold many dangers. Mud and snow can make the jeep trail impassable for all vehicles in early summer, so before August 1, check with the SNRA first or plan to hike.

From the trailhead (7,160 feet), go .2 mile back to the main road and up it .1 mile to a gate. Go through the gate, leaving it the way you found it, and .2 mile farther on turn right at a junction with the road up Railroad Ridge (669). In the next 2 miles, it climbs 1,000 feet up a sagebrush hillside in the sun. The surface has rocks and deep ruts.

Where the road forks at 2.7 miles take the right (north) branch. At 3.2 miles, in trees beside a stream, is a large campsite. Beyond here, the road is often in better shape than it is lower down. At 3.8 miles (9,090 feet), the road divides again not shown on the topographic map.) Take the right branch, which turns northeast.

The road climbs 600 feet in .8 mile. At 4.6 miles, it hairpins 180 degrees to the west. At this bend (9,760 feet) the French Creek Jeep Trail (670), turns off to the north, but it becomes a pack trail part way down.

From this junction, keep west on the road along the top of the ridge. Soon the road splits briefly to avoid a washout . At 5.9 miles (10,320 feet), the road divides again. The north branch of the road is an old mine road and peters out. Park if you haven't already, and walk left (southwest) on a faint jeep trail to the ridge summit at 6.3 miles. This track is not shown on the topographic map and shouldn't be driven because of rare plants.

To view Crater Lake below, walk north of the road a few yards. Beyond the ridge summit, the faint track continues to a notch at 6.6 miles. To look down on Tin Cup and Gunsight Lakes, climb south cross-country from the notch about 500 feet to the top of a rocky knoll (10,817 feet). at 7 miles. Descend 100 yards to the west toward another notch to see Tin Cup and the unnamed lake north of it called Gunsight Lake. Climbing down to these lakes from the sandy saddle (10,400 feet) east of the knoll is dangerous, but possible for experts. It is much safer to reach Tin Cup and Gunsight Lakes by hiking cross-country up Gunsight Creek from Quicksand Meadows.

100.

Walker Lake

Round trip: 15 miles from Livingston Mill; connects with trails to Frog Lake and Island Lake and a cross-country route to the Big Boulder Lakes.
Elevation gain: 2,079 feet **Highest point:** 9,239 feet
Maps: Livingston Creek, Boulder Chain Lakes
Trailhead GPS: 44 07.896, 114 30.753
Difficulty: strenuous; time: 12 hours or two days
Access: On Idaho 75, 37.6 miles east of Stanley, turn south on the East Fork Salmon River Road, and go 18.2 miles. Then turn right (northwest) on the dirt Livingston Mill Road (667) and drive 4.2 miles. At a sign for the Big Boulder Trailhead, turn left and go .2 mile to the trailhead.

What you'll see: A village of weathered brown cabins stands near the trailhead. From the lower part of the trail the view is of brown and white rock layers that resemble melting vanilla ice cream on chocolate cake. Bordering Quicksand Meadows farther up the trail, pink, brown, rust, and white stripes and patches form a crazy quilt on Granite Peak. North of aqua-green Walker Lake, triangular towers crown the double summit of a burnt orange and white peak. Above the upper end of the lake, the tips of White Cloud peaks resemble icebergs when the morning sun shines on them.
Directions: From the trailhead (7,160 feet), the trail skirts Big Boulder Creek through sagebrush flats then follows an old road with a view of red rock towers across Big Boulder Creek. At 1.5 miles, it bridges the creek and becomes single track. The turnoff to Frog Lakes is at 2.1 miles (7,700 feet). This trail, the Livingston - Castle Divide Trail, goes over that divide and all the way to Chamberlain Lakes. On the way, it passes Frog Lake 7.6 miles from Livingston Mill after a 1,804-foot elevation gain and 700-foot elevation loss.
Beyond the Frog Lake Junction, the trail to Walker and Island Lakes crosses Big Boulder Creek in two sections. The first of these is spanned by three planed footlogs. Beyond here, the trail climbs through sagebrush, lodgepoles, and aspens and is very hot on summer afternoons. At 3.1 miles it is above a large meadow. After a steep grade, it goes above a 100-foot gorge. Then it circles the large meadow called Quicksand Meadows. This is shown as a flat, wooded area on the map. At 4.2 miles a side trail leads down into the meadows. The main trail goes around the meadows on the north, high above and crosses Gunsight Creek at 4.5 miles on a double footlog. Then it turns south along the hillside above Gunsight Creek to Big Boulder Creek and stays on its right (north) side.
The quicksand is in the lower meadows and is dangerous to stock.

Quicksand is caused by water upwelling underneath sand with such force to equal the weight of the sand, and thus separates the sand grains making it possible for an object on it to sink. A person floats more easily in quicksand than in water. because it is denser, but their feet could get stuck as I have seen. To get out of quicksand, a person needs only to lie down and work their feet out. A horse would have to be pulled out.

Beyond the meadows the trail switchbacks up a talus slope, then climbs through trees, with views of the striped peak on the left. At 5.3 miles across the canyon, the combined outlets of Island and Goat Lakes rush down in a cascade and waterfall. At 5.6 miles the trail crosses that creek on double footlogs. At 6.2 miles is a junction of the trails to Island and Walker lakes. The trail to Walker Lake is not shown on the topographic map but is an official maintained trail. The Walker Lake trail a rocky section south of a granite knoll and then descends to a pond, which it skirts on the left. Between the pond and another bigger one it crosses the creek on a double log to the right (north) side at about 7 miles. The trail continues up and down over granite benches and through trees to the lake at 7.5 miles. At one point there is a steep dropoff straight ahead where a misleading fisherman trail goes off to the right. There are several campsites along the shore all the way to the upper end. The distance to Walker Lake is longer than it used to be because of the reroute around Quicksand Meadows.

101.

BIG BOULDER LAKES

This one-way section: 2 miles, 801-foot elevation gain on a cross-country route from the lower end of Walker Lake

Round trip: 19 miles from Livingston Mill to the highest lake; connects with a cross-country route from Island Lake to the Big Boulder lakes.

Elevation gain: 2,880 feet **Highest point:** 10,040 feet
Map: Boulder Chain Lakes; Livingston
Trailhead GPS: 44 07.896, 114 30.753
Difficulty: cross-country from Walker Lake; time: 2 to 3 days
Access: Following directions for Walker Lake, hike 7.5 miles from the Livingston Mill trailhead to that lake.

What you'll see: From above, the three Big Boulder Lakes resemble three sapphire blue platters with turquoise rims set among white China. To the southeast, is the gray, orange, and cream-colored patchwork of Granite Peak. Above them to the west, a scalloped, ridge of white rock gleams in the morning sunlight. In the afternoon, when the sun shines on the other side of the ridge, the light fades to pearl gray. Glacial moraines surround the upper lake, Cirque Lake, but the ice on

230

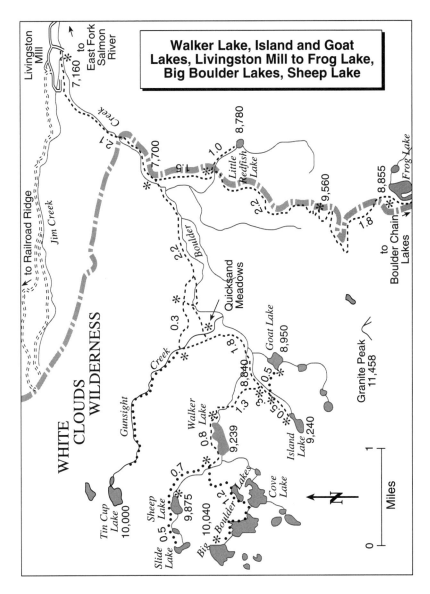

Walker Lake, Island and Goat
Lakes, Livingston Mill to Frog Lake,
Big Boulder Lakes, Sheep Lake

and within the moraines has stopped moving, so it is no longer classi-
fied as a glacier or even a rock glacier (moving ice that is hidden by
rocks.)

Directions: The lower end of Walker Lake (9,239 feet), where this
hike description begins, is 7.5 miles and a 2,079-foot climb from Livingston Mill. Begin by taking the trail along the north shore .5 mile to
the upper end of Walker Lake.

Turn right (east) and go up the right (north) branch of an inlet,

231

Big Boulder Lakes - Cirque Lake

called Bighorn Creek. Where a stream joins it from the left at .8 mile, turn west across the inlet and go up the left (south) side of a stream, which is not shown on the map. Cross to the right of this stream and go out into a flat meadow. From here turn left and climb south between ledges to the top of a low ridge above Hook Lake. Then drop to the east end of that lake and go around it and head south between granite benches. You should come out on the stream between Cove (9,842 feet) and Sapphire lakes (9,888 feet) at 1.5 miles. Go around the north side of Sapphire Lake and up an inlet to Cirque Lake (10,640 feet) at 2 miles.

It is also possible to reach the Big Boulder Lakes by two other routes. One is to climb the cliffs beside an unnamed inlet that flows into the west end of Walker Lake. There is also a route from Island Lake, but it is less obvious. To find it, go to the northeast corner of Island Lake. Then go north 300 feet up a gully to the top of a ridge at 9,600 feet. Turn left (west) along the ridge to a tiny pond (shown as an open area on the map) and follow the 9,800-foot contour line west to Cove Lake, the lowest of the Big Boulder Lakes, at 1 mile.

102.

SHEEP AND SLIDE LAKES

This one-way section: 2 miles, 636-foot gain by a cross-country route from the lower end of Walker Lake

Round trip: 15.2 miles from Livingston Mill
Elevation gain: 2,715 feet **Highest point:** 9,875 feet
Map: Boulder Chain Lakes; Livingston
Trailhead GPS: 44 07.896, 114 30.753
Difficulty: cross-country above Walker Lake; time: 2 to 3 days
Access: Using directions for Walker Lake, hike 7.5 miles from the
Livingston Mill trailhead to that lake (a 2,079-foot climb).

What you'll see: Granite benches and ledges softened by wildflower
meadows surround Sheep Lake. Below it, patchwork designs decorate
the wall of Granite Peak. The pinnacles and jumbled cliffs of a peach-
colored mountain rise 1,200 feet above the east side of the lake. Two
matching rock triangles stand at the head of the canyon above the
granite shelves that hold Neck and Slide Lakes.
Directions: From the lower end of Walker Lake (9,239 feet), hike .5
mile along the right (north) side of the lake to the upper end. Then
climb along the right (east) side of the right (north) branch of the
inlet, which is called Bighorn Creek.
Keep straight ahead at .8 mile where a side stream comes in from the
flat place on the left (west) that marks a route to the Big Boulder Lakes.
Continue along the east side of Bighorn Creek to Sheep Lake (9,875
feet) at 1.5 miles. There are only one or two small campsites. To reach
Slide Lake (10,200 feet), 320 feet above Sheep Lake, walk .5 mile up its
inlet passing a narrow pond called Neck Lake on the way.

103.

ISLAND AND GOAT LAKES

This one-way section: .8 mile, 400-foot elevation gain; additional .5
mile and 100-foot gain and 200-foot elevation loss for Goat Lake
Round trip: 14 miles to Island Lake from Livingston Mill
Elevation gain: 2,080 feet **Highest point:** 9,240 feet
Maps: Boulder Chain Lakes, Livingston Creek
Trailhead GPS: 44 07.896, 114 30.753
Difficulty: strenuous; time: 9 to 11 hours or 2 days
Access: Following directions for Walker Lake, hike 6.2 miles from
Livingston Mill to the junction of the Island and Walker Lake trails.

What you'll see: The aquamarine water of Island Lake holds two
islands, one big enough for whitebark pines and the other just a granite pancake. Granite benches surround the lake except for a narrow
boulder-dotted meadow at the upper end and a 200-foot cliff beside it.
Above the green water of nearby Goat Lake, gray, cream, and chocolate
stripes wander east across Granite Peak to a jumble of pinnacles.
Directions: From the Walker Lake-Island Lake Junction (8,840 feet),
the Island Lake Trail at first climbs the canyon at a distance from the

233

gorge of the lake's outlet. In a boggy meadow beyond the gorge at .3 mile, you can climb to the left (east) cross-country over a 100-foot ridge to Goat Lake (8,950 feet). To do this, when you reach the boggy meadow, look east to a saddle between a rock knoll and a ridge. Head for this saddle .1 mile from the trail. From the saddle, descend 200 feet through the trees to the lake, .5 mile from the trail. Back at the boggy meadow, the main trail to Island Lake runs along above a second gorge, crosses a side creek and reaches the lake (9,240 feet) at a campsite at .8 mile.

![104.]

LIVINGSTON MILL TO FROG LAKE

Round trip: 15.2 miles from Livingston Mill; connects with trail to the Boulder Chain Lakes
Elevation gain: 2,400 feet **Highest point:** 9,560 feet
Elevation loss (return climb): 705 feet
Maps: Livingston Creek, Boulder Chain Lakes
Trailhead GPS: 44 07.896, 114 30.753
Difficulty: strenuous; time: 2 to 3 days
Access: On Idaho 75, 37.6 miles east of Stanley, turn south on the East Fork Salmon River Road. Drive 18.2 miles and turn right (northwest) on the dirt Livingston Mill Road (667) and drive 4.2 miles. At a sign for the Big Boulder trailhead, turn left and go .2 mile to the trailhead parking.

What you'll see: Southwest of the summit of this trail, two snow-filled ravines furrow the charcoal gray face of Castle Peak. To the right of the peak are the orange needles of Serrate Ridge and the cathedral of Merriam Peak. West of the trail summit, burnt orange patches and stripes pattern the white face of Granite Peak. On the far side of the summit, the trail drops to the yellow water lilies of Frog and Little Frog Lakes.
Directions: From the trailhead (7,160 feet), the trail goes along the creek through sagebrush flats, past the old brown cabins of Livingston Mill at .5 mile. Keep away–the buildings are private property and some contain toxic chemicals. Beyond them, the trail follows the route of an old road across the creek from red towers. It bridges Big Boulder Creek in a small meadow at 1.5 miles.
At a junction at 2.1 miles, turn south on the Frog Lake Trail. It switchbacks through a forest underlain by dead-tree jackstraws. The trail climbs gently and even small streams have bridges. At 3.6 miles is a junction with a 1-mile side trail to Little Redfish Lake (8,780 feet), 400 feet above. This lake in marsh grass and water lilies is surrounded by wooded ridges.
The main trail zigzags up, crossing and recrossing streams across Big Boulder Creek from open grass and orange mountains. At a corner

234

Livingston Mill

at 4 miles, white peaks appear behind the Big Boulder Lakes. The trail climbs through open areas, flattens out in lodgepoles, and passes a pond at 5.1 miles.

Next, long switchbacks lead to a divide (9,560 feet) at the west end of Red Ridge at 5.8 miles. From it the stripes and patches of Granite Peak are close. As the trail descends, it turns west for .2 mile, then zips back to the east. At 6.5 miles, it goes down a creek through meadows. It reaches a pond beside Frog Lake (8,855 feet) at 7.6 miles. Little Frog Lake is .2 mile to the east.

105.

FROG LAKE AND THE BOULDER CHAIN LAKES

This one-way section: 4.3 miles, 908-foot elevation gain, 120-foot loss from Frog Lake (It is .7 mile and 900 feet extra cross-country to reach the two highest lakes, Headwall and Lonesome.)

Round trip: 23.8 miles to Scoop Lake (the last on the trail) from Livingston Mill; provides cross-country access to Shallow, Scree, and Quiet lakes; connects with the trail to Walker Lake.

235

Hatchet Lake

Elevation gain: 3,308 feet **Highest point:** 9,643 feet at Scoop Lake

Elevation loss (return climb): 825 feet

Map: Boulder Chain Lakes; Livingston Creek

Trailhead GPS: 44 07.896, 114 30.753

Difficulty: strenuous; time: 3 to 4 days

Access: Following directions for Livingston Mill to Frog Lake, hike 7.6 miles to that lake

What you'll see: A glacier strung these eleven lakes on a creek like blue beads on a necklace. A ridge of orange slabs and pinnacles links the first five of the lakes. On this ridge above the second lake, Hatchet Lake, stands a tower with owl-like ears. Above the trail to the first lake from Frog Lake, the dark snow-slashed face of Castle Peak looms ahead.

Directions: From Frog Lake (8,855 feet), the trail drops through trees with the view of Castle Peak ahead. At 1 mile, it bridges the outlet of Willow Lake (8,735 feet). The trail goes around the lake on the left (south) side near campsites. Sites are also 200 yards southeast off-trail at a pond called Waterdog Lake.

The trail climbs through trees to Hatchet Lake (8,884 feet) at 1.5 miles. Blue-green water, marsh grass, and the pinnacle with ears distinguish this lake. Campsites are off-trail on the northeast side. The trail comes close to this lake only at the outlet, which it fords. In .2 mile, it crosses the inlet from the third lake, 8,939-foot Shelf Lake. Forest, and rock shelves stand on the north side of this lake and the eared mountain on the south.

As the trail passes Shelf Lake, it climbs next to the cliffs of the orange mountain. It goes through trees under the owl-eared tower to boulders and turf on the south shore of the fourth lake, Sliderock Lake (8,978 feet), at 2 miles. Campsites are located behind rock peninsulas.

The trail circles the head of the lake, and crosses the inlet to the north side on rocks. It then goes along the north shore of the fifth lake, Lodgepole Lake (9,008 feet). Here on the south, the orange ridge sheds rocks into the water, and on the north, an inlet flows into the lake through a tongue of golden sand.

236

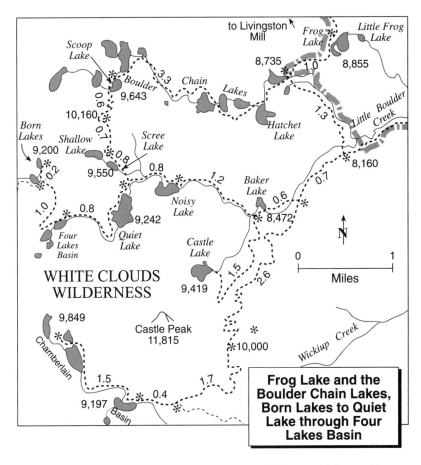

Frog Lake and the Boulder Chain Lakes, Born Lakes to Quiet Lake through Four Lakes Basin

Now there is a one-mile gap in the chain of lakes, and the trail stays away from Boulder Chain Lakes Creek, climbing steeply over rock benches and through forest. At 3.4 miles, it crosses to the west side of the creek, then east and west again just below Hourglass Lake at 3.7 miles.

This upper basin holds three lakes: Hidden (9,517 feet), Hammock (9,514 feet) and Hourglass (9,731 feet), which sit below splintered pale-gray peaks. Campsites are abundant. The trail continues up a shelf to the ninth lake, Scoop Lake (9,643 feet) at 4.3 miles. This lake, the last lake on the trail, is in a hollow of solid rock with a few stunted white-bark pines.

The trail keeps on up through a pass called Windy Devil (10,160 feet) at 4.9 miles. The two upper lakes, Headwall (9,755 feet) and Lonesome (10,435 feet), are off-trail and above timberline. They can be reached by going around the west side of Scoop Lake on the trail and ascending its inlet cross-country for 990 vertical feet for .7 mile.

From Windy Devil Pass, the trail climbs onto a shelf (10,200 feet),

237

passes a pond, and ends 557 feet and 1.5 miles above Scoop Lake. Trying to go over the off-trail pass sometimes called the Devils Staircase from here to Born (Boorn) Lakes can be fatal.

106.

LITTLE BOULDER CREEK TRAIL TO THE BOULDER CHAIN LAKES

Round trip: 15.6 miles from the East Fork of the Salmon River to Scoop Lake, the highest lake on the trail; connects with trails to Castle Divide and Frog Lake

Elevation gain: 1,915 feet

Highest point: 8,135 feet

Maps: Bowery Creek, Boulder Chain Lakes

Trail beginning GPS: 44 05.056, 114 26.727

Difficulty: strenuous; time: 9 hours

Access: On Idaho 75, 37.6 miles east of Stanley, turn south on the East Fork of the Salmon River Road. Drive 14.6 miles on pavement, and 5 miles on gravel to a parking area and transfer camp for the Little Boulder Creek Trail. From here, walk .4 mile south along the road to the trail. (There is no room to park where the trail begins.) Those with horses should park their horse trailers at the corrals 1 mile farther up the East Fork where Sheep and Wickiup creeks enter the river.

What you'll see: The Little Boulder Creek Trail is the shortest route to the Boulder Chain Lakes and Baker Lake. This trail was reopened in 1991 after the Forest Service built a 3-mile road around the property of a landowner who had blocked access to the upper end of the East Fork of the Salmon River Road for 13 years. From this trail, there are fine views of Castle Peak. One is from a meadow at 3.4 miles and another is from the large meadow at the junction with the Livingston Mill - Castle Divide Trail at 6 miles. Photographs of the view from this meadow showing the face of Castle Peak and its companion, Merriam Peak, have appeared in many books and national magazines, especially during the controversy over mining in the White Clouds in the early 1970's. This controversy led to the formation of the Sawtooth National Recreation Area in 1972.

Directions: The mileage given here is from the trail beginning not the transfer camp, which is .4 mile farther on. From the road at 6,200 feet, the first 1.8 miles of the trail climb 1,000 feet through sagebrush with only two groves of trees and no water. The trail is the southern one of three trails the map shows joining.

At first as it climbs the trail heads along the East Fork canyon. At .5 mile, it descends into a grassy area and then climbs through an aspen grove. Then it angles uphill in the sagebrush again with scattered Douglas firs and rocky bluffs. At .9 mile, the trail parallels the red rock formations of Red Ridge across Little Boulder Creek and reaches a grove

238

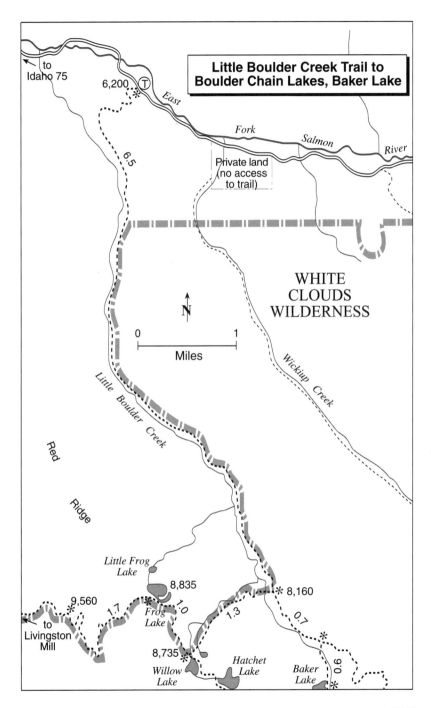

to
Idaho 75

6,200
T

East

Fork

Salmon

River

Private land
(no access
to trail)

6.5

WHITE
CLOUDS
WILDERNESS

N

0   1

Miles

Wickiup Creek

Little Boulder Creek

Red

Ridge

Little Frog
Lake

8,835

9,560

1.7

1.0

1.3

8,160

0.7

to
Livingston
Mill

Frog
Lake

8,735

Willow
Lake

Hatchet
Lake

Baker
Lake

0.6

239

of Douglas firs which provide the first shade at 1.1 miles.

It enters forest at last at 1.8 miles and comes close to Little Boulder Creek for the first time at 2.8 miles. A meadow with willows at 3.4 miles offers the first view of Castle Peak. The trail continues climbing along the creek to a second large meadow at 6 miles. At the upper end at 6.5 miles (8,160 feet), it joins the Livingston Mill-Castle Divide Trail.

At this junction, turn right (north) up Boulder Chain Lakes Creek. The trail fords Little Boulder Creek at 6.6 miles. At 7 miles, it is on an open sagebrush slope decorated with aspens. It heads up the wooded canyon of the outlet of the Boulder Chain Lakes and crosses the outlet of Waterdog Lake at 7.6 miles. Waterdog is just a little pond off trail. Willow Lake at 7.8 miles is considered the first of the Boulder Chain Lakes.

107.

BAKER LAKE

This one-way section: 1.3 miles from the Little Boulder Creek trail at its 6.5-mile point.

Round trip: 15.6 miles from beginning of the Little Boulder Creek trail at the East Fork Road, connects with Castle Divide trail, and cross-country routes to Castle and Quiet lakes.

Elevation gain: 2,252 feet **Highest point:** 8,472 feet
Map: Boulder Chain Lakes
Trail beginning GPS: 44 05.056, 114 26.727 at the East Fork Road
Difficulty: strenuous; time: 3 to 4 days
Access: Following directions for Little Boulder Creek Trail to the Boulder Chain Lakes, hike 6.5 miles up that trail to the junction with the Castle Divide Trail.

What you'll see: Marsh grass edges shallow, green Baker Lake beneath pearl gray granite ridges and orange towers of Merriam Peak. To the left of it, the furrowed dark-gray face of Castle Peak peers over a wooded ridge. If the Sawtooth National Recreation Area hadn't been formed in 1972, this ridge would now be an open pit molybdenum mine.

Directions: From the junction (8,160 feet) of the Little Boulder and the Castle Divide trails, keep straight ahead on the Castle Divide Trail and climb wooded slopes for .7 mile to the signed spur trail to the lake. Turn right (west) on this trail and drop to a prospect. Cross the outlet and climb a few feet to the lake (8,472 feet) at 1.3 miles. There are several campsites. Baker Lake can also be reached from the lowest Chamberlain Lake (9,197 feet) in 6.3 miles by climbing over 10,000-foot Castle Divide. (That lake is 7.4 miles from the closest trailhead, which is Three Cabins Creek.)

108.

CASTLE LAKE

This one-way section: 1.5 miles, 947-foot elevation gain, 40-foot loss from Baker Lake
Round trip: 18.6 miles from the beginning of the Little Boulder Creek trail
Elevation gain: 3,208 feet **Highest point:** 9,419 feet
Elevation loss (return climb): 1,320 feet
Map: Boulder Chain Lakes
Trail beginning GPS: 44 05.056, 114 26.727 at the East Fork Road
Difficulty: cross-country for experts; time: 3 to 4 days
Access: Following directions for Little Boulder Creek to the Boulder Chain Lakes, and for Baker Lake hike 7.8 miles to Baker Lake.

What you'll see: Two snow-filled chimneys form a "V" on the charcoal gray face of Castle Peak above Castle Lake. The lake is so deep and the mountain so dark that the water is navy blue. Talus slopes surround the lake except for ledges, benches, and whitebark pines at the lower end. At the north corner of the lake below the orange sawteeth of Merriam Peak and Serrate Ridge, a solid-rock peninsula sprinkled with bonsai-like trees encloses a small turquoise bay. Note that the route to Castle Lake is slippery and has a dropoff of several hundred feet. Avoid camping in the lake basin because it is a fragile alpine area.
Directions: From the outlet of Baker Lake (8,472 feet), take the right (west) of two old mining roads which leave the lake from the west side of a log bridge over the outlet. These roads are not maintained, so they may no longer be obvious. The west road crosses a stream at .1 mile. At .4 mile, just past a clearcut area, the main trail over Castle Divide is close enough to see its blazes. Continue on the road across another stream, and around two switchbacks to a split at .5 mile. Take the left branch up a ridge (9,204 feet). Where the road splits again at 1 mile, take the right (west) branch downhill, then go up across a ravine.
Beyond the ravine, turn left (south) off the road up a sandy ridge to a spring and old log cabin. Go straight up the ridge above the cabin to a .4-mile long narrow flat area of grass and talus shown on the map as an open area at (9,300 feet. This area has no water in or near it. You can also reach here by descending 500 feet in .5 mile from the trail over Castle Divide. To do this, cut west along the south edge of the timber.
From the 9,300-foot flat open area, the route to Castle Lake is slippery and only for experts. It angles up the ridge of white gravel to the right toward Baker Lake. Where gravel covers solid rock, use extreme caution. Circle the end of the ridge and then drop west to the lake (9,419 feet) at 1.5 miles.

Castle Lake

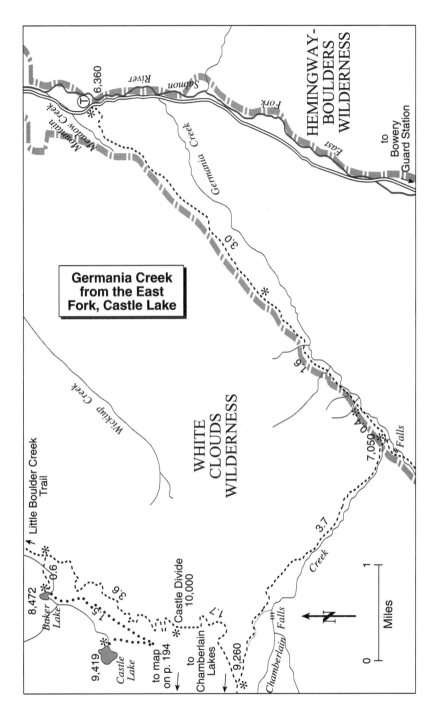

Germania Creek
from the East
Fork, Castle Lake

HEMINGWAY-
BOULDERS
WILDERNESS

to
Bowery
Guard Station

East Fork

Salmon River

6,360

Germania Creek

Mountain Meadow Creek

3.0

WHITE
CLOUDS
WILDERNESS

Wickiup Creek

1.6

7,050

0.4

Falls

Little Boulder Creek Trail

8,472
Baker Lake

0.6

3.6

1.5

Castle Divide
10,000

to map
on p. 194

to
Chamberlain
Lakes

9,419
Castle Lake

9,260

3.7

Creek

Chamberlain Falls

N

Miles

0   1

109.

BAKER LAKE TO NOISY AND QUIET LAKES

This one-way section: 2 miles, 770-foot elevation gain from Baker
Lake
Round trip: 19.6 miles from the Little Boulder Creek trailhead.
Elevation gain: 3,482 feet **Highest point:** 9,242 feet
Elevation loss (return climb): 1,280 feet

Map: Boulder Chain Lakes
Trail beginning GPS: 44 05.056, 114 26.727 at the East Fork Road
Difficulty: cross-country for experts; time: 3 to 4 days
Access: Following directions for Little Boulder Creek to the Boulder
Chain Lakes and for Baker Lake, hike 7.8 miles to Baker Lake.

What you'll see: A pointed orange and gray peak guards the upper
end of jade-green Noisy Lake. From the south side of the lake, apricot
and gray cliffs climb the side of Serrate Ridge, with, a waterfall splash-
ing down in a niche. Above Quiet Lake, Castle Peak spreads out into a
network of avalanche troughs and outcrops resembling roof gables.
From the upper end of this lake, the orange pleats and sawteeth of Serrate Ridge zigzag along. The cross-country climb up the ledges above
Baker Lake is difficult and can be hazardous for those with backpacks.
Directions: At Baker Lake (8,472 feet), cross the log bridge over the
outlet if it is still there or ford it, go around the south side of the lake,
ignoring the old mine road leading toward Castle Lake. Ford the inlet
in a marsh and walk up its right (west) side to a talus slope with grass
below it. A waterfall appears to the right on Slickenside Creek, which
joins the inlet here. Climb northwest up ledges beside this creek, staying well to the right of it. Descending these ledges with a pack is more
difficult than going up, but this is rugged hiking even going uphill.
At the top of the ledges, 400 feet above Baker Lake, continue along
the right (north) side of the creek through forest and granite benches
to Noisy Lake (8,997 feet) at 1.2 miles.
Then edge the north side of the lake in woods, cross the inlet on slippery logs, and climb along the left (south) side of this inlet to the lower
end of Quiet Lake (9,242 feet) at 2 miles. To continue to the upper end
at 2.5 miles, ford the outlet and go along the west shore of the lake
across grass and talus.

Scree Lake

THE BOULDER CHAIN LAKES TO SHALLOW, SCREE, AND QUIET LAKES

This one-way section: 2.1 miles, 397-foot elevation gain, 918-foot elevation loss from the ninth Boulder Chain Lake (Scoop Lake)
Round trip: 26.4 miles from the East Fork Salmon River Road
Elevation gain: 3,825 feet **Highest point:** 10,160 feet
Elevation loss (return climb): 1,743 feet
Map: Boulder Chain Lakes
Trail beginning GPS: 44 05.056, 114 26.727 at the East Fork Road
Difficulty: expert; time: 4 to 5 days
Access: Following directions under Little Boulder Creek Trail to the Boulder Chain Lakes and Frog Lake and the Boulder Chain Lakes, hike 11.1 miles for the Little Boulder Creek Trail to the ninth lake, Scoop Lake.

What you'll see: The triangular towers of Serrate Ridge zigzag across the canyon from the turquoise water and pale orange granite of Scree Lake. At Shallow Lake, .2 mile above it, blocks of granite create white islands above the water and pale green rectangles beneath it. Above the head of the lake, a gray tower guards a dangerous notch called the Devils Staircase. Less than a mile to the north of Shallow Lake is the ninth Boulder Chain Lake, Scoop Lake, which is shaped like the scoop of an earth mover. From it the trail climbs south through a pass called Windy Devil, goes out onto a shelf and ends. From the shelf, hikers can descend cross-country to Shallow and Scree Lakes, and then climb down a hidden slot in the rocks to Quiet Lake.
Directions: From Scoop Lake (9,643 feet), the trail switchbacks across talus to the pass in the ridge called Windy Devil at .8 mile. From the trail, you can see the tenth lake, Headwall, on a rocky shelf to the west. Snow lingers on the trail here as late as mid-August. Beyond the pass, the trail turns right (west) and climbs an additional 150 feet to a flat, rocky basin where it ends 1.5 miles from Scoop Lake.
Back at .7 mile where the trail turned right (west) out into the basin, keep straight ahead off- trail to Shallow Lake (9,635 feet). Descend a ridge to the lake at 1.3 miles. From here, continue down the north side of its outlet to Scree Lake (9,550 feet). A few campsites are along this creek.
To descend from here to Quiet Lake, go around the north side of Scree Lake and then down its outlet on the left (northeast). Angle east away from the creek a few yards to find the secret slot in the cliffs. Descend the slot and follow the canyon of the outlet until it bends to the left (east) and the pink granite ledges stop. Then ford the creek and to the south side and go south away from it. In .2 mile is the lower end of Quirt Lake ((9,242 feet)) at 2.1 miles.

111.

GERMANIA CREEK FROM THE EAST FORK TO CHAMBERLAIN CREEK

Round trip: 10 miles from the Germania Creek trailhead on the East Fork of the Salmon River to Chamberlain Creek; trail continues to Three Cabins Creek; connects with Chamberlain Creek and Bowery Cutoff trails.
Elevation gain: 680 feet **Highest point:** 7,040 feet
Elevation loss (return climb): 440 feet
Maps: Bowery Creek, Boulder Chain Lakes
Trailhead GPS: 44 03.005, 114 27.889
Difficulty: strenuous to expert; time: 9 hours
Access: On Idaho 75, 37.6 miles east of Stanley, turn south on the East Fork of the Salmon River Road. It is paved for 14.6 miles, gravel for 2.9 miles, and dirt for the last 5.3 miles. The trail begins at a parking area 22.8 miles from the highway (3.2 miles beyond the Little Boulder Transfer Camp.)

What you'll see: Brown, peach and dark gray cliffs line the canyon walls above this trail, which follows the canyon of Germania Creek only after the first 3.5 miles. The farther up you travel, the higher and more dramatic are the cliffs, and the closer are the fluted triangular peaks in the distance. There is lots of sagebrush, with some Douglas fir. Aspens and willows line the creek and the few side streams, but the area is very dry with only two-inch high grasses between the sagebrush. There are no campsites for the first 4.5 miles because there is either no water or no flat ground. Upriver from Chamberlain Creek .2 mile, waterfalls on Germania Creek are hidden from the trail, and up Chamberlain Creek is another set of falls.

Directions: Reaching Chamberlain Creek requires fording 30-foot-wide Germania Creek twice, so this hike is best for late summer if you plan to go all the way to Chamberlain Creek. Earlier in the summer, it is easier to reach Chamberlain Creek from the Three Cabins Creek Trailhead at the upper end of Germania Creek because the two fords of Germania Creek on that part of the trail are not as wide and deep.

From the trailhead (6,360 feet), the trail climbs around a crumbly rock outcrop, and then in rolling sagebrush. It splits into three trails as it climbs a steep, rocky hill at .5 mile. The center trail is the most direct but steepest. Beyond the top of the hill, the trails rejoin and head down into the little canyon formed by Mountain Meadow Creek. Here the trail goes over talus for 150 yards at the edge of willows. Then it comes out on a flat dry meadow surrounded by sagebrush. Above on the right, are pink and brown cliffs, and on the left is a wooded hill with more cliffs. Beyond the meadow, the trail descends 100 feet to a dry wash at 1.5 miles. Here you can see into the canyon of Germania

Creek on the left.

Now the trail climbs beside a 200-foot rock knoll and at 2 miles is on the right side of its summit. The trail goes through a little defile that is filled with firs and then descends 100 feet. There are 500-foot brown cliffs to the left along Germania Creek Canyon, which is still .3 mile away. The trail climbs past the right side of another knoll through aspens, staying 200 feet below its crumbly, summit at 3 miles. On the right are more peach and brown cliffs. Next the trail descends 250 feet. Part way down it splits, into two branches. Keep to the right here through the aspens because it is level, though muddy. After the branches rejoin at 3.3 miles, the trail crosses a small creek.

Beyond this creek, the trail climbs the left side of a knoll, goes over talus for 100 yards, and descends onto a sagebrush flat. After a short climb, it crosses another stream at 3.6 miles. Here you can see Germania Creek rushing along below and a knoll of brown rock columns ahead on the right. At 4.2 miles, the trail crosses another stream. The trail goes along in willows and rounded river stones to an apparent ford at 4.4 miles. Instead of crossing, the trail goes up around a little knoll and then along in the grass beside willows. It reaches a ford to the left (south) side of the creek shown on the map at 4.6 miles. You have to ford here because 60-foot brown cliffs drop into the water on the right (northwest) The creek is 20 feet wide and knee-deep in early August.

The trail fords back in 500 yards and continues along open and wooded flats to a ford of Chamberlain Creek at 5 miles (7,050 feet). Just before this ford, a little-used trail turns right (northwest) up Chamberlain Creek. It leads 3.7 miles to the Chamberlain Lakes. After fording Chamberlain Creek, the Germania Creek Trail crosses a sagebrush hillside and climbs in woods where gray rock knolls between the trail and the creek hide Germania Creek Falls. From here it is 6.2 miles and a 1,210-foot climb from Chamberlain Creek up Germania Creek to Three Cabins Creek Beyond the hidden falls, the trail fords to the south side of the creek into a meadow. Just beyond the meadow on a steep bank is a junction with the Bowery Cutoff Trail. That trail leads 4.5 miles in a 1,600-foot climb and 2,000-foot descent to the Bowery Guard Station, which is just beyond the end of the road up the East Fork of the Salmon River.

Titus Lake in the Smoky Mountains

TRAILS IN THE SMOKY MOUNTAINS

On the east side of Idaho 75, across from the Boulders rises a small section of the Smoky Mountains,. This range runs east and west along the South Fork of the Boise River. A few close together trails that are in these Smokies provide easy hikes. One of the mountains in this range is Baldy the main ski hill at Sun Valley. On my first time in the Smokes I took my mother and four of my kids to Baker Lake. The trail then was one mile straight up. It was such a steep trail l had to hike most of it myself to see how far it was before my mother would agree to go on up it. Since then the trail has been made into a two-mile much more gentle walk. The Smokies are more rounded with cliffs only here and there, but you may see pikas in the rocks carrying grass and plants to their burrows for winter food or hear their warning cries of "peep, peep!"

GALENA AREA

112.

HEADWATERS OF THE SALMON RIVER

Round trip: 5 miles from first crossing of the river beyond Chemetkan Campground; connects with the trail down Big Smoky Creek to the South Fork of the Boise River Road

Elevation gain: 700 feet **Highest point:** 8,300 feet

Maps: Frenchman Creek, Galena

GPS at official trailhead: 43 48.826, 114 45.144; GPS at first ford of river: 43 49.686, 114 95.309.

Difficulty: easy; time: 4 hours

Access: From Idaho 75, at the bottom of the Galena Summit grade in Sawtooth Valley, 34.1 miles north of Ketchum, (26.8 miles south of Stanley) turn left (south) at a sign for the Salmon River Road. Two branches from the highway join to form this gravel road (216). At 1 mile, turn right at a sign for Chemetkan Campground. (The road to the left is the section of The Old Toll Road that climbs from here to Galena Summit (220) and is open to motor vehicles.) At 3.2 miles, just before the campground, the road fords a creek and becomes primitive. Continue 1.5 miles beyond the campground on this road to a ford of the river 4.7 miles from the highway. Park before the ford because driving across the river here stirs up silt that can damage salmon spawning habitat downstream. By early fall, there is often no water in the river here and you can drive farther.

250

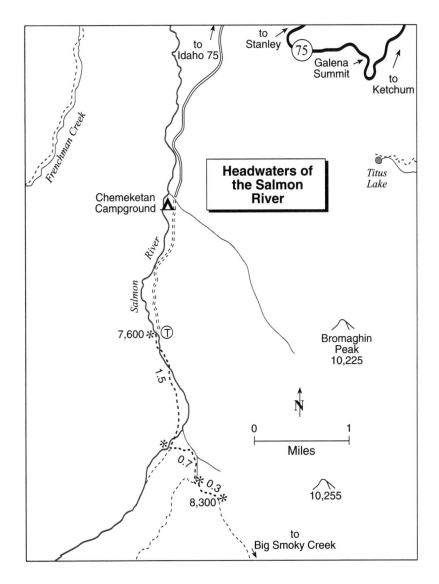

What you'll see: This easy hike leads you to the place where one of the two highest branches of the main Salmon River begins in a wild-flower meadow. This meadow is just below the divide between the Salmon River and the Boise River drainages. East of the meadow, two lumpy, gray shoulders of a peak named Bromaghin (10,225 feet) over-look the infant river. In the meadow, rivulets collect into a three-foot wide stream which rushes down a ravine for a mile to join the other branch and begin the Salmon River. (The beginning of the slightly longer branch to the west is more difficult to reach and requires cross-

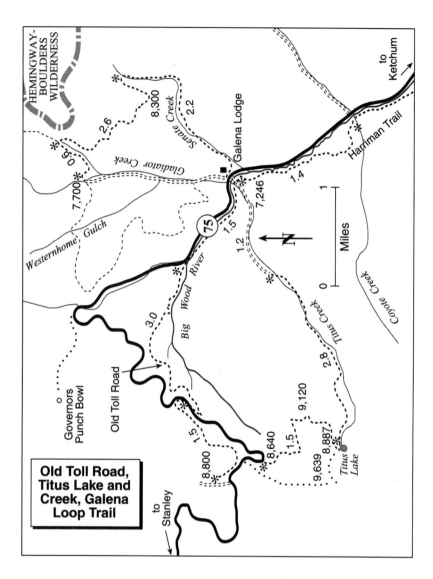

country hiking.) Beyond the end of the meadow and the divide, tiers of cliffs decorate the canyon wall of Big Smoky Creek, a tributary of the Boise River. The headwaters of the Salmon River divide the Sawtooth Mountains on the west and north from the Smoky Mountains on the east and south.

Directions: Park before the ford 4.7 miles from the highway (7,600 feet), ford the river and walk up the road. It fords the river or a branch of it four more times in the next .3 mile. There are no logs for hikers, so if the water is deep, it is easiest to wade the river only once to the

right (west) side and walk cross-country between the pieces of road.
From the last of the fords, walk up the jeep trail as it climbs gently
up and down in forest. At 1.1 miles, it fords the east branch of the river
to the left (east) where there are some campsites in a grassy area. At 1.3
miles, the road branches. Follow the left (east) branch here to a closed
gate at 1.5 miles. (The other branch is blocked off in about 150 yards.)
The gate is the official trailhead, but driving this far is not recommended unless your car has four-wheel drive and a high wheelbase.

Take a path around the gate and continue walking up the old road
which makes two switchbacks and then winds south along the edge of
a 60-foot gorge. At 2.2 miles, turn left (east) off the jeep trail onto a pack
trail. This trail drops into the lower end of the meadow and fords the
three-foot wide river at 2.3 miles, which begins as springs in the
meadow. The trail goes around the left (northeast) side of the meadow
to the divide (8,300 feet) at 2.5 miles. From here, the Big Smoky Creek
Trail descends 2,920 feet in 18.5 miles to the Canyon Campground,
which can be reached by road from Fairfield or Featherville. For a
view of the rugged canyon of Big Smoky Creek, continue downhill .5
mile.

If you want to see the longer tributary of the river, go back .3 mile to
where you left the old jeep trail. Turn left (south) and walk up the jeep
trail as it climbs 200 feet to a view of Bromaghin Peak and the second
branch of the river. To reach the head of the longer branch, continue
along the old jeep trail, which goes along the side of the ridge to a saddle at 1.5 miles. Then leave the track, go west cross-country along the
ridge, and descend to the center stream at 2.2 miles from the saddle (4.4
miles from where you parked before the ford).

113.

TITUS LAKE AND TITUS CREEK

Round trip: 3 miles from the Titus Lake Trailhead on Highway 75;
through trip to Titus Creek Road 4.3 miles
Elevation gain: 480 feet
Elevation loss (return climb): 233 feet
Highest point: 9,120 feet
Map: Galena
Trailhead GPS: 43 52.039, 114 42.984; trail beginning on Titus Creek
Road: 43 51.996, 114 40.496
Difficulty: easy except slippery sections, expert for cross-country
side trip to peak; time: 3 ? hours
Access: On Idaho 75, 29.3 miles north of Ketchum (31.7 miles south
of Stanley), park .3 mile south of Galena Summit in a large turnout on
the east side of the road.

What you'll see: In July, once the snow melts, blueflax, shooting

Old Toll Road

star, phlox, and arrowleaf balsamroot color the slopes along the trail to Titus Lake. Willows and mountain bluebells separate its cloudy emerald green water from a marshy meadow. A gray and orange ridge of crumbled ledges overlooks the miniature lake. Southeast across Titus Creek, grooves divide the scalloped cliffs of the canyon wall into lobes. On the southwest, cliffs and snowbanks slope up to the pointed top of Bromaghin Peak. Please keep off the meadows at the lower end of the lake to avoid damaging the plants and grasses

From the summits of either of two unnamed peaks north of the lake, the jagged mountains of six ranges stretch in every direction. They are the Sawtooths, Salmon River Mountains, White Clouds, Boulders, Pioneers, and Smokies. An alternate route to or from the lake via the Titus Creek Trail provides a shady walk with views of the Boulder Mountains and of the peaks at the head of Titus Creek.

Directions: Watching carefully for traffic, go west across the highway from the large parking area (8,640 feet). This trailhead parking is at the curve of the highest big hairpin south of Galena Summit. Walk south along a wide trail for 100 yards to where a trail turns off to the left (southeast). Take this trail across a small creek at .1 mile and another at .5 mile. Here it turns left (east) in forest and runs along the side of a ridge, gradually climbing to the top of a wrinkle in the ridge (9,000 feet) at .8 mile. Then it climbs south over another wrinkle at 1 mile (9,120 feet). From here, it dips southwest into the canyon of the north branch of Titus Creek. As it starts down, it is steep and slippery. Watch your step:. I fell here several years ago and broke my wrist. At 1.2 miles, the trail turns west and descends 233 feet to the lake (8,887 feet) at 1.5 miles.

Experts can climb cross-country to the west .3 mile above the lake onto a saddle between Peaks 9,921 and 9,636 and walk up either peak for a view. It is also possible to walk north from Peak 9,636 down the ridge to Galena Summit, or climb it from there. By this route it is 1.5 miles from the lake to the highway.

It is also fun to return by way of Titus Creek. That trail descends 1,320 feet in 2.8 miles to a road (188) that leads 1.2 miles to the highway across from Galena Lodge. To find this trail at the lake, take a path going off to the left (east) along the near side of the meadow by the outlet. Stay close to the creek, and you will find the trail in the sagebrush .descending to Titus Creek. At 1 mile, it moves away from the creek into a forest of lodgepoles and Douglas fir. After crossing a side stream twice, it goes over a rocky point where there are cliffs below. Then it switchbacks to the right and fords the creek to the right (southeast) side at 2 miles. Now the ground flattens out and the trail traverses boggy places.

At 2.3 miles, it reaches an old road, but is still the trail. At 2.6 miles it fords the creek to the left (north) side and becomes an official road (188) A big parking area is at 2.8 miles (7,560 feet). This flat area is 1.2 miles from the highway, which it meets across from Galena Lodge.

On the trail and road, be sure to watch for horses. Guided rides go up the Titus Creek Road and trail every day. Be sure to give any horses plenty of room. If in a car, stop, and if on the trail step downhill to let them by, and say something so the horses will know you are a person.

114.

THE OLD TOLL ROAD

Through trip: 6 miles from Galena Summit to Galena Lodge, where it connects with the Harriman Trail. At the Galena Summit end, it continues as a dirt road (220) open to vehicles that leads down into Sawtooth Valley. The trip requires a car shuttle or is a 12 mile round trip.
Elevation gain: 100 feet **Highest point:** 8,800 feet
Elevation loss: 1,510 feet
Maps: Galena, Horton Peak
GPS at summit: 43 52.378, 114 42.984
Difficulty: easy; time: 4 hours
Access: On Idaho 75, drive 27.3 miles north of Ketchum to Galena Summit. Descend the other side .2 mile, turn right uphill onto a spur road and park. Walk up this dirt road 100 yards to where it branches, then take the right branch and look for a trail to the right (south).

What you'll see: Following the section of this historic road from Galena Summit down to Galena Lodge will give you an idea of what it must have been like to drive a horse and wagon or a Model T up and down this grade. It has superb views of the crumbling gray and beige cliffs of the Boulder Mountains. In the upper section, you can see the walls of hand-placed stone that support the old road bed. Part way down the lower section are the remnants of a wooden trestle that once spanned a small branch of the Big Wood River.

Galena Lodge, where this hike ends, is a mountain biking and cross-country ski center. Its site was once in Galena, the first town in the area, beginning in 1879. Before then no one had settled in the upper Wood River area because of Indian problems even though Warren Callahan discovered the lead ore, galena, there in 1864.

Directions: These directions start at the Galena Summit end of this trail section because that allows you a hike or ride that is all downhill. A new trail connects the spur road from the highway to the top of the Old Toll Road at 8,800 feet. This trail starts out parallel to the highway 100 feet above it. It climbs gently to a point right above Galena Summit at .2 mile. Then the toll road descends to the east with a great view of the Boulder Mountains across the canyon of the Big Wood River ahead. Except for omitting the big curve at the Titus Lake trailhead, and going back into side canyons, the track continues to parallel the highway. At .5 mile, it goes into a side canyon and is overgrown with trees. When it comes back out again, it is just above the highway on a sagebrush slope with scattered trees. Here you can see some of the rock work as it crosses the gullies. At 1.2 miles, the track goes back into another side canyon, and hairpins around a rocky knoll. Just above the highway, the road narrows to a trail where the roadbed has collapsed. It widens to road width just before it crosses the highway to the south side at 1.5 miles.

Be sure to watch carefully for traffic, including bicycles, as you cross the highway. From here the trail cuts down to the west (right), then switchbacks down into a grassy area at the edge of forest. It parallels the highway once more at 2 miles. It is now single track instead of the old road it was above the highway. At 2.3 miles, the trail heads into the same canyon where it rounded the knoll above the highway. As you approach where the canyon curves south, you can see the Alexander Ross sign 200 feet above. The trail fords a creek at this curve. After running below outcrops, it goes back into another canyon and crosses the creek a second time at 2.5 miles. This canyon is not shown on the maps.

Next, the trail comes out onto sagebrush, curves around a knoll with a rock nubbin, and hairpins to the right. It goes across a gully on fill, and then hairpins again in sagebrush. Now you are walking above a grassy area, parallel to the highway, The trail now leaves the old road bed, and descends a short steep slope to cross a creek on planks at 3 miles. Upstream a few yards, you can see the remnants of an old wooden trestle.

The track follows the canyon of the creek and turns south with it. Now a wooded hill and gullies separate the toll road from the highway. At 4.2 miles, the track hairpins to the left and you can see the highway below. It switchbacks right and comes out beside the highway at 4.5 miles, with a branch of the Big Wood River between it and the pavement. There is a pullout next to the highway here.

Turn south on a faint track and follow the highway. In 200 yards, after the side creek joins the Big Wood River, the trail crosses the river on a log bridge, so that the river is between the toll road and the highway. Next it goes through boggy grass, crosses Enid Creek at 5 miles, and goes uphill into forest.

After the trail nears the highway again, it splits. The steep right-hand trail looks well used. However, the toll road goes off to the left here close to the highway, where the tread becomes distinct. It climbs up on a wooded bench where you can see Galena Lodge and its parking area across the highway. On the bench are piles of old boards – all that is left of the settlement of Galena. The trail passes cabins (private property) and meets the Titus Creek Road (188) at 6 miles (7,320 feet). The Titus Creek Road leads a few yards east to the highway just south of Galena Lodge, passing the upper end of the Harriman Trail on the way.

PRAIRIE CREEK AREA

115.

MILL LAKE

Round trip: 4 miles from the Prairie Creek Road

Miner Lake

Elevation gain: 1,060 feet **Highest point:** 8,222 feet
Map: Galena
Trailhead GPS: 43 48.342, 114 36.458
Difficulty: moderate; time: 4 hours
Access: On Idaho 75, drive 19 miles north of Ketchum. Turn left (west) onto the gravel Prairie Creek Road (179) and drive 2.2 miles to a sign for Mill Lake.

What you'll see: Driftwood and dark gray talus surround the aqua-green water of Mill Lake below the crumbled cliffs and pointed cap of Norton Peak. From the peak, square crags form a wall. on the west side of the lake An outcrop high above the opposite side of the lake resembles a lover's leap. There is no real inlet, so the water line lowers as the summer passes.

Directions: At a sign for Mill Lake, turn left off the main road and park near the creek. The trail begins by fording Prairie Creek at 7,160 feet into forest. This will be difficult in early summer. At first, the trail is an old jeep track that is open to motorcycles but not to motor vehicles. At .5 mile, it crosses Mill Creek to the right (west) side, shrinks to single track, and begins to climb. At 1 mile, it returns to the east side of the creek and enters a valley of wildflowers. After 200 yards, the trail climbs into forest to the left, then curves right, climbing steeply. At 1.3 miles, it recrosses the creek and then goes along to the right of a big open area. The next part is the hardest because it has no shade and climbs 300 feet over ball-bearing gravel. Be very careful here. Just before the lake (8,222 feet), it tops a little rise and descends to the woods along the east shore at 2 miles.

116.

MINER LAKE

Round trip: 8 miles from the Prairie Creek trailhead; connects with trails to Norton and to Prairie lakes.
Elevation gain: 1,570 feet **Highest point:** 8,770 feet
Map: Galena
Trailhead GPS: 43 48.233, 114 38.604
Difficulty: moderate; time: 6 hours
Access: On Idaho 75, drive 19 miles north of Ketchum. Turn left (west) onto the gravel Prairie Creek Road (179) and go 2.6 miles. The trail starts on the left (south) side of the parking area.

What you'll see: Bleached driftwood and feathery horsetails surround the jade green water of Miner Lake. Under the water, logs create brown stripes. On the south talus slopes and wildflowers climb to the pointed top of Norton Peak. On the east the crags above have shed many rocks onto the shore.

Directions: From the Prairie Creek Road (7,200 feet), the trail first fords the West Fork of Prairie Creek and turns south. It climbs for 1 mile along the west (right) side of Prairie Creek, beside emerald green moss and yellow monkey flower. At a meadow at 1.2 miles, the view back is of pink, gray, and cream stripes of the Boulder Mountains. A second meadow is at 1.7 miles and another is at 2 miles.

The trail to Miner Lake splits off to the southeast at 2.5 miles (7,680 feet). That trail is closed to motorcycles and is not recommended for mountain bikes. The Prairie Creek Trail is open to both. Take the Miner Lake Trail across Prairie Creek and into the woods. In the next 1.5 miles, it climbs 1,100 feet. At 3.5 miles, it crosses the outlet of the lake to a paintbrush meadow. It continues through forest and meadows below a talus ridge to the lake (8,770 feet) at 4 miles. Just before the lake is a junction with a trail to Prairie Lakes, and on the far side of Miner Lake, a faint trail over a pass to Norton Lakes climbs the headwall.

117.

PRAIRIE LAKES

This one-way section: 2.5 miles with 1,020 feet elevation gain from the Miner Lake junction

Round trip: 10 miles from Prairie Creek trailhead; connects with trails to Miner Lake and to the West Fork of Norton Creek

Elevation gain: 1,500 feet **Highest point:** 8,701 feet

Map: Galena

Trailhead GPS: 43 48.233, 114 38.604

Difficulty: moderate; time: 7 hours

Access: On Idaho 75, drive 19 miles north of Ketchum. Turn left (west) onto the gravel Prairie Creek Road (179) and go 2.6 miles The trail starts on the left (south) side of the parking area.

What you'll see: On the way to the lake, furrowed and cracked peaks line Prairie Creek Canyon. Logs thatched with bright green grass edge the apple green water of the largest Prairie Lake. Twisted stripes of chocolate brown etch the face of a peak south of the lake.

Directions: This hike description begin at the Miner Lake Junction (7,680 feet), 2.5 miles up the Miner-Prairie Lakes Trail. To reach Prairie Lakes, continue straight ahead. Cliffs hang over the trail at 1.2 miles. At 2.2 miles, in a marshy meadow, it crosses Prairie Creek and reaches the largest lake (8,701 feet) at 2.5 miles. A large campsite is on the south shore. Two miniature lakes hide 200 yards over a rise to the east. A third tiny lake is .5 mile to the northwest of them. A trail leads to Miner Lake from here that allows a loop hike. Beyond the largest Prairie Lake, a trail leads over a pass and down the West Fork of Norton Creek to the Norton Lakes trailhead.

260

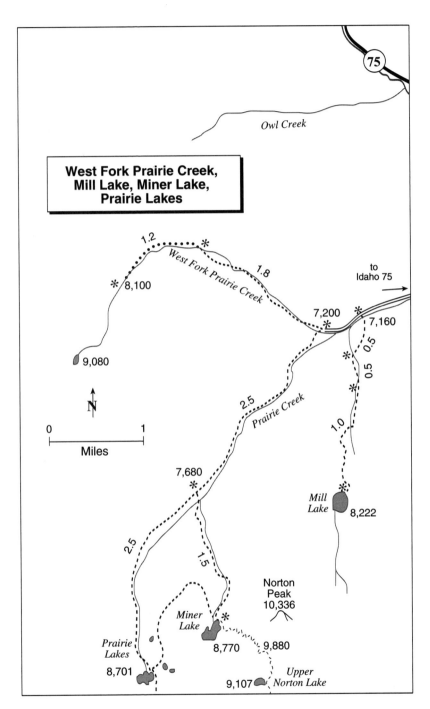

West Fork Prairie Creek,
Mill Lake, Miner Lake,
Prairie Lakes

Owl Creek

1.2

West Fork Prairie Creek

1.8

to
Idaho 75

* 8,100

7,200

7,160

0.5

0.5

9,080

N

0   1

Miles

2.5

Prairie Creek

1.0

7,680

Mill
Lake

8,222

2.5

1.5

Norton
Peak
10,336

Miner
Lake

*

Prairie
Lakes

8,770

9,880

8,701

9,107

Upper
Norton Lake

261

118.

WEST FORK PRAIRIE CREEK

Round trip: 6 miles from the Prairie Creek Road
Elevation gain: 880 feet **Highest point:** 8,080 feet
Map: Galena
Trailhead GPS: 43 48.233, 114 38.604
Difficulty: expert; time: 5 to 6 hours
Access: On Idaho 75, drive north of Ketchum for 19 miles. Turn left (west) onto the gravel Prairie Creek Road (179). Drive 2.6 miles to its end. This trail angles off to the right (west).

What you'll see: This faint trail provides a pleasant early summer walk through wildflowers to a meadow with a view of fluted peaks streaked with snow. Flowers varying with the season include forget-me-not, cinquefoil, penstemon, umbrella plant, phlox, horsemint, arnica, mountain bluebell and arrowleaf balsamroot, Above the flowers rise high cliffs of dark gray, purple, and yellow orange. The trail is little used, perhaps because it fords the creek near the beginning.

Directions: From the Prairie Creek Road at 7,200 feet, the trail angles off to the right (northwest) across a rocky flat that is usually full of wildflowers. At 350 yards, the trail climbs along talus above the creek. Then it drops and fords the creek to the left (southwest). By mid-July, the creek often runs underground a few feet above the ford. You can cross without getting your feet wet.

Next, the trail climbs away from the creek into woods. Across the creek at a big talus slope with charcoal gray cliffs above, you may see mountain goats. At .3 mile, is an open area with scattered aspens and Douglas fir. Across the canyon, talus slope and cliffs continue. The trail descends to a flat area of sagebrush and snowbrush beside the creek, which has water in it again. Then it goes 100 feet up into forest above a beaver pond. As the forest dwindles, the trail follows the creek bottom. At 1 mile, it crosses a small side creek and climbs to the left up a rocky step in the canyon. Just below the step Is a 40-foot-long pool. By mid-July, the creek lacks water above the step for several hundred yards.

Now the trail cuts over to the right of the dry creek below multicolored cliffs At 1.2 miles, the trail crosses back to the left side of the canyon in gravel. Now the trail goes level along the edge of willows, and then at the edge of a meadow. At 1.8 miles, it goes through forest then out into willows. Here it crosses the creek to the right (north) side and becomes faint.

Continue as best you can through willows, forest and sagebrush above the creek. At 2.2 miles, it crosses a rockslide with a definite tread. Ahead are avalanched trees and triangular peaks with snow filling their pleats. The route goes up onto a rocky slope right below an avalanche chute. Stay right (north) of the creek as you follow the path

262

to where it disappears in a wildflower meadow (8,100 feet) at 3 miles. One mile and 850 feet above it to the southwest is a tiny lake (9,100 feet), which you can reach by hiking cross-country.

NORTH FORK AREA

119.

THE HARRIMAN TRAIL

Through trip: 19.2 miles from Galena Lodge to the Sawtooth National Recreation Area Headquarters; connects with the Old Toll Road to Galena Summit.

Elevation gain or loss: 1,060 feet, plus ups and downs not on maps
Highest point: 7,500 feet

Maps: Amber Lakes, Easley Hot Springs, Galena; and the brochure "Summer Trails: The Harriman Trail and Galena Lodge"

The Harriman Trail

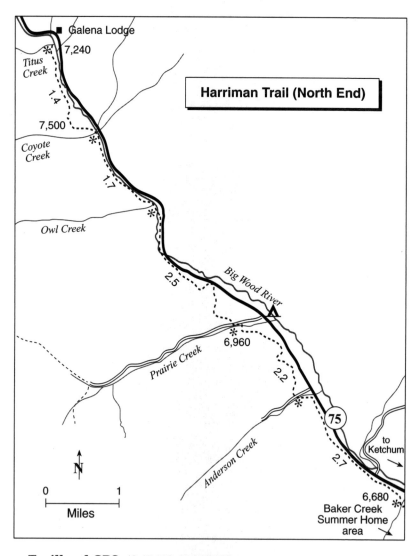

Trailhead GPS: 43 47.118, 114 25.197

Difficulty: Easy to strenuous depending on distance time: 12 hours for the whole trail on foot. In winter it is a groomed cross-country ski trail.

Access: There are five main access points along the trail: the Sawtooth National Recreation Area Headquarters 8 miles north of Ketchum on Idaho 75, the Wood River Campground, Baker Creek, Prairie Creek, and Galena Lodge.

What you'll see: You will see many aspens along the trail, so its

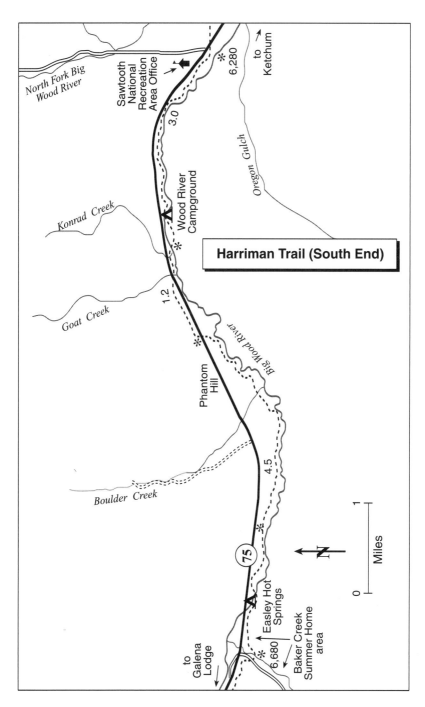

Harriman Trail (South End)

North Fork Big Wood River

Sawtooth National Recreation Area Office

to Ketchum

6,280

3.0

Oregon Gulch

Konrad Creek

Wood River Campground

Goat Creek

1.2

Big Wood River

Phantom Hill

Boulder Creek

4.5

75

N

Miles

1

0

Easley Hot Springs

Baker Creek Summer Home area

6,680

to Galena Lodge

265

logo is aspen leaves. In the fall, the aspens blaze gold and orange, and in summer wildflowers create a multicolored display. The most interesting part of the trail is the upper 5.6 miles between Galena Lodge and Prairie Creek. That's because it climbs over two rocky viewpoints, Hawk's Hill, and a mountain goat viewing site. South of Prairie Creek the pink and gray cliffs and twisted stripes of Easley Peak (11,108 feet), Silver Peak (11,112 feet), and Boulder Peak (10,981 feet) stand across the river.

Directions: The surface of the whole trail is fine gravel and it is the width of a narrow road to allow room for a ski groomer in winter. People starting on the trail at its beginning at the SNRA Headquarters must park at the headquarters and carefully cross the highway to the trailhead because there is no parking where the trail starts and no crosswalk.

I recommend that through hikers and mountain bikers start at the upper end, to take advantage of the trail's 1,000-foot descent. The trail has a lot of ups and downs that are not included in this 1,000 feet, and which are difficult to calculate since the elevation changes aren't shown on the maps. Many people will start from the lower end because it is closer to Ketchum and Sun Valley. Therefore, this description starts at the lower end. Distances given here may not agree with all mile markers.

The trail begins by curving over to the Big Wood River and back and wanders along near the highway in aspens. At .6 mile, it crosses the road into the North Fork Campground. The trail continues as before winding along in the aspens. At the Wood River Campground road, it turns left (west) on the campground road and follows it across the river into the day use area at 2.5 miles.

From the day use parking the trail climbs a hillside and then up and along in lodgepoles and Douglas firs. It passes under cliffs and towers, and at 3 miles crosses back to the north side of the river on the Murphy Bridge. The wide steel and wood bridge was named for a cross-country skier, Dick Murphy, who was killed in a plane crash in 1985.

Within .2 mile, the trail crosses the highway to its north side to avoid wetlands. It goes along in the sagebrush and then returns to the south side of the highway at 4.2 miles and detours around the hill known as Phantom Hill at 4.7 miles and then goes close to the river.

The trail crosses the road to the Cathedral Pines Camp at 7 miles. At 7.5 miles, it crosses the road to the Easley swimming pool and enters Easley Campground, detours to the right around it and returns to the river. At 7.9 miles, it crosses a slough of the river and the river itself to the left (south) side on bridges. The trail goes west through the Boulder View Campground, and angles off to the left through sagebrush toward a cabin area. From here, is an excellent view of the pink and gray stripes of the Boulder Mountains. Now the river is across the highway from the trail until a couple of miles northwest of Prairie Creek.

Beyond the cabins, the trail goes into lodgepoles and reaches a sign in memory of Pamela Harriman, wife of Averell Harriman, the founder of Sun Valley. She helped get the original funding for the trail. The trail crosses Baker Creek (6,680 feet) on a cement bridge at 8.7

miles. Then it runs north along the creek and crosses the Baker Creek Road. There is no parking at or near this crossing. Those starting their hike or bike ride here, should park in the parking lot on the east side of the highway and walk from there along the Baker Creek Road to the trail. There is no parking right at the trail.

From the Baker Creek Road, the trail curves over near the highway, and goes along close to it. in the open. This section of the trail is less interesting and is hot on a sunny day. Soon there are cabins above. The trail curves back into the forest, crosses the Anderson Creek Road at 11.4 miles, and hairpins back toward the highway. It continues northwest in sagebrush, climbing up on a bench and passing a small hot spring. It angles away from the highway and crosses the gravel road to the Central Idaho 4-H camp at 12 miles. The next section goes up-and-down through forest. A bridge over Prairie Creek and a crossing of the Prairie Creek Road are at 13.6 miles.

A few yards to the left (west) is a large parking area. From here, the trail goes off to the left, into forest. Soon the trail turns away from the highway, climbing to cross a bridge over a small stream at 14.6 miles. It is called the Community Bridge to honor the many local donors who gave money to build it.

At 14.7 miles, the trail has climbed to the top of a ridge. Here a footpath goes northeast 30 yards to a mountain goat viewing site on top of an outcrop. Back on the trail, you go downhill past a natural rock bench at 14.9 miles. The trail descends farther, then climbs past an aspen grove and over some hills.

You are now are right across the river and highway from rock teeth on a hill. There is a tall outcrop between the trail and the river. The trail passes left of a large meadow. It curves and goes up and down, and at 16.1 miles goes over Owl Creek on a bridge. It then crosses the Owl Creek Road, a 4-wheel drive road that fords the river here. This road goes 4 miles up Owl Creek to a fine view of Bromaghin Peak.

Now the trail goes along level in sagebrush and woods. At 16.4 miles, it is beneath crumbly outcrops and across from big rock teeth. Next the trail crosses Coyote Creek, which has a picnic table at 17.8 miles, and heads back toward the highway. It climbs steeply, and goes along the highway in lodgepoles. It curves into a gully and out among small outcrops. It climbs to the top of an enormous outcrop that forms three giant stairsteps. The summit of this outcrop, known as Hawk's Hill, is at 18.5 miles.

The trail descends and curves back toward the highway. Here you can look back at the stairsteps of Hawk's Hill. The trail winds along in lodgepoles above willows, goes over a couple of little creeks, crosses Titus Creek on a bridge, and arrives at the upper trailhead (7,240 feet) at 19.2 miles. (31 kilometers from the trail's beginning). There is parking next to the highway or across it at Galena Lodge.

TRAILS IN THE BOULDER MOUNTAINS

Grand Prize Gulch

THE BOULDER MOUNTAINS

The Boulders are southeast of the White Clouds. You can see several of the peaks with swirling gray and pink stripes from Idaho 75 between Ketchum and Galena Summit They can also be reached from the road up the East Fork of the Salmon River from near Clayton. Lakes are scarce and tend to dry up in late summer. Many of the trails are poor, overgrown, and hard to follow, especially in the eastern section that is now the Jim McClure-Jerry Peak Wilderness. This wilderness is on the Salmon-Challis Forest and and managed by the Middle Fork District of that forest and by the Challis Field Office of the Bureau of Land Management, not the Sawtooth National Recreation Area. Because this wilderness is dry, only the tops of the mountains have timber. The peaks have gentle summits and any drama is found in the shapes of brown outcrops, which resemble gargoyles, ships or anything you can think up. Many of the plants are desert species, such as cacti, pinon pines, and evening primrose. The eastern Boulders are so dry that when I sat on a cactus at lunch one day it was so dried out that the spines were so floppy they didn't stick me.

Several years before that, when I went into the Boulders for the first time my Suburban got stuck in the creek at the bottom of the Boulder Basin Road. I had my mother and four of my kids with me. I had just started doing hikes for my guidebook and thought it would be a short hike because we could drive part way. We ended up having to walk along the highway a couple of miles to the swimming pool at Easley's where the woman in charge persuaded the director of the church camp there to pull us out with his backhoe. Later that summer I hired a babysitter and did the hike alone. It was supposed to be a road but there were few signs and even the road was hard to find and follow.

TRAILS IN THE BOULDER MOUNTAINS

POLE CREEK AREA

*120.

GOVERNORS PUNCHBOWL

Through trip: 4 miles

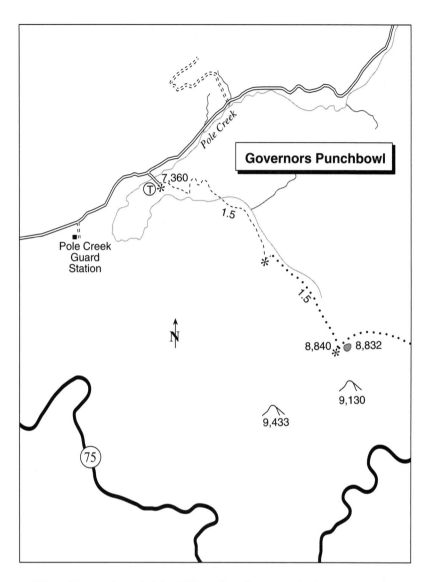

Pole Creek

Governors Punchbowl

7,360

1.5

Pole Creek
Guard
Station

1.5

N

8,840   8,832

9,130

9,433

75

Elevation gain: 1,360 feet **Elevation loss:** 960 feet
Highest point: 8,760 feet
Map: Horton Peak
Trailhead GPS: N 43 degrees, 54' 48.3", W 114 degrees, 42' 55.4". N 43
55 0.73, W 114 43 46.6
Difficulty: cross country for experts following route of old trail and
old stock driveway
Time: 6 hours
Access: To reach Pole Creek trailhead, turn east off Idaho 75 0.5

The Governors Punchbowl in late summer when it's dry

mile south of Smiley Creek Lodge onto the Pole Creek Road. Go 3.1 miles up Pole Creek , turn right, and go .2 mile. At the end of the new side road is a circle drive and on the southeast side of it a wide trail is signed Corrals ATV Trail.

What you'll see: This route to the Governors Punchbowl is much shadier and gentler than the steep climb from the highway on the old stock driveway. There are only traces of trail tread whichever way you go. When Alexander Ross discovered Galena Summit in 1824, he also discovered the pond and named it the Governors Punchbowl for George Simpson, who at the time was the "governor" of the Hudson Bay Fur Company in Vancouver, Washington. Some historians think Ross went over the divide above the Punchbowl, not over Galena Summit on this first trip, so the hike gives you a chance to follow in the probable footsteps of this famous explorer. It also gives you an excellent view of the Boulder Mountains.

Directions: Take the Corrals ATV trail, which soon crosses Pole Creek on a wide plank bridge. Continue walking up the trail, which climbs to a junction, where a sign, Corrals ATV trail , points to the right, and Rainbow to the left (east). Turn left here. The trail steepens and zigzags several times before fording Rainbow Creek. After another 200 feet of climb in forest, it descends to a branch of Rainbow Creek. About one mile from the trailhead, an old road turns off to the right. It

271

is closed to motorized travel. Walk up this road for about a half mile until it starts to go along the base of a talus slope on rocks.

Here turn left (east) off trail. This point is at N 43 degrees, 54' 3 W 114 degrees, 43' 46 over a small forested hill and down to Rainbow Creek. The distance from the road to the creek is about 0.3 mile. Now go up the canyon of Rainbow Creek, staying on its right (southwest) side in the woods. The aspen groves on the opposite side of the creek look tempting but have poor footing because of rocks. In the woods look for game trails and traces and blazes of the old trail that used to run up this canyon. At 2 miles is a grassy opening about 200 yards long. After this the route goes back into forest, until a series of meadows begin at 2.5 miles. The meadows lead up to a low point on the south skyline. In early summer these meadows are full of wildflowers. When the meadows end just below the divide, climb up about 200 feet through open forest to the divide, which has an excellent view of the Boulder Mountains, especially of Galena Peak.

Walk a few feet northwest until you overlook the murky green water of the Punchbowl, which is only about 250 yards long. By September the Punchbowl often has no water. An old road or a remnant of the old trail angles down about 100 vertical feet to the north end of the Punchbowl, which is about 2.5 miles from the trailhead.

From the Punchbowl there is supposed to be a pack trail down a stock driveway to where Idaho 75 crosses Horse Creek, but there are only traces of it. The route meets the highway at the first hairpin curve as the highway starts up Galena Summit from Galena Lodge. The slope descends about 1,000 feet in a mile on sagebrush slopes that are hot even in the fall. A compass or GPS will help make sure you are descending into the right canyon. If you get too far to the right (south) you'll end up on a extreme drop to the highway. The GPS at the small parking place at Horse Creek is N 43 degrees, 53', 47.0", W 114 degrees, 40', 52.3" The author recommends returning to Pole Creek from the Punchbowl, rather than descending to the highway at Horse Creek.

121.

GRAND PRIZE GULCH

Round trip: 9.4 miles from a spur road off the Pole Creek - Germania Creek Road to the top of a divide with Galena Gulch and a tiny lake; connects with West Fork East Fork trail to the Bowery trailhead

Elevation gain: 1,860 feet to top of the divide; additional 100 feet to a lake; **Highest point:** 9,560 feet

Map: Horton Peak

Trailhead GPS: 43 56.177, 114 41.564

Difficulty: expert; time: 7 hours

Access: On Idaho 75 turn right (east) 24.5 miles south of Stanley (36.4 miles north of Ketchum) onto the gravel Pole Creek - Germania

Creek Road (194). Keep right at the Pole Creek - Valley Road Junction at 2.3 miles. At 6.5 miles, turn right (east) on a dirt road (402) at a sign for Grand Prize Gulch and drive down to near where the road ends at the creek at 6.7 miles,.

What you'll see: The divide between the Grand Prize Gulch and Galena Gulch trails, has a view of high orange and charcoal gray peaks and crumbly cliffs typical of the Boulder Mountains. To the north are the creamy summits of the White Clouds. Near the divide, four rounded towers overlook a tiny amber lake.

Directions: From the trailhead (7,700 feet), ford Pole Creek and walk up the old closed road through small lodgepoles, avoiding side roads. At 1.5 miles, the old road fords the side creek to the east and switchbacks above it. Young trees are sprinkled over an old avalanche area across the creek. At a meadow, where a road branches to the right, keep straight ahead. At 2.3 miles, the road turns left uphill to a prospect. Turn off onto a trail to the right (signed "trail") that continues up the canyon.

The trail crosses a flat meadow, climbs to the low point (9,040 feet) on the skyline ahead at 3.3 miles, and levels out. At 3.5 miles, a cairn (9,040 feet) marks a junction with the Gladiator Creek Divide Trail which crosses the Boulder Mountains to a trailhead near Galena Lodge on Idaho 75.

Continue 100 yards on the main trail down the West Fork of the East Fork of the Salmon River. Then turn left onto the Galena Gulch Trail shown on the map. There is no path or sign for the trail. (The main trail descends the West Fork of the East Fork and the East Fork 9.5 miles with a 2,240-foot elevation loss to Bowery Guard Station.)

As you follow the route of the Galena Gulch Trail here toward the divide, it splits into paths which don't connect. Generally, the route angles northeast below a spring, which dries up in late summer. Then it circles below a rock knoll and heads straight up to the saddle (9,560 feet) at 4.2 miles.

To reach a tiny amber lake (9,620 feet) from the saddle, walk northeast between rock benches. This lake at 4.7 miles makes a fine destination, especially for those with children. Those with more energy will want to climb northeast from the divide and then north to look down on Deer Lakes from 9,960 feet. (See the detailed description for reaching the viewpoint under Galena Gulch.)

122.

GALENA GULCH

Round trip: 8 miles from the Pole Creek - Germania Creek Road;

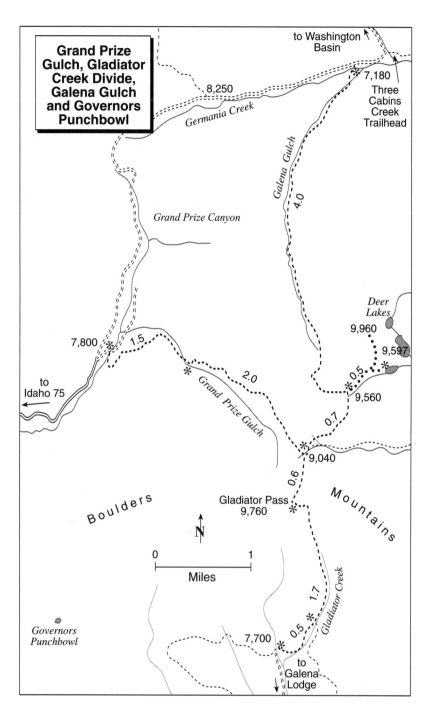

Grand Prize Gulch, Gladiator Creek Divide, Galena Gulch and Governors Punchbowl

to Washington Basin

8,250

Germania Creek

Grand Prize Canyon

Galena Gulch

4.0

7,180

Three Cabins Creek Trailhead

Deer Lakes

9,960

9,597

7,800

1.5

to Idaho 75

Grand Prize Gulch

2.0

0.5

9,560

0.7

9,040

0.6

Gladiator Pass 9,760

Boulders

N

0   1

Miles

Mountains

Gladiator Creek

1.7

0.5

Governors Punchbowl

7,700

to Galena Lodge

connects with the Grand Prize and West Fork East Fork Salmon River trails

Elevation gain: 1,680 feet; a cross-country side trip to view Deer Lakes is an additional 1 mile and 600-foot elevation gain **Highest point:** 9,560 feet

Map: Horton Peak

Trailhead GPS: 43 58.877, 114 38.009

Difficulty: expert; time: 7 hours

Access: From Idaho 75, turn right (east) 36.4miles north of Ketchum (24.5 miles south of Stanley) onto the gravel and primitive Pole Creek-Germania Creek Road (194 and then 197). Drive over Pole Creek Summit to a ford of Germania Creek at 11.8 miles.

What you'll see: In Galena Gulch, lumpy ridges banded with gray and apricot overlook a canyon of avalanche slopes crowded with lodgepoles. The trail offers a view north of the white, gold, and red peaks around Washington Basin in the White Clouds. From the head of the canyon, you look south at a dark gray tooth on a wall of crumbly cliffs. From a ridge above the divide, Deer Lakes are spread out below hidden cliffs in a basin of gray rock and whitebark pines. The upper lake resembles a melting green guitar.

Directions: To find the Galena Gulch Trail, drive across the first of two fords before the Three Cabins Creek trailhead, which is where the road changes to a jeep trail. (These fords are not shown on the map.) The trail begins just beyond (east) of the first ford (7,680 feet) at a "no motorized vehicles" sign.

The trail crosses a tiny stream in moss, and soon goes left (east) over Galena Gulch Creek. It leads uphill away from the creek through Douglas firs, then returns to the creek now in a ravine. At 1 mile is an avalanche area with young lodgepoles. As the trail crosses a second grass-covered avalanche area at 1.3 miles, it disappears, but reappears in the woods beyond.

There are several more avalanche areas with grassy slopes and downed timber before the 3 mile point. Use the topographic map to find the trail beyond each avalanche area. Below a meadow at 3.2 miles, the trail fords the creek back to the right (west) side.

It curves up into forest beneath outcrops, and over a rock knoll. Above a little meadow, the trail turns 90 degrees to the right (southwest). Walk along the right (west) side of the meadow to its upper end, then at 3.5 miles cross its tiny stream to the south side and watch for blazes. The trail stays at the edge of the forest below the rocky headwall until it crosses a scree slope just before the saddle (9,560 feet) at 4 miles.

To see Deer Lakes, go northeast from the saddle up the sandy ridge, which levels out at 9,960 feet. There you will see the summit of an unnamed peak is ahead. Now turn left and walk north until you are 1 mile from the saddle and the lakes appear below under hidden cliffs. To the left (north) of these cliffs are steep scree slopes, which experts could descend to the lakes, (9,490 and 9,597 feet).

GALENA AREA

123.

GLADIATOR PASS

Round trip: 5.6 miles from trailhead above Galena Lodge; connects with Grand Prize, and West Fork East Fork of the Salmon River trails.
Elevation gain: 2,060 feet **Highest point:** 9,760 feet
Maps: Galena, Horton Peak
Trailhead GPS: 43 53.678; 114 39.322
Difficulty: strenuous; time: 5 hours
Access: From Idaho 75, 23.5 miles north of Ketchum (37.5 miles south of Stanley), turn right into the parking area for Galena Lodge. From the far end of it drive a dirt road (189). At .7 mile is a junction with a road that goes off to the right and over a creek. Keep straight ahead up a steep, rocky hill. Continue through forest to the trailhead in a grassy spot at 1.6 miles.

What you'll see: This trail climbs so steeply with so many views that it seems like a slow glass elevator. On the way, it passes through two grassy basins that stairstep up the headwall of the canyon, which is dark gray and burnt-orange towers. From the pass, to the east you can see knobby gray and orange ridges and to the north white peaks of the White Clouds and the white and orange-gray wall of Castle Peak.
Directions: At the trailhead (7,700 feet), the western part of the Galena Grinder Trail goes off to the left. Take the other trail, which goes to the right and gradually turns north. At .5 mile, it steepens and goes through forest onto a sagebrush slope. Here it passes a junction with the east half of the Galena Grinder trail.
The trail climbs with few switchbacks. At .8 mile, where a gray peak with a brown summit is visible, it crosses a talus slope. It passes a grove of trees, and at 1.5 miles is between young whitebark pines opposite orange mine tailings. Then it crosses to the right (east) of the creek, which is dry most of the summer.
At 1.7 miles is the lower of the two grassy basins. At the head of this basin, where the creek trickles down a gray outcrop, the trail climbs to the right to a second, smaller basin at 2 miles. Then it goes up through whitebark pines to the divide (9,760 feet) at 2.2 miles.
The trail turns east along the divide, and then descends over talus. After a 520-foot descent in .6 mile, it joins the Grand Prize Gulch Trail. This junction is 100 yards south of the junction with the West Fork of the East Fork and Galena Gulch trails.

124.

GALENA LODGE TRAILS: THE GALENA GRINDER

Loop trip: 9 miles from Galena Lodge for the whole loop
Elevation gain: 1,000 feet **Highest point:** 8,300 feet
Maps: Galena, Horton Peak; a brochure "Summer Trails: The Harriman Trail and Galena Lodge"
GPS at Galena Lodge: 43 52.345, 114 39.326
Difficulty: strenuous; time: 7 hours
Access: On Idaho 75, 23.5 miles north of Ketchum (37.5 miles south of Stanley), park at Galena Lodge.

What you'll see: The hike is a sample of the trail complex that has been developed at Galena Lodge. From this half of the longest trail, the Galena Grinder, you get an excellent view of Galena Peak and the Smoky Mountains across the Big Wood River to the west. The peak in the Smokies with cliffs along the top is called Bromaghin. An old jeep trail, which begins where the Galena Grinder crosses Senate Creek, provides cross-country access to a basin of wildflowers right below the crumbly face of Galena Peak. The Galena Lodge trails include Psycho, Rip and Tear, and the Cherry Creek loop.

Directions: To begin the east section of the Galena Grinder, from the lodge parking lot (7,240 feet) walk south along a road behind the lodge parallel to the highway. At 200 yards it curves left (east) downhill to the Senate Creek Road (186). Walk northeast up that road, ignoring cross-country ski signs. The road goes along the left edge of a meadow perpendicular to the highway. At .5 mile, turn off onto a road that goes off to the right at a 90-degree angle. In another .5 mile, the road crosses Senate Creek on a culvert, and goes along the right (south) side of the creek. The road curves east. The route of the road differs from the topographic map. Avoid a road to the left at a T-intersection at 1 mile and another to the right in a Y intersection at 1.2 miles.

Stay on the main road, which climbs along an avalanche area and curves north to a split in the canyon at 1.6 miles. Take the road that leads north up the left branch, which turns into a trail. It leads along the base of an opening to the next little canyon and a big avalanche area. It continues up the right side of this canyon in sagebrush. Where the canyon steepens at 2.2 miles, the trail makes a hairpin turn to the southwest as it crosses a usually dry creek.

From the hairpin turn, the Galena Grinder trail goes southwest up the side of the canyon into forest. At 2.7 miles, it reaches its high point (8,300 feet) and turns northwest. From then on, it winds downhill, still in the trees. Avoid a blocked-off road leading left. The trail winds in and out of gullies and a dry wash. There are more curves and switchbacks than shown on the maps. Beyond the wash at 4.2 miles, the trail climbs into the canyon of Gladiator Creek and goes north up it for about .3 mile. Here the trail passes log cabin ruins, and at 4.8 miles it crosses Gladiator Creek, which is dry most of the summer. Just beyond the creek is a junction with the trail up the creek to Gladiator Pass.

Turn left (southwest) down Gladiator Creek to its trailhead at 5.4 miles. From here, you can walk down the dirt road to the lodge at 7 miles. Or you can hike the west half of the Grinder. To do this continue straight ahead at the Gladiator trailhead and climb uphill on the trail. It winds along in the wooded hills for about 4.5 miles that are much closer to the highway than the miles you just hiked. Landmarks on this half are Westernhome Gulch at 5.2 miles, a half mile of trail that is very close to the highway at 6.5 miles, and joining another trail, called Psycho at 7.5 miles. This part of the Galena Grinder joins the Gladiator Creek Road at 8.5 miles, .5 mile above the lodge. Because the hike begins and ends on dirt roads a car shuttle will shorten it by a couple of miles.

EASLEY AREA

125.

SILVER LAKE

Round trip: 3.2 miles from the end of the Silver Creek Road
Elevation gain: 1,242 feet **Highest point:** 9,642 feet
Map: Easley Hot Springs
Trail beginning GPS: 43 49.222, 114 32.572
Difficulty: cross-country for experts; time: 5 to 6 hours
Access: On Idaho 75, 15.2 miles north of Ketchum, turn right (east) at a sign for Silver Creek (road 174). For those driving south, the turnoff is 13.8 miles south of Galena Summit. Drive across the bridge and avoiding a road to the left at .2 mile, continue up the primitive road through sagebrush and grass-covered hills to the end of the road at 3.4 miles. Four-wheel-drive is required for the last mile.

What you'll see: Silver-gray mountains, rock benches, whitebark pines, and subalpine firs ring the clear green water of Silver Lake. Between the lake and the mountain rim, ponds and meadows fill dents in gray and orange talus. Above the trail near the beginning of the hike, white rock between gray layers resembles dripping icing. Here and along the first part of the route in July, the hillsides are awash in cobalt blue penstemon, a white variety of lupine, and other wildflowers. It is one of the finest wildflower displays in the SNRA. Note that the last part of the route is steep and difficult to find, so the hike will seem much longer than the mileage.

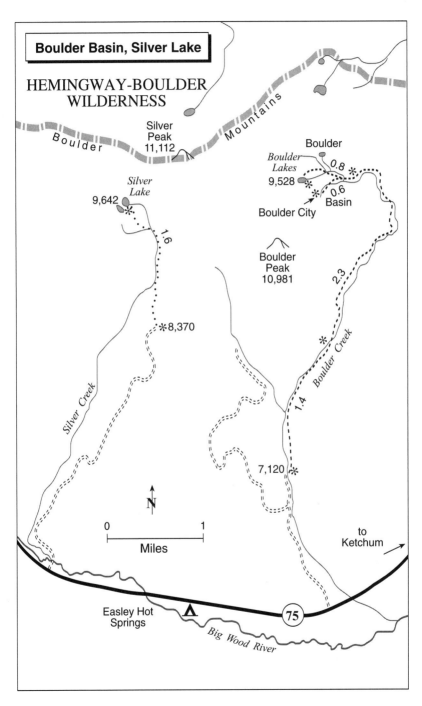

Boulder Basin, Silver Lake

HEMINGWAY-BOULDER WILDERNESS

Boulder Mountains

Silver Peak 11,112

Silver Lake

9,642

1.6

*8,370

Silver Creek

Boulder Peak 10,981

Boulder

Boulder Lakes 9,528

0.8

0.6

Basin

Boulder City

2.3

Boulder Creek

1.4

7,120

N

0 — 1

Miles

to Ketchum

Easley Hot Springs

75

Big Wood River

279

Cabin in Boulder Basin

Directions: After you drive over the bridge and climb the hill, the road descends into a big meadow at 1 mile. There is a hump in the road as it starts uphill just beyond here, so leave passenger cars in the meadow. The road curves over to the right as it climbs along sagebrush hills., and soon has big rocks in it. At 2.7 miles, where the road switchbacks up the hillside, 4-wheel drive is required. Above the switchbacks, avoid a track to the left. Stay to the right on the more well-worn road, which drops over a small knoll and climbs again. At 3.4 miles, the road splits again. The left branch is blocked off and the right branch ends in aspens. Park at or near this junction (8,370 feet).

Begin hiking by climbing the steep left branch to its end in 150 yards. From here the route continues more gently across the slopes of lupine and penstemon. At .2 mile is a grove of firs and spruces. Beyond the trees, at .4 mile, descend into and climb out of a ravine. At .5 mile, go to the right under a 15-foot outcrop just before another ravine. On the other side of this ravine are trees on a sandy hillside and in another ravine. At .9 mile, you come out on an open basin with plants and grasses beside the cascading creek. Stay to the right of the creek at the edge of the talus.

At 1.2 miles the creek splits into two cascades. It is 500 more vertical feet to the lake. Using the map for guidance, cross the right-hand stream, go over to the left stream, and climb its right (north) side. In 200 yards this cascade divides. Ignore the left branch and continue up the right side of the right branch. As the slope steepens, switchback and forth to make it easier. The route goes left of a pale orange knoll at 1.4 miles, and comes to a place where the creek splashes over a

280

Silver Lake route

bluff ahead.

Cross the creek to the left and follow a faint path to the top of this bluff. Walk along rock benches left (west) of a bog and then north to the lake (9,642 feet) at 1.6 miles. There are three miniature lakes nearby. Two of them, 200 yards southwest of Silver Lake and 40 feet higher, are separated from the mountain wall by great mounds of orange talus.

126.

BOULDER BASIN

Round trip: 8.6 miles from the first ford to Boulder City; an additional 1.6 miles round trip to see the largest lake; connects with the old South Fork East Fork Trail to the East Fork of the Salmon River

Elevation gain: 2,000 feet from ford to City, 360 feet more for lake
Highest point: 9,528 feet
Maps: Easley Hot Springs, Amber Lakes
GPS at ford: 43 48.008, 114 30.983
Difficulty: strenuous; time: 8 hours
Access: On Idaho 75, 12.7 miles north of Ketchum turn east on the primitive Boulder Creek Road (184). In .2 mile keep straight ahead where the old road branches to the right across the creek

Keep right at 1.1 miles where the Left Fork of Boulder Creek Road turns uphill to the left. To reach the trailhead, continue on the extremely rocky road up the left (west) side of Boulder Creek. This road fords Boulder Creek to the right (east) side 1.5 miles (7,120 feet) from the highway. (Required 4-wheel drive). The upper parts of the jeep trail are rough enough to damage 4-wheel drive vehicles.

The forest and topographic maps do not show this ford.

What you'll see: A rusty boiler, and the remnants of a mill and log cabins mark the location of Boulder City. High above, a rusted tramway stretches up the mountain to an old mine below crinkled peaks. Nearby, below rock buttresses, in late summer the meadows that fringe a small aquamarine lake are sprinkled with gentians. Above the lake, stripes of pink, white and orange ruck swirl across the face of Boulder Peak. Those who like movie westerns may be interested to know that the main set for Clint Eastwood's 1985 movie *Pale Rider* was on the flat area next to Boulder Creek near the highway.

Directions: Recent high use by jeeps and ATVs makes this hike more pleasant if you go on weekdays or in the fall. The mileage given here starts where the road fords Boulder Creek to the east side 1.5 miles from the highway. On the other side of it, the road goes through sagebrush to a campsite in the woods at .5 mile. The next ford is at 1.4 miles. The road crosses the creek to the west side here. It is safer to drive 4-wheel drive vehicles only a short distance beyond this ford because the road is so steep and rocky.

From the ford walk along the road which skirts the base of a talus slope for .4 mile. In the trees beyond this, the road splits. There are several more splits in the next mile. Most of these soon rejoin. Water runs over all of them and some have mud holes. By the time the track fords the creek in a big mud hole to the north at 3.1 miles, there is probably only one road.

Among trees at 3.3 miles, the road makes a sharp left (west) turn. At 3.5 miles, it crosses a branch of the creek to the left (south) in a meadow. At 3.7 miles (9,100 feet), the road splits again. The right fork leads to tiny lakes at the head of the canyon, and the left fork leads to Boulder City.

To see Boulder City, follow the left branch, which crosses to the south side of the creek in a ravine at 3.9 miles. The road fords another creek at 4.2 miles and goes out into a basin below the talus and crags at 4.3 miles (9,200 feet). The remains of cabins, a mill, and a tramway are

Rock formations along Murdock Creek

found here. Please remember that these remnants are historical and treat them with respect.

To see the lakes, take the right branch back at the road junction. It goes through woods north of the creek, which runs in a gorge. At 4.2 miles, the creek comes out into a meadow and the road fords the creek to the left (south). At a T-intersection at 4.3 miles, take the left branch around a hairpin turn .8 mile to the largest lake (9,528 feet).

The right branch at the "T" intersection climbs 1 mile over talus and past tiny ponds to a divide at 10,560 feet. From here, an unmaintained trail descends the South Fork of the East Fork of the Salmon River 3,400 feet in 7.5 miles to the trail along the East Fork at a point 4.5 miles above Bowery Guard Station.

NORTH FORK BIG WOOD RIVER AREA

127.

MURDOCK CREEK

Round trip: 7 miles from the end of the Murdock Creek Road, which branches off the North Fork Big Wood River Road
Elevation gain: 1,060 feet **Highest point:** 7,560 feet

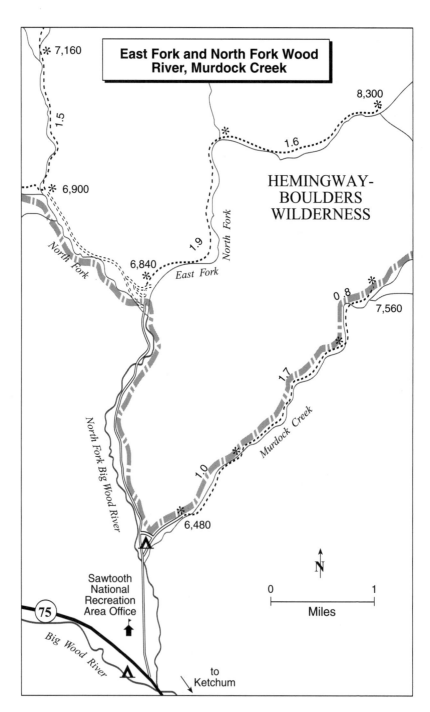

East Fork and North Fork Wood River, Murdock Creek

* 7,160

1.5

8,300
*

*
1.6

* 6,900

HEMINGWAY-
BOULDERS
WILDERNESS

North Fork

North Fork

1.9

6,840
*

East Fork

*
0.8

7,560

North Fork

1.7

Murdock Creek

North Fork Big Wood River

1.0

*

* 6,480

Sawtooth
National
Recreation
Area Office

N

0   1

Miles

75

Big Wood River

to
Ketchum

284

Map: Amber Lakes
Trailhead GPS: 43 48.403, 114 24.885
Difficulty: moderate except the first mile is for wheelchairs; time: 6 hours
Access: From Sun Valley Road in Ketchum, drive north on Idaho 75 for 8 miles. Turn right (east) at the SNRA Headquarters onto the gravel North Fork Big Wood River Road (146). At 1.2 miles from the highway, turn right on the Murdock Creek Road and drive .4 mile to a parking area.

What you'll see: This trail runs along the canyon beside a green cloud of willows. It passes tall outcrops, one like a skull and another like a rough-hewn castle. There are three crossings of the creek. At the second of these, the creek is braided in gravel. Here two miniature waterfalls cascade down emerald moss. The first two crossings are on bridges. The mountain at the head of the canyon appears as gentle as a pile of sand. The upper part of the trail is little used, so it is a good place to see wildlife.

Directions: Beginning at 6,480 feet, the trail goes along the left (northwest) side of the creek in sagebrush. At .2 mile, it bridges the creek to the right side and leads through grassy areas and Douglas firs to a bridge to the left at 1 mile. Now the trail is no longer constructed for wheelchairs. At 1.3 miles, where the creek and hillside come close, the trail climbs above the creek and goes along a steep canyon wall. It drops again and at 1.5 miles passes a 30-foot castle-like outcrop Ahead is a long, narrow valley full of willows.

Next the trail climbs over a small, gray outcrop, goes along a steep open hillside and then into Douglas firs. It drops to the creek and passes between cottonwoods and the skull-shaped gray outcrop at 2 miles. The trail then alternates steep hillsides of sagebrush and talus with grassy flats next to the creek. At 2.5 miles, the canyon curves left and a gully of aspens is on the opposite canyon wall. The canyon widens, the willows disappear, and the trail fords the creek at 2.7 miles to the right side.

Beyond this ford, the trail climbs away from the creek and turns left. Across the creek is a pale outcrop shaped like eyes and eyebrows. On the trail side, is a flat area in the forest with campsites. The trail descends, goes over the creek to the left (west) at 3 miles. Past a gully with an early-season stream, the trail curves left into the canyon of another creek. The official trail ends at this side creek (7,560 feet) at 3.5 miles.

128.

EAST FORK NORTH FORK BIG WOOD RIVER

Round trip: 7 miles from the end of the East Fork North Fork Big

Wood River Road

Elevation gain: 1,460 feet **Highest point:** 8,300 feet at the end of the official trail

Maps: Amber Lakes, Rock Roll Canyon

Trailhead GPS: 43 50.404, 114 25.050

Difficulty: expert; time: 8 hours

Access: From Idaho 75, at SNRA Headquarters 8 miles north of Ketchum, drive the North Fork Big Wood River Road (146) to a side road for the East Fork trail .3 mile past Camp Manapu. Turn right on this road. When it branches, take the right branch to avoid a very steep hill. This branch curves around the hill and intersects two branches of the steep road. Avoid a track going off to the right (east) toward the creek. Instead go left (northeast) on the more well-worn road to the trailhead .4 mile from the main road (146).

What you'll see: This trail is a pleasant walk below crumbly apricot and gray peaks. Halfway up, an enormous snowbank covered with the pine needles of many avalanches spans the creek. Beyond this the trail dwindles, and disappears before the canyon forks at 3.5 miles.

Directions: From the trailhead (6,840 feet), the trail goes along grassy slopes and through Douglas firs at 1 mile, is an open area across from talus that is crosshatched with game trails. Then the trail goes through timber close to the creek and at 1.2 miles, climbs above the creek below more talus.

It ascends an open hillside and at 1.3 miles reaches the needle-covered snowbank at 1.9 miles, where it fords a side creek at 7,650 feet. The trail returns to forest that has three narrow open areas between 2 and 2.5 miles. At 2.5 miles below a pinkish-gray mountain, willows line the canyon, which gradually curves left.

After another open area. the trail is hard to find in thick timber and, after crossing two small creeks, it ends. A few yards farther the canyon forks at 3.5 miles (8,300 feet). Here you see a a wide peak of apricot-colored talus up the canyon. From the end of the trail, it is possible to climb cross-country over a 10,000-foot divide to a trail along the West Fork of Trail Creek.

129.

WEST FORK NORTH FORK BIG WOOD RIVER AND WINDOW LAKE

Round trip: 7.6 miles to the end of the West Fork trail, 9 miles; 3.8 miles extra (cross-country) for Window Lake, which is in a side canyon; connects with the Amber Lakes trail

Elevation gain: 2,260 feet to end West Fork, 3,122 feet to Window Lake **Highest point:** 10,022 feet

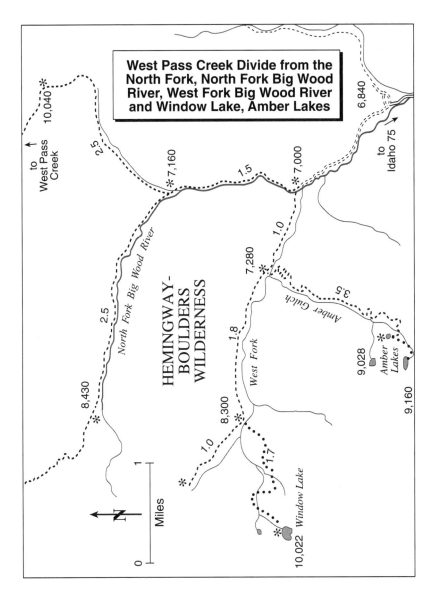

West Pass Creek Divide from the North Fork, North Fork Big Wood River, West Fork Big Wood River and Window Lake, Amber Lakes

Maps: Amber Lakes, Easley Hot Springs

Trailhead GPS: 43 51.200, 114 26.207

Difficulty: expert; time: 7 hours for the end of the West Fork trail, 10 hours for Window Lake

Access: From Idaho 75, turn right (east), 8 miles north of Ketchum, at the SNRA Headquarters. Drive 5.3 miles on North Fork Big Wood River Road (146) to its end

What you'll see: At the end of this trail is a valley of wildflowers below sheer-walled peaks. Here a feathery waterfall glides down a niche in a black cliff. If you choose the rough cross-country route to Window Lake instead, you will find an alpine garden of alpine buttercup, dwarf lupine and red and white mountain heathers among pink, orange and gray rocks. On a knoll below crumbling peaks, stand dwarfed whitebark pines. The way to Window Lake is steep, hazardous, and hard to find. Because the lake is in a fragile alpine area, avoid camping at it.

Directions: The trail begins by fording the North Fork of the Big Wood River to the west bank. This ford can be hazardous in early summer. (At the trailhead DO NOT follow a path that goes up the North Fork on its right side before the ford because it takes you into the wrong canyon.) On the far side of the ford, the trail angles to the left and then back to the right above the creek. In an avalanche area of young trees, it descends to the creek and runs along its right hand (north) side. Across from Amber Gulch at 1 mile, the trail angles up to the right onto a wooded bench, to a junction with the Amber Gulch trail. The West Fork trail heads uphill from this junction away from the creek.

In meadows at 1.5 miles, the tread becomes faint. Here the view ahead is of peaks above Window Lake. At the head of the open area a path close to a waterfall is not the trail; the correct route is uphill from it. At 2.3 miles, the trail reappears in the trees 100 feet above the creek and climbs in woods. When it descends 100 feet at 2.6 miles, a wooded side canyon appears across the creek, but it is not the canyon of Window Lake.

At 2.8 miles, a narrow open area extends southwest up a ridge that is across the main creek. This open strip is the easiest route to Window Lake. To climb this, leave the trail at 2.8 miles (8,300 feet), cross the creek to the left and start climbing. At 3.5 miles, where the hillside becomes gentler turn right (west) to two streams. The right (north) one of these is the outlet of Window Lake.

Keep left of both streams at first. In .1 mile, the left stream splits. Climb the right branch of this, which is usually dry, up a ravine. The ravine leads to a large flat grassy area at 9,400 feet.

From the flat area, go right (north) to the outlet of Window Lake and cross it to the north side below a waterfall at 3.8 miles. Climb away from the creek around a rock bench, and return to it at 4.1 miles where it meets a creek from a pond. Ford back to the left (south) of the creek and walk over rock benches to the lake (10,022 feet) at 4.5 miles.

If you want to go to the end of the trail instead of the lake, do not turn off at 2.8 miles. Stay on the trail, which gradually turns northwest into an open valley of grass and rocks at 3 miles where the feathery waterfall is in the distance. The trail ends below the waterfall at 3.8 miles (9,160 feet).

130.

AMBER LAKES

Round trip: 9 miles to the end of the trail at a pond; 1 mile additional to see the lower lake; 1.6 miles for the upper lake; connects with the West Fork North Fork Big Wood River Trail

Elevation gain: 2,260 feet **Highest point:** 9,160 feet

Map: Amber Lakes

Trailhead GPS: 43 51.200, 114 26.207

Difficulty: strenuous to end of trail; expert for lakes; time: 10 hours to see both lakes

Access: From Idaho 75, turn right (east) 8 miles north of Ketchum at the SNRA Headquarters. Drive 5.3 miles on gravel and dirt North Fork Big Wood River Road (146) to its end.

What you'll see: Sometimes the two tiny Amber Lakes reflect the amber color of the peaks above, but on other days, they reflect the blue of the sky. Jumbled silver logs from old avalanches line the edges of both lakes. In late summer the lakes dwindle to tiny pools or even dry up. From the trail you get excellent views of the striped Boulder Mountains.

Directions: The ford of the North Fork of the Big Wood River at the beginning of the hike can be hazardous or impassable in early summer. The trail starts on the west side of the parking loop by fording the North Fork. (At the trailhead DO NOT follow a path that goes up the North Fork on its right side before the crossing because it takes you into the wrong canyon.) Beyond the ford the trail goes along above the West Fork on its north side. The Amber Gulch turnoff (7,280 feet) at 1 mile is on a bench in the woods. That trail drops to ford the West Fork of the North Fork and it can be difficult in early summer.

Next the trail crosses a small creek and switchbacks up through the woods in seven long switchbacks. Then it makes a long curve into the gulch. At 2.2 miles the trail zigzags up into a boulder field and back down. It stays on the side of the gulch. Along the creek below are aspen groves. At 3 miles, the trail goes along the left side of a grassy bowl and then up a wooded ridge to another grassy valley at 3.5 miles. The outlet of the upper lake cascades into it. Now, the trail switchbacks up the right (east) side of this outlet into meadows. It goes to the right across the meadows and ends at a small pond at 4.5 miles. By fall, the pond often is just a basin of gray rocks. It is best to avoid camping at the lakes because their alpine plants are fragile and the growing season very short.

To reach the lower lake from the end of the trail at the pond, go north 200 yards into the canyon of that lake's outlet. Cut below a boulder field and cross to the north (right) side of the outlet. Then climb

Upper Amber Lake

along it until rocks interfere. Now cross to the left side and climb through steep forest to the rocky shore. To reach the upper lake from the pond, follow the meadows below it to the south, and then go up the lake's outlet. As you climb, the trees thin out, and the creek curves west and north around a knoll to the lake (9,160 feet) It is about .8 mile from the pond and a 400-foot climb.

131.

NORTH FORK BIG WOOD RIVER

Round trip: 8 miles from the end of the North Fork Big Wood River Road to the end of a definite trail in meadows; connects with the trail to West Pass Creek Divide.
Elevation gain: 1,620 feet **Highest point:** 8,480 feet
Elevation loss (return climb): 40 feet
Maps: Amber Lakes, Ryan Peak
Trailhead GPS: 43 51.210, 114 26.182
Difficulty: moderate; time: 6 to 7 hours
Access: On Idaho 75, 8 miles north of Sun Valley Road in Ketchum, turn right (east) at the SNRA Headquarters. Drive 5.3 miles on the dirt North Fork Big Wood River Road (146) to its end.

What you'll see: This hike is through wildflower meadows under orange and gray crags, with waterfalls hiding in chasms. The meadows are avalanche areas that are being filled in by subalpine firs. From the upper trail, the pleated top of Kent Peak bars the canyon. At 4 miles, the trail disappears in downed timber, but energetic experts can hike cross-country for another 1.5 miles and 1,800 vertical feet to a 10,300-foot divide overlooking Ibex Creek.

Directions: From the north side of the parking (6,900 feet), the trail climbs 80-feet over a wooded ridge at .2 mile, then drops to the edge of the creek. Next it goes up and down gently in the woods and returns to the creek at a grassy flat at .4 mile. Here the horse trail fords the river to the west bank. The foot trail climbs along an open hillside to a sagebrush flat at .6 mile. Although its tread is good, a couple of steep places in this stretch are slippery. After woods at .8 mile, the horse trail rejoins from across the North Fork.

Next the trail crosses two branches of a stream, and goes along talus. At 1.3 miles, after another side stream, you reach a side creek that is often dry. The trail turns 90 degrees to the right in forest, then turns 90 degrees back to the left. When it comes out onto a narrow sagebrush area, look for a cairn at 1.5 miles. The cairn marks a trail turning off to the right for West Pass Creek Divide.

Keep on the main trail, which returns to the edge of the creek in willows. The first of the wildflower meadows is at 2 miles, where the creek runs in cascades and then in a gorge. Cairns mark the route through the meadows.

At 2.4 miles, the trail crosses a side stream and climbs an outcrop. At a gully, it ascends a bluff to the left. At 2.6 miles, it is beside waterfalls in a gorge. It levels out at a campsite and at 2.7 miles, enters another long meadow. At the far end at 3.6 miles, the trail climbs another bluff into more woods. A third, much shorter open area with downed trees is at 3.7 miles. Here, the trail fords a side creek, but it does not go cross the river and back as shown on the map. Beyond where the river splits into a "Y" at 3.8 miles, the trail enters woods and at 4 miles (8,480 feet) disappears in downed timber.

132.

WEST PASS CREEK DIVIDE FROM THE NORTH FORK BIG WOOD RIVER

Round trip: 8 miles from the end of the North Fork Big Wood River Road; connects with a trail up West Pass Creek, a tributary of the East Fork of the Salmon River
Elevation gain: 3,140 feet **Highest point:** 10,040 feet
Maps: Amber Lakes, Ryan Peak
Trailhead GPS: 43 51.210, 114 26.182

North Fork Big Wood River Canyon

Difficulty: strenuous; time: 8 hours
Access: On Idaho 75, 8 miles north of Ketchum, turn right (east) on the North Fork Big Wood River Road (146) at the SNRA Headquarters. Drive 5.3 miles on the gravel and dirt road to its end.

What you'll see: Across West Pass Creek from this divide, Glassford Peak and the peaks around it are red, gold, and orange. To the east of these peaks, float the white peaks of the White Clouds. Just above the divide, the orange-streaked cliffs of Ryan Peak merge with the crinkled wall and towers of Kent Peak.

Directions: This trail climbs almost 2,880 feet in 2.5 miles, so you need to plan for the steep ascent with extra water and snacks. For the first 1.5 miles detailed directions are given under the North Fork Wood River. On this trail at 1.5 miles, just beyond a long sagebrush area, the trail turns 90 degrees to the right for 100 yards. Then it makes a hairpin turn to the left and goes straight up the canyon into a flat sagebrush area (7,160 feet). Here cairns mark an unsigned trail to the right (east). This is the trail to West Pass Creek Divide.

Turn off onto it, looking for blazes in the forest to find the right route. The trail angles up the canyon for 200 yards, and then makes two switchbacks; each one is 400 yards long. At 2 miles, it comes to the edge of a side canyon of the North Fork above a waterfall. From here, it turns up the side canyon on an open slope. It goes over two small side creeks, dry in late summer, and then below a grove of Douglas firs.

At the head of a gorge at 2.8 miles, the trail comes close to the branch of the North Fork. After crossing a third side creek, it climbs scree and talus. At 3 miles, the main creek splits in a basin of tiny subalpine firs.

The trail curves left (west) up the left branch of the creek in whitebark pines near a lumpy campsite at 3.2 miles. It edges the creek at 3.4

Homestead cabin on the East Fork of the Salmon River

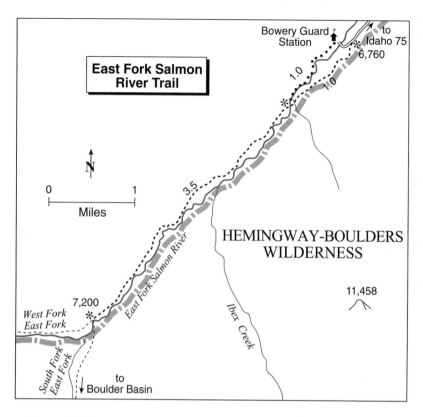

miles and disappears in moss. Then it winds northwest up a steep rocky slope onto a talus ridge dotted with whitebark pines. At 3.7 miles, it runs left of a gully across from a burnt orange outcrop. It goes into a grass and talus basin at 3.8 miles. After climbing above this basin, the trail disappears in turf and reaches the divide (10,040 feet) at 4 miles. On the other side, it descends 2,000 feet in 5 miles into the canyon of West Pass Creek to where the West Pass Creek Road is blocked off, 5 miles below the pass and 3.2 miles above the East Fork of the Salmon River Road.

BOWERY AREA

133.

EAST FORK SALMON RIVER TRAIL

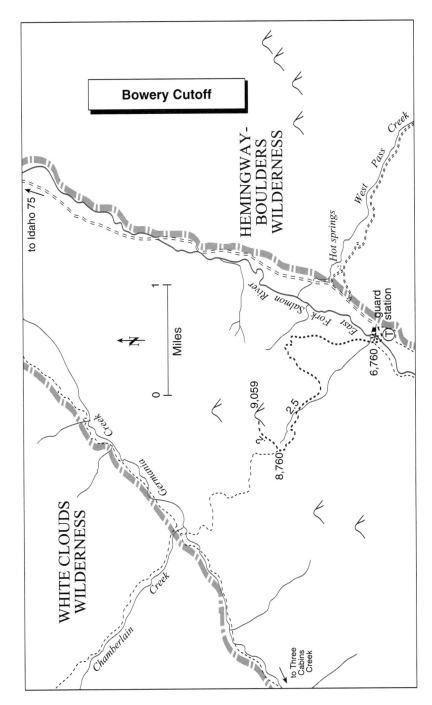

Bowery Cutoff

HEMINGWAY-
BOULDERS
WILDERNESS

WHITE CLOUDS
WILDERNESS

to Idaho 75

West Pass Creek

Hot springs

East Fork Salmon River

guard station

6,760

9,059

2.5

8,760

Germania Creek

Chamberlain Creek

to Three Cabins Creek

N

Miles

0   1

South side of Castle Peak from the Bowery Cutoff

Round trip: 9 miles from the Bowery trailhead to the junction of the South Fork East Fork and West Fork East Fork of the Salmon River trails; connects with Grand Prize Gulch and Gladiator Pass trails
Elevation gain: 440 feet **Highest point:** 7,200 feet
Maps: Ryan Peak, Galena Peak
Trailhead GPS: 43 58.607, 114 29.759
Difficulty: moderate; time: 6 ? hours
Access: From Idaho 75, 37.6 miles east of Stanley, turn right (south) on the East Fork of the Salmon River Road. The first 14.6 miles are paved, then it is gravel and dirt for 9 more miles (road 120). After that, it is primitive. It ends at 28.3 miles at a gate .2 mile before the Bowery Guard Station.

What you'll see: This hike leads toward an alpine headwall that is much more impressive from close up. In early to midsummer, the headwall holds patches of snow. Triangular gray peaks flank the rectangular top of Galena Peak, which marks the center. Cool weather is best for this hike, as the trail follows the blue-green curves of the East Fork in sagebrush

Directions: If you take the trail from the trailhead (6,800 feet), it fords the river at 1 mile. This ford is difficult until midsummer. To avoid it, squeeze through the log fence and walk the dirt road to the guard station. This route allows you to cross the river on the station's road bridge.

From the guard station walk 50 yards northwest to the Bowery Cutoff Trail and a few yards up it. At a T-intersection, turn left (southwest) on a path up the river. Follow it for about a mile to meet the main trail on the upriver side of the ford. This path climbs a sagebrush bench 50 feet above the river, passing a rounded gray knoll on the opposite bank. Then it drops to the river and runs along it between outcrops on a steep slope. Beyond a marshy area it meets the main trail on the west side of the ford. From here on you may find traces of the old road that used to go up the canyon.

From the ford, the trail runs along open sagebrush slopes, skirting a patch of forest at 2 miles. Wooded ridges form the left side of the canyon. On the right side, sagebrush, scattered Douglas firs, and outcrops rise to four pinkish-gray peaks. At 2.3 miles, there is a view of cliffs, a rounded mountain, and up Ibex Creek, a gray rock tooth. At 3.1 miles, the trail crosses a side creek and drops to a meadow beside the river.

From the meadow, the trail jogs up to the right then turns back up the canyon keeping well above the river. At 3.7 miles, it fords a side creek in trees that frame a view of the headwall.

At 3.9 miles, the trail drops to the edge of willows and climbs back up onto sagebrush slopes. It goes over a side stream at 4 miles. At 4.5 miles, it is beside the river at 7,200 feet.

Here the South Fork of the East Fork and the West Fork of the East Fork diverge, and trails lead up both canyons. There is no sign or trail tread for the South Fork Trail. To find that trail, look across the river for a "closed to motorized travel" sign. You have to ford the river to reach the trail, which leads over a 10,600-foot pass to Boulder Basin, 13 miles from the trailhead. It is seldom maintained and isn't shown on current maps.

From the junction, the West Fork East Fork Trail goes straight ahead, climbing sagebrush slopes into forest below two prominent wooded peaks with gray rock summits. This trail goes 5 more miles with a 1,840-foot climb to join the Galena Gulch and Grand Prize Gulch trails. On the way, it gives cross-country access to an unnamed lake at 9,550 feet, 1.5 miles south of the trail.

134.

BOWERY CUTOFF

Round trip: 5 miles to a divide; additional .4 mile to viewpoint of Castle Peak; connects with the East Fork Salmon River and Germania Creek trails

Elevation gain: 2,000 feet plus 200 feet up hill for view

Highest point: 8,760 at the divide

Maps: Ryan Peak, Galena Peak

GPS at trailhead: 43 58.509, 114 29.922

Difficulty: strenuous; steep and gullied; time: 5 to 7 hours plus driving time

Access: From Idaho 75, 37.6 miles east of Stanley, turn south on the East Fork Salmon River Road (120) and drive 28.5 miles to a gate .2 mile before the Bowery Guard Station. The trail begins behind the guard station.

What you'll see: From the summit of the trail you must climb about 200 more feet up a hill to see the gray, white, and red view of Castle Peak that is the goal of this hike. As the trail curves into the canyon of a creek on the way up, it passes beneath a complex cliff of rounded towers decorated with white dashes of rock. This steep hike is best for a cool day because there is no shade.

Directions: From the small parking area at the main trailhead, squeeze through the log fence and walk .2 mile along a road and over a bridge to the guard station. The trail begins behind the guard station. A few yards up the slope, turn right at a T-intersection. (The left branch goes to the ford on the main trail.) The trail to the right crosses a stream and goes through a hard-to-open gate. Please try to leave the gate the way you found it.

From here the trail leads east for 1 mile through the sagebrush to a line of quaking aspen. Here it switchbacks twice before turning back toward the guard station and returning to the canyon of the stream by the guard station high above it. The trail curves into this canyon around the base of a towered cliff at 1.7 miles. It ascends the steep canyon beside aspens and Doug firs. A short switchback has difficult footing. At 2 miles the trail crosses the little stream to the left (west)

298

side and continues climbing. There are no more cliffs, just sagebrush hills topped with whitebark pines. Now you can look out at a wide sweep of the Boulder Mountains. In the next half mile, the trail switchbacks three times in passing aspen groves. You also see a crumpled, pointed peak to the west. Finally, the trail levels on the right of a wooded area. This is the divide, but the forest on the far side blocks the view. To see Castle Peak and the canyon of Germania Creek, you have to climb the small, steep hill on the right (9,059). In doing so, please zigzag across the hill, to avoid causing more erosion of the path.

From the hill you can look down into the canyon of Germania Creek, which is lined with charcoal gray cliffs. Across Germania Creek, you can see the gray, white, and red-orange summit of Castle Peak. The unique view of Castle Peak from here is worth the long, steep climb.

From its summit, the trail descends 1,660 feet in 2 steep miles to the Germania Creek Trail, meeting it 6 miles below Three Cabins Creek.

135.

WEST PASS CREEK DIVIDE FROM THE EAST FORK SALMON RIVER

Round trip: 10 miles from end of West Pass Creek Road; connects with trail from North Fork Wood River.
Elevation gain: 2,720 feet **Highest point:** 10,040 feet
Map: Ryan Peak
Trail beginning GPS: 43 57.134, 114 26.542
Difficulty: expert; time: 8 to 9 hours
Access: On Idaho 75, 37.6 miles east of Stanley, turn right (south) on the East Fork of the Salmon River Road. Drive 14.6 miles on pavement, 9 miles on gravel and dirt, (road 120) and 2.4 miles on a primitive road to the West Pass Creek Road (063), which begins 28 miles from the highway. Turn left (east) and drive 3.2 miles on a rough, primitive road to a flat grassy area where the road is closed to motor vehicles.

What you'll see: This sketchy trail goes through long open grassy areas with views of gray, orange and rusty red peaks. Above the trail beginning high gray bluffs look melted and dripping. At its upper end, the trail is just a line of rock cairns. Because it is rarely used, it provides a great place to see wildlife.

Directions: Just beyond the gated private property near the end of the road to Bowery, two roads turn off to the left (south). The first goes to a hot spring. Take the second, which goes up West Pass Creek. They meet each other just beyond a path down to the hot springs. The road is steep and rutted at first, then has mud holes , but after the first mile is a little better.

From the place 3.2 miles from the turnoff where the road is blocked

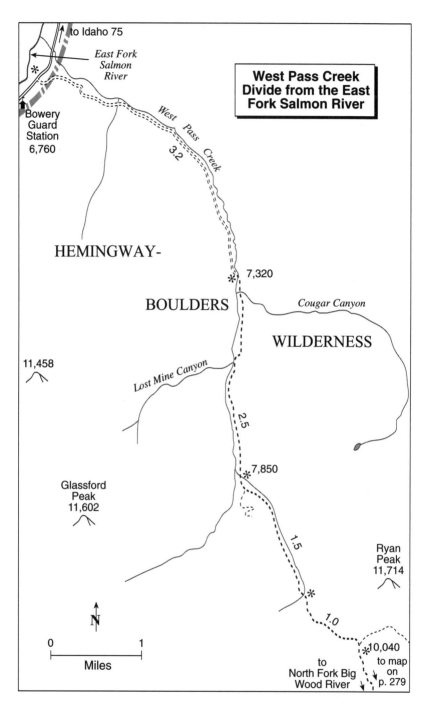

to Idaho 75

East Fork
Salmon
River

Bowery
Guard
Station
6,760

West Pass Creek

3.2

**West Pass Creek
Divide from the East
Fork Salmon River**

HEMINGWAY-

7,320

Cougar Canyon

BOULDERS

WILDERNESS

11,458

Lost Mine Canyon

2.5

7,850

Glassford
Peak
11,602

1.5

Ryan
Peak
11,714

N

0   1

Miles

1.0

10,040

to
North Fork Big
Wood River

to map
on
p. 279

300

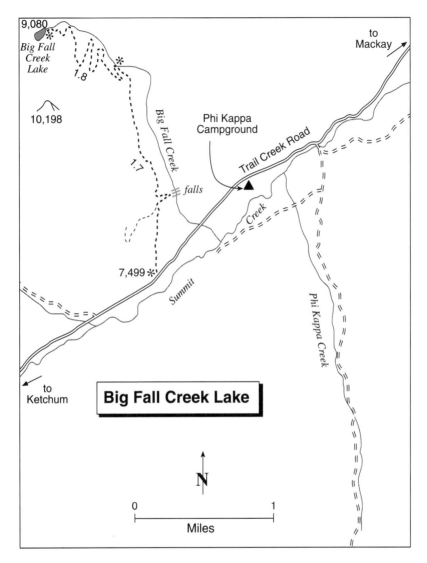

Big Fall Creek Lake

off at 7,320 feet start hiking along the closed road. It leads along the right side of the creek for 150 yards, then fords the creek to the west side in willows. The ford can be dangerous in early summer.

Once across, follow the old road as it climbs up the canyon. At .3 mile, it fords little Cougar Creek. The road alternates Douglas firs with open areas where you can look across at aspens in avalanche areas.

At 1 mile, the road steepens and curves right and then left. It comes into a big open area where you see a blocky peak at the head of Lost Mine Canyon to the right and pointed peaks straight ahead. It returns to forest and continues to climb, crossing two tiny creeks. At 2.5 miles,

Big Fall Creek Lake

the track drops to West Pass Creek and fords it back to the right (west) side (7,850 feet). Now watch for a blazed trail going off to the left 150 yards beyond the ford and turn off the road onto it. The road keeps on going another .7 mile to a former mine on the side of Lost Mine Canyon.

Next , the trail climbs on through forest and open areas. At an open area at 3 miles are two ruined log cabins. Soon, the trail is on a steep wooded hillside above the creek. At 3.5 miles, the trail crosses loose talus and goes among small trees on an old avalanche. Soon the grasses between the trees obscure the trail tread. At the head of the canyon you can see a level, green ridge that appears to be West Pass Creek Divide, but instead it is the divide between Ryan and Kent Peaks.

At 3.8 miles, is a long open area of boulders. Here only cairns show the route. On the trail (right) side of the canyon rise three rock towers. At 4 miles, the open area ends, opposite the gorge of a side creek on the other side of the canyon. Here you cross a side creek, then turn left (east) and ford the main creek. Beyond the ford, faint traces of the trail go straight up a steep hillside.

At 4.5 miles is a rocky slope with a few whitebark pines. Below are mounds of boulders and above rise burnt orange summits. Follow the cairns to the left away from the boulders in the canyon bottom. The route switchbacks up the rocky hill that hides the divide. Then it climbs past a little meadow and zigzags through a ravine to the top of the divide (10,040 feet) at 5 miles.

OUTSIDE THE SAWTOOTH NATIONAL RECREATION AREA

TRAIL CREEK AREA

*136.

BIG FALL CREEK LAKE

Round trip: 7 miles
Elevation gain: 1,540 feet **Highest point:** 9,100 feet
Map: Phi Kappa Mountain
Trailhead GPS: N 43 51 05.5 W 114 13 48.9
Difficulty: strenuous
Time: 6 to 7 hours

Access: From Ketchum take Sun Valley Road east past the golf course and the Hemingway Memorial. It turns into Trail Creek Road and after 8 miles is a dirt one-lane rocky road with no guard rail. Go 2.5 miles past Trail Creek Summit at 12 miles , and find a sign for Big Fall Creek Lake on the south side of the road facing east. The former jeep trail is now an ATV trail and is closed to full size vehicles.

What you'll see: The lake sits in a wildflower-filled basin under a high gray peak topped with lumpy cliffs. From the trail there is an excellent view of the Devils Bedstead, and other cliff-covered mountains in the Pioneers to the south.

Directions: The trail follows an old road that begins with a steep climb in the open and then goes into a Douglas fir forest. In the forest it switchbacks left (west) and passes an old cabin with a tree on its roof. Beyond the cabin the track curves north along the side of a ridge and at 1 mile comes out in the open and crosses avalanche slides.

At 1.7 miles the trail comes to a creek and turns away from it in forest. It is now steep and covered with sharp rocks. At 1.8 miles it begins long switchbacks to the north and then south again at 2.1 miles. It gets even steeper , and at 2.5 miles switches south and then north again. At 2.8 miles the track reaches a high point under a high reddish mountain. Here a branch goes up to the left to a mine. Take the road to the right that goes downhill around the end of a ridge. Soon you are above an old mining cabin. Where the road turns to go down to the cabin, take a side road that goes uphill to a clump of trees and ends at 3 miles.

From here take a path that leads northwest, well above the creek on open, grassy slopes. It soon curves left and then switchbacks right at a steep, slippery corner. It continues around the curve of a hill and comes out into a grassy bowl with the lake at 3.5 miles. A campsite is in a clump of trees on the left (east) side of the lake.

*137.

TOOLBOX CREEK

Round trip: 6 miles
Elevation gain: 1360 feet **Highest point:** 8,800 feet
Maps: Herd Peak, Meridian Peak
Trailhead GPS: N 43 56 39.9 W 114 14 17.6 W
Difficulty: moderate to strenuous time: 6 hours
Access: From Ketchum drive east on Sun Valley Road, which becomes rough and rocky Trail Creek Road. At 18.5 miles turn left (north) on the dirt North Fork Big Lost River Road. At Toolbox Creek at 25 miles, turn right on a two wheel track and drive about 200 yards to the trailhead.

What you'll see: From the two divides on this trail you get a view of the white side of Castle Peak and its shoulders to the west and of rugged brown and pale sand peaks to the north. You can also look south at the swooping gray mountains on the other side of the North Fork of the Big Lost River.

Directions: The trail starts at a gate in a fence a few yards beyond the end of the road. It goes along in willows and after 100 yards crosses

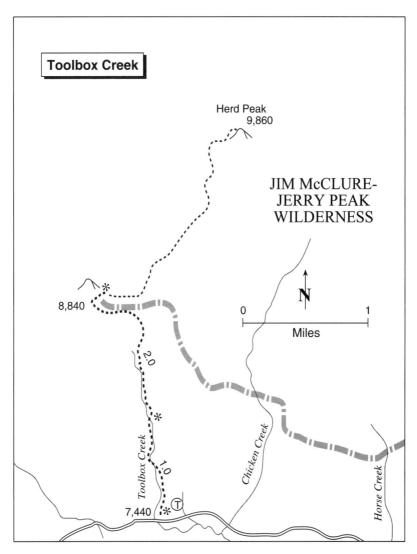

Toolbox Creek

Herd Peak
9,860

JIM McCLURE-
JERRY PEAK
WILDERNESS

N

8,840

0   Miles   1

2.0

Toolbox Creek

Chicken Creek

1.0

Horse Creek

7,440   T

to the left (north) side of the creek. It climbs a little in a Douglas fir forest and then alternates sagebrush, willows, and meadows, At 1 mile the
trail crosses back to the right side of the creek in a flat grassy area
with a possible campsite. The trail climbs along the creek through
meadow and patches of forest, getting steeper as it goes. Now and then
you can look back across the North Fork to gray peaks beyond it,

The creek ends at a spring where the trail begins to curve west into
a forest of mixed lodgepole and subalpine fir. On the map the trail is
shown going straight up a ridge to the right, but it doesn't. Instead it
makes a very long switchback to the left ((west) and then turns straight

305

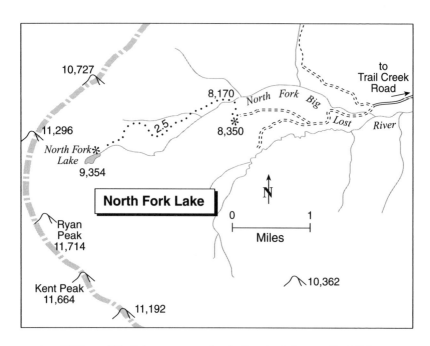

North Fork Lake

Labels on map: 10,727 · 8,170 · North Fork Big · to Trail Creek Road · 11,296 · 2.5 · 8,350 · Lost · River · North Fork Lake · 9,354 · N · 0 · 1 · Miles · Ryan Peak 11,714 · Kent Peak 11,664 · 11,192 · 10,362

up to a little saddle It has gone so far before turning up that it has gone off the Herd Peak map, so figuring out where you are is confusing. You are looking across Meridian Creek. On the saddle the trail comes to an unsigned T intersection. Take the right branch and avoid a path that goes up a rounded hill ahead. The trail skirts the base of that hill and at 3 miles comes to another saddle, with a view to the north. If you want to climb Herd Peak from here the trail goes straight up a steep high ridge to the east that is a shoulder of the peak, and follows along the side and top of it in another 1,000 feet of climb to the summit at 5 miles.

138.

NORTH FORK LAKE

Round trip: 5 miles from the North Fork of the Big Lost River Road
Elevation gain: 1,184 feet **Highest point:** 9,354 feet
Elevation loss (return climb): 190 feet
Maps: Meridian Peak, Ryan Peak
Trail beginning GPS: 43 55.490, 114 21.089
Difficulty: cross-country for experts; time: 7 hours
Access: In Ketchum, go east on Sun Valley Road, which turns into Trail Creek Road over Trail Creek Summit. A slow speed on the rocky road will help avoid flat tires. At 20.4 miles, turn left (west) on the dirt

North Fork Lake

North Fork of the Big Lost River Road (128). Pass the turnoff for Hunter Creek Summit at 31.7 miles and cross the North Fork on a bridge. At 32.1 miles, the road splits. Take the left branch uphill. At a Y at 32.9 miles, take the right branch along a ridge. Park where the road comes to a grove of aspens on the crest of the ridge before it turns downhill at 33.9 miles.

What you'll see: North Fork Lake is unique because its strip of aquamarine water separates a gray mountain wall from an orange one. At the head of the lake, orange rock meets gray rock in a row of orange cylinders divided by strips of gray. The peak on the south side of the lake is gray, and the mountain on the north is orange. There are stripes where the two colors meet at the head of the lake.

Directions: From the aspen grove (8,360 feet), walk down the road to the right (north) off the ridge. It switchbacks to the right and passes a junction with a jeep road coming from the right. Then it winds down through meadows to the North Fork at .5 mile. Once at the North Fork (8,170 feet), ford the creek to the north side and climb away from it a few yards to find the sketchy trail. It goes only about a mile before fading. Continuing to the lake from the end of it is steep and confusing. The upper creek runs in a gorge, so you can't just follow the creek.

The trail first goes along a lodgepole bench at a distance from the creek. Then it heads back toward it, crossing a side creek. It goes out into sagebrush, back into woods, and at 1.5 miles, enters a big meadow. A trail sign points to the right, and the trail goes uphill around the upper edge of the meadow and along the lower edge of a sagebrush slope above forest until it appears to end in woods. Six hundred feet of the climb is left with not much of a path.

The best route goes right (northwest) to the top of the sagebrush ridge. Then turn west and follow the crest of a little ridge above a creek that parallels the main canyon. Where the slopes to the left become less steep, turn left (south), aiming for the flat summit of the ridge. If you cut over too soon, you will end up on cliffs or a very steep slope. Once in the main canyon, just follow it, which is no longer steep, to a small flat meadow and then the lake (9,354 feet) at 2.5 miles.

JIM MCCLURE-JERRY PEAK WILDERNESS

Salmon-Challis National Forest and Challis Field Office, Bureau of Land Management

EAST FORK SALMON RIVER AREA

*139.

Lake Basin

Round trip: 15 miles
Elevation gain: 2,140 feet **Highest point:** 8,360 feet
Map: Herd Lake
Trailhead GPS: N 44 06 19.5, We 114 14 25.5
Difficulty: Expert **Time:** 2 to 3 days
Access: From Stanley drive northeast on Idaho 75 for 36,7 miles to the East Fork Salmon River Road. Turn south and follow this road for 10 miles to the Herd Lake Road. Turn left (east) and go 5 miles to the upper Herd Creek trailhead

What you'll see: This is a trek into the wildest country you can imagine, where the few trails are overgrown with sagebrush and over-looked by the brown cliffs of unnamed peaks. You will see beaver ponds, tiny cacti, and in season the white flowers of evening primrose. There are no blazes or cairns and few signs, and the trails are often faint.

Directions: From the Herd Lake Road, the trail (No. 51) climbs over a low ridge of grass and sagebrush and soon enters the wilderness. At 0.3 mile the trail splits. Straight ahead is a barbed wire fence. Take the branch to the right which leads downhill through a gate. Beyond the gate the trail continues through sagebrush high above the meanders of Herd Creek. Now and then it descends into and climbs out of ravines. Few of these are signed and few are labeled on the map. At 1.0 mile it crosses Pine Gulch and at 1.3 miles Bull Gulch, just beyond the border of the Salmon-Challis National Forest

At 1.8 miles an unmarked trail comes in from the south from East Pass Creek. Its tread and that of its branch up Sagebrush Creek is faint in those canyons. At 2 miles the canyon forms a narrow Y and there is a sign here for East Pass Creek, but no trail. You can look up the canyon of that creek past partly-timbered hills to a double-pointed peak.

The trail descends to go right along the creek through willows and meadows with nettles, and is overgrown. It is now going up the East Fork of Herd Creek. At about 2.8 miles the trail goes into the creek for 75 yards below a pointed outcrop. Here you can ford to the west side, follow a sketchy path, and ford back to the east. Just before Hell Canyon at about 4.8 miles you can camp on a narrow grass and sagebrush flat on the west side of the main creek. Above them rise two gullies filled with Douglas firs.

At 5.8 miles a larger side canyon goes up to the left (east) and the trail follows this canyon, which is the canyon of Lake Basin Creek. It is confusing because the trail is faint and has side paths. At 6 miles the canyon splits again. The most well worn path fords the creek here to the right (south) side. Beyond the ford are two indistinct paths. One goes straight up the sagebrush hill ahead and one turns left and climbs the creek a few yards from it. This is NOT the canyon of Lake Basin Creek. And that path soon disappears on a steep slope. If you keep going up that slope you will see at about 6.3 miles a path on the other side of the creek. It leads through sagebrush basins under high brown outcrops. A basin at 6.5 miles contains an old corral right by the creek. From the corral a trail crosses back over the creek to the south and

A pond in Lake Basin

climbs low hills to a small pond in willows. This pond is on the map at
6.8 miles. Here you meet the official trail that has come up the ridge
from the first ford as a faint trace. Beyond the pond that trail goes
south up a low ridge. Two faint trails branch from its top. One
descends to Lake Basin Creek ahead and soon ends The other goes
southeast along the top of the ridge and down the end of it. . This
branch is the main trail. There is no path from the ford on the other
branch. The main trail, which is very faint, descends the end of the little ridge and continues through the sagebrush, climbing to the two

310

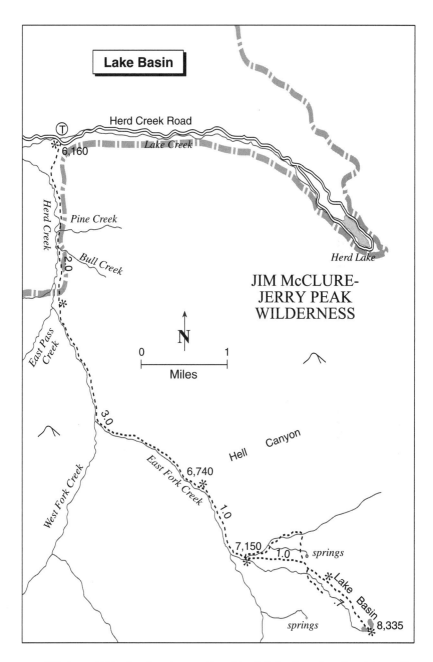

Lake Basin

Herd Creek Road

T

*6,160

Lake Creek

Herd Creek

Pine Creek

Bull Creek

2.0

East Pass Creek

Herd Lake

JIM McCLURE-
JERRY PEAK
WILDERNESS

N

0   1

Miles

3.0

West Fork Creek

East Fork Creek

Hell   Canyon

6,740
*

1.0

7,150
*

1.0   *springs*

Lake Basin

.7

springs

8,335
*

small lakes of the basin at 7.7 miles. Each lake is only about 0.1 mile across. They are similar to the pond -- in willows and alders below hills that lack timber. From the lakes two branches of the Trail 51, the trail

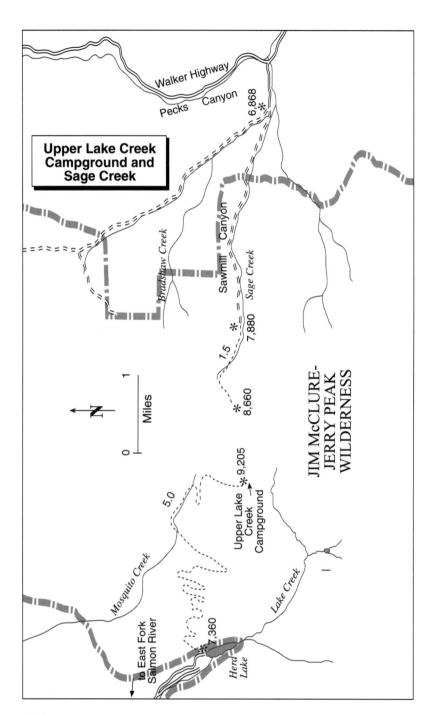

Upper Lake Creek
Campground and
Sage Creek

Walker Highway

Pecks Canyon

6,868 *

Bradshaw Creek

Sawmill Canyon

Sage Creek

1.5 * 7,880

* 8,660

N

1

Miles

0

5.0

Mosquito Creek

Upper Lake Creek Campground

9,205 *

JIM McCLURE-
JERRY PEAK
WILDERNESS

Lake Creek

to East Fork Salmon River

7,360 *

Herd Lake

you have followed all the way from the Herd Lake Road, are supposed to lead to the top of the ridge above the lakes and southwest along it to Herd Peak but there is little evidence of either one.

*140.

Upper Lake Creek Campground

Round trip: 10 miles
Elevation gain: 1,850 feet **Highest point:** 9,150 feet
Map: Herd Lake
Trailhead GPS: N 44 05 33.2, W 114 10 39.6
Difficulty: strenuous to expert **Time:** 8 hours

Access: From Stanley, drive 37.6 miles northeast on Idaho 75 to the East Fork Salmon River Road. Go south up that road for 10 miles to the Herd Lake Road. Turn right (east) here and drive 9.2 miles to the end of the road at an overlook above Herd Lake

What you'll see: You follow an old road not open to motorized travel) through slopes of black talus, fir and mountain mahogany, past sharp peaks to a defunct campground. At the beginning is a view of Herd Lake among hills of grass and sagebrush topped with forest.

Directions: The old road that is now a trail starts out at a blockade of large

View from Upper Lake Creek Campground Trail (Chris Fuller photo)

313

rocks and goes uphill in gradual curves under occasional 20 to 30 foot outcrops. At the north end of a switchback at 1.8 miles a spring sends out a trickle of water below the trail. Just beyond the next loop, which extends to the south, the track climbs 20 vertical feet all at once through big rocks and continues through this talus for 150 yards.

At about 3.4 miles the track goes along the left (north) side of a meadow with a dry streambed in it. By 3.6 miles in July the stream has water and groves of lodgepoles on the far side of the stream provide possible campsites. At 3.7 miles the old road crosses the stream on a culvert to the right and goes across the face of a wooded hill. After 1/4 mile it switches back and comes out on the west side of a canyon that runs north-south. It goes south along this open hillside to the head of the canyon where it goes into forest and curves east. In 200 yards it turns into the old campground. The campground has two picnic tables and a vault toilet but no water. Beyond the campground the old road fades and disappears. On the Salmon-Challis Forest map the campground is shown as much closer to Sage Creek than it is.

*141.

BOWERY CREEK

Round trip: 9.6 miles
Elevation gain: 2,190 feet; **Highest point:** 8,640 feet
Elevation loss: 100 feet
Maps: Bowery Creek, Bowery Peak
Trailhead GPS: N 44 01 46.7 W 114 27 48.5
Difficulty: strenuous **Time:** 8 to 9 hours
Access: Drive east of Stanley on Idaho 75 for 37.5 miles. Turn right (south) on the East Fork Salmon River Road and drive 28.3 miles to the old Bowery Creek trailhead next to the river.

What you'll see: This canyon gives a view of the white side and shoulders of Castle Peak across the East Fork. You also can look up at a long line of brown cliffs and the pale sandy top of Bowery Peak. In the fall the many aspens blush with gold and orange. From the divide you can look over into the canyon of East Pass Creek.

Directions: From the parking area, walk back up to the East Fork Road and along it 200 yards to the sign. Then go down the trail to the river and wade across it, taking care to put your feet between the large rocks. It was still knee deep in late September, so in early summer would be impassable. Because of this ford it is a trail meant for horses. On the other side the trail begins by going south until it meets the old trail at .2 mile. Here it turns uphill and climbs through an aspen grove. The trail then goes along an open sagebrush hillside, with an occasional aspen grove. At .6 mile it crosses Narrow Canyon Creek. After a long stretch of more sagebrush with the view of Castle Peak and more

314

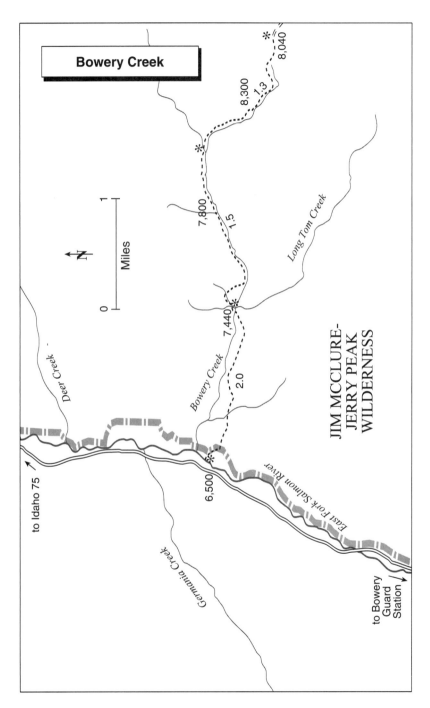

Bowery Creek

to Idaho 75

Deer Creek

N
Miles
0   1

8,040
8,300
1.3
7,800
1.5
7,440
2.0
6,500

Long Tom Creek

Bowery Creek

East Fork Salmon River

Germania Creek

JIM MCCLURE-
JERRY PEAK
WILDERNESS

to Bowery
Guard
Station

Herd Lake

aspens it makes a slow descent to Bowery Creek and at 2 miles fords it to the north side. Now the trail climbs away from the creek through an aspen grove and then a sagebrush slope. Until it is under the wall of brown cliffs. It then returns to the creek and goes along in meadows, sagebrush and aspens. At 3 miles the trail crosses an unnamed side creek in aspens. The next half mile is alongside a series of meadows. At 3.5 miles it curves into a larger meadow with campsites and crosses Bowery Creek, now small, back to the south side. After this the trail climbs in woods and at about 4 miles splits with an unsigned branch going off to the left. Keep on the right branch, signed 244. The trail now climbs in the open to a saddle at 4.8 miles (8,640 feet), and on the other side drops into the canyon of East Pass Creek.

*142.

SAGE CREEK

Round trip: about 3 miles to end of old roadbed
Elevation gain: 600 feet **Highest point:** 8,400 feet
Maps: Jerry Peak, Herd Lake
Trailhead GPS: N 44 05 14.1, W 114 05 22.4
Difficulty: expert **time:** 4 hours from trailhead to end of former road
Access: On Idaho 75 drive 37.5 miles northeast of Stanley to the East Fork Salmon River Road. Turn right (south) here and go 6.4 miles to Road Creek. Turn left (east) here and drive to a junction at 13.4 miles with the Dry Gulch Road. Turn right (south) here. The road is labeled Walker Way on the maps. It goes along side of hills and through Peck's Canyon, which is full of mountain mahogany and blocky limestone cliffs, to a junction with the Sage Creek Road at 19.7 miles. You can also reach this junction from the Trail Creek Road by way of Walker Way. The turnoff is about five miles from US 93. Turn right (west) on the Sage Creek Road. If you have 4-wheel drive and high clearance, you can drive 3.2 miles to where the road is closed to motor vehicles. If not, you'll need to park somewhere before that.

What you will see: The Challis Field Office of the BLM says this is a user-created off-highway (OHV) trail. If so, it is so over grown with sagebrush it must be an old one. This track goes up the remote canyon of Sage Creek toward the old road that leads from Herd Lake to a campground called Upper Lake Creek. The canyon is full of sagebrush and Douglas firs, and the walls are high peaks with brown cliffs and towers. Those who are willing to do some rough cross country hiking may be able to reach the campground, but since it has no view and no water it's probably not worth it from this side However, the access up Road Creek and through Peck's Canyon is scenic, and so is the first part of the hike.

Directions: From the place where the road is blocked off the road continues for about 300 yards before it dwindles into three paths. Two of them go up either side of the creek in a tangle of timber and bushes. Take the third which crosses the creek to the left side and goes straight uphill for about 50 vertical feet where it becomes (or meets) an old road that is overgrown with sagebrush. This is the trail you follow. Continue up it for over a mile. At about 1.2 or 1.3 miles it curves to the left and steepens. At about 1.5 miles it pretty much disappears as it climbs the headwall of the canyon. The challis BLM office says the road goes through to the Upper Lake Creek Campground, but I doubt it. The upper end of Sage Creek is a fine destination in itself because the canyon is lined with rugged mountains that are worth photographing.

*143.

EAST PASS CREEK FROM HUNTER CREEK SUMMIT

Round trip: 12 miles to waterfall
Elevation gain: 1,280 feet; **Highest point:** 9,400 feet
Elevation loss (return climb): 1,360 feet
Map: Meridian Peak
Difficulty: strenuous due to steepness, erosion and creek crossings; time: 2 to 3 days
Access: From Idaho 75 at Ketchum, turn east on Sun Valley Road. Go past Sun Valley and drive Forest Road 408 over Trail Creek Summit at 12 miles. The road turns to rocky gravel at 8.4 miles. Flat tires are frequent. The road turns to 208 at the summit. At 19 miles turn left on the North Fork of Lost River Road. Drive this road, which soon becomes dirt to the turnoff for the Hunter Creek Trail at 31.4 miles. Continue on the rutted and rocky 4 wheel drive road for 1.2 miles to its end on a sagebrush slope.

What you'll see: The view of the rugged, snow-streaked mountains such as Ryan and Kent Peaks at the head of the North Fork of the Big Lost River is magnificent, beginning at the trailhead. You can also see the sandy white summits of Bowery and Sheep peaks down the canyon. East Pass Creek has meadows of sagebrush and grass in the valley bottom and partly timbered walls.

Directions: From the no motor vehicles sign, the trail climbs the sagebrush hill to the right, travels level for a bit, then drops into forest and fords the creek to the north side. As you go along there are many crossings of small side creeks. At about one mile the trail comes back to the east (right) side of the main creek.

At 1.25 miles it goes to the left side again and then right at 1.6. At 2 miles it crosses back to the left and goes up steeply, making one long switchback as it goes. At 2.2 miles the trail goes over to the right of a

East Pass Creek (Chris Fuller photo)

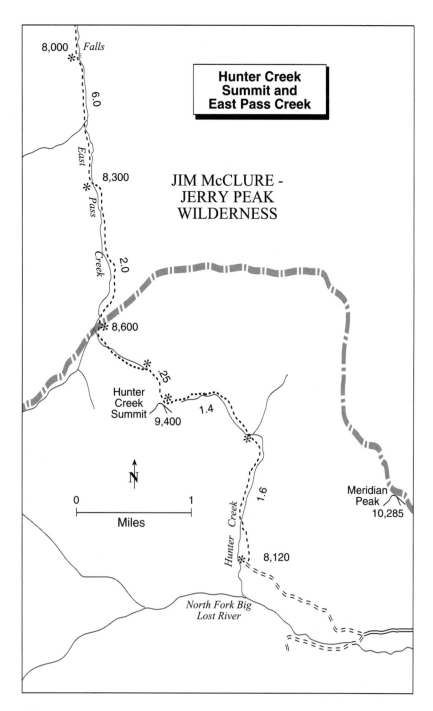

8,000 *Falls*

6.0

East

8,300

Pass

**Hunter Creek
Summit and
East Pass Creek**

JIM McCLURE -
JERRY PEAK
WILDERNESS

Creek

2.0

8,600

.25

Hunter
Creek
Summit
9,400

1.4

N

0   1

Miles

Hunter Creek

1.6

Meridian
Peak
10,285

8,120

*North Fork Big
Lost River*

side creek and from there to the summit goes straight up the right side of that now dry creek. The footing is difficult with pebbles sliding on hard dirt. At about 1.8 miles you pass a flat, mossy meadow, where you might be able to camp early in the summer before the creek dries up. At about 3.5 miles you reach the summit, which is in another meadow, which is drier. You can't see out to any mountains.

A trail junction with no signs is here. The right branch is a stock driveway along the ridge. Follow it for about 1/4 mile for a view of the peaks in both directions. The left branch goes downhill, first along the face of the ridge in forest and then straight down. It is steep, alternating grassy slopes with patches of forest. At about 3.5 miles the trail crosses a little stream to the left side. Just beyond it and a few feet uphill is a big flat grassy place where people have camped. There are too many trees to see out.

Beyond the campsite the trail heads straight downhill through forest and a couple of big open grassy areas. At 4 miles the trail joins one that comes in from the left (south) and proceeds to follow the canyon of East Pass Creek at a distance above it. The trail soon crosses a couple of side creeks, than arrives at a big flat meadow at 5 miles. with a view up the canyon of peaks at its head. After more sagebrush and some forest you come to a second meadow. Just beyond it is a big outfitters camp with some pole tent bases. Soon you reach an open slope of sagebrush and grass where the trail disappears. Cut down toward the main creek to find it again. There is soon a repeat of the big sagebrush and grass area, and then at 6 miles the trail crosses the creek to the left (north) side on a plank footbridge.

It is another mile and 500 feet of descent to where you can go over to the creek to see a waterfall. Two miles below this is a junction with the trail that comes over a divide from Bowery Creek. Below here the trail fades out within a mile and the canyon bottom is too rugged and remote to recommend descending it any farther.

APPENDIX

OTHER TRAILS AND ROUTES

The trails listed here are of three kinds: trails the author hasn't hiked, trails she found disappointing, and cross-country hikes that are not described in detail in the text. The descriptions of the cross-country routes listed here tell in which hikes brief directions for them are given. Elevations are given for the unnamed lakes to help identify where they are located. (Several other cross-country routes are described in complete detail as hikes in the text.) For trails that intersect other trails described in the hike writeups, but which the author hasn't hiked, brief information is given in the appropriate hike description. These trails and the hike descriptions in which they are mentioned are listed here. For trails that don't intersect any described trails, the brief information is given here in the appendix.

SAWTOOTHS

ALTURAS SHORE: From dirt road off the Alturas Lake Road (205) 3.5 miles to Inlet Day Use Area, Elevation gain: 200 feet, elevation loss 200 feet, Maps: Alturas Lake, Snowyside Peak. Trail removed from book because it was rerouted onto old road way above lake shore because of many fallen trees. The rerouting took away the view and it is still difficult to follow due to downed timber.

AZURE LAKE: in Johnson Lake Junction to Johnson Lake and Pats Lake

BENCH CREEK TRAIL: Access: Highway 21. From Highway 21, .4 mile south of the road to Bull Trout Lake, southeast to Swamp Creek Trail, .1 mile north of Marten Lake. Only .7 mile of this trail is in the SNRA. 5.5 miles, 1,280-foot elevation gain, 644-foot loss. Map: Banner Summit

BENEDICT CREEK TRAIL: in Ingeborg, Rock Slide, and Benedict Lakes

CIRQUE LAKE (9,020 feet): In Baron Creek Trail to Baron Lakes

DECKER CREEK: an abandoned trail that is now impassable due to dead trees that mostly fell during the winter of 2015-16. From the Bull Moose trail 200 yards from its lower end to Decker Creek and up it and a ridge to the trail between Hell Roaring and Redfish lakes.5.3 miles, 1,450 feet gain, highest point, 8,470 feet. Maps: Obsidian, Mt. Cramer

DIAMOND LAKE: in Scenic Lakes Junction to High Pass and the Johnson Lake Junction

DUTCH LAKE: From primitive road (195) .5 mile south of Thatcher Creek Campground on Idaho 21. Goes 1 mile to lily-covered lake in woods. 160 feet elevation gain. No view out. A path leads from end of ridge on primitive road up and along it to pond and then the lake. Map:

Dutch Lake

Banner Summit.

ELK CREEK TRAIL: in Observation Peak

FISHHOOK CREEK NATURE TRAIL: From Redfish Lake Visitor Center. From the center it makes a .3-mile loop through a marsh and along the creek. Map: Stanley

FLAT TOP LAKES: in Scenic Lakes

ESTHER LAKE (8,556 feet) AND OTHER LAKES ALONG INLET OF IMOGENE LAKE: in Imogene Lake

FINGER OF FATE LAKE (8,200 feet): in Hell Roaring Lake

GOAT CREEK LAKES ABOVE GRANDJEAN (SUCH AS WARBONNET LAKES): Directions are deliberately not given because crossing into the upper end of Goat Creek canyon from Redfish Canyon can be dangerous, and hiking up Goat Creek from the South Fork of the Payette leads through much downed timber.

HIDDEN LAKE: (No trail) From Highway 75 at Trap Creek Campground. Although a trail is shown on the topographic map, it does not exist. Only cow paths wander over the meadows in the area. From the campground, walk up the chain of meadows along Meadow Creek, then at 1.5 miles climb up onto a ridge to the right (north) and follow it to the lake at 2 miles. (300-foot elevation gain). Reaching the lake is difficult and hazardous because of bogs, downed timber, and lack of landmarks. A compass is required. When you get there, all you see are wooded hills. Map: Elk Meadow

JOE DALEY TRAIL: in Queens River

JOHNSON CREEK TRAIL (lower end near Graham): Must drive through the North Fork of the Boise River to reach trailhead. The trail runs from just above the Johnson Creek Campground east and north to the Bayhouse Trail. Upper end of the trail is covered in the text. Between the campground and the Bayhouse Trail there are four fords of the creek. The area along the trail burned in the 1994 fires. 5 miles, 700-foot elevation gain. The trail also leads from the campground down Johnson Creek to the Deer Park guard station. Both of these sections are not in the SNRA. Another trail climbs above the part of the section that goes to Deer Park, providing access to Warrior Lakes and the summit of Swanholm Peak. Maps: Swanholm Peak, Nahneke Mountain

LAKES ON SIDE OF MCGOWN PEAK (8,575 and 8,609 feet): in North Alpine Way Trail to Stanley Lake

NEINMEYER CREEK TRAIL: From Johnson Creek Trail, .6 mile south of Bayhouse Trail Junction near Graham, southeast over Grouse Creek Pass down to Black Warrior Creek. Then it goes over another divide and down to the Little Queens River, 6.2 miles from the trailhead. Much of the area along the trail has burned in the last ten years. 7.6 miles, 2,320-foot elevation gain, 2,080-foot elevation loss. Map: Nahneke Mountain

NORTH FORK BOISE RIVER TRAIL: From the South Fork Payette River Trail 3.8 miles above Grandjean south to the Bayhouse Trail 1 mile east of the Graham Road. North end begins with a 120-foot ford of South Fork of Payette, which can be dangerous or impassable in early summer. The south end connects with a 1-mile trail to the Graham Road. This road is a very rough, primitive road recommended only for skilled drivers in 4-wheel drive vehicles with a high wheelbase. The area along the trail burned in the 1994 fires. 11.8 miles, 2,271-foot elevation gain, 1,656-foot elevation loss. Maps: Edaho Mountain, Nahneke Mountain, Swanholm Peak

PARKS PEAK LAKE (8,723 FEET): in Farley to Toxaway Lakes

PICKET MOUNTAIN TRAIL: From the North Fork Boise River Trail near Grandjean over Picket Mountain (within 100 feet of summit) and out of the SNRA to a junction with the Wapiti Creek Trail, from Grandjean. The area along the trail burned in the 1994 fires. 4.5 miles, 1,404-foot elevation gain, 280-foot elevation loss. Map: Edaho Mountain

QUEENS RIVER LAKE (8,702 FEET): in Queens River Canyon to Pats Lake Junction

REDFISH RIDGE: in Grand Mogul Trail

SAWMILL CREEK TRAIL: Non-system trail from road to Vienna goes 1 mile up creek and ends in rock slides and downed timber. There are only bits of trail after that. Hikers can use it and a difficult cross-country route to reach a tiny, shallow lake (8,700 feet) at the head of the canyon, but the view is not very good. Map: Frenchman Creek.

SWAMP CREEK TRAIL: From .7 mile south of Thatcher Creek Campground on Highway 21 to Trap Creek Trail at Marten Lake. 6 miles, 910-foot elevation gain. Overgrown and boggy. Map: Banner Summit.

324

THREE ISLAND LAKE: in Ingeborg, Rock Island and Benedict Lakes

TRAILER LAKES: in Trail Creek Lakes

WHITE CLOUDS

BLUETT CREEK TRAIL: From East Fork Salmon River Road west and then north to Big Lake Creek Trail 5.8 miles from trailhead. Not signed, not maintained, not on topographic map. 6 miles, 2,500-foot elevation gain. Map: Potaman Peak

CHAMBERLAIN CREEK TRAIL: in Germania Creek from East Fork Salmon River and in Germania Creek from Three Cabins Creek to Chamberlain Creek

FISHER CREEK LAKE (7,550 feet): There is a steep and slippery cross-country route from the Fourth of July Creek Road north to the location of a former tiny lake. A trail seen going northwest descends Pass Creek instead. Must ford 4-foot wide canal at beginning. Drought has dried up the lake except perhaps in early spring. Good view of Sawtooths and of cream and gray towers on wooded ridge above the present dry meadow. 1 mile, 240-foot elevation gain, 160-foot elevation loss (return climb). Map: Obsidian

GARLAND CREEK TRAIL: in Rough and Garland lakes.

LITTLE REDFISH LAKE: in Livingston Mill to Frog Lake

MARTIN CREEK TRAIL: in Boundary Creek, Casino Lakes and Big Casino Creek

OCALKENS LAKES (8,872 and 9,040 feet): This discontinued trail begins at the end of the Slate Creek Road , which begins 23.7 miles east of Stanley. It is 7 miles from Highway 75 to the trailhead. 4 miles, 2,050 feet elevation gain. The lakes have views of creamy white peaks with charcoal gray outcrops and the curving multicolored stripes of the Chinese Wall. The Forest Service discontinued maintaining the trail more than 20 years ago to create a trailless, non-motorized area for wildlife protection. The beginning of the old trail is difficult to find. From the trailhead, take the path across the landslide, then follow the old mining road past the mining ruins, and ford the outlet of Hoodoo Lake. Where the old road to Hoodoo Lake turns off to the right, keep straight ahead on the remaining track into an area full of downed small trees. Just before this old road ends, look uphill to the right through more downed timber for the trail. The timber was felled to keep motorcycles out of this non-motorized area. About half way up the trail a washout beyond a ford has narrowed the trail enough to make it difficult for some horseback riders. The continuation of the former trail from Ocalkens Lakes up to Iron Basin and over into Warm Springs Creek is difficult to find and follow. It disappears altogether in Iron Basin. Maps: Livingston Creek, Robinson Bar

POLE CREEK GUARD STATION: From parking area at end of a side road from the Pole Creek-Germania Creek Road .2 mile to historic log guard station. Map: Horton Peak

SECOND WASHINGTON LAKE (9,440 feet): in Fourth of July and Washington lakes

STRAWBERRY BASIN: This former mining road led to the best view of the whitest peaks of the White Clouds. It has now been plowed under. The plowing makes the surface so difficult to hike, the hike description was removed from the text for the 5th edition. However, with two trekking poles, good route-finding skills and conditioning, and plenty of patience you can still hike to the view. With caution, you can also use the route to return from a climb of Blackmon Peak. It is a 6.4-mile round trip and 960-foot elevation gain to the viewpoint. Map: Washington Peak

SUNNY GULCH TRAIL: in Boundary Creek, Casino Lakes, and Big Casino Creek, and in Little Casino Creek

WICKIUP CREEK TRAIL: Access to the trail from the East Fork Salmon River Road is BLOCKED by posted private property where it begins near the corrals at the mouths of Wickiup and Sheep Creeks. Goes southwest and then northwest to unmarked junction with Castle Divide Trail .6 mile north of divide. Not maintained. 7 miles, 3,140-foot elevation gain. Maps: Bowery Creek, Boulder Chain Lakes.

BOULDERS

KONRAD CREEK TRAIL: Goes up only the lower 1.5 miles of Konrad Creek. Not on topographic map. Location of the trail on forest map is wrong. Goes up Konrad Creek on west side, crossing to the east at .7 mile. Does not connect with Amber Lakes Trail. Map: Amber Lakes.

SOUTH FORK EAST FORK SALMON RIVER TRAIL: in East Fork Salmon River Trail

WEST FORK EAST FORK SALMON RIVER TRAIL: in East Fork Salmon River Trail

SMOKIES

TITUS LAKE RIDGE: a cross-country route described in Titus Lake and Titus Creek

GUIDE TO TRIPS

Suggestions for loop or through trips

ALTURAS LAKE TO STANLEY LAKE: From Alturas Lake over Mattingly Creek Divide, down Mattingly Creek, up the Middle Fork of the Boise then to Spangle Lakes, then to Ardeth and Edna Lakes, down across the South Fork of the Payette and up to Hidden Lake, then over Cramer Divide to Cramer Lakes, down to Flatrock Junction on Redfish Creek, over Baron Divide to Baron Lakes, down Baron Creek to the North Fork of Baron Creek, up the North Fork to Sawtooth and McGown Lakes, over a divide to Stanley Lake Creek and down to Stanley Lake. 70 miles; 9 to 12 days.

GRANDJEAN LOOP: From Grandjean to Baron, Alpine, Cramer, Hidden, and Elk Lakes and back to Grandjean. 43 miles; 4 to 6 days. Possible side trips to Edna and Spangle lakes.

HELL ROARING CREEK LOOP: From Hell Roaring trailhead to

Hell Roaring, Imogene, Edith, Edna, Hidden, Cramer, Alpine, Baron, and Trail Creek Lakes, down Stanley Lake Creek to the Alpine Way and south on it to Marshall, and Redfish Lakes, then to Decker Lakes and back to Hell Roaring Creek. 92 miles; 11 to 14 days. Possible side trips to Profile, Spangle, Sawtooth, Bench, and Goat lakes.

POWERPLANT CAMPGROUND AT ATLANTA TO GRAND-JEAN: From the campground up the Middle Fork of the Boise to Rock Creek and Spangle Lakes, then to Ardeth, Edna, Cramer, and Baron Lakes and down to Grandjean. 74 miles; 7 to 10 days. Possible side trips to Ingeborg, Rock Slide, Camp, Heart, and Benedict lakes.

QUEENS RIVER TO GRANDJEAN: from the Queens River Trailhead up the Queens River, then to Everly Lake, down Benedict Creek and down the South Fork of the Payette River to Grandjean. 41 miles; 5 days. Possible side trips to Arrowhead, Pats, and Plummer lakes.

LIVINGSTON MILL TO LITTLE BOULDER CREEK: From Livingston Mill trailhead to Walker, Frog, Boulder Chain and Baker Lakes and down to the Little Boulder Creek trailhead. 35 miles; 5 to 7 days. Possible side trips to Big Boulder, Island, Goat, Shallow, Scree, Quiet, Noisy, and Castle lakes.

GERMANIA CREEK LOOP: From the Three Cabins Creek trailhead down Germania Creek to the Bowery Cutoff, over the Bowery Cutoff to Bowery Guard Station, up the East Fork of the Salmon River and West Fork of the Salmon River trails, and down Galena Gulch, then along the Pole Creek-Germania Creek Road to Three Cabins Creek. 26 miles; 3 to 4 days.

GERMANIA CREEK TO LITTLE BOULDER CREEK: From the Three Cabins Creek trailhead to Chamberlain Lakes, over Castle Divide, down to Baker Lake, and down Little Boulder Creek. 21 miles; 3 to 5 days. Possible side trips to Washington Basin, Castle, Noisy, Quiet, Scree, Shallow, and the Boulder Chain lakes.

Suggestions by difficulty

EASY (not more than 7 miles; less than 1,000-foot elevation gain; no cross-country travel): Elk Meadows, Farley Lake, Fishhook Creek, Fourth of July Lake, Headwaters of the Salmon River, Hell Roaring Lake, Jimmy Smith Lake, The Old Toll Road, Phyllis Lake, Redfish Lake to Flatrock Junction, Yellow Belly Lake

MODERATE (5 to 10 miles and 1,000 to 1,800-foot elevation gain, no cross-country travel):
Alpine Way From Iron Creek to Stanley Lake, Bench Lakes, Galena Gulch, Galena Grinder (part), Grand Mogul Trail, Lower Warm Springs Creek, Mays Creek to McDonald Lake, Marten and Kelly Lakes, Mill Lake, Miner Lake, Murdock Creek, Pettit Lake Over Ridge to McDonald Lake, Sawtooth Lake, Warm Springs Meadows. Some hikes of moderate distance and elevation gain are not listed as moderate because they are cross-country, have difficult footing, or the trail disappears in places. Many people may feel the moderate hikes should be listed as strenuous, especially if they are carrying backpacks, or haven't taken long hikes for several years.

STRENUOUS (over 10 miles and over 1,800 feet elevation gain, no cross-country travel): Those hikes not listed in other categories are strenuous. Some people may feel the hikes the author has listed as strenuous should be called exhausting!

PARTLY OR ALL CROSS-COUNTRY (for experienced hikers only): Alpine Creek Lakes, Bench Lakes 3, 4, and 5, Big Boulder Lakes, Born (Boorn) Lakes, Castle Lake, Decker Lakes, Elizabeth Lake, Four Lakes Basin, Goat Lake (Sawtooths), Goat Lake (White Clouds), Hanson Lakes, Heart Lake (Sawtooths), Heart and Six Lakes (White Clouds), Lake Basin, Lake Jon, Leggit Lake (trail disappears), Lightning Lake, Lucille and Profile Lakes, Mill-Holman Loop, North Fork Lake, Noisy and Quiet Lakes, Rainbow Lake, Rough Lake, Saddleback Lakes, Shallow and Scree Lakes, Sheep Lake, Silver Lake, Sullivan Lake, Thompson Cirque Lake, Upper Redfish Lakes, and West Fork Prairie Creek. (To protect fragile soils and plants, do not camp at these lakes, take only small parties, and in the cross-country part walk on rock where possible.)

EXPERT (poor footing and/or route difficult to find): Alpine Creek Lakes, Amber Lakes from end of trail to lakes, Big Boulder Lakes, Castle Lake, East Fork North Fork, Elizabeth Lake, Four Lakes Basin, Galena Gulch, Goat Lake, Huckleberry Creek, Leggit Lake, Profile Lake, North Fork Lake, Noisy and Quiet Lakes, Rainbow Lake, Rough Lake, Saddleback Lakes, Scenic Lakes, Shallow and Scree Lakes, Silver Lake, Sullivan Lake, Thompson Cirque Lake, Upper Redfish lakes, West Fork North Fork Wood River. (These areas are fragile; avoid camping in the lake basins.)

Amount of use

LIKELY TO BE OVERCROWDED: Alice Lake, Alpine Lake (Redfish), Alpine Lake (Iron Creek), Baron Lakes, Bench Lakes, Boulder Chain Lakes, Cramer Lakes, Farley Lake, Fishhook Creek, Fourth of July Lake, Frog Lake, Hell Roaring Lake, Imogene Lake, Sawtooth Lake, Toxaway Lake, Twin Lakes, Walker Lake, Washington Lake, Williams Creek

SELDOM VISITED: Benedict, Rock Slide, and Ingeborg Lakes, Bowery Creek, Bowery Cutoff, Hanson Lakes, Camp and Heart Lakes, Casino and Garland Lakes, Elizabeth Lake, Elk Lake to Hidden Lake Junction, Everly and Plummer Lakes, Frenchman Creek, Germania Creek from the East, Grand Mogul Trail, Johnson Lake, Leggit Lake, Lookout Mountain, Lower Warm Springs, Marten and Kelly Lakes, North Fork Wood River, Pats and Arrowhead Lakes, Noisy and Quiet Lakes, Rock Creek to Spangle Lakes, Rough Lake, Sawtooth View and Nip Peak, Scenic Lakes, The Boulder Chain Lakes to Shallow, Scree and Quiet Lakes, Sullivan Lake, Upper Lake Campground, Washington Basin, Washington Basin Lake, West Pass Creek Divide

RARELY VISITED: Bayhouse and Johnson Creek Trails, Bowery Cutoff, Champion Creek, Decker Lakes to Redfish Inlet, East Fork North Fork Wood River, East Fork Salmon River, Galena Gulch, Gladiator Creek Divide, Huckleberry Creek, Hunter Creek Summit and East Pass Creek, Lake Basin, Little Casino Creek, Mattingly Creek, Mays Creek to McDonald Lake, Timpa Lake, Toolbox Creek, West Pass Creek Divide from the East

Overnight trips

TWO OR THREE DAYS REQUIRED ON FOOT: Baker Lake, Baron Lakes, Boulder Chain Lakes, Browns Lake, Chamberlain Lakes, Edna Lake, Lake Basin, Leggit Lake, Livingston Mill to Frog Lake, Mattingly Creek, North Fork Baron Creek, Observation Peak, Sand Mountain Pass and the Imogene Divide, Scenic Lakes

THREE TO FIVE DAYS ON FOOT: Ardeth and Spangle Lakes, Arrowhead Lake, Everly and Plummer Lakes, Hidden Lake, Ingeborg, Rock Slide, and Benedict Lakes, Timpa Lake.

Opening dates

OPEN ABOUT JULY 1 IN AN AVERAGE YEAR (except that stream crossings will still be high and difficult): Alpine Way Trail, Alpine Lake (near Sawtooth Lake), Bench Lakes, Bridalveil Falls, Champion Creek, Elk Lake, Farley Lake (from Pettit), Fishhook Creek, Frenchman Creek, Grand Mogul Trail, Grand Prize Gulch, Jimmy Smith Lake, Marshall Lake, Mays Creek, Middle Fork Boise to Rock Creek, Murdock Creek, Sullivan Lake, Upper Lake Creek Campground, Williams Creek

NOT OPEN UNTIL EARLY OR MID-AUGUST: Alpine-Baron Divide, Ardeth-Spangle Divide, Big Boulder Lakes, Castle Divide, Cramer Divide, Ingeborg, Rockslide, and Benedict Lakes, Elizabeth Lake from Stanley Lake, Four Lakes Basin, High Pass, Imogene Divide, Windy Devil Pass above Scoop Lake, Pats Lake Divide (latest pass in the SNRA to open), Sand Mountain Pass, Snowyside Pass

Difficult access roads

Graham Guard Station (4-wheel drive and skilled driver required), Hell Roaring Creek upper trailhead (4-wheel drive required), Phyllis Lake (described here as a hike), Railroad Ridge (described here as a hike), Washington Basin Jeep Trail (described here as a hike), West Pass Creek from Bowery Guard Station, Yellow Belly Lake

Suggested trails for mountain biking

Boundary Creek, Casino Lakes and Big Casino Creek, Decker Flat Road (from the Salmon River bridge across Idaho 21 from the Sawtooth Valley Work Center to the Redfish Lake Road; watch for traffic near the Redfish Lake end), East Fork Salmon River, Elk Meadow loop, Frenchman Creek, Galena Loop Trail and other Galena Lodge trails, Germania Creek from the East, Grand Prize Gulch, Harriman Trail, Headwaters of the Salmon River, Little Boulder Creek, Livingston Mill to Frog Lake, Marten and Kelly Lakes, Mattingly Creek Divide to the ford of Alturas Creek, Nip and Tuck (a dirt road from Lower Stanley to the Stanley Creek Road near the Stanley Lake turnoff on Idaho 21), Pole Creek Road (from Idaho 21 south of Smiley Creek Lodge as far as Grand Prize Gulch), Smiley Creek Road (described as the access road for the Smiley Creek Trail), Stanley Lake Creek to Bridalveil Falls, The Meadows on Warm Springs Creek, The Old Toll Road, Valley Creek Road (this is the old highway, parallel to Idaho 21 from the Stanley

329

Lake Creek Road north to near the Sheep Trail Campground), *Valley Road (parallels Idaho 21 on the east side from the Pole Creek-Germania Creek Road to near the Fourth of July Creek Road), Williams Creek (for the safest travel make a loop by going up the Fisher Creek Road and returning down the Williams Creek Trail.) The author does not recommend the Fourth of July Creek Road as a mountain bike ride because of the heavy automobile traffic.

Sources of information

Sawtooth National Recreation Area Headquarters, 5 North Canyon Road, Ketchum ID 83340. It is just off the highway 8 miles north of Ketchum on Idaho 75. www.fs.usda.gov/sawtooth, 208-727-5000

Stanley Ranger Station, HC 64, Box 9900, Stanley, ID 83278, (5 miles south of Stanley on Idaho 75) 208-774-3681

Redfish Lake Visitors Center at Redfish Lake, 208-774-3376 (summer only)

Lowman Ranger Station (on Idaho 21, 1.5 miles east of Lowman), 208-259-3361

Boise National Forest and Bureau of Land Management Visitors' Center, 1249 S. Vinnell Way, Boise ID 83705, 208-373-4007; www.fs.usda.gov/boise

Sawtooth Society, P.O. Box 268, Boise ID 83701, 208-387-0852 (for information on volunteer opportunities), PO Box 209, Stanley, ID 63278. www.sawtoothsociety.org

Idaho Department of Fish and Game, 600 S. Walnut, Boise ID 83706, 208-334-3700, www.fishandgame.idaho.gov (for information on fishing regulations and fish stocking)

Idaho Outfitters and Guides Association, P.O. Box 95, Boise, ID 83701. 1-800-49-IDAHO or 208-342-1919, www.ioga.org.

National Weather Service www.weather.gov (For five-day forecasts for Ketchum or Stanley)

To order this book and the author's other books www.trailguide-books.com

Suggested reading

Alt, David D. and Donald W. Hyndman, Roadside Geology of Idaho, Missoula, Montana: Mountain Press, 1989.

Berger, Karen, Hiking Light Handbook: Carry Less, Enjoy More, Emmaus, Pennsylvania: Backpacker, 2004.

Bradley, Jim., Environmental Outfitting, Moose Creek Ranger District, Idaho: Nez Perce National Forest, 1975.

Brower, David, Sierra Club Wilderness Handbook, New York: Ballentine Books, 1971.

Cox, Steven M. et al, editors, Mountaineering, the Freedom of the Hills, Seattle, Washington: The Mountaineers, the most current revision

Craighead, John J. and Frank C., Field Guide to Rocky Mountain Wildflowers, Boston: Houghton Mifflin Co., 1963.

Derig, Betty, and Margaret Fuller, Wild Berries of the West, Missoula, Montana: Mountain Press, 2001.

330

Duft, Joseph, and Robert Moseley, Alpine Wildflowers of the Rocky Mountains, Missoula, Montana: Mountain Press, 1989.

Earle, A. Scott, Idaho Mountain Wildflowers, Boise, Idaho: Larkspur Books, 2008.

Elser, Smoke and Bill Brown, Packin' In On Mules and Horses, Missoula, Montana: Mountain Press, 1987.

Fuller, Margaret, Mountains: A Natural History and Hiking Guide, New York: John Wiley & Sons, 1989.

Fuller, Margaret, Forest Fires: An Introduction to Wildland Fire Behavior, Management, Firefighting, and Prevention, New York: John Wiley & Sons, 1991.

Fuller, Margaret and Jerry Painter, Trails of Eastern Idaho: expanded and updated third edition, Weiser, Idaho: 2010.

Fuller, Margaret, Trails of the Frank Church-River of No Return Wilderness: expanded and updated second edition, Weiser, Idaho: Trail Guide Books, 2002, 2006.

Fuller, Margaret, Trails of Western Idaho: expanded and updated third Edition, Weiser, Idaho: Trail Guide Books, 2003, 2006.

Fuller, Margaret and Van Grunsven, Anita, The Weiser River Trail: Idaho's Longest Rail Trail, Cambridge, Idaho: Friends of the Weiser River Trail, 2015, third edition

Harmon, David, Llamas On the Trail: A Packer's Guide. Missoula, Montana: Mountain Press, 1992.

Harvey, Mark, The National Outdoor Leadership School's Wilderness Guide: The Classic Handbook, Revised and Updated, New York: Fireside Books (Simon & Schuster), 1989.

Letham, Lawrence, GPS Made Easy, Seattle, Washington: The Mountaineers Books, 2003.

Little, Elbert L., The Audubon Society Field Guide to North American Trees, Western Region, New York: Alfred A. Knopf, 1980.

Lopez, Tom, Idaho: A Climbing Guide, (Second edition with changed title), Seattle, Washington: The Mountaineers, 2000.

LeFavour, Nicole and Lisk, Mark. Sawtooth White Cloud, Caldwell, Idaho: Caxton Press, 2016

Maley, Terry, Exploring Idaho Geology, Boise, Idaho: Mineral Land Publications, 1979.

Off Belay, Renton, Washington, February 1975: (descriptions of early climbs)

    Bachman, Ben, "Sawtooth Prolog," page 4.

    Stur, Louis, "Sawtooth Pioneering," page 10.

    Bachman, Ben, and Smutek, Ray, "Sawtooth Mountaineering," page 18.

National Geographic Society Field Guide to the Birds of North America, Washington D.C.: National Geographic Society, 2002.

Rember, John, Traplines: Coming Home to Sawtooth Valley. New York: Pantheon, 2003.

Simer, Peter, The National Outdoor Leadership School's Wilderness Guide, New York: Simon & Schuster, 1985.

Spellenberg, Richard, The Audubon Society's Field Guide to North American Wildflowers, Western Region, New York: Alfred A. Knopf, 1979

331

Townsend, Chris, The Backpackers' Handbook. Camden, Maine: Ragged Mountain Press/McGraw Hill 2005.

Whitaker, John O. Jr., The Audubon Society's Field Guide to North American Mammals, New York: Alfred A. Knopf, 1980

Wilkerson, James A., Hypothermia, Frostbite, and Other Cold Injuries, Seattle, Washington: The Mountaineers, 1986.

Yarber, Esther and McGown, Edna, Stanley-Sawtooth Country, Salt Lake City, Utah: Publishers Press, 1976.

BASIC BACKPACKING EQUIPMENT

CLOTHING:
- ❏ broken-in hiking boots
- ❏ wool or acrylic boot socks
- ❏ *long pants
- ❏ *long-sleeved shirt
- ❏ sweater or fleece jacket
- ❏ *insulated jacket
- ❏ *wool hat
- ❏ sun hat
- ❏ *rain poncho or jacket
- ❏ rain pants or chaps
- ❏ *sunglasses
- ❏ complete change of clothes
- ❏ mosquito headnet

GENERAL:
- ❏ comfortable backpack with padded straps and padded waist-band
- ❏ *topographic map
- ❏ *flashlight
- ❏ plastic trowel
- ❏ extra batteries and bulbs
- ❏ toilet paper
- ❏ *compass
- ❏ 30 feet of 1/8" nylon rope
- ❏ plastic bags
- ❏ signal mirror and whistle

COOKING:
- ❏ aluminum cooking pots (2)
- ❏ cup and spoon per person
- ❏ utensils (at least an extra spoon)
- ❏ backpacking stove
- ❏ folding plastic washbasin
- ❏ extra fuel
- ❏ biodegradeable soap

- ❏ work gloves or pot gripper
- ❏ pot scrubber (nylon filament)
- ❏ *extra food
- ❏ *pocket knife
- ❏ *firestarter
- ❏ *waterproof matches
- ❏ *water filter or extra kettle and fuel for boiling water

SLEEPING:
- ❏ tent (breathable fabric with water-proof rainfly)
- ❏ tent "footprint" (waterproof ground cloth cut to the exact size of the tent floor) to put under tent to keep water out OR small tarp to put INSIDE the tent to stop floor leaks in wet weather.
- ❏ down- or synthetic-fill three-season sleeping bag, packed inside plastic bag and waterproof stuff sack
- ❏ waffle-patterned, closed-cell foam pad or foam-filled air mattress

FIRST AID:
- ❏ mosquito repellent
- ❏ sunburn cream
- ❏ lip salve
- ❏ *minimum first aid kit: pain pills, Moleskin, Bandaids, gauze, adhesive tape, antibiotic ointment, electrolyte-replacing drink powder to treat shock, other items and prescriptions recommended by your doctor

* indicates essential items for every hiker

OPTIONAL
❏ set of handheld two-way radios to communicate with other members of your party (There is no cell phone coverage, and satellite phones often work only on high ridges. Most handheld radios send a signal up to only 2 miles.)
❏ GPS unit and practice in using it (does not replace topo map)

❏ playing cards or small games
❏ small toys for kids
❏ camera with extra cards and charged batteries
❏ paperback book
❏ fishing equipment
❏ trekking poles or walking stick
❏ guidebook or copied pages
❏ extra batteries or solar recharger for optional electronics

ABOUT THE AUTHOR

Margaret Fuller is best known for writing five guidebooks to Idaho trails and keeping them up-to-date. The hiking books are Trails of the Sawtooth and Boulder-White Cloud Mountains, Trails of Western Idaho, Trails of the Frank Church – River of No Return Wilderness, Trails of Eastern Idaho (with co-author Jerry Painter), and The Weiser River Trail: Idaho's Longest Rail Trail (with coauthor Anita Van Grunsven.) She has also written three natural history books: Forest Fires: An Introduction to Wildland Fire Behavior, Management, Firefighting, and Prevention; Mountains: A Natural History and Hiking Guide; and Wild Berries of the West (with co-author Betty Derig). To learn more about Margaret's books, view her website at www.trail-guidebooks.com.

The first edition of Trails of the Sawtooth and White Cloud Mountains, published in 1979, was the first comprehensive guidebook to trails in any one area of Idaho. In 1982, the year Trails of Western Idaho was first published, Margaret received the Writer of the Year Award from the Idaho Writer's League. In 1989, the then three hiking guidebooks were endorsed by the Idaho Centennial Commission as official centennial publications. In 1991, Margaret received the Achievement Award from the Idaho Trails Council. In 1991, Forest Fires won first place for books in the Northwest Outdoor Writers' annual contest. In 1996, she received the Women of Today and Tomorrow Award for the outdoors from the Silver Sage Girl Scout Council. That year she was elected to membership in the Society of Woman Geographers (an international organization). In 2003, Outdoor Idaho (Idaho Public Television, Channel 4) profiled Margaret on a program about older Idahoans who have con-

Margaret Fuller on Washington Peak (photo by Dottie Greenwood)

tributed to the knowledge of Idaho's outdoors and who are still active in it. In 2010, Margaret received the Keith and Pat Axline Award for Environmental Activism from the Idaho Conservation League. In 2014

Margaret and her coauthors Doug Fuller and Jerry Painter received a Skade Award from the International Skiing History Association for Ski the Great Potato: Idaho Ski Areas, Past and Present.

Margaret was born and raised in Palo Alto, California, and received a B.A. in biology from Stanford University. She has taught backpacking and mountain ecology in workshops and community education courses and has given more than 250 slide shows about Idaho mountains to community, church and school groups. In doing research for her books she has hiked over 6,000 miles. When she started doing the hikes for the first edition of the Sawtooth book in 1973, she often took at least three of her children along, and sometimes all five. Her husband Wayne would join them when he could get away from his law practice. The family lived in Caldwell for 28 years before moving to Weiser when Wayne was appointed a district judge in 1985. Now Wayne is retired and he and Margaret have seven grandchildren who hike with them.

INDEX

Alice Lake 61, 71-75, 78-79, 189, 328

Alpine Lake to Baron Lakes 16-117

Alpine, Sawtooth, and McGown Lakes 119, 141

Alpine Creek Lakes 59, 328

Alturas Lake Shore 327

Amber Lakes 20, 286, 289, 326, 328

Ardeth Lake 83-85, 143-144, 166

Atlanta 20, 22-23, 31, 66-67, 148, 154, 158, 160-165, 327

Baker Lake 20, 25, 200-201, 238, 240-241, 244, 250, 327, 329

Baker Lake to Noisy and Quiet Lakes 244

Baron Creek Trail to Baron Lakes 137-138, 322

Bayhouse and Johnson Creek Trails 144,328

Bench Lakes 108-111, 327-329

Benedict Lake 143, 166, 322, 325, 327, 329

Big Boulder Lakes 20, 229-230, 232-233, 235, 328-239

Big Fall Creek Lake 302-303

Born (Boorn) Lakes 20, 196-200, 203-204, 216, 238, 328

Born (Boorn) Lakes to Quiet Lake through Four Lakes Basin 199

Boulder Basin 269, 280-281, 297

Boulder Chain Lakes 20, 187, 234-235, 237-238, 240-241, 244, 246, 326-329

Boulder Chain Lakes to Shallow, Scree, and Quiet Lake 20, 246, 328

Boundary Creek, Casino Lakes, and Big Casino Creek 206, 326

Bowery Creek 20, 314, 317, 321, 326, 328

Bowery Cutoff 183, 185, 247-248, 296-298, 327-328

Bridalveil Falls and Hanson Lakes 126, 129

Browns Lake 156, 329

Cabin Lakes 70

Camp and Heart Lakes 165, 167, 328

Casino Lakes 206-210, 325, 326, 329

Castle Lake 20, 241-244, 327, 328

Chamberlain Lakes from Three Cabins Creek 20, 186, 201

Champion Lakes 176-181, 183, 189

Champion Creek 21,175-177, 189-191, 328, 329

Cramer Lakes 94, 111-112, 114-117, 119, 328

Cramer Lakes to Edna Lake 115

Crater Lake 20, 219-220, 228

Decker Creek to Redfish Inlet Transfer Camp 94

Decker Lakes 91-92, 94, 327, 328

East Fork Salmon River Trail 273, 294, 326

East Fork North Fork Big Wood River 20, 285

East Pass Creek 20, 309, 314, 317-319, 321, 328

Edith Lake 81-82, 84, 86

Edna Lake to Ardeth and Spangle Lakes 84

Edna Lake 78, 81, 83-85, 115-116, 142-143, 165, 326, 329

Elizabeth Lake 127, 128, 130, 131, 133, 328, 329

336

Elk Lake 115, 141-144, 326, 328, 329

Elk Meadow 127-129, 133, 327, 329

Eureka Gulch 25, 62-64

Everly Lake 151-152, 327

Farley Lake to Toxaway Lake 84

Farley Lake 75, 78-80, 83-84, 327, 328, 329

Fishhook Creek Meadow 103, 105

Flatrock Junction to Cramer Lakes 113, 115, 117

Flatrock Junction 111-119, 326, 327

Flatrock Junction to Alpine Lake 116-117

Four Lakes Basin 20, 199, 328, 329

Fourth of July and Washington Lakes 195-196, 199-200, 325

French Creek 221-222, 226, 228

Frenchman Creek 56, 328, 329

Frog Lake and the Boulder Chain Lakes 235, 246

From Alice Lake over Snowyside Pass to Toxaway Lake 75

Galena Lodge Trails: The Galena Grinder 277, 329

Galena Gulch 272-276.298, 327, 328

Garland Lakes 207-208, 210-213, 325, 328

Germania Creek from the East Fork to Chamberlain Creek 247

Germania Creek Trail: Three Cabins Creek to Chamberlain Creek 183

Gladiator Pass Trail 297

Goat Falls and Lake 121

Goat Creek Lakes 323

Governors Punchbowl from Pole Creek 269

Graham 144-147, 152, 156-157, 324, 329

Grand Prize Gulch 173, 177, 186, 268, 272, 276, 297-298, 329

Grand Mogul Trail 94, 100, 324, 327-329

Grandjean 20, 22, 23, 27, 31, 83, 115-116, 126, 130, 133-134, 137, 138, 141-144, 147, 323, 324, 326, 327

Hanson Lakes 126, 129, 328

Headwaters of the Salmon River 8, 23, 250, 252, 327, 329

Heart Lake (Sawtooths) 167, 328

Heart and Six Lakes 183, 191, 328

Hell Roaring Lake 85, 87-88, 90-94, 100, 102, 323, 327, 328

Hell Roaring Lake to Decker Creek and Lakes 92

Hemingway-Boulders Wilderness 6, 18, 20, 51

Herd Lake 309, 311, 313, 316-317,

Herd Peak 306, 313

Hoodoo Lake 20, 216-217, 325

Horton Peak 175-176, 187

Huckleberry Creek 90-92, 98, 328

Hunter Creek Summit and East Pass Creek 20, 318, 328

Imogene Lake 81-82, 85, 88, 96, 97, 323, 328

Ingeborg Lake 166, 328

Ingeborg, Rock Slide, and Benedict Lakes 166, 322

Island and Goat Lakes 20, 233, 250

Jim McClure-Jerry Peak Wilderness 18, 20, 51, 269, 308

Jimmy Smith Lake 30, 222-224, 226, 327, 329

Johnson Lake Junction to Johnson Lake and Pats Lake 157, 322

337

Kelly Lake 130-131, 133, 327, 328, 329

Lake Basin 20, 308-310, 328, 329

Lake Jon 102, 104, 328

Leggit Lake 162, 328, 329

Lightning Lake 192, 194-195, 328

Lily Pond (Lily Lake) 103

Little Casino Creek 207, 209-210, 326, 328

Little Queens River to Scenic Lakes Junction 153, 155

Little Boulder Creek Trail to the Boulder Chain Lakes 20, 238, 240, 246

Livingston Mill to Frog Lake 234, 325, 329

Lookout Mountain 211, 213, 328

Lower Warm Springs Creek 20, 215, 327

Marshall Lake 105-107, 109, 120, 329

Marten and Kelly Lakes 130, 131, 327, 328, 329

Mattingly Creek 63-64, 66-67, 158, 162, 326, 328, 329

Mattingly Creek Divide 64

Mays Creek Trail to McDonald Lake 86

McDonald Lake 74, 79, 86, 88, 327, 328

McGown Lakes 21, 119-121, 129, 141, 326

Middle Fork Boise River: Rock Creek to Spangle Lakes 165

Middle Fork Boise River: Powerplant Campground to Rock Creek 158, 162

Mill Gulch 54

Mill-Holman Creek Loop 220

Mill Lake 257, 259, 327

Miner Lake 258-260, 327

Murdock Creek 20, 283, 285, 327, 329

Noisy Lake 20, 244

Noisy and Quiet Lakes 244, 328

North Fork Big Wood River 283, 290

North Fork Lake 306-308, 328

North Baron Trail to Sawtooth Lake 138

Observation Peak 126, 129-130, 323, 329

Ocalkens Lakes 325

Old Toll Road 250, 254, 256, 263, 327, 329

Pats Lake Junction to Everly and Plummer Lakes 151

Pats Lake Junction to Pats Lake 152

Pettit Lake Over Ridge to McDonald Lake 74, 327

Phyllis Lake 192, 194-196, 327, 329

Plummer Lake 151-152, 327, 328, 329

Prairie Lakes 259, 260

Profile Lake 96-98, 328

Queens River Canyon to Pats Lake Junction 147, 324

Quiet Lake 20, 199-200, 235, 240, 244, 246, 328

Railroad Ridge 173, 220-222, 226-228, 329

Rainbow Lake 175-176, 328

Redfish Inlet to Flatrock Junction 111

Rock Slide Lake 166

Rough and Garland Lakes 210, 325

Saddleback Lakes 111-113, 328

Sage Creek 20, 314, 317-318

Sand Mountain Pass to Imogene Lake 85

Sawtooth View and Nip Peak 169, 328

Sawtooth Lake 119-121, 123, 129, 130, 133, 137, 138, 140, 141, 327, 328, 329

Scenic Lakes 153-156, 322, 323,

Backpackers at Twin Lakes

328, 329
  Scenic Lakes Junction to
Browns Lake, High Pass, and
Johnson Lake Junction 156
  Scoop Lake 236-238, 246, 329
  Scree Lake 172, 245, 246, 328,
329
  Shallow Lake 97, 115, 246, 324
  Sheep Lake 20, 233, 328
  Silver Lake 278, 281, 328
  Six Lakes 183, 191, 328
  Smiley Creek Trail 57, 329
  South Fork Champion Creek
and Rainbow Lake 175
  South Fork Payette River:
Grandjean to Elk Lake 141, 144
  South Fork Payette River: Elk
Lake to Hidden Lake Junction
142
  Spangle Lakes 83-85, 115, 144,
158, 162, 165-167, 326-329
  Strawberry Basin 30, 325
  Sullivan Lake 223-224, 226, 328,

329
  Tenlake Creek Trail to Ardeth
Lake
  The Lily Pond 96, 99, 102-104
  The Alpine Way from Redfish
Lake to Marshall Lake and Iron
Creek 106
  The Alpine Way from Iron
Creek to Stanley Lake 103
  The Meadows on Warm
Springs Creek 202, 329
  The Harriman Trail 42, 256,
257, 263-264, 277
  Timpa Lake 158, 162, 163, 165,
328, 329
  Thompson Cirque (Profile)
Lake 107
  Titus Lake and Titus Creek
253, 326
  Toll Road 250, 254-257, 263, 327,
329
  Toolbox Creek 20, 304, 328
  Toxaway Lake to Edna Lake 83

Toxaway Lake 71, 73, 75, 77-82, 84, 86, 324, 328

Trail Creek Lakes 21, 123, 126, 130, 133, 135, 137, 141, 325, 327

Trailer Lakes 133-134, 136, 325

Upper Lake Creek Campground 20, 313, 318, 329

Upper Redfish Lakes 117, 328

Walker Lake 20, 229-233, 23, 328

Washington Basin Lake 180, 328

Washington Lake to Castle Divide and Baker Lake Junction 20, 200

Washington Basin 24-25, 176, 177, 179-183-187, 189, 201, 275, 327, 328, 329

Washington Peak 177, 179-180, 183, 191, 326, 334

Washington Lake 20, 195-196, 199-201, 325, 328

West Pass Creek Divide from the East Fork Salmon River 299

West Fork Prairie Creek 262, 328

West Fork North Fork Big Wood River and Window Lake 20, 286

West Pass Creek Divide from the North Fork Big Wood River 20, 291

White Clouds Wilderness 172

Williams Creek Trail 204, 206, 215, 330

Yurt Lake 109

Window Lake 20, 286-288

Yellow Belly Lake 74, 77-79, 82-86, 88, 166, 187, 327, 329